D1525876

SUPPLY CHAIN

Project Management

A Structured Collaborative and Measurable Approach

Second Edition

Series on Resource Management

James B. Ayers

SUPPLY CHAIN

Project Management

A Structured Collaborative and Measurable Approach

Second Edition

CRC Press
Taylor & Francis Group
Boca Raton   London   New York

CRC Press is an imprint of the
Taylor & Francis Group, an **Informa** business

AN AUERBACH BOOK

WITHDRAWN

ROBERT VAN PELT B...
MICHIGAN ...CH...
HOUGHTON, MICHIGAN

Auerbach Publications
Taylor & Francis Group
6000 Broken Sound Parkway NW, Suite 300
Boca Raton, FL 33487-2742

© 2010 by Taylor and Francis Group, LLC
Auerbach Publications is an imprint of Taylor & Francis Group, an Informa business

No claim to original U.S. Government works

Printed in the United States of America on acid-free paper
10 9 8 7 6 5 4 3 2 1

International Standard Book Number: 978-1-4200-8392-7 (Hardback)

This book contains information obtained from authentic and highly regarded sources. Reasonable efforts
have been made to publish reliable data and information, but the author and publisher cannot assume
responsibility for the validity of all materials or the consequences of their use. The authors and publishers
have attempted to trace the copyright holders of all material reproduced in this publication and apologize to
copyright holders if permission to publish in this form has not been obtained. If any copyright material has
not been acknowledged please write and let us know so we may rectify in any future reprint.

Except as permitted under U.S. Copyright Law, no part of this book may be reprinted, reproduced, transmitted, or utilized in any form by any electronic, mechanical, or other means, now known or hereafter invented,
including photocopying, microfilming, and recording, or in any information storage or retrieval system,
without written permission from the publishers.

For permission to photocopy or use material electronically from this work, please access www.copyright.
com (http://www.copyright.com/) or contact the Copyright Clearance Center, Inc. (CCC), 222 Rosewood
Drive, Danvers, MA 01923, 978-750-8400. CCC is a not-for-profit organization that provides licenses and
registration for a variety of users. For organizations that have been granted a photocopy license by the CCC,
a separate system of payment has been arranged.

Trademark Notice: Product or corporate names may be trademarks or registered trademarks, and are used
only for identification and explanation without intent to infringe.

Library of Congress Cataloging-in-Publication Data

Ayers, James B.
    Supply chain project management : a structured collaborative and measurable
approach / James B. Ayers. -- 2nd ed.
        p. cm.
    Includes bibliographical references and index.
    ISBN 978-1-4200-8392-7 (hardcover : alk. paper)
    1. Business logistics. I. Title.

HD38.5.A94 2010
658.7--dc22   2009028808

**Visit the Taylor & Francis Web site at
http://www.taylorandfrancis.com**

**and the Auerbach Web site at
http://www.auerbach-publications.com**

Dedication

To MoJo and Alex—the dream team teens. What a project!

MAR 2 5 2010

Contents

Copyright Information

Trademarked entities mentioned in this book:

A Guide to the Business Analysis Body of Knowledge (BABOK) is a registered trademark of the International Institute of Business Analysis (IIBA).

A Guide to the Project Management Body of Knowledge (PMBOK Guide) is a registered trademark of the Project Management Institute.

CBAP is a registered trademark of the Certified Business Analysis Professional™ program of the International Institute of Business Analysis (IIBA).

Cisco is a registered trademark of Cisco Systems, Inc. and/or its affiliates in the United States and certain other countries.

CPFR (Collaborative Planning, Forecasting & Replenishment) is a registered trademark of the Voluntary Interindustry Commerce Standards Association (VICS).

C.P.P. (Certified Professional Purchaser) is a registered trademark of the Purchasing Management Association of Canada (PMAC).

CSCMP is a registered trademark of the Council of Supply Chain Management Professionals.

Demand Flow is a registered trademark of the John Costanza Institute of Technology.

EVA (Economic Value Added) is trademarked by Stern Stewart and Company.

Excel is a registered trademark of Microsoft Corporation in the United States and/or other countries.

Holiday Inn is a registered trademark of the InterContinental Hotels Group.

Honda Civic and Honda CR-V are trademarks of Honda, Inc.

ITIL (Information Technology Infrastructure Library) is a registered trademark of The APM Group Limited.

Keds is a registered trademark of The Stride Rite® Corporation.

MinuteClinics is a registered trademark of CVS/pharmacy.

OPM3 (Operations Project Management Maturity Model) is a registered trademark of the Project Management Institute.

PMI is a registered trademark of the Project Management Institute.

SCOR-model (Supply-Chain Operations Reference-model) is a trademark of the Supply-Chain Council.

SFIA (Skills for the Information Age) is a registered trademark of the SFIA Foundation Limited.

ThinkPad is a registered trademark of Lenovo.

Tupperware is a registered trademark of Tupperware Brands Corporation.

UNIX is a registered trademark of Linus Torvalds.

Visio is a registered trademark of Microsoft Corporation in the United States and/or other countries.

Corporate trademarks mentioned in this book:

Coca Cola, CVS/pharmacy, Dell Computers, Enterprise Rent-A-Car, FedEx, General Electric, General Motors, IBM, Intel, Lenovo, and UPS.

Preface

Why This Book?

Other books in this series, like the *Handbook of Supply Chain Management* and *Retail Supply Chain Management,* assert that managing supply chains requires new ways of doing traditional management tasks. These "old" tasks include making and delivering products and services, developing new products and services, and a host of administrative tasks. The emergence of supply chain management (SCM) has made the job of performing these tasks both harder and easier. Going alone in today's world, without collaborating with supply chain partners, may be a dead-end strategy for many companies. For some companies, it will be hard to innovate the ways they work with partners. Multicompany collaboration will also challenge management's project management capabilities. "Structured, collaborative, and measurable" will supplant dictated instructions to subordinates inside the walls.

In other ways, however, successful collaboration will make life easier. Managers have the opportunity to widen their circles, involving partners with mutual interests in making their businesses a success. These partners bring brains, brawn, and money to the multicompany "enterprise." Collaboration could be the shortest path to "breakthroughs" that create new market space with little or no competition.

At the time this book's manuscript was shipped to Auerbach Publications, U.S. and world economies were somewhere in a sharp business decline. The length of the downturn was unknown at the time; hopefully, it is over when you find time to spend with this book. The thought is that the content of this book becomes more pertinent in tough economic times. Margins for error are lower, and second chances may not present themselves.

Achieving supply chain transformation requires inspiration and perspiration. "Structured, collaborative, and measurable"—terms in the subtitle of this book— are undoubtedly virtues worth pursuing. But, in a supply chain world, how? This book addresses that question. Fundamentally, managers have the choices represented in the table that follows. On one side is "business as usual"; on the other is the "structured, collaborative, and measurable approach" that blends project management with supply chain management knowledge and practice:

Business as Usual	Structured, Collaborative, Measurable Approach
Functional initiatives	Multicompany initiatives
"Program" mentality, ambiguous goals	"Project" mentality, "make it happen"
Current market space	New market space
Narrow solutions	Broad solutions
Led by technical staff	Led by senior management
Systems first, processes later	Processes first, systems as enablers
Measured by return on investment (ROI)	Measured by competitive improvement
Get it done in your spare time	Dedicated resources
Launch and forget	Monitor and track

Business as usual, as the term implies, is the rule, not the exception. The first hurdle is enlisting different parts of the organization in the supply chain effort. If that can be accomplished, moving to a multicompany effort is often the next hurdle. One can debate which of these two stages is more difficult. Recent surveys indicate it's the first—aligning the internal organization.

How the Book Is Organized

This book is divided into three sections and includes two appendices.

Section I: SCM Execution—Foundation Concepts

The first chapter orients you to the book's layout and describes the book's foundations. These include knowledge and practice in both SCM and project management. The remaining chapters in Section I describe SCM knowledge areas—essential building blocks for strategy execution. Chapter 4 summarizes five management tasks that managers must perform differently to be successful.

Section II: Project Management and SCM

Section II turns to structured approaches for project management and supply chain analysis and documentation. Chapter 5 opens the second section with a discussion of "maturity models" for project management. The maturity model is a tool to measure progress in implementing what we preach in the book. Since the first edition, the Project Management Institute (PMI) and the Council of Supply Chain Management Professionals (CSCMP) have "inundated" the practitioner community with process models and self-evaluation yardsticks that measure maturity in their disciplines. These are on top of previous models from organizations like the Supply-Chain Council, which maintains its Supply-Chain Operations Reference-model (SCOR-model). These are summarized for project management knowledge and practice application (Chapter 5) and for SCM knowledge and practice application (Chapter 10).

Other chapters are devoted to standards promulgated by national organizations for project management and SCM. PMI maintains *A Guide to the Project Management Body of Knowledge (PMBOK Guide)*, which is covered in Chapter 6 and Chapter 7. The CSCMP has published its *Supply Chain Management Process Standards*, described in Chapter 8. Chapter 9 uses experience from IT projects to develop a working list of root causes for project failures. Section III project processes address these common project management shortcomings.

Section III: SCM Project Processes

This section contains templates for an expansive supply chain project. It borrows *PMBOK Guide* process standards for the recommended project structure. Section 3 is designed to help practitioners shape their own efforts, particularly those who want cross-functional and multicompany participation.

Appendices

Appendix A is a list of deliverables from Section III project management process templates and summarizes responsibilities for executing those processes. Appendix B describes project responsibilities for stakeholders and participants in project processes.

How Should You Use This Book?

There are likely to be two types of reader: The first is a supply chain practitioner seeking background on project management. The other is a project management practitioner wanting knowledge of SCM. Section II fills gaps for the former; Section I for the latter. Here are some suggestions: Start with Chapter 1 for a quick overview. Pick topics of interest and explore the applicable chapters. Each is designed as an explanation of its topics. For those charged with managing a supply chain improvement project, Section III should be very helpful.

Good luck in your pursuit of supply chain project management success.

Acknowledgments

My consulting career has required working on or running numerous projects. Unfortunately, that experience hasn't included all that much formal training in project management. Learning on the job, guided by some fine examples and intuition, has seemed adequate. Drew Gierman, who shepherded the first edition, suggested the Project Management Institute (PMI) as a source for the project management side of the SCM/project management "cocktail." That was an inspired suggestion; managing supply chain projects is too important—and complex—to be left to casual approaches. I also thank the late Ray O'Connell for overseeing this edition and helping me fill my time with writing projects.

Several reviewers checked my work in progress. Chris Christensen and Lars Rosqvist, both experts in project management, reviewed Section II covering project management, and made many important suggestions. Chris also certified the compliance of the course based on this book and its predecessor for PMI's Registered Education Provider (R.E.P.) program. Dave Malmberg of CGR Management Consultants reviewed Chapter 9 defining root causes of project management shortcomings. Dave has experienced many supply chain technology project successes—and failures.

About the Author

James B. Ayers is a principal with CGR Management Consultants (www.ayers-consulting.com) in Los Angeles, California. He consults in strategy and operations improvement with clients of all sizes across many manufacturing, distribution, and service industries inside the United States and internationally. Services include strategy development, profit improvement, and new product development.

Jim has authored or edited books and numerous articles on supply chain management. His books include *Making Supply Chain Management Work: Design, Implementation, Partnerships, Technology, and Profits*; *Retail Supply Chain Management,* co-authored with Mary Ann Odegaard; and two editions of *The Handbook of Supply Chain Management.*

Jim holds a bachelor's degree with distinction from the U.S. Naval Academy, and master's degrees in business administration and industrial engineering from Stanford University. As a naval officer, he served on submarines. Jim is also a member of the Project Management Institute, the Society of Manufacturing Engineers, and the Council of Supply Chain Management Professionals. He is a Certified Management Consultant (CMC) of the Institute of Management Consultants.

SCM EXECUTION— FOUNDATION CONCEPTS

I

Chapter 1, the first of four chapters in this section, describes the book's foundations. These include knowledge and practice in both SCM and project management. Chapter 1 orients the reader to the book's layout. Remaining chapters in Section I describe SCM knowledge areas – essential building blocks for strategy execution. Chapter 4 summarizes five management tasks that managers must perform differently to be successful.

Chapter 1

Purpose and Overview

This chapter describes this book's purpose and its plan to achieve the contract with readers implicit in the title.

This work complements the *Handbook of Supply Chain Management,* which its publisher characterizes as a "best seller."[1] The *Handbook*'s first edition dates from 2001; a second edition came out in 2006. Both editions examined the emerging supply chain management (SCM) discipline. SCM doesn't change management goals but does call for new knowledge, practices, and skills in achieving them. The *Handbook* described the knowledge and practice skills needed by managers to effectively apply SCM—in other words, *what* needs to be done.

This book focuses on the implementation process, which is *how* to do it. The underlying premise is that the design and improvement of supply chains requires organized projects that exploit best practices from project management knowledge and practice. Commenters like academics, analysts, and senior managers at times debate the relative value of strategy and tactics. Great strategies that go unimplemented have little value. On the other hand, well-executed projects unguided by strategy may also produce little value. Whatever benefits they bring to their organizations are purely accidental. Drivers of supply chain change, described in some detail in Chapter 3, add to the urgency of integrating the SCM and project management disciplines.

1.1 Book's Purpose

SCM is not just a "left brain" discipline, that is, totally analytical. SCM application requires "right brain" intuitive strategy making as well. The science of the optimal

Table 1.1   Roles for This Book

Title Component	Role for This Book
Supply Chain	The "supply chain" term continues to be defined. This book contributes to that definition and seeks to advance the level of knowledge and practice.
Project Management	Project management knowledge and practice have much to offer any improvement endeavor. We describe the project management practices that support implementation of supply chain strategies.
Structured	A tenet of project management is a disciplined, not casual, structure. Structured approaches increase the chances of success.
Collaborative	Collaboration among an organization's functional departments and along the supply chain is indispensable to success. The need for coordination in planning and executing supply chain strategy, design, and execution makes project management all the more crucial.
Measurable	SCM projects should move an organization from where it is to where it wants to go. The book describes frameworks for self-assessment and ongoing tracking of progress.

has to be tempered by the art of the possible. That is, SCM extends beyond managing the thousands of transactions needed to get a product from producer to user. SCM also requires "right brain" thinking to develop strategies that meet the needs of underserved markets. The purpose of this book can be stated in the following way:

To enable managers to use both SCM and project management knowledge and practice to develop and execute supply chain strategies.

The extended title of this book embraces the themes necessary to fulfill this mission. Table 1.1 lists title components and describes how the book addresses each element. We hope you will find the implicit promises achieved.

To achieve the book's goals, it should address knowledge and practice in both the project management and SCM disciplines. Figure 1.1 illustrates this, showing four components that comprise supply chain project management. "Knowledge" is more "right brain" and embraces skills developed by experience and education that require judgment in their application. "Practice" is "left brain" and encompasses models, procedures, vocabulary, standards, and tools that ease the job of applying knowledge.

The scope of knowledge and practice in both the project management and SCM disciplines is very, very broad. It would be impossible to capture everything in either discipline in a single book, even one much larger than this one. In fact,

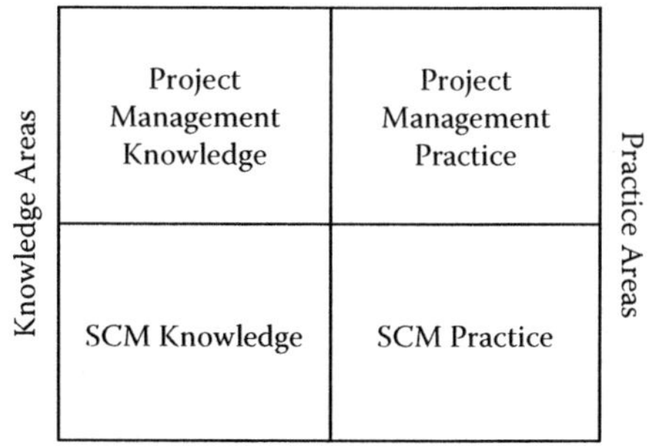

Figure 1.1   Component disciplines for supply chain project management.

a consistent feedback theme comments positively on its brevity. Here, we can provide a foundation drawing from a number of authoritative sources. An ample Bibliography points toward additional resources.

Our target audience consists of managers charged with supply chain improvement efforts. Many company initiatives are pursued without a synthesis of disciplines. After all, a busy manager can't be expert in every discipline he or she needs. This book should help those seeking to proceed in a disciplined way to avoid missteps or even disasters. As many have found, missteps and disasters are all too common. These can be costly in terms of lost business, wasted money, and frustration.

1.2 Project Management and SCM Knowledge Areas

Section 2 reviews project management knowledge and practice. The principal source is the Project Management Institute (PMI). PMI describes its knowledge areas in *A Guide to the Project Management Body of Knowledge (PMBOK Guide),*[2] which is a Certified Global Standard for the project management discipline. The fourth edition was published at year-end 2008. *PMBOK Guide* frameworks in the form of project structures, descriptions of the knowledge areas, and project processes will aid you in improving SCM project execution. Table 1.2 lists the project management knowledge areas described in the *PMBOK Guide,* and SCM knowledge areas from the *Handbook of Supply Chain Management.*

PMI describes SCM as an "application area" for project management knowledge and practice. An application area is a field that, by the nature of the work done there, relies on projects to fulfill its missions. Projects, as the *PMBOK Guide* defines them, are temporary, unique efforts leading to a "product, service, or result." Examples of other project management application areas are plentiful, including construction, software development, and new product development. Projects are taking an increasing share of the work done in many organizations, displacing ongoing, repetitive operations. PMI refers to this phenomenon as "management by projects." Management consulting is another industry that is "managed by projects."

Table 1.2   Knowledge Areas for Project Management and Supply Chain Management

Project Management	Supply Chain Management
1. Project Integration Management	1. Designing Supply Chains for Strategic Advantage
2. Project Scope Management	2. Implementing Collaborative Relationships
3. Project Time Management	3. Forging Supply Chain Partnerships
4. Project Cost Management	4. Managing Supply Chain Information
5. Project Quality Management	5. Removing Cost from the Supply Chain
6. Project Human Resource Management	
7. Project Communications Management	
8. Project Risk Management	
9. Project Procurement Management	

PMI offers organizations the opportunity to develop "application area extensions." These extensions become PMI standards if they undergo the rigors of the PMI Project Management Standard-Setting process. Although we view SCM as an excellent candidate for such certification, we haven't pursued this approval.

SCM knowledge and practice, in our view, is broad and includes strategy development, measuring performance and costs, and how we organize. It has roots in, but is not limited to, logistics, which includes procurement, manufacturing, transportation, and warehousing. Other disciplines related to SCM include operations research, competitive analysis, financial planning, industrial engineering, accounting, finance, mechanical engineering, and process re-engineering.

SCM brings these knowledge areas together. The *Handbook of Supply Chain Management* synthesizes this knowledge and practice into five management tasks that need to be performed with increasing levels of proficiency. This book employs these as knowledge areas for SCM, as shown in Table 1.2. Like the *PMBOK Guide* relies on knowledge areas to structure its project management processes, we use the five SCM knowledge areas to recommend SCM improvement project processes. These are the subjects of Section III.

1.3 Book Road Map

Figure 1.2 is a road map to guide you through the three major sections of the book.

Section I, SCM Execution—Foundation Concepts, describes why environmental change challenges management and the SCM skills needed to deal with that change.

Chapter 2 explores the ways "supply chain" and "supply chain management" might be defined. There are multiple viewpoints and definitions. Chapter 3 describes SCM change drivers and Chapter 4 recaps the five SCM management tasks.

Section II, Project Management and SCM, focuses on knowledge and practice in project management. This overview introduces models and techniques used in these disciplines. It also includes a chapter on reference models from the Council of Supply Chain Management Professionals (CSCMP) and the Supply-Chain

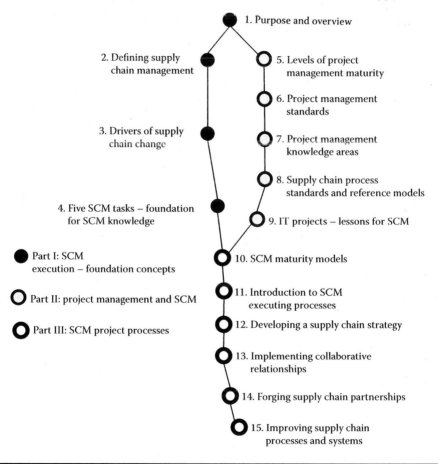

Figure 1.2   Book road map.

Council. It begins with a discussion of project management maturity measurement (Chapter 5). "Maturity" in this context calibrates the organization's utilization of formal project management approaches.

Chapter 6 continues with a summary of terminology used by project management professionals. Project management terminology, as well as SCM terminology, varies from organization to organization. This book's Glossary aids in standardizing vocabulary.

Chapter 7 describes the nine project management knowledge areas and related processes for managing projects.

Chapter 8, Supply Chain Process Standards and Reference Models, contributes to the book's goal of structure for improvement efforts.

Information technology is an important enabler of supply chain processes. Many IT projects fail to meet their goals. We dedicate Chapter 9 to project management "lessons learned" from IT projects gone awry and industry efforts to correct the problems. These lessons point to root causes that project designs must address.

Section III, SCM Project Processes, integrates Section I and Section II concepts and tools into project templates for implementing change. The section begins with a discussion of maturity models for SCM (Chapter 10). Like the project management maturity models, they gauge readiness and capability for pursuing competitive improvement from SCM. The descriptions enable you to locate your current state and plan for moving to the proverbial next level of maturity. This injects the element of measurability into all supply chain efforts.

Chapter 11 lifts features of effective project management described in Section II for inclusion in a template for SCM projects.

Chapters 12 through 15 describe processes within the SCM knowledge areas for executing supply chain improvement projects.

Figure 1.3 organizes book topics into the four categories that define world-class supply chain project management—project management knowledge and practice and SCM knowledge and practice. Chapters 2 through 11 focus on one of the four categories. Chapters 12 through 15 integrate knowledge and practice from all four categories, symbolized by the circle around the four in Figure 1.3.

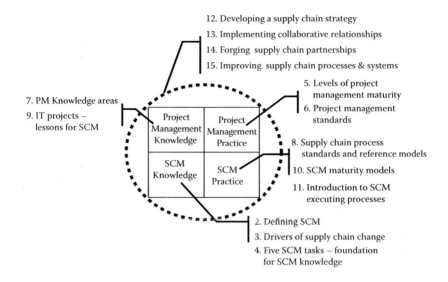

Figure 1.3   Book chapters/topics organized by category.

Notes

1. James B. Ayers, *Handbook of Supply Chain Management*, 2nd ed. (Boca Raton, FL: Auerbach Publications, 2006).
2. PMI Global Standard, *A Guide to the Project Management Body of Knowledge (PMBOK Guide)*, 4th ed. (Project Management Institute, 2008).

Chapter 2

Defining Supply Chain Management

Its people, its industry, its history, and its products frame an organization's view of supply chain management (SCM). This chapter recognizes different SCM interpretations for different companies. There is no right, absolute view of SCM. However, each organization should have a working definition that fits its needs. This should include SCM scope, goals, participation, and plan for implementation. Most companies define SCM too narrowly. This chapter should increase awareness of choices faced in defining SCM and guide you toward making choices.

Efforts to define SCM are warranted. SCM is relatively new in the business lexicon, and its definition varies from user to user. Before going far in this book, we need to get our arms around the "space" we call SCM. Chapter 9 describes examples of failed projects that trace their root causes to ignoring this need.

Unless there's agreement in the organization about what SCM is, it's going to be tough to get on with improvement projects conducted under that banner. Methodologies described in this book will help companies reach agreement on what constitutes SCM as it applies to their situation. The definition should include, but not necessarily be limited to, the scope, goals, participation, and management plan for SCM efforts.

2.1 Seven Principles of SCM

The periodical *Supply Chain Management Review* (*SCMR*) has charted the evolution of the SCM discipline. In its first edition in the spring of 1997, *SCMR* laid out basic

SCM principles in what has become its most requested article. It republished the article in its ten-year anniversary issue in 2007.[1] The seven time-tested principles listed in Table 2.1 offer value to the organization trying to define how SCM applies to them. The "Comments" column contains observations that reinforce or expand on each principle. The authors of the article explain that each principle brings one or more of three types of financial benefit: revenue growth, asset utilization, and cost reduction.

The list suggests that companies' goals and opportunities might be reviewed for improvement. Revenue growth results from tailoring the supply chain to the customer requirements, enabling faster penetration of new products or increases in market share. Asset utilization refers to fixed assets like plants and equipment, logistics resources like vehicles and warehouses, and working capital like inventory and receivables. Cost reduction means costs all along the chain, going beyond direct costs for purchased materials to less-visible overhead and quality costs.

2.2 Professional Organization Perspectives

This section describes perspectives from three organizations whose members have stakes in the direction of SCM. The first, the Council of Supply Chain Management Professionals (CSCMP), has taken a leadership position in terms of defining what a supply chain is and what constitutes SCM. The organization itself reflects the evolution of the SCM discipline; until 2005, its name was the Council of Logistics Management (CLM). The name change recognized the broadening of the discipline. The backgrounds of its members—all individuals, not companies—are diverse, with heavy participation from third-party logistics provider organizations, transportation companies, and distribution center operators. CSCMP has defined SCM on its Web site (www.cscmp.org) and distinguishes it from the logistics discipline where it had its roots:

> Supply chain management encompasses the planning and management of all activities involved in sourcing and procurement, conversion, and all logistics management activities. Importantly, it also includes coordination and collaboration with channel partners, which can be suppliers, intermediaries, third-party service providers, and customers.

SCM, according to CSCMP, is an "integrating function" that links business functions and processes in a cohesive multicompany "business model." The scope of these functions includes marketing, sales, product design, finance, and information technology. Because of its previous life as CLM and to avoid confusion of terms, CSCMP defines "logistics management" as:

> that part of supply chain management that plans, implements, and controls the efficient, effective forward and reverse flow and storage of

Table 2.1   The Seven Principles of SCM

	Principles	Comments
1	Segment customers based on service needs and customize the supply chain to serve each profitably. Supports revenue growth.	This implies the possibility of multiple supply chains or, at a minimum, built-in flexibility in supply chain design to meet the requirements of customer segments.
2	Customize the logistics network to segment service requirements and profitability. Supports asset utilization.	"Logistics networks" should be interpreted broadly beyond physical distribution to all aspects of customer interaction.
3	Listen to market signals and align demand and plan accordingly. Have "consistent" forecasts and "optimal" resource allocation. Supports asset utilization.	Today, practitioners seek to capture the "voice" of the customer in the design of the supply chain and in the replenishment decisions required in daily operation. Many seek to "immunize" themselves from reliance on forecasts, using actual demand as much to "pull" products through the chain.
4	Differentiate the product closer to the customer and speed conversion across the supply chain. Supports cost reduction and asset utilization.	Postponement and synchronization are initiatives in this direction. Such efforts call on participation by marketing, sales, and engineering functions.
5	Manage sourcing strategically to reduce the often-unseen total cost of ownership (TCO) for purchased materials and services. Supports cost reduction.	Many organizations associate SCM with the purchasing function. And many purchasing organizations are viewed as paper-pushing, even clerical, functions ill-equipped to act strategically.
6	Develop a supply chain-wide, enterprise technology strategy that supports multiple levels of decision making and provides visibility over the flow of products, services, and information. Supports asset utilization.	The *SCMR* authors note that systems must cover short-term transactional needs, intermediate planning, and strategic analysis. Such systems must go beyond churning out data to providing information that decision makers can act on in a timely way.

(continued on next page)

Table 2.1 (continued)   The Seven Principles of SCM

	Principles	Comments
7	Adopt vertical or end-to-end measures for each channel to gauge multicompany success in reaching end users effectively and efficiently. Supports revenue growth, asset utilization, and cost reduction.	The *SCMR* authors point to tools like activity-based costing to clarify supply chain costs. In traditional costs, overhead is applied evenly rather than to the root "driver" of the cost. Activity-based costs also enable shared scorecards with trading partners.

Source: Adapted from David L. Anderson, Frank F. Britt, and Donavon J. Favre, "The Seven Principles of Supply Chain Management," *Supply Chain Management Review* (April 2007): 41–6.

goods, services, and related information between the point of origin and the point of consumption in order to meet customers' requirements.

CSCMP holds that logistics covers planning and execution at strategic, operational, and tactical levels.

Another organization representing those at the other end of most businesses—the inbound side—is the Purchasing Management Association of Canada (PMAC). Its vision is "to be the recognized leader in the development and advancement of world-class strategic supply chain management."[2] This translates into a mission to be "dedicated to serving the needs of the strategy supply chain management practitioner and enterprises." PMAC does this through continuous learning, practice standards, research, and networking. At the time of writing this book, the members had approved an effort to change the name of their certification credential, the C.P.P. (Certified Professional Purchaser). A new title will be something more reflective of the organization's direction and the strategic contribution made by many in the purchasing function. To this end, the association encourages practitioners to enroll in their Strategic Supply Chain Management Leadership program.

APICS, the Association for Operations Management, also weighs in through its comprehensive dictionary of terms.[3] This organization has also gone through the name change process. "APICS" stands for American Production and Inventory Control Society. Many terms in the Glossary of this book are adapted from the twelfth edition of the *APICS Dictionary*. The organization has long association with manufacturing information systems, notably MRP's[4] transformation of product planning, scheduling, and replenishment. Following are the *Dictionary*'s definitions of supply chain and SCM:

Supply chain: The global network used to deliver products and services from raw materials to end customers through an engineered flow of information, physical distribution, and cash.

Supply chain management: The design, planning, execution, control, and monitoring of supply chain activities with the objective of creating net value, building a competitive infrastructure, leveraging worldwide logistics, synchronizing supply with demand, and measuring performance globally.

Both APICS definitions portray supply chain and SCM as a branch of learning that cuts across many traditional disciplines. Like CSCMP and PMAC, the definitions also hold that SCM goes beyond organization boundaries and supports a business model through which an enterprise differentiates itself. For a private company in a competitive market, this means winning in the marketplace through gains in market share and profits. For the public agency, it means successfully fulfilling the organization's mission in a cost effective manner. The challenge to all organizations, as PMAC illustrates, is the need to acquire and train those that must execute supply chain strategies. Unfortunately for many companies, the chief resource is limited to employees composed of specialists whose skills are too narrow to tackle supply chain projects.

2.3 Competing Supply Chain to Supply Chain

Strategic SCM, as described earlier, reflects a belief that competition will shift from a company-to-company basis to a supply-chain-to-supply-chain basis. However, the shape of supply chain versus supply chain competition is a nuanced subject. A survey, also reported in *SCMR*, examines the perceptions and realities around supply chain versus supply chain competition.[5] The survey was sponsored by the Integrated Supply Chain Management (ISCM) program at the Massachusetts Institute of Technology (MIT) and canvassed thirty supply chain experts from industry, academia, and consulting.

The MIT authors' report has important implications for framing SCM and projects that implement supply chain change. The survey addresses questions like the following:

Do we actually compete as supply chains, or as individual companies?
What effect does industry structure have on our supply chain decisions?
Is there a continuum for competing on a supply chain basis?
Is there a single supply chain model for competing in an industry?

Over 70 percent of respondents said that supply chain versus supply chain competition was real. However, there was far less agreement on the meaning of such competition. By interpreting responses, the surveyors reported three different scenarios for supply chain versus supply chain competition:

Scenario 1: Literally competing supply chain versus supply chain. This entails groups of companies competing with each other. The entity, in this scenario, is the group comprising the supply chain. Groups are either formal or informal. There is little overlap of companies among competing supply chains.

Scenario 2: Supply chain network capabilities. In this model, individual companies are the principal competitive entity, not the multicompany chains in Scenario 1. These individual companies compete on the basis of their supply networks. The networks support one of two "subscenarios":

Scenario 2A: The way most supply chains develop. The supply chain evolves by providing a capability to compete on cost and service beyond the reach of a single company.

Scenario 2B: A unique network consciously erected in a short period of time by a lead company.

Scenario 3: Supply chain networks headed by a channel master. A single powerful company dictates "terms of trade" in the channel. Examples include Wal-Mart Stores, Inc. in retail, Dell in computers, and the U.S. government for its prime contractors.

According to the MIT authors, Scenario 1 has many difficulties in reaching true supply chain versus supply chain competition. First, there are often common suppliers in rival supply chains. This is a barrier to any supply chain being truly unique, at least over those parts of the chain that are common. Second, investments by a customer in one of its suppliers may end up benefiting rivals if that investment is used to meet their needs. Third, proprietary information is difficult to hold close if a supplier can "signal" innovations to rivals with whom it is working. Finally, information sharing sufficient to establish a proprietary chain is hindered by the threat of disclosure.

The MIT authors also point out that some suppliers compete with their customers. This happens when the component supplier or its sister divisions have competing end products. It is also the case in aftermarket support where the component supplier has control of the design and components in critical subsystems built into their customers' products. The authors report success with supply chain versus supply chain in industries like fashion, food production, products based on proprietary technology or raw materials, or geographically focused supply chains. A vertically integrated company can also compete supply chain versus supply chain because it is relatively independent.

Supply chain versus supply chain doesn't work, in the MIT authors' view, in industries with "channel masters" like automobiles, commercial aircraft, and personal computers. Dominant customers, like Boeing and Airbus, use a multitude of suppliers, many of which serve both companies.

This doesn't mean that companies who serve a channel master shouldn't use SCM to improve their competitive positions. Scenario 2 is the traditional way a supply chain develops. A company has a product it wants to sell. It picks suppliers based on the competencies it needs, including competencies in SCM. If it needs "widgets," it goes to the "best" widget maker. "Best" here may mean the fastest, the cheapest, the most flexible, or the one having the best technology. If that maker is already providing widgets to competitors, like Intel provides its chips to competing computer companies, it may look elsewhere. Or, it may accept that there is no choice, or that it doesn't make much difference.

Scenario 2B provides a more proactive approach to improving competitive position. A company seeking to join such a chain might design a focused "activity system" using techniques recommended in Chapter 4. Our view is that the MIT survey doesn't emphasize the differences between Scenarios 2A and 2B enough. A 2B company has the opportunity to design a differentiated supply chain or activity system focused on the needs of its customers, whether the customer is Boeing-like or a small business.

In Scenario 3, the channel master makes the rules. However, most channel masters have plenty of choices. So, a company needs to strive to be the best supplier available in its chosen category. SCM is an important tool in doing so, both in the way it picks its own suppliers and the way it supports the channel master.

Which scenario best describes your situation? The answer will lead a company along different paths to supply chain improvement. A vertically integrated company, for example, will re-examine prospects for farming out supply chain activities. A manufacturer whose suppliers and distributors "sleep with the enemy" may be more selective and reduce the number of business partners. If this isn't possible, then improvement efforts will focus on building internal capabilities.

2.4 The Value Chain and Other Perspectives

This section describes other perspectives that either help define SCM or contribute to confusion around its definition. They are also presented here to guide you toward the definition you choose for your own organization.

2.4.1 Supply Chain Definitions

The second edition of the *Handbook of Supply Chain Management*[6] proposes definitions of the terms "supply chain" and "supply chain management." These are repeated in this section; they have held up well since initial publication of the *Handbook:*

> Supply chain: Product life cycle processes comprising physical, information, financial, and knowledge flows whose purpose is to satisfy enduser requirements with physical products and services from multiple, linked suppliers.

The definition says that the supply chain is made up of processes. Processes in a manufacturer include sourcing material, designing products, manufacturing, transporting, fixing, and selling physical products and related services. The term "product life cycle" has at least two meanings: the selling life cycle and the usage life cycle. For long-life products as well as many services, these aren't the same. The selling window may be far shorter than the product's useful life. Examples are automobiles, computers, life insurance policies, and thirty-year mortgages. All must be supported long after newer products take the place of older ones. For this reason, product support after the sale can be an important—if not the most important and plausible—supply chain component. In these cases, the prospect for seller longevity is a factor in the purchasing decision.

Physical, information, and financial flows are traditional supply chain dimensions. However, a very common viewpoint of supply chains as purchasing or physical distribution is limiting. Information and financial components can be as important as physical flow.

Also omitted from many supply chain definitions is the role of knowledge inputs in supply chain processes. Knowledge is the driver behind many new products and processes, the source of growth through innovation. Supply chain processes for new products require coordination of intellectual input (the design) with physical inputs (components, prototypes, factories, distribution channels, and the like). Such knowledge produces better designed, more user friendly, and more stylish products. Increasingly, products sold to consumers rely on a knowledge input—software—to distinguish them and make them work. There is also a need for consulting with customers in the course of purchasing complex products. This consultation helps the buyer understand the options that meet his or her requirements.

The supply chain should support the satisfaction of end-user requirements. These requirements give rise to the fundamental mission of supply chains: matching supply and demand. As noted earlier in this chapter, there may be a range of customer/end-user market segments. An integral part of SCM is designing and implementing supply chain operations to profitably satisfy these segments. Note that a customer who buys a product may not be the end-user. An example is a household in which the homemaker shops for food consumed by the family.

A supply chain also has multiple, linked suppliers. From the customer/end-user viewpoint, a supply chain exists when there are multiple enterprises backing the last-link enterprise that delivers the product or service. Under this condition, the neighborhood barber would not constitute a supply chain although a chain of barbershops would.

Flow in the supply chain is two-way. Many consider supply chains only in terms of forward flow from suppliers to end users. So, SCM definitions take on a limited sourcing–logistics flavor. For the physical processes, this is largely true. But, supply chain design must include backward flows for product returns, payments and rebates, replenishment orders, repair, and other reasons. Government agencies have passed regulations that assign companies responsibility for the ultimate disposal of the products they sell. For example, electronics manufacturers have to take back and recycle parts and materials from the products that they have sold.

Services, including those provided by non-manufacturing enterprises, also have supply chains. Production planning for the research and development department, which produces designs and not products, can benefit from the same techniques used by product manufacturers. FedEx and UPS operate service businesses but they employ complex supply chains to service customer shipments. A software company is challenged to constantly improve its product through upgrades, so it too has a supply chain for its knowledge-based product.

Following is the *Handbook*'s definition of SCM:

> Supply chain management: Design, maintenance, and operation of supply chain processes, including those that make up extended product features, for satisfaction of end-user needs.

Note the use of the term "extended product." Examples of extended product features include company image, after-sales services, financing, and availability. These are within the scope of SCM.

Other authors and practitioners use other terminology. For example, as noted earlier in this chapter, supply chains are frequently referred to as "networks." The chain analogy infers linear movement of product, information, and money. The reality is closer to simultaneous, concurrent processes. So, "network" may be the better term in many situations.

Also, many take a "company-centric" view and split the "chain" between "supply" and "demand" at the company level. This is the case if the company is in the middle of the chain, several steps away from end users. The company-centric enterprise sees the "supply" chain as providing incoming materials to the company— the upstream side. The "demand" chain constitutes the downstream side from the company to the end user. We favor the view that the "supply chain" represents all the resources needed to satisfy end-user needs. In other words, to the end user, it's all a supply chain.

2.4.2 The "Value Chain"

"Supply chain," the term, gets confused with the term "value chain," which Michael Porter introduced in his books, *Competitive Strategy*[7] and *Competitive Advantage*.[8] Porter's books are important contributions to strategic planning. Within a company, the value chain includes generic product or customer-touching activities, including inbound logistics, operations, outbound logistics, marketing and sales, and service. Supporting these are other activities like procurement, technology development, human resource management, and infrastructure. Each linked company has its own value chain comprising these functions.

Porter also adds profit margin to his value chain. This represents the difference between the prices paid by customers and the cost of the functions required to deliver them. Higher profits signal that the enterprise deploys its capabilities in a way that delivers more value to customers as measured by their willingness to pay for it. Enterprise strategy in this framework leverages value chain components to increase these profits.

Supply chain activities are a subset of the value chain. Notably, inbound logistics, operations, and outbound logistics are certainly supply chain activities. Excluded from some definitions of supply chain are activities like human resources, marketing and sales, and technology development. But, it is harder and harder to discern any difference between supply chain activities and value chain activities. Our view is that the two are nearly synonymous. Certainly, a review of the enabling processes in supply chain reference models from CSCMP and the Supply-Chain Council support this view. We include Task 1 Designing Supply Chains for Strategic Advantage as an SCM knowledge area. A project management template in Chapter 12 describes how to produce a supply chain strategy.

2.4.3 Viewpoints Encountered in Industry

There are several models found in enterprises. Most companies will fit one of the six in Table 2.2. The views are arranged from the narrowest supply chain point of view to the broadest. For each, there's a description and a best guess of what kind of manager would lead a supply chain improvement project in a company with that particular viewpoint.

In Viewpoint 1, Functional, there is no supply chain function. Traditional departments, like purchasing, manufacturing, or distribution, are independent, tied together only by a reporting relationship to a CEO or COO. A supply chain project would be difficult to implement in such a company if functional executives aren't aligned to the goals of the project. A company heavily dependent on suppliers will pick a procurement executive as the supply chain executive, as shown in

Table 2.2 Viewpoints toward SCM

	Viewpoint	Focus	Supply Chain Executive
1	Functional	None; stand-alone department	None
2	Procurement	Incoming "supplies"	From procurement
3	Logistics	Distribution to channels	From distribution
4	Information	Integration through technology	From IT or operations
5	Process re-engineering	Cost reduction	From operations
6	Strategic	Profit-adding capabilities	Up-and-coming manager

Viewpoint 2. Cost reductions might focus on the bill of materials. Large engineered-product companies like those in aerospace or automotive often fit this model.

A company dependent on its downstream activities might hold Viewpoint 3, Logistics. In these organizations, the distribution executive advances to the lead supply chain role. Industries with high distribution costs, relative to raw material and manufacturing costs, could logically follow this direction. Examples include apparel, food, and consumer goods.

An information-intensive company might hold Viewpoint 4 and bestow supply chain project management responsibility on a technical person. Companies serving a channel master might feel responsiveness to their customers lies in technology links and would make the choice of a tech-savvy manager. Process re-engineering companies, representing Viewpoint 5, pursue programs (like Six Sigma or lean) that focus on process improvement. They are often in mature industries where continuous cost reduction is mandatory to stay in the game.

The Strategic Viewpoint is the broadest viewpoint. It recognizes that SCM is a strategic enabler. Section 3 project processes will lay out a pathway to implement this viewpoint. Our view is that SCM holds value for improving strategies, and a company that fails to take a strategic view forfeits an opportunity to improve its lot in life.

2.5 Implications for SCM Project Management

Our definition of SCM will set the limits for projects pursued under the supply chain banner. An important element of supply chain project management knowledge is "Scope Management." Chapter 7 and Chapter 12 describe this knowledge area in the Guide to Project Management Body of Knowledge and its implications for project definition. A company's viewpoint can expand or limit the scope it is willing to pursue. In too many companies, there is no true supply-chain-responsible manager. There are only functional mangers from procurement or distribution departments given a new title. Without the recognition that managing supply chains requires a new perspective, a company is likely to be disappointed in pursuing supply chain improvement projects.

Notes

1. David L. Anderson, Frank F. Britt, and Donavon J. Favre, "The Seven Principles of Supply Chain Management," *Supply Chain Management Review* (April 2007): 41–6.
2. Purchasing Management Association of Canada, *Annual Report, 2007–2008*.
3. John H. Blackstone Jr., *APICS Dictionary*, 12th ed. (APICS—The Association for Operations Management, 2008).

4. MRP refers to computer applications for material requirements planning, material resource planning, or manufacturing resource planning. Many of these systems have been expanded into ERP systems (enterprise resource planning).

5. James B. Rice Jr. and Richard M. Hoppe, "Supply Chain versus Supply Chain: The Hype and the Reality," *Supply Chain Management Review* (September/October, 2001): 46–54.

6. James B. Ayers, *Handbook of Supply Chain Management*, 2nd ed. (Boca Raton: Auerbach Publications, 2006), Chapter 1.

7. Michael E. Porter, *Competitive Strategy: Techniques for Analyzing Industries and Competitors* (New York: The Free Press, 1980).

8. Michael E. Porter, *Competitive Advantage: Creating and Sustaining Superior Performance* (New York: The Free Press, 1985).

Chapter 3

Drivers of Supply Chain Change

According to Charles Darwin, it's not the strongest of the species that survive, not the most intelligent, but the one most responsive to change. This chapter addresses change drivers fueling supply chain improvement projects. Awareness of root causes for change helps the supply chain manager formulate projects.

3.1 Drivers Are Important

Two hundred years after his birth, Darwin's theories have been confirmed repeatedly. Unlike slower moving changes in the species, drivers of supply chain change are visible and widely reported in the press. However, supply chain managers don't necessarily connect these drivers to what they do on a daily basis. Also, the drivers are beyond the power of an individual manager, particularly one immersed in day-to-day supply chain activity, to influence. This chapter explains how change drivers are a force in many supply chain projects. Awareness helps supply chain managers get a jump on competition by leading in responding to change forces. In initiating a project as described in Chapter 12, those formulating projects should understand each project's "roots" in the form of change drivers. As a practical matter, this attention should point the project manager at the issues that the project must address.

This chapter should find practical application as a checklist. You should examine each change driver and the potential impact on your operation. This should also lead to questions about whether the organization's project portfolio is sufficient in terms of dealing with the drivers. A new project might result to fill a gap.

Table 3.1 SCM Driver Definitions

	SCM Drivers	Definition
1	PESTEL	An acronym for "political, economic, social, technological, environmental, legislative." Includes advances in both product and process technology. Examples are materials, production equipment, software, and artistic input. Encompasses economic conditions, societal values, and regulation.
2	Extended products	The necessity for value-adding features and related services beyond the physical or "base" product. Such features and services often accompany the commoditization of the base product.
3	Globalization	Having to source and sell worldwide. Includes cross-border trade for raw material, manufacturing support, distribution, and sales to customers and end users.
4	Flexibility imperative	The competitive advantage derived from fast responses to environmental changes and shorter product life cycles. Flexibility has many dimensions, including product mix, volume, and features.
5	Process-centered management	Improvement of processes, not functions. Shifting focus to multicompany business processes as a basis for improvement efforts away from departments and one's own company boundaries.
6	Collaboration	Using intracompany and intercompany cooperative efforts to meet mutual goals.

Table 3.1 provides a working definition of each driver. Figure 3.1 models the connections among the drivers.

In Figure 3.1, the whole process is pushed forward by PESTEL, which is an acronym for political, economic, social, technological, environmental, and legislative factors. These factors are external to the supply chain but act on it through the continuous improvement driver.

Unlike PESTEL factors, all the other drivers take place inside the supply chain. Three drivers—extended products, globalization, and flexibility imperative—act in different ways, described later. All three shape products and services offered by the supply chain and the operations that deliver them. Two-headed arrows connect these three drivers to signify simultaneous, collaborative interaction. In effect, the three "digest" the impact of the drivers and transform them into requirements for processes and collaboration.

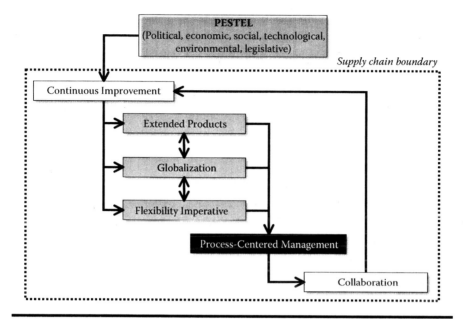

Figure 3.1 Drivers of supply chain change.

The next driver is process-centered management, encompassing the requirements for multicompany supply chain processes. These, in turn, produce needed collaboration, the last driver. Collaborations set in motion more innovations in the form of tactical and strategic continuous improvement changes. The following sections discuss the drivers and how each contributes to supply chain change.

3.2 PESTEL

The model in Figure 3.1 shows the six PESTEL components as the "engine" of external changes acting on supply chains and their managers. They are shown outside the boundary of the supply chain. PESTEL factors influence both products and processes, and any of the six PESTEL factors will force an organization to innovate. For example, a totally new product technology will require new suppliers and ways to make and distribute a product. A process technology innovation may alter the way the product is produced, making it better or lowering its cost. Either type of innovation can broaden the market and bring on the need for supply chain change. Other innovations may lie in the way the product is delivered or in the supply chain itself. In the last few years, the "green" movement, reflecting concern with the environment, has focused attention on the "carbon footprint" resulting from supply chain operations. Getting goods to market involves transportation, packaging, and—for some products—recycling at the end of the product's life. In response, many supply chain managers are changing their supply chains to lower their environmental impact.

Forbes, in its eighty-fifth anniversary issue, listed what it considered the eighty-five most important innovations since its founding in 1917.[1] When they were introduced, the innovations undoubtedly affected their industries and their supply chains. The effect on supply chains might have been indirect, in the case of new materials, fundamental technology advances, and process innovations; or direct, as noted in several of the supply chain innovations listed in the article.

Some of the product, process, and supply chain innovations described in the article, along with the date of the innovation, are given in the following tables. The first table entails technology used in products. The names in italics are those given by *Forbes* as they appeared in the article:

Breakthroughs in fundamental technologies	*Bell Telephone Laboratories,* which developed transistors, data networking, and many other innovations (1925)
	Synthetic Rubber that forms the basis of many products today, like cable insulation and wet suits (1929)
	Transistors (1947)
	Recombinant DNA, using gene splicing (1976)
New materials	*Wallboard,* which reduced building costs (1933)
	Nylon (1934)
Technology without new material embedded in product designs	*Frozen Food,* by Clarence Birdseye (1924)
	Integrated Circuits that shrunk discrete components onto chips (1959)
Artistic content like motion pictures, books, and music	The *LP,* or long-playing record (1948)
	e-Entertainment beginning with Nolan Bushnell's Pong game (1972)

The following innovations impacted processes, including those used in supply chains:

Advances in process and production technology	*Electronic Digital Computer* (1942)
	Microprocessor, which miniaturized computers (1971)
Software for managing and executing processes	*Relational Database* from Edgar Codd of IBM (1970)
	UNIX/C Programming, which enabled cross-platform applications (1972)
	Spreadsheet, the "killer app" for personal computers (1979)

Innovation in management techniques and roles in society	*Business Management* by Alfred Sloan of General Motors, which formalized corporate structures (1923)
	Value Investing, which brought science to stock and bond valuation and perhaps many of the motivating measures of industry performance (1934)
	United Auto Workers, that pioneered extended benefits for employees (1935)
	Conglomerates, diversified holding companies (1952)
	Consumerism spurred by Ralph Nader (1965)
Methods of communication	*Pulse Code Modulation* that transferred signals into electronic zeroes and ones pulses (1937)
	Fiber Optics for high-capacity communication (1956)
	Modem for data transfer over phone lines (1962)
	Telstar I, the first commercial communications satellite (1962)
	The Internet (1969)
	Ethernet used to connect computers into networks (1972)
	World Wide Web that widened access to the Internet (1991)

You should certainly be able to draw a line between innovations like the Internet and microprocessors to supply chain design. The following examples might be considered "pure" or "nearly pure" examples of innovation in the way supply chains operate. No one should be surprised that these direct examples have made this short list of innovations. Also, the innovations include many examples of "extended products" or product/service designs focused on market segments.

Mass marketing of products	*Keds Sneakers* (1917)
	Tupperware, using new plastics marketed door to door (1947)
	Mutual Funds as a new way to sell securities to the public (1924)
	Holiday Inn, utilizing standardized franchises (1952)
	Fast Food with franchised food outlets (1955)
	Containerized Shipping, speeding up transport of goods (1956)
	Point of Sales data by Sam Walton, leading to information sharing (1962)

(continued on next page)

	Discount Brokerage, offering basic services at low cost (1973)
	Index Fund with formula investment policies offering low cost (1976)
	Customized Mass Retail from Dell that bypassed distributors (1984)
	Internet Business, as embodied at Amazon (1995)

Figure 3.2 depicts the interaction of product, process, and supply chain innovation driven by PESTEL factors. The interactions can overlap or be sequential in their timing. Overlapping innovation is more common. New products, changes in process technology, or new markets often emerge at the same time. These may be characterized either as a threat to competitive position or an opportunity to improve it. Due to department specialization in most organizations, awareness of the need to change might reside in different departments. For example, the manufacturing manager may understand the importance of a process improvement but the CEO, marketing, and finance managers may not. Also the parties involved may or may not come together until things no longer work well and management is forced to react. Only at that time may the organization make a coordinated effort to change—perhaps too little, too late.

Without PESTEL-driven innovation, the push for supply chain change would be much more limited than it is. Product innovation increases the value of products to customers. This in turn generates the profits needed to attract new investment, enriches producers, and fuels more innovation. The supply chain is called upon to produce the products that generate the profit. Porter's value chain model discussed in Section 2.4.2 describes this profit contribution. For high-growth innovative products, this is not a minimal profit based on cost but the kind of profit enjoyed by those vigilant and capable enough to exploit the opportunity.

Another driver arises from process innovation. Even without new products or markets, few can stand still in the face of competition. This is a powerful driver for

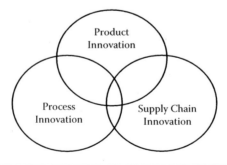

Figure 3.2   Interaction of product, process, and supply chain innovations.

improving supply chains. As process innovations improve cost and service, products become more affordable, increasing potential markets.

The consulting firm McKinsey encapsulated the effects of process innovation by examining U.S. retail sales leader Wal-Mart.[2] Bradford Johnson notes that, in 1987, Wal-Mart had only 9 percent of market share but was 40 percent more productive than competitors as measured by sales per employee. By 1995, through "big box" stores, electronic communication with suppliers, low prices, and central distribution centers, Wal-Mart had a 27-percent share and a productivity advantage of 48 percent.

From 1995 to 1999, competitors played catch-up, but Wal-Mart maintained its edge. McKinsey's study reported how Wal-Mart achieved the gains:

■ Managerial innovations: These had nothing to do with IT (information technology). An example cited is cross-training employees to increase flexibility in their assignment.
■ Focused IT investments: These enhanced its low-price objective and did not include more recent investments in real-time sales data collection and dissemination.
■ Higher-value goods: This reflected the market's desire for more upscale products. For example, the $30 shirt costs as much to sell as the $20 shirt but the margin is much higher.

Wal-Mart is an example of the continuous improvement driver for supply chain projects. The company uses its supply chain capability to identify products that yield the highest profit. For a retailer bringing thousands of products to market, pegging profitability at the product level is a vital, if not daunting, task. Relying on market data, not the intuition of buyers and merchandisers, is key. The demand-driven supply chain, addressed in Chapter 15, seeks innovations that replace forecasts with actual demand in making replenishment decisions.

What about the company with no confusion about where profitability lies? This is often the case when the product is based on intellectual property (IP), which often provides a monopoly position. An article in *The Wall Street Journal* (*WSJ*) described the implications of this product category.[3] Products based on IP are fundamentally different. Almost all the cost is in development, and almost 100 percent of every sales dollar is pure profit. Is supply chain management (SCM) important in supporting products high on IP? The answer is yes, there are at least three ways SCM supports IP monopoly products along their life cycle.

First, effective supply chain processes speed money-making products to market. Glitches that cause delays in product introduction leave money on the table. Also, according to Bill Gates as quoted in the *WSJ* article, such products require "monopoly power" when your product becomes an industry standard. A reliable supply chain is a requirement to establish this position. Without the domination, up-front investments will be total losses, not total profits.

Second, reducing lost sales requires adequate supplies to meet demand. Money-making products produce no profit if the sale is lost due to a stockout.

Finally, the innovative product is not innovative forever. It may die a sudden death as it matures if costs aren't in line with the competition. In mature markets where there is no monopoly, supply chain excellence becomes all the more important, as the Wal-Mart example illustrates. Section 4.2 describes how SCM practices should vary over the product life cycle.

3.3 Extended Products

Figure 3.1 illustrates how innovations forced on the supply chain by PESTEL forces feed the next SCM driver, extended products. Our definition in Chapter 2 describes the supply chain as "physical, information, financial, and knowledge flows whose purpose is to satisfy end-user requirements with physical products and services from multiple, linked suppliers." This includes a lot of intangible services as well as tangible products. In fact, as a *WSJ* article stated, "manufacturers find themselves increasingly in the service sector."[4] The article attributes the trend to manufacturers turning to services because that is "where the money is." Offering such services is also necessary to stand out from a crowded field.

The base product is the physical form of the product—its shape, features, and functionality. The term "form factor" is used in technology circles to describe the base product. The extended product includes other features that influence our purchasing decision. For the automobile shown in Figure 3.3, examples include the dealer network, financing, ease of doing business with the company and its representatives, the warranty, and brand image.

Few products and services are commodities in the strictest sense. In fact, features of the extended product may outweigh the importance of the base product,

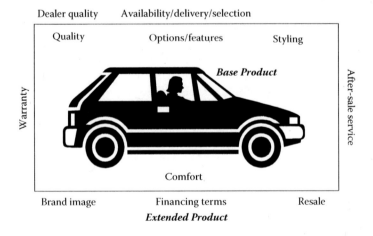

Figure 3.3   Base and extended products.

which customers may view as indistinguishable from competing brands. General Electric's former CEO, Jack Welch, points to service development associated with hardware production as fundamental to his success at General Electric.[5]

Along with this trend comes shorter life cycles for product-producing businesses and a shift in their assets, as reported in a *WSJ* article.[6] The article charts the trend in the value of total assets away from tangibles like inventory and factories to intangibles like IP, reputation, and technology. Since 1955, tangibles have declined from 78 percent to 53 percent. The article also reports that investments in intangibles such as research and development, software, and advertising have more than doubled as a percentage of gross national product (GNP) in the United States since 1978. How is the extended product a driver for supply chain change? In Figure 3.3, several extended product features for an automobile rely on supply chain design:

■ Availability/delivery/selection: Supply chain processes like inventory management, the ways orders are placed, a reliable supplier base, and physical distribution determine these features.
■ After-sales service and dealer quality: At the time of purchase, a customer enters a long-term relationship with the car company and its dealer. In fact, many auto dealers make little profit on the sale of a vehicle but rake it in after the sale.
■ Accessibility and ease of doing business: Interactions with a company can involve a host of customer contacts over the product's life cycle. These can draw key suppliers to the original equipment manufacturer (OEM). So, good choices are important to the OEM's success.

In an ideal world, the supply chain manager will methodically monitor the product and process innovations coming his or her way. The manager then makes changes to the supply chain to incorporate the innovation. Or, in a slightly less ideal world, the manager slots each innovation into the "best fit" supply chain already in place. However, many fall short of achieving this ideal. In fact, base product and extended product management are likely in separate functions. Base products reside in engineering and manufacturing departments, and marketing and sales functions rule over extended products. Managers may also assume every innovation fits into an existing supply chain, and inertia makes it hard to change supply chains. Everyone understands how things work now, and changes require investments in retraining, systems, staff, and facilities.

3.4 Globalization

For supply chain managers, globalization influences range from upstream suppliers to downstream customers. For smaller manufacturers who export to other countries, their executives must monitor not only production lines but also the currency markets.[7] The shift to "offshore" sourcing, usually to cut material cost, provides opportunities for jobs and investment in developing countries. When this occurs, globalization puts new money in people's pockets, widening markets for company products. For example, the Chinese demand for Rolls Royce is limited because relatively few can afford any car at all. But, as Chinese companies grow through exports, car buyers—even for the Rolls—are created.

Carly Fiorina, CEO of Hewlett-Packard, captured the potential for expanding markets around the world.[8] Her comments cited a speech by Bill Moyers[9] that profiled a village of 100 people that mirrored the global community:

- Fifty-seven people are from Asia, twenty-one from Europe, fourteen from the Western Hemisphere, and eight from Africa.
- Thirty are Christian.
- Eighty live in substandard housing.
- Fifty suffer from malnutrition.
- Twenty have never had a drink of clean water.
- Seventy can't read.
- Sixty-five have never made a phone call.
- Thirty-five have never made more than $2 a day.
- One is college-educated, and one owns a computer.

The profile demonstrates that there is much to do to raise living standards and create markets. Through globalization, many more could enjoy the benefits of the kind of prosperity advanced economies provide.

The numbers cited by Ms. Fiorina also demonstrate the "distance" between rich and poor in terms of living standards. In the global economy, this distance between rich and poor is as important as physical distance. Pankaj Ghemawat expanded the concept of distance in an article in the *Harvard Business Review*.[10] His definition of "distance" takes into account factors beyond the physical definition. He proposes a framework called "CAGE" because it addresses cultural, administrative, geographic, and economic distance.

Applying CAGE to a country like China puts the large population in that country into perspective. Despite the potential implicit in a large population (over 1.3 billion people), China is further away than the simple geographic distance implies. Ghemawat cites income level, multiple dialects, reliance on personal connections, high taxes, duties, government intervention in business, and corruption as factors that increase his definition of distance. With CAGE as a tool, he encourages managers to take an expansive view. According to his research, factors that decrease distance the most include having a common colonizer, currency, or joint membership in a trading block. All of these trump physical distance and common borders—principal measures of physical distance—in calculating CAGE distance. In fact, CAGE holds that the economic and social factors in PESTEL are likely to be the most important of the six factors.

Another globalization trend is the need for factories and their supply chains to serve broader, international markets. An example is Bombardier Transportation, which delivers rail equipment and aftermarket components for rail equipment for use around the globe. Through multiple acquisitions, the company had accumulated twenty-one manufacturing sites in Europe with 25,000 employees. Factory proliferation had become common because national governments favored local suppliers for their rail systems. The situation called for closing duplicate or redundant manufacturing capacity, a process referred to as "rationalizing" a supply chain. Propelling this trend had been the privatization of national rail systems. Unlike some government buyers, hard-nosed private operating companies go looking for the best deal for equipment and parts regardless of location. An important criterion for whether a plant had a future or not is that any surviving plants had to be competitive in export markets, capable of selling outside their home country.

This process had also been propelled by decisions of the European Court of Justice. The court rejected "golden shares" that had enabled countries to block acquisitions of local companies by outsiders. The purpose cited by the court is to remove "restrictions on the movement of capital between member states and third countries." In PESTEL terms, Bombardier Transportation's business was impacted by political, legislative, and economic factors.

China, a source for many components, is turning its attention to U.S. markets.[11] According to *Forbes,* Chinese companies, formerly anonymous hardware manufacturers, will seek to sell their own brands in U.S. markets. Examples include Haier Group, a maker of appliances and ranked #1 among Chinese companies in global brand "influence." Haier has over $15 billion in sales and has targeted a threefold increase in sales to the United States. Huawei Technologies serves the same markets as Cisco for network equipment. The company also wants to triple its export sales. To make these goals a reality, the companies are fast obtaining marketing and sales expertise.

In summary, the examples portray three globalization-related drivers for supply chain projects: new sources, new markets, and rationalization. New sources expand options upstream in the supply chain. New markets do the same downstream. Rationalization calls for restructuring—shifting one's own operations to different locales—to meet globalization challenges that diminish the relative importance of home country markets.

3.5 Flexibility Imperative—The Ultimate Capability

The last driver arising from the momentum for continuous improvement is the supply chain flexibility imperative. Absence of flexibility only works if an organization has no need to "flex" its supply chain as the environment changes. Since this is rare, there is an "imperative" for most supply chains to be flexible. Absence of supply chain flexibility also characterizes organizations serving different customers with different needs through a "one size fits all" approach. Chapter 4 describes this need further; Chapter 12 explains how to design and implement focused supply chains that provide flexible responses to customer and end-user needs.

The Wall Street Journal described the advantage enjoyed by Honda from its ability to change its product mix more quickly than it competitors.[12] The author described how Honda's plant in Ohio could shift from producing Civic models to the longer, taller CR-V in five minutes. Competitors who have traditionally designed their plants for specialization require investments of hundreds of millions to make similar conversions.

"Flexibility" is a term with different meanings to different people. The need for flexibility raises to an art form management decisions about what "flexible" actually is and what is needed in the way of supply chain flexibility. Later, this chapter describes a way to specify with rigor what a supply chain needs in the way of flexibility.

Others have tackled the job of defining flexibility. Flexibility and adaptability have performance metrics in the Supply-Chain Operations Reference-model (SCOR-model) maintained by the Supply-Chain Council. The five Level 1 SCOR-model metrics are of two types: (1) customer-facing metrics are reliability and responsiveness in addition to flexibility, and (2) internal-facing metrics are cost and asset utilization. The latter includes both working and fixed capital. Without flexibility and adaptability, the other four metrics are unlikely to be achieved. The only exception is in rare supply chains that enjoy firm orders, long-term visibility of market demand, and monopoly power. Peter Bolstorff provided an example of the use of SCOR-model metrics in a consumer products company.[13] The case describes how the company used the metrics to set goals for eleven supply chain projects in its portfolio. An analysis forecasted expected improvements in each SCOR-model metric that was used to calculate financial benefits. With objectives for each project established, Bolstorff recommends formal project charters to launch the projects, one of the tools of project management covered in this book.

Flexibility can be achieved in a number of ways. If a car dealer provides same-day delivery of either a blue, black, or red car to a customer, that dealer is considered "flexible" because he can quickly deliver a range of choices. For this, his supply chain might receive high marks from the SCOR-model for satisfying customers. However, the dealer may achieve flexibility by carrying a great deal of inventory, so all three colors are readily available on demand. This will hurt the internal-facing metrics, cost and asset utilization. However, if the dealer didn't carry inventory but had a supply chain that could create the car to order (just-in-time), its supply chain would not only be externally flexible but also internally cost- and asset-efficient. In the make-to-order example, the supply chain uses a different way to satisfy the customer's need.

Earlier, we stated that "flexibility" could have many meanings. The SCOR-model defines it as being able to move across a range of outputs without penalty.

The *APICS Dictionary* provides two sets of meanings: one for manufacturing systems and one for supply chains. For manufacturing systems, the *Dictionary* lists six categories of flexibility[14]:

- mix flexibility (the Honda plant example cited earlier),
- design changeover flexibility,
- modification flexibility,
- volume flexibility,
- rerouting flexibility, and
- material flexibility.

One might expect these types of flexibility in a factory but they are no less applicable to an entire supply chain because supplier flexibility may be necessary to make the OEM flexible.

At the supply chain level, the *Dictionary* includes the ability to mitigate the following uncertainties:

- demand forecast uncertainty,
- supply continuity variability,
- cycle time (end-to-end process time) plus lead time (market-driven delivery commitment) variability, and
- transit time plus customs-clearance time variability in the face of changing volume.

Most, if not all, supply chain and production planning is based on expectations for these parameters. Note that all four mention "variability" as the main culprit. In today's world, for example, reliable, non-varying lead times are likely to be more highly prized than shorter, variable lead times. This supply chain view holds that flexibility is the ability to adapt when expectations (for demand, supply continuity, cycle time, and transit time) prove false.

A broader view maintains that flexibility exists at three levels:

1. management mind-set (recognition of the need for flexibility and an ability to define what kind of flexibility is needed, supply chain design must rigorously specify and incorporate flexibility),
2. long-term (matching supply chain design with customer requirements), and
3. short-term (lead time and production flexibility).

The levels are interdependent. That is, a company must have #1 in order to get #2, and it must have #2 in order to get #3. The SCOR-model focuses on #3 and is quiet on #1 and #2. The APICS definitions are strong on production planning and scheduling for long and short-term needs but lacking in terms of considering external-facing, customer-oriented requirements for flexibility. The next sections define the three levels and their implications for defining supply chain flexibility and incorporating it into supply chain design.

3.5.1 Management Mind-Set

If you accept that change is a constant in the marketplace, then you must accept that flexibility is a necessity. As mentioned earlier, flexibility becomes the foundation for achieving any of the other high-level metrics in the SCOR-model for service and cost. In essence, being "flexible" means having the ability to move to where the supply chain needs to be with regard to reliability, responsiveness, cost, and asset utilization. Without flexibility to cope with changing conditions, there can be no reliable delivery, no responsiveness to customers, no efficiency, and no appropriate use of assets. "A clock that's stopped is accurate twice a day." This observation continues with the notion that a clock that's stopped, that's stuck and doesn't move, is of little value. Inflexible supply chains are like this. Possibly, they were correct at a single point in time. But, as markets and products changed, unchanging supply chains jeopardized the company's future.

For flexibility to be a reality, it has to be a real priority in the minds of managers. Often, it is simpler to define when the correct mind-set is absent rather than when it's present. Symptoms of mind-set absence appear in what executives measure and how they organize. Symptoms to look for that indicate the absence of planning for flexibility include the following:

- Company strategies are silent on the need for flexibility.
- Supply chain departments are frozen and unlinked. Separate budgets shape each function—purchasing, product design, manufacturing, product support, and distribution.
- The primary measure for supply chain managers is cost. A common metric is "supply chain cost per dollar of sales."
- Management is pursuing an inventory reduction campaign. Inventory is an effect, not a cause.
- Buyers are measured on unit costs of purchased material as they appear on purchase orders.
- Lost sales aren't estimated and tracked. No one is accountable for them.
- Inventory and other capital assets are "free." Their costs are not weighed in performance measures for any of the functions.

The presence of any of these should raise alarms. However, absence of any of the symptoms is not sufficient for achieving a management mind-set. Management must articulate the types of flexibility needed for the business. For that task, they need strategies for competing through SCM. Chapter 12 and Chapter 15 incorporate flexibility definition into project processes. There, we apply the approach described in the following section.

3.5.2 Defining Needed Flexibility

David Upton has focused on the flexibility topic, and has recommended a methodology for incorporating flexibility into planning manufacturing systems.[15] His definition of flexibility, similar to that provided by APICS and the SCOR-model, is stated in the following way:

> Flexibility is the ability to change or react with little penalty in time, effort, cost, or performance.

Upton proposes three dimensions for defining flexibility. The framework can easily be translated from the manufacturing system level, where he proposed it, to the supply chain. Table 3.2 summarizes the framework and provides examples.

Upton recognizes the problems that go with defining flexibility. Just saying "we need to be flexible" is inadequate, due to the many possible interpretations. To define the form of needed flexibility, Upton poses three questions, shown in the "Description" column in Table 3.2:

Table 3.2 Characterization of Flexibility

	Component	Description	Examples
1	Dimensions	What is it that requires flexibility?	Different input materials Product mix Different volumes
2	Time horizons	What is the period over which flexibility is required? • Operational: seconds to days • Tactical: days to months • Strategic: months to years	Operational: schedule changes, daily shipments Tactical: quarterly changes in mix, use of materials Strategic: long-range changes often requiring capital
3	Elements	In what way should we be flexible? • Range: by how much the dimension must be able to change • Mobility: low transition costs for moving in a range • Uniformity: the ability to be consistent over a range	Range: volumes of output, sizes of product, range of products Mobility: having low setup costs to change product mix Uniformity: building the ability to maintain service, process yield, and cost

What parameter requires flexibility? That is, in what "dimension" is flexibility needed? The six manufacturing system components identified by APICS and listed earlier are examples of dimensions.

What is the time horizon? The answer to this question identifies the "time horizon." Upton uses operational, tactical, and strategic for short (seconds, minutes, hours), medium (hours, days, weeks), and long time horizons (weeks, months, years).

What element must be flexible? This question addresses "elements" of flexibility. Upton describes range, mobility, and uniformity as the three elements likely to be encountered.

A range element will specify the limits of performance. For example, if volume flexibility (dimension) over a short period is sought (time horizon), the range will specify the high and low operating volumes (element). Mobility refers to the penalty of moving from one state in the range to another. For example, if there is little cost in moving from 100 units per hour to 150 units per hour, then mobility is high. On the other hand, if it is very difficult to make this change, mobility is low. Honda, cited earlier, has designed its factories to reduce this penalty. Uniformity refers to performance over a range. For example, if the move from 100 units to 150 units causes little change in the lead time for the product, then flexibility is high.

Figure 3.4 illustrates a supply chain flexibility specification, defining supply chain flexibility requirements for product mix, volume, and customer response time.

- Product mix changes are required over an operational time frame that, in this case, is daily. The element of flexibility is mobility. So, any product mix can be made at any time each day with the supply chain moving quickly from delivering one build-to-order product to another. A sandwich shop exemplifies this type of flexibility in a short time frame, with any sandwich on the menu being produced to order in minutes.
- Product volume in this example is the ability to change overall volume up or down in a tactical, or intermediate, time frame. A monthly time horizon

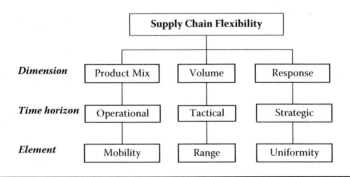

Figure 3.4   Defining flexibility (example).

likely fits the sandwich shop. So, the sandwich shop might adjust its schedule up or down based on the expected business level by month. If the shop were across the street from a college, then staff levels would be higher during the school year and lower during summer vacation. The range component would specify the product volumes used to set the high and low staffing levels.

■ Response time provides a standard that is competitive at the sandwich shop chain level. It is a "uniformity" element, meaning that customer response time must be uniform over the range of volumes in which the supply chain must operate. So, each sandwich shop in the chain must provide service within minutes at both high- and low-volume levels.

Flexibility specifications are "imperative" because they drive design of supply chain processes and shape collaboration with supply chain partners. Static specifications are not acceptable; the Upton method enables definition of ranges of operations and expectations for customer service. Also, many executives seek some kind of visual cockpit for their operations. A display based on defined flexibility parameters is an excellent view of the state of operations.

3.6 Process-Centered Management

Another driver of supply chain change is a focus on processes in driving improvements. Awareness of the importance of processes is not new. Re-engineering, the lean movement, total quality management (TQM), and Six Sigma are familiar process-oriented initiatives. But, there are barriers in the form of departmental and company boundaries that inhibit one from taking a process perspective. There is also often a "tension" between those wanting to focus on process and those wanting to bring technology, just because it's available, into the company. Jack Welch, in the previously cited interview, talks about "world peace" projects requiring complex IT.[16] In his first decade as General Electric's CEO, he approved many of these projects. His term, "world peace," refers to the overhyped promises made to promote such projects. The promises assured that the massive projects would be the ultimate answer to all shortcomings. When the promised results were never delivered, Welch reports he got a lot smarter and certainly more skeptical. In his second decade as CEO, only projects that produced tangible, fast results moved forward.

What is the implication for SCM? Is top-down, the process perspective, or bottom-up, the department perspective, the right model for SCM projects? Table 3.3 describes three scenarios framing how projects for supply chain improvement are formulated, justified, and managed. Scenario #1 in Table 3.3 is bottom-up, originating in the department. A project might be the purchase of a machine tool in the manufacturing department. "We cut our labor by 60 percent" is a claim that might describe results from such a project. Yet, it is likely a local savings, involving that portion of the process where the tool is used.

Table 3.3   Three Scenarios for Developing Supply Chain Projects

	Level	Sponsorship	Example Approaches	Goal	Justification
1	Function	Department head	Machine tools, new production equipment	Department improvement	Return on investment, savings
2	Company, business unit	CEO	Enterprise systems, expansions/ contractions	Business unit improvement	Revenue increase or cost reduction
3	Supply chain	CEO, customer, supplier, alliance	Information sharing, investment sharing	Supply chain competitiveness	Revenue and profit increase

Scenario #2 is top-down at the business-unit level, with projects that cross department boundaries. A customer relationship management (CRM) system is an example. "We increased our sales 5 percent" describes a claim of success for the system. However, an auditor might have difficulty tracing any "hard" return revenue increases to the system. Scenario #3 is "beyond" top-down because it extends beyond company boundaries. Projects in this category seek to reduce total cost in the supply chain. There are many obstacles to projects of this type. If supply chain partners are to be more involved in a company's improvement efforts, those companies must also be willing to rely on process-centered management approaches. To be effective at the supply chain level, Scenario #3 in Table 3.3 (a process focus, i.e., top-down) is a necessity. Reasons include avoiding local optimums at the expense of the overall process, the interdependence of departments and businesses in the supply chain, and the advantages of shared knowledge to solve problems.

But, there are also many obstacles that include physical separation, suspicion, poor cost accounting, fear of trade secret disclosure, counterproductive performance measures, and lack of skills or numbers. So, collaboration to improve processes is not easy. But, the beginning is a process-centered management focus with process definitions that extend beyond the boundaries of the business unit. The project management processes described in Section 3 will help you implement process-centered approaches at the supply chain level.

3.7 Collaboration

Few today dispute the need for collaboration in improving supply chains. Implementation, however, faces obstacles associated with working across company boundaries. This section takes a closer look at the collaboration driver. In Figure 3.1, collaboration plays a key role in generating continuous improvement in supply chain design.

3.7.1 Definitions of Collaboration

A big push for collaboration is technology-based. To many practitioners, the term "collaboration" is a code word for "information sharing," which is in turn code for "new systems." So, supply chain information applications, a category of software products, has emerged to support collaboration. These products enable sharing of transaction data like production and inventory data, online auctions, marketplaces for buying and selling, and scheduling production and delivery along the supply chain.

It should be no surprise, then, that definitions of collaboration have an IT tone. Table 3.4 shows the definitions of collaboration by industry analysts from three prominent research organizations.[17] At the time of presentation, these analysts represented organizations that report on technology employed along the supply chain.

As shown in Table 3.4, all three analysts described collaboration as a three-stage process. The levels begin with simpler forms of information sharing that are relatively easy to automate. They proceed to higher levels that involve joint decision making. These may be aided by technology but are essentially powered by management decision-making processes that are difficult to automate. Of the three, we favor the Forrester Research version because it captures the widest range of decision-making activity going beyond transactions to supply chain structuring. It

Table 3.4 Definitions of the Term "Collaboration"

	Company Represented		
Company	Yankee Group	AMR Research	Forrester Research
Analyst	Jon Derome	Larry Lapide	Navi Radjou
Level 1	Exchange of structured data	Execution (routine documents like purchase orders)	Monitor, watch the process together
Level 2	Free-form interactive sharing (Web tools, chats, online)	Information sharing, mostly one-way	Manage, coordinate activities
Level 3	Process collaboration (structured, mix of human and automated exchange)	Collaborative relationship (joint planning and scheduling, coordinated execution)	Optimize, joint decision making, win–win partnerships across network

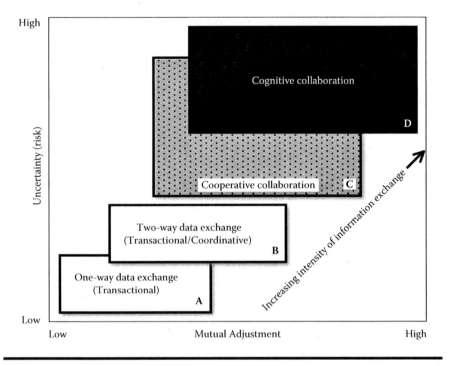

Figure 3.5   Collaboration road map.

also most clearly covers collaboration processes like strategic planning and sharing of needed investment to compete on a supply chain basis. Section 4.4 describes an expanded framework for collaboration.

A collaboration technical team working on the SCOR-model developed another collaboration framework. The team objective was to model different forms of collaboration to better associate those forms with individual SCOR-model activities. The resulting model, called a "collaboration road map," is depicted in Figure 3.5. The team adopted the following definition of "collaboration":

> A relationship built on trust that is benchmarked by the commitment to the team objective and where consensus may not always be achievable but where nothing takes place without the commitment of all involved.

The collaboration team defined motivations for collaboration in terms of a "hierarchy of business needs." The levels are comparable to Abraham Maslow's familiar hierarchy of needs: survival, safety, social and belonging, esteem and aesthetic, and self-actualization. Following is the collaboration hierarchy derived from this framework:

1. business survival,
2. sustained business activity,
3. sustained growth and market recognition,
4. channel master control, and
5. value chain leadership.

If your trading partner customer dictates to you, your choices are limited. Your motivating force is likely to be Level 1 or 2 in the hierarchy. On the other hand, Levels 3, 4, and 5 might drive the organization to carve out new space on the competitive landscape, as described in Section 4.4.2.1. At this point, the supply chain project moves beyond a traditional cost reduction to expanding market share and revenues.

The team defined three levels of collaboration that could support moves to higher levels in the hierarchy. The collaboration levels range from lower to higher levels in Figure 3.5:

- Data exchange collaboration, where partners (internal or external) exchange information as required, principally to complete day-to-day transactions. Data exchange can be one-way ("A" in the figure) or two-way ("B" in the figure).
- Cooperative collaboration ("C" in the figure), where partners (internal or external) share systems and tools so that all have access to information simultaneously.
- Cognitive collaboration ("D" in the figure) is the highest level requiring "joint, concurrent intellectual and cognitive activity between partners." This level embraces information sharing to reach joint decisions.

The committee originated the term "collaboratory" to characterize a partnership between parties. A collaboratory includes the business, cultural, and system environment needed to build and operate a linkage between partners. The collaboratory is intangible, based on trust and predictability, and involves work requiring intellectual skills to set it up.

On the vertical axis in Figure 3.5 is "uncertainty," which is also "risk," according to *A Guide to the Project Management Body of Knowledge (PMBOK Guide)*. The horizontal axis in Figure 3.5 measures "mutual adjustment." Low levels of uncertainty and mutual adjustment mean that, even if a transaction has a wide range of potential outcomes, these outcomes will bring little disruption to either party's operation. Business will go on "as usual" under most scenarios. Higher levels of uncertainty and mutual adjustment drive the need for more collaboration. "Intensity of information exchange" is measured by volume, range of participants, frequency, and complexity. As mutual adjustment and uncertainty increase, so does the need for increasing intensity of information exchange.

In transaction settings, low intensity is associated with readily available commodity products at widely known market prices. It is likely such a transaction can be completed by a simple one-way information transaction, as in Box A in Figure 3.5. For example, a buyer goes to the bookstore for a book. The book is in stock; the buyer buys the book and leaves the store. Communication is one-way from the book buyer to the bookstore. To the extent that any of these three conditions grows more uncertain, the intensity of information exchange increases. In Box B, the book buyer goes online and orders the book. The seller confirms the order by e-mail and notifies the buyer when the book is shipped. In this setting, there is two-way communication between buyer and seller.

High levels of mutual adjustment go with potentially disruptive outcomes. So, a multicompany supply chain project through a cognitive collaboratory in Box D needs to anticipate these outcomes and possible reactions. As an example, the auto assembly plant receiving just-in-time components shuts down if a single part is missing. The "cognitive collaboratory" to set the system up could assure capacity at the supplier, qualify new parts, put supplier plants close to assembly plants, require buffer stocks, set up real-time communications, and continuously monitor the financial and operating health of the supplier. Indeed, the lower levels of collaboration (Boxes A, B, C) may have resulted from a Box D collaboratory.

A *WSJ* article illustrates the need for cooperative forms of collaboration in Box C.[18] The article tells the story of the Grant J. Hunt Company, a distributor of fruits and vegetables headquartered in The Dalles, Oregon. The company buys produce from farmers and sells their products to supermarket chains, wholesalers, and restaurant-supply companies. The article recounts the experience of its president, Grant Hunt, in evaluating business-to-business (BTB) exchanges. An auction Web site would have produce farmers bid for Hunt's business. The proposed tool reflects the view that potatoes and other produce are commodities: sold in markets readily adaptable to online trading, characteristic of Box B.

However, Hunt's experience showed there is more to the buying and selling of fruits and vegetables than meets the eye. In the first place, the company has positioned itself as a partner with its suppliers and grocery store customers. Its Web site states the company is "more than fruits and veggies." Its extended product services include merchandising programs to promote produce in stores, category management for specific crops, crop updates and estimates to educate retailers, and a trucking service. Being more than fruits and veggies wasn't necessarily consistent with arm's-length auction sites that could create distance between trading partners.

Table 3.5 summarizes the result of trial implementation of the exchange.[19] Selling produce turned out not to be like selling books. In fact, much of the over-the-phone collaboration centered on advising customers about market conditions, not completing transactions. Also, as it turns out, produce (including potatoes) has many variations, and the type the buyer wanted wasn't always available. Hunt's staff had to work out alternatives with customers. Using a Box A or Box B business exchange model failed. Cooperative collaboration, in Box C of Figure 3.5, was the best model for the company. The lesson of the Hunt case is that one has to examine

Table 3.5   BTB Exchange Transactions: Promises and Realities

The Promise	The Reality
Joining an exchange would bring new customers.	The exchanges were seen to attract customers with marginal credit ratings. An Internet-posted offer to sell cherries produced no bidders in four days.
The exchange would streamline transactions bringing "incalculable efficiencies."	The existing infrastructure (faxes, phones, etc.) is not that inefficient. The exchange systems wouldn't link to homegrown systems. The result was duplication.
The Internet would increase business.	The best way to get business was to hit the phones and call suppliers and customers. The Internet alone wouldn't attract incremental business. Much of the service consists of advising suppliers and customers on market conditions. It is difficult to automate this function, and it wasn't offered by the exchange.
Big customers would require Web-based transactions.	Big customers said they wanted to shift business to the exchanges but—as of the date of the article—weren't able to follow through.
The Internet would improve visibility along the supply chain.	It was important to keep some prices and transactions confidential; the Internet opened the terms of these transactions to too many parties.
The exchange fee was competitive.	The fee of 1% to 2% was a steep price in a narrow-margin business like produce distribution.
The software would work.	The software wasn't ready for use. Several of the early providers that Hunt encountered left the business.
The software was flexible.	The systems wouldn't allow Hunt to changes prices quickly in response to market conditions. The software had difficulty processing abnormal transactions like returns. It failed on four of nine transactions selected for a test. The software had difficulty classifying different types of potatoes. Different distributors used different codes for the same type of potato.
The Hunt systems were outmoded.	They did work, however, and supply chain partners had grown accustomed to using them.

buyer–seller relationships in the supply chain in some detail to establish the real needs for collaboration.

3.7.2 Stage 3 (Multicompany) SCM

This chapter cites good examples of industry responses to the need for supply chain change. But, what form might collaboration take at a strategic level? An earlier article outlined a vision for "Stage 3" supply chain collaboration efforts.[20] The term "Stage 3" comes from the third, or supply chain, level as described in Table 3.3. Chapter 14 is a project blueprint for establishing this type of collaboration. Following is a list of some multicompany SCM features:

- Shared goals that include both strategic and tactical improvements. An example of the former is increased market share; an example of the latter is lower cost or reduced inventory.
- A team effort that includes representatives from participating companies.
- As needed, an honest broker to facilitate the effort. This can be a trusted team member or third party like a consultant.
- A multicompany CEO or senior management steering committee. This group would be responsible for the results of the collaboration.
- Contracting that distributes costs and rewards based on contributions. Negotiations over costs and profits shouldn't fall back on a standard buyer–seller, arm's-length, low purchase price model.
- Process integration using appropriate technology and continuous improvement.

The last bullet item also closes the loop, as shown in Figure 3.1, taking collaboration back to further supply chain innovation. A Stage 3 effort shouldn't be a one-shot affair; after the initial effort, improvements should continue. Once established, the supply chain partnership becomes a source of innovations.

3.8 Know Your Drivers

This chapter has addressed factors that make supply chain change a way of life. Some companies will be slow in recognizing which of these drivers affects them the most. However, the drivers will be there, exerting a force for change, even if it's not recognized in the organization. But, the need for coming to grips with change is inevitable. As we move on in this book, we explore in greater depth ways you can be successful at proactively managing the drivers rather than having them manage you. A prerequisite for proactive management is knowing which drivers are acting on you.

Notes

1. David Armstrong, Monte Burke, Emily Lambert, Nathan Vardi, and Rob Wherry, "85 Innovations," *Forbes*, December 2002, 124–210.
2. Bradford C. Johnson, "Retail: The Walmart Effect," *The McKinsey Quarterly* (no. 1, 2002): 4042.
3. Alan Murray, "Intellectual Property: Old Rules Don't Apply," *The Wall Street Journal,* August 23, 2001, A1.
4. Clare Ansberry, "Manufacturers Find Themselves Increasingly in the Service Sector," *The Wall Street Journal*, February 10, 2003, A2.
5. A conversation with Jack Welch, MSI Executive Series (Internet broadcast), April 16, 2002.
6. Greg Ip, "Why Many High Fliers Built on Big Ideas Are Such Fast Fallers," *The Wall Street Journal,* April 4, 2002, A1.
7. Michael M. Phillips, "Ship Those Boxes: Check the Euro!" *The Wall Street Journal,* February 7, 2003, C1.
8. Carleton S. Fiorina, "Widening the Communities of Knowledge," *Town Hall SpeakerDigest* (December 18, 2001): 104.
9. Bill Moyers is an American journalist with the Public Broadcasting System.
10. Pankaj Ghemawat, "Distance Still Matters: The Hard Reality of Global Expansion," *Harvard Business Review* (September 2001): 137–147.
11. Kerry A. Dolan and Quentin Hardy, "The Challenge from China," *Forbes*, May 13, 2002, 73–76.
12. Kate Linebaugh, "Honda's Flexible Plants Provide Edge," *The Wall Street Journal,* September 22, 2008, B1.
13. Peter L. Bolstorff, "From Chaos to Control with SCOR Metrics," *CSCMP Supply Chain Quarterly* (Quarter 2/2008): 65–73.
14. John H. Blackstone Jr., *APICS Dictionary,* 12th ed. (APICS—The Association for Operations Management, 2008), 52.
15. David M. Upton, "The Management of Manufacturing Flexibility," *California Business Review* (Winter 1994): 72–89.
16. A conversation with Jack Welch.
17. Larry Lapide, Jon Derome, and Navi Radjou, Analysts panel discussion: "Supply-Chain World North America: Extending Collaboration to End-to-End Synchronization," April 2002.
18. Lee Gomes, "How Lower Tech Gear Beat Web 'Exchange' at Their Own Game," *The Wall Street Journal*, March 16, 2001, A1.
19. A copy of this table appeared in *Supply Chain Myths and Realities,* by James B. Ayers (Auerbach Publications, 2001), 10.
20. James B. Ayers, Craig Gustin, and Scott Stephens, "Re-engineering the Supply Chain," *Information Strategy: The Executive's Journal* (Fall 1997): 13–18.

Chapter 4

Five SCM Tasks—
Foundation for
SCM Knowledge

This chapter summarizes five management tasks employed as a foundation for supply chain management (SCM) knowledge. They are also the basis for SCM project processes described in Section 3.

Chapter 1 introduced five managerial tasks, referred to in Table 1.2 as supply chain knowledge areas, which will change with the emergence of SCM. The five tasks, also the subject of the *Handbook of Supply Chain Management*, have always been important components of the managerial workload. However, the drivers of supply chain change, described in Chapter 3, require new ways of performing these traditional tasks. Table 4.1 lists the five tasks, along with the project management themes associated with each. Chapters 12 through 15 incorporate tools and concepts that constitute supply chain knowledge areas into project management execution tasks.

4.1 Introduction to the Five SCM Tasks

Task 1 is supply chain strategy design. It is consistent with the view, described in Chapter 2, that company strategy should include the supply chain. SCM is more than procurement or distribution—activities that conventional management practice views as costs to be controlled, not sources of strategic advantage. With regard

49

Table 4.1   Five Tasks for Better SCM

	Task	Description	Section 3 Chapter
1	Designing Supply Chains for Strategic Advantage	Marketplace success requires supply chain innovation. Supply chain design should support the company's strategy for competing.	12
2	Implementing Collaborative Relationships	Organization form, responsibilities, and measures enable or inhibit supply chain innovation. The place to begin is at home. Task 2 covers relationships inside the organization.	13
3	Forging Supply Chain Partnerships	Outside partners must participate to be successful. Old paradigms must be discarded. Effective project management requires an organized, multicompany approach.	14
4	Managing Supply Chain Information	Opportunities to succeed wildly or fail miserably abound. Information systems must support supply chain processes.	15
5	Removing Cost from the Supply Chain	Effective change requires understanding and managing root causes of cost in operating processes. The task embodies goals for both service and cost.	

to change drivers from Chapter 3, PESTEL,* extended products, flexibility, and globalization are all drivers of change addressed in supply chain strategic planning. (Refer to Figure 3.1).

Task 2 refers to internal collaboration. This collaboration is between departments or functions in the organization that need to work together. Gaining such collaboration is not trivial. A Webcast and report released in October 2008 by *Supply Chain Management Review* (*SCMR*) reports that overcoming interior boundaries remains the biggest barrier to supply chain improvement in most companies.[1] Companies tinker continuously with organization structures and performance measures. But, reorganizing alone is insufficient for gaining lasting improvement.

---

* PESTEL is an acronym for political, economic, social, technical, environment, and legislative factors.

Effectively partnering with external partners is the goal of Task 3. Different types of partnership are required for each situation. The task describes the alternative forms of partnership and where each form fits best. Also, roles in the supply chain are changing, with companies offloading some functions to partners while incorporating or cultivating others as core competencies. Effective performance of Tasks 2 and 3 produces collaboration leading to continuous improvement, our primary driver of supply chain change.

Tasks 4 and 5 reflect the drive for process-centered management, another of the drivers identified in Chapter 3. Information technology management providers flood the marketplace with products and accompanying claims for their efficacy. A growing consensus is that, to effectively manage supply chain information (our Task 4), the process to be improved must be the primary focus. Cost cutting (Task 5) will never go out of style and is always an important SCM component. However, it too must be process-focused, as supply chain costs are consequences of process design. One objective of process improvement efforts in manufacturing and distribution companies is to replace forecasts with actual demand in replenishment decisions—what this book and others in the series refer to as the demand-driven supply chain. The demand-driven supply chain is compared frequently with the forecast-driven supply chain. Not to be ignored in all this is the need, while cutting costs, to maintain competitive levels of service.

Barriers to effective SCM are outdated paradigms that dominate relationships in supply chains. The buyer–seller arm's-length relationship is an example. Unintended consequences can be the result of measures geared at cutting material costs. Also, many costs are little understood. Too few organizations work effectively to reduce costs simply because they don't understand the root causes for the costs they are trying to cut.

This is a "how to" book. Chapters 12 through 15 describe the project management processes needed to execute the SCM tasks. The remainder of this chapter highlights knowledge, practice in the form of tools, and terminology for performing these tasks. Section 3 will place all of these into project execution tasks.

4.2 Task 1: Designing Supply Chains for Strategic Advantage

Managers in supply chain functions can no longer limit themselves to single disciplines like procurement, manufacturing, or distribution. Section 2.2 noted the shift to a broader view by many professional organizations, including APICS, the Council of Supply Chain Management Professionals (CSCMP), and the Purchasing Management Association of Canada (PMAC). Managers also need an understanding of company markets, needs filled by company products, and the competitive landscape. A trait of low-performing companies is ignorance of these dynamics—also a finding of the 2008 *SCMR* survey cited earlier. This leads to static supply chain designs that leave the company vulnerable to competitors.

4.2.1 The Nature of Markets and Products

Fundamental to developing supply chain strategies is awareness of market segments. Market segmentation is a long-used tool of marketing and sales organizations. Segments are customer or user groups with common characteristics. In the automobile market, BMW caters to a different segment, often loosely referred to as "high end," than Saturn, which caters to the "low end" cost-sensitive segment. It is also likely that the BMW buyer will have different expectations for extended product services than the Saturn buyer. To be a successful dealer for either of these products, you must understand and design your business model and supply chain to match those expectations.

Figure 4.1 illustrates the danger of ignoring this advice. The figure shows a typical supply chain from a company's suppliers to its customers, shown as three distinct segments. Figure 4.1 also shows four of the six top-level Supply-Chain Operations Reference-model (SCOR-model) processes: PLAN, SOURCE, MAKE, and DELIVER. The other two, RETURN and ENABLE, are omitted for the sake of brevity. Instead of there being one "monolithic" customer on the right, there are three customer segments, numbered 1, 2, and 3. Cost may be the basis that defines these segments, with some segments being cost-sensitive; others may view service as more important. Quality might be another basis for segmentation. Some segments may be especially demanding in terms of requiring high quality; others may be satisfied with lower quality. Examination of extended product features, described in Section 3.3, can also lead to alternate definitions of segments. Following is a list of some successful companies that have employed segmentation and supply chain excellence to differentiate their offerings:

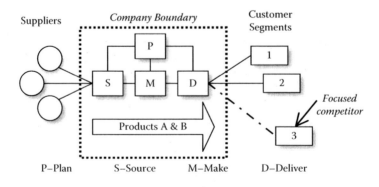

Figure 4.1 Penalty for poor SCM strategies.

- Enterprise Rent-A-Car established off-airport rentals focusing on non-travelers' rental car needs.
- IKEA Group, the furniture maker, sells low-cost, unassembled furniture in a self-service environment. Its target segment is the buyer wanting stylish furniture and willing to put it together—or pay extra to have someone else do it.
- Contract manufacturers in the electronics industry serve original equipment manufacturers (OEMs) with manufacturing and logistics capabilities tailored to each customer's needs.
- U.S. manufacturers in globalizing industries, who face lower-cost importers, recast their supply chains for greater flexibility and fast response.

Segmentation requires companies to make choices about their supply chain design. Those who use a single supply chain design to serve several segments are at risk. Eventually, a competitor will sniff out opportunities to do a better job serving one or more of the segments (Segment #3 in Figure 4.1). The competitor will then run off with that business, also shown in Figure 4.1. They'll do this by responding to that segment's needs with better prices, service, base and extended product features, or quality than that provided by a "one size fits all" supply chain.

A second product-market dynamic is the product life cycle, shown in Figure 4.2. A new product starts life with low sales, shown as the inception phase. At inception, the product is both produced and marketed through an existing supply chain. Alternately, if the product's markets are new to the company, the company must build its supply chain from scratch or market its products through existing outside distribution channels. In this stage, most companies will adjust supply chain processes because product design and market preferences are likely to be fluid.

If the product is successful, the product moves into the growth phase. Growth brings prosperity, and profits are plentiful. Often, the supply chain for the product

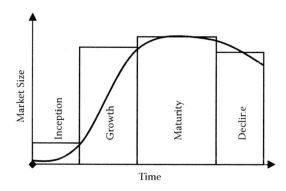

Figure 4.2   The product life cycle.

can't keep up, and products are hard to get because demand exceeds supply. At this point, competitors enter the market, sharing in the riches.

As sales level off, the market for the product enters the maturity phase. Competitors are still there, attracted by fat profits enjoyed during the growth phase. Design changes increasingly fail to produce incremental sales because the product is "good enough." Competitors also quickly copy design changes. Margins tighten, and a battle for market share ensues. Now, a company may want to outsource supply chain tasks to specialists. This expands the company's competencies with specialists who can lower costs and provide paths to new markets. In the last stage, decline, sales drop. As they do, those who aren't competitive exit the market.

Marshall Fisher promotes the idea that different product types require different types of supply chain.[2] He observes two types of products: innovative and functional. With regard to the product life cycle, innovative products are those in the inception and growth phases. Functional products, like those we buy every day, are in maturity or decline stages. Fisher argues that innovative products require responsive supply chains, and that functional products require cost-effective supply chains. This is because the higher profit margins that go with innovative products justify "inefficient" supply chain practices like fat inventories, expedited shipping, and other exceptional expenses that assure supply to eager customers.

Figure 4.3 combines Fisher's insight with the product life cycle model. In the inception and growth phases, competitive battles are centered on the product itself, the base product as shown in Figure 3.3. The primary supply chain mission is to assure supply. As the product matures, the basis for competitiveness shifts from the base product to the supply chain, including the chain's extended product features. Base product features become increasingly commodity-like with only minor

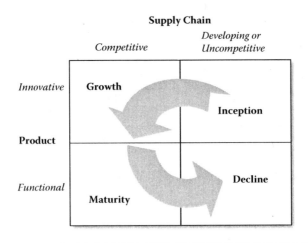

Figure 4.3   Market positions of products.

differences among them. The supply chain, loaded with extended product features as described in Section 3.3, must also be cost-effective for the product to survive.

A mismatch occurs when the responsive model is used for functional products or the cost-effective model is used for innovative products. For innovative products, the cost-effective model leads to lost sales or surplus goods. Thus, a supply chain manager measured on costs for logistics and inventory may hurt the company's bottom line by pursuing these objectives. The damage comes from being too tight-fisted when there is robust demand that goes unmet. For functional products, customer service can be too good, leading to excessive inventory and other inefficiencies.

Few measure financial losses from either lost sales or excessive supply chain cost. In the best of worlds, such a measure would be an estimate. So, accountants are reluctant to ascribe "phantom" numbers requiring guesses about a "cost" like lost sales. Fisher refers to these costs as "market mediation" costs. However, lost sales, write-offs, and too-high operating expense are real costs incurred from failing to match supply and demand, a primary supply chain mission. When such costs will make a difference to decision makers, they should be estimated, considered a cost of doing business, and targeted for reduction.

Can a product be both innovative and functional at the same time? The answer is yes, if you define the product in terms of its extended product features. For example, the cloth maker that can deliver a commodity material base product to support a "hot" fashion trend inside a week has an innovative extended product (fast delivery) by virtue of its flexibility. The same material ordered nine months in advance from a Chinese manufacturer for a lower unit price is a functional product. The Grant J. Hunt Company, introduced in Section 3.7, is another example. The produce Hunt sells is functional but the ample free advice is an extended product feature accompanying its fruits and vegetables. For manufacturers caught in the globalization vice, extended product features, based on supply chain flexibility, may be their best recourse.

Dr. Hau Lee, the Stanford University supply chain expert, also uses a functional and innovative product framework to classify uncertainties in upstream supply and downstream demand[3]:

Scenario #	Supply Uncertainty	Demand Uncertainty	Examples
1	High	High, innovative products	New products, semiconductors
2	Low	High, innovative products	Fashion apparel, toys, music
3	High	Low, functional products	Weather-dependent produce, precious metals
4	Low	Low, functional products	Basic apparel, grocery products

In this framework, supply chains low on demand and supply uncertainty (Scenario #4) should stress efficiency. These chains are particularly enhanced by demand information relayed up the chain. Matching that demand with reliable supply enables a lean supply chain characterized by increases in inventory turns and utilization of pipeline resources like trucks and shelf space. Low demand, high supply uncertainty supply chains (Scenario #3) should build risk-hedging methods into their supply chain processes. This could be the result of formally developed business continuity plans (BCPs) that call for multiple suppliers for critical components, inventory buffers, and information sharing along the supply chain.

High demand, low supply uncertainty supply chains (Scenario #2) must emphasize responsiveness. No factories in China for these supply chains; response times must be minimized, and flexibility is key. An example business continuity strategy could be contingency stocks of raw materials ready to be configured into end products, a postponement approach. Supply chains where both demand and supply are uncertain (Scenario #1) require what Lee calls "agility." This may come in the form of a "network" of flexible manufacturing resources making up the "virtual" enterprise. Designing products with as many common parts as possible can also mitigate such a situation.

4.2.2 Model for Competing through SCM

"Actions speak louder than words" is an old saying. Organizations don't always practice what they preach. A way to understand an organization's strategy is to examine the projects underway at the company. Figure 4.4 is a model for competing through

Level 1 Function	Level 2 Company	Level 3 Supply Chain
	Strategic Changes basis for competition Proprietary product/process technology Market-based justification Broad sponsorship	
	Non-Strategic Fixes a problem Non-proprietary technology ROI, cash flow justification Functional sponsorship	

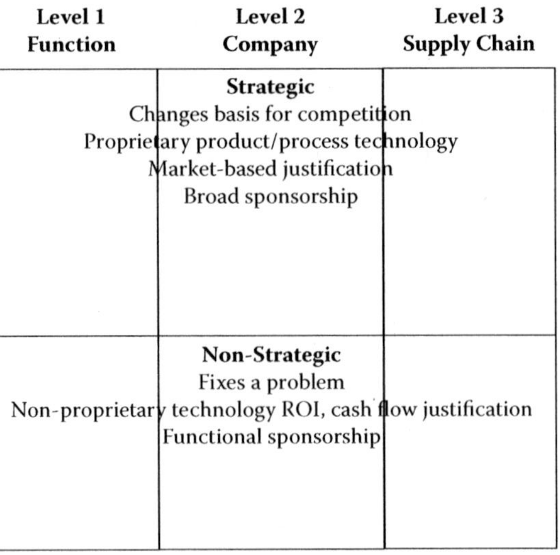

Figure 4.4 Types of supply chain improvement projects.

SCM, utilizing the three-level model introduced in Section 3.7.2. The model displays the levels of project (function, company, supply chain) from left to right, and the type of project (strategic or non-strategic) from top to bottom. The figure also lists criteria for identifying strategic and non-strategic projects.

The way most companies work leads to projects in the lower left-hand corner. A climate that encourages fast payback projects supports non-strategic functional projects. Lack of internal collaboration also leads to selection of projects confined to a single function. If companies improve internal collaboration, Task 2 in our list of SCM tasks, more projects will occur at the company or business-unit level. Effective collaboration along the supply chain will add projects at Level 3. The model in Figure 4.4 should aid those implementing supply chain strategies. Its use assures that strategy making is indeed generating a portfolio of strategic projects to implement those strategies.

4.2.3 SCM Strategy Tools

There are many views of what a supply chain strategy might be. What content should such a strategy have? Should the supply chain strategy be separate from the rest of the company's strategy? How does a company incorporate the drivers described in Chapter 3 into their SCM strategy? Our view is summarized by the following propositions:

- Operating processes, including all those we associate with the supply chain, can be a source of competitive advantage and are as important as other strategy elements like product mix or design.
- The supply chain is not only a cost of doing business but also an opportunity for improving competitive position by delivering better service along with base and extended products.
- SCM should be intertwined with the company "strategy." It may be at the center of the strategy (like Dell's direct model) or supportive of that strategy.
- SCM as a strategy is necessary but not sufficient. The other factors like customer selection, product mix and design, the social–political environment, financial constraints, and other factors must also be considered.
- Supply chain measures should support strategic goals.

There are many ways to develop strategies that incorporate these propositions. Two are described here. The first approach, using best practices from industry organizations like the CSCMP and the Supply-Chain Council, produces a narrower, operations-oriented strategy for improvement. Users must take additional steps to link these best practices with other strategic components. The second approach, activity systems, produces a broader strategy that defines needed supply chain processes and incorporates other strategic components. The two approaches employed together can produce operating improvements along with new strategic directions.

4.2.3.1 Industry Best Practice Approach

The SCOR-model, described in more detail in Chapter 8, recommends metrics as a basis for a supply chain strategy. An article by Peter Bolstorff, cited in Chapter 3, expands on this approach.[4] The product line metrics enable identification of key success factors and comparison of one's own company to competitors. This process is supported by flowcharts using processes at Level 3 in the SCOR-model to define implementation projects. A supply chain strategy, based on improving in areas judged to be the most important to the business, arises from this comparison.

The SCOR-model contains many metrics spread throughout its three levels. There are metrics for customer-facing and internal-facing measurement. Many SCOR-model users follow an approach similar to that shown in Table 4.2, which shows the top, or Level 1, SCOR-model metrics, in this case for Version 9.0. The table points out "where to go" in terms of supply chain improvement using the following steps:

1. Pick the performance attributes or metric of most importance to your business, product line, or customer segments (column 2).
2. Set priorities for the metrics. In which areas does the company have to excel (column 1)?
3. Compare or benchmark your company's current performance against competitors (column 5). Identify the best opportunities for improvement. Such best practices are listed in the SCOR-model and the CSCMP's *Supply Chain Management Process Standards (Process Standards).*[5] Use current measures to establish an "as-is" baseline that measures performance for the current supply chain.
4. Develop strategies to close performance gaps.

Table 4.2 shows the SCOR-model top-level metrics in the customer-facing and internal-facing categories (columns 3 and 4). Customer-facing metrics are those that measure performance attributes that are visible to customers. Examples are delivery performance and lead time. Internal-facing components, mostly financial, are those of concern to internal stakeholders, namely, owners and managers of the business. In this case, the company has decided that two Level 1 metrics don't apply—"NA" for not applicable (Step 1). Perhaps all raw materials are commodity-like and readily available from a variety of suppliers. So, Downside Supply Chain Adaptability and Return on Working Capital aren't relevant.

For Step 2, the company ranks the priority for the metric. This company ranks the most important metrics as an "A" and metrics of low importance as a "C." The last three columns, "Competitive Assessment" collectively evaluate the company's position relative to competitors. The data shows the company is underperforming in customer-facing areas ("Underperforming Competitors" column) and overperforming in internal-facing ones ("Exceeds Competitors" column). From Table 4.2,

Table 4.2   Using the SCOR-model to Define a Supply Chain Strategy

1	2	3 Customer-Facing			4 Internal-Facing		5 Competitive Assessment		
Priority	SCOR-model Level 1 Metrics	Reliability	Responsiveness	Agility	Cost	Assets	Underperforms Competitors	Exceeds Competitors	Opportunity
C	Perfect Order Fulfillment	•					■		
A	Order Fulfillment Cycle Time		•				■		
A	Upside Supply Chain Flexibility			•			■		■
A	Upside Supply Chain Adaptability			•				■	
NA	Downside Supply Chain Adaptability			•				NA	
A	Supply Chain Management Cost				•			■	
C	Cost of Goods Sold				•			■	
C	Cash-to-Cash Cycle Time					•		■	
C	Return on Supply Chain Fixed Assets					•		■	
NA	Return on Working Capital					•		NA	

Note: Priorities: A = high priority, B = medium priority, C = low priority, NA = not applicable.

you should conclude that the company stresses financial performance over customer service. At Step 4, the analysis identifies Upside Supply Chain Flexibility as an opportunity for improvement. Perhaps improvement here will improve customer service while retaining expected financial performance.

The illustration describes the essence of the SCOR-model approach. There are many alternatives for gathering and presenting the gathered information. Note that the SCOR-model approach focuses on the measures directed at managing production and distribution processes, those that produce the base product. In Chapter 3, we identified the "extended product" as a basis for competition. In setting priorities for performance attributes and identifying opportunities for improvement, a company should consider other strategy elements like extended product features. However, this has to be a concerted effort involving functions beyond those most closely associated with the supply chain—procurement, manufacturing, and distribution. The next section describes an approach that does this.

4.2.3.2 Activity Systems

Michael Porter, a strategic planning expert, has formulated the activity system approach.[6] Along with other writings, Porter's premise is that competitiveness arises from a network of company "activities" performed differently than in rival companies. These multiple activities are linked, making competitor replication difficult—certainly far more difficult than replicating any single activity. Armed with unique activity systems, the organization can better withstand competitive attacks. A procedure for strategy development using this framework includes the following steps:

1. Pick attractive market segments for your products. (Section 4.4.1 describes a related concept called "spheres" or "businesses inside the business.")
2. Choose how to compete for the attractive segments.
3. Develop themes to support each choice.
4. Design activities containing operating processes that support the themes.
5. Link the activities into an activity system.

Making choices, required in Steps 1 and 2, is hard for many executives. One might be forced to forsake customer segments or drop products, choosing to serve one customer and not another. This is counterintuitive, especially if one believes any revenue, regardless of profitability, is better than no revenue at all. Also, using the sphere technique described later, the company may end up with multiple supply chains, each tailored to the needs of different segments. This may add complexity or seem to require outright duplication leading to increased operating costs and assets.

By creating activity system uniqueness, the company escapes "commoditization" where rivals compete solely on price. Our example in Table 4.2 is likely competing on price. But, the company's customer service is deemed below industry standards. If it doesn't improve its customer service, the company's only way to compete is to grind out cost reductions. So far, it seems to have succeeded. But, the future is in doubt if competitors attack profitable segments with strategies designed around unique activity systems.

Herman Miller Inc., a market leader that designs, manufactures, and sells furniture systems and products for offices and health care facilities, undertook a classic overhaul of the supply chain for one of its divisions at the time, Miller SQA. The initials stood for "simple, quick, and affordable," themes that targeted the price-sensitive market for its office products. Motivations for the project and the resulting design have been widely emulated in the industry.[7] Miller's office furniture includes chairs, panel systems, desks, and file cabinets. These are built to order with different designs and mixes of components. At the time of the case, customers ordered through dealers or the Miller SQA sales force. The back-and-forth nature of major purchases could take many weeks. Also, delays in delivery may have led to "buyer's remorse" and cancellation of orders. Before Herman Miller implemented its new "model," competitive lead times were four to six weeks for delivery plus another couple of weeks for installation. Often, furniture was shipped by the manufacturer, stored at the local dealer, and then installed at the customer's site.

In its effort, Herman Miller worked to transform its entire "value chain," not just a piece of it. Miller defined this chain as having the following components, also shown in Table 4.3 as "phases" in the fulfillment process:

- customer contact to order entry,
- order entry to shipment, and
- shipment to installation.

It was important to Herman Miller to take this holistic approach. Manufacturing only represented 20 percent of total lead time. If other components couldn't be reduced, customers would see little difference. After implementing the new supply chain, Miller was capable of reliably filling orders in ten days. An important consideration in achieving short lead times was the susceptibility to order changes and outright cancellation. Miller also sought to increase the financial return on its business. Their measure was EVA (economic value added), which, in essence, assigns the cost of working capital and fixed assets to process cost. A particular concern to Miller was the cost of inventory. This also meant reducing the cash-to-cash cycle and lowering inventory and manufacturing assets. Traditional accounting doesn't always assign the cost of working capital and fixed assets to processes. So, financial statements often ignore an important cost. The broad

Table 4.3   Herman Miller Supply Chain Activities

Phase	Activity/ Process	Description
Customer Contact to Order Entry	Easy customer interface	An activity driven by the philosophy of quickly providing information to customers about the product to facilitate decisions.
	Order entry tool: "1.1"	Online catalog showing products. Acts as order entry mechanism. Transmits the order to the factory.
	Visualization tool: "Z-Axis"	Keeps running price. Generates bill of material. Enables the customer to view the layout in three dimensions; hence, the name "Z-Axis."
Order Entry to Shipment	Build-to-order	A production system capable of delaying production until after the order is received.
	"Production Metering Center"	A raw material facility that processes incoming materials, staging them for production. Interfaces with suppliers, enables low raw material inventory.
	ERP	Enterprise resource planning system. Stores bill of materials and financial data.
	"Expert Scheduling"	A proprietary application and accompanying manual interventions for scheduling production. It is continuous, avoiding MRP problems associated with periodic updates.
	MES	Manufacturing execution system. System that assigns work orders to production lines.
	Visibility	Information sharing so that trading partners know what others are doing.
	New contracting	Altered terms for suppliers. Shifted inventory responsibility and set tight schedules for delivery.
	"SupplyNet"	Supplier information sharing. Internet tool for sharing material status throughout the supply chain. Includes stock at Miller and its suppliers.
Shipment to Installation	Direct delivery	Delivery to the end-user sites, bypassing dealers' warehouse facilities and the associated handling costs and time delays.

Table 4.3 (continued)   Herman Miller Supply Chain Activities

Phase	Activity/ Process	Description
	Multi-order shipping	Shift from a reliance on less than truckload to full truckload. Enables efficient routing of multiple orders on a single truck.
All	Empowered customer service	Ability of customers to contact a person who can answer questions and make decisions on the customers' behalf. Contact points are staffed to provide high levels of access.

strategy to maximize EVA was to shift replenishment decisions from forecast-driven to demand-driven.

The Miller team followed an important project management principle. White paper guidance by project management practitioners has produced the "100% rule,"[8] which states (in project management argot):

> The next-level decomposition of a WBS [Work Breakdown Structure] element must represent 100% of the work applicable to the next higher (parent) level.

Miller's decision to include end-to-end processes to scope their project adheres to this principle. With regard to the model in Figure 4.4, the effort became a Level 3 supply chain effort. Herman Miller used a combination of management savvy, lean manufacturing techniques, and technology to achieve its ends. We can derive an activity system using the activity systems components Miller exploited to accomplish its goals. These are depicted in Table 4.3 and Figure 4.5.

Herman Miller's intent was to rely on its established reputation for product quality and shift the basis of competition to fast, efficient service. Miller SQA (simple, quick, affordable) provides the themes for this approach, our Step 3. Our version of the Miller activity system adds maximizing EVA as a theme; it was a motivator and target metric to measure the effectiveness of the effort. EVA improvement would come from reductions in lost revenue, lower inventory, faster collection of revenue, and increases in plant utilization.

Figure 4.5 shows the linkages between activities. If Figure 4.5 resembles a spider web, it's no accident. Lines connect themes (shown in circles) and activities (in boxes). The activities that directly support the themes are also darkened; build-to-order manufacturing, easy customer interface, and direct delivery. Supporting these activities are other activities. For example, the "Z-Axis" application is part of an order entry program. New contracting altered the relationship with suppliers, including requiring suppliers to hold inventory and make frequent deliveries from plants in Southwest

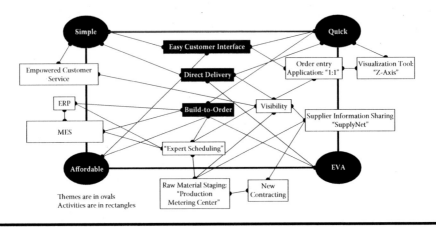

Figure 4.5   Herman Miller activity system.

Michigan. This enabled a third-party "Production Metering Center," managed by Menlo Logistics, that processed raw materials to supply build-to-order production lines. Miller has since made the Metering Center an internal function.

The activity system is a powerful tool for building company strategies, including missions for the supply chain. The tool enables internal collaboration by drawing on all functions to coordinate what otherwise might be disparate, department-level efforts. It also supports responses to the SCM drivers described in Chapter 3. By identifying how the company will compete, the process should define flexibility requirements. Activity systems, because they are operationally focused, also support process-centered management. Strategy making with the activity system approach develops supply chain process needs and shows where those processes fit the strategic picture. Finally, where gaps in internal operations need to be filled, collaboration with outside partners can fill the holes. Working with suppliers and local dealers was an important element in implementing the Miller system.

4.2.4   New Products and Processes

Chapter 3 put product and process innovation as the central driver of supply chain change. Figure 4.6 summarizes different types of innovations. The lower right-hand quadrant represents the *status quo.* From there, each type of innovation can move the organization in a different direction. The upper right-hand quadrant (new product, existing process) describes companies with a constant flow of new products. The music company that produces many new releases has a well-used supply chain; so does the restaurant chain that churns out new menu items. In these cases, products continuously take new shapes but process changes are incremental. A large part of what the company does is to operate the "machine" that brings new products to market.

Process

	New	Existing
Product New	Radically New Product	Repetitive Products: Movies, Restaurant Menus
Existing	Process Breakthrough: Herman Miller, Internet	Current Product/Process Mix

Figure 4.6 Types of product and process innovation.

The lower left-hand quadrant (existing product, new process) happens when a process innovation radically alters the economics of an industry or even enables new products. Process improvements that pack more functions on smaller and smaller silicon chips are an example. Supply chain innovation, like Herman Miller's, also lies in this quadrant. The Internet's role in marketing and selling merchandise is another example of process innovation. A flexible machine tool that can quickly shift from one part to another is another innovation that adds flexibility to the supply chain.

The upper left-hand quadrant brings changes in both product and process dimensions. These can be breakthrough core products or the fruits of advanced R&D. Technology products like personal computers and copiers were such products when they first reached their markets. Their success required new supply chains to support production and sales of the new technology. Process-centered management calls for concurrent development of both product and process. This has the benefit of faster development, a benefit in an era of shrinking product life cycles. Project management processes should be ready to accelerate supply chain process improvements in response to new product introductions or development of more competitive processes.

4.3 Task 2: Implementing Collaborative Relationships (see Table 4.4)

Task 2 turns inward to issues of collaboration within company walls. One can hardly argue that the company's ability to manage itself and its supply chain initiatives isn't a requisite for improvement. For example, if one wants to develop an activity system like Herman Miller's, boundaries must be extended to many departments in order to comply with PMI's "100% rule." These include not only

Table 4.4   Alternative Organization Forms

Type of Organization	Preferred When:	Not Preferred When:
Functional/ process-centric	Narrow product line or small organization All products have similar processes and common needs for cost, service, and flexibility Mature business (Stage 3 and 4 life cycle products) with low growth or design change Capital intensive production technology Dominant production competence required, technical excellence required in a focused area	Diverse product/ customer base, particularly where the strategic plan must address multiple market segments Products in several life cycle stages Flexibility important in adjusting to changing conditions
Product-centric	Multiple products with differing process technologies New product undergoing changes in growth markets (Stages 1 and 2) Cost-driven business, functional products Homogeneous customer base—one or only a few segments Uncertain supply environment, weak supplier base	Serving varied customer base with differing requirements Relatively low cost production technology Cost secondary to service in production decision Little in the way of process technology innovation
Customer-centric	Strategy that targets attractive segments Alliances needed in distribution channels Outsource capabilities readily available Style driven business requiring fast response, innovative products Market segments demanding different extended product features Heterogeneous customer base/many segments Uncertain demand environment, difficult forecasting	Too many segments to serve Lack of scale could cause loss of focus Price sensitive market

manufacturing but also sales, procurement, product, engineering, systems development, and finance.

Also, functional departments, often focused on their own issues, must work with other departments toward a common goal—in Miller's case, improving EVA. To keep things going, top management must be involved with timely decisions, moral encouragement, and financial support. The organization structure and performance measures also must also be "in sync" with the direction sought, topics addressed in Chapter 12 and Chapter 13 project process descriptions.

In this chapter, we discuss the "boundary" issues regarding the scope of the improvement effort. This involves market segmentation as discussed earlier, company organizations, and dividing the overall supply chain into logical "chunks" for activity systems. We call these chunks "spheres" or "businesses within (or inside) the business." A sphere is made up of customer–product–operations combinations. Such a sphere is carved out if the organization needs a separate activity system and accompanying supply chain. For Herman Miller, the activity system in Figure 4.5 was targeted at the economy buyer. Later, success with those customers made perfectly good sense for other segments.

A decision regarding organization structure also falls under this task. The best organization for the future is often not the one currently in place, so here we describe the basic options (Table 4.4) for changing it:

- functional/process-centric (depicted in Figure 4.7),
- product-centric (depicted in Figure 4.8), and
- customer-centric (depicted in Figure 4.9).

The next sections discuss the choices available and the environments that support each alternative.

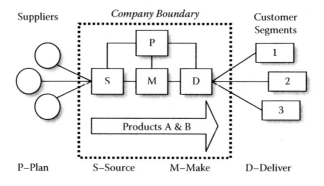

Figure 4.7 Functional, process-centric organization.

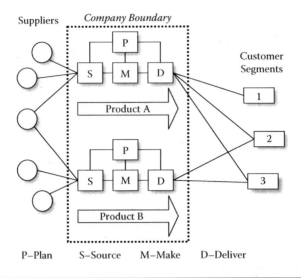

Figure 4.8   Product-centric organization.

4.3.1 Functional or Process-Centric Organizations

The first organization type (Figure 4.7) is functional or process-centric. This type defines most mature organizations with "one size fits all" supply chains. Typical functional departments in a manufacturing company include manufacturing operations, distribution, procurement, customer service, and finance. Like Figure 4.1, Figure 4.7 uses the SCOR-model core management processes—PLAN, SOURCE, MAKE, and DELIVER—to model the supply chain structure. The figure shows three suppliers and three market segments (1, 2, and 3). Both company products (A and B) flow through the same functions. In this structure, operations processing the work product (MAKE) may also be functionally organized with equipment distributed into work centers organized by type of equipment.

The functional organization with its focus on specialization by work units in the organization is often the product of relentless cost reduction through ratcheting down department budgets. As such, the functional structure usually does a good job of producing "local optimums" in terms of cost. Examples are the cheapest possible raw materials (low-cost SOURCE), production processes with low labor cost (low-cost MAKE), and cost-optimized distribution channels (low-cost DELIVER). The functional organization also is likely to rely on Level 1 improvement project types, those populating Level 1 on the left in Figure 4.4. Most of these are non-strategic, aimed at local cost reductions.

The functional, process-centric organization may fit smaller organizations. In small companies, informal lines of communication facilitate collaboration across functions because there is little physical separation. A narrow product line also fits

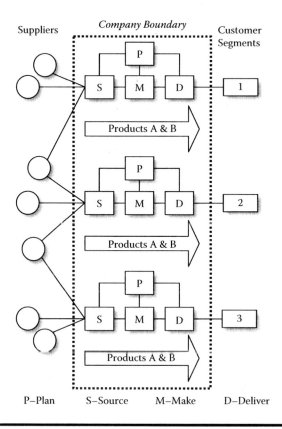

Figure 4.9   Customer-centric organization.

well into the functional organization; so does the firm that is a product line specialist and needn't worry about the problems that go with a complex product portfolio
or multiple customer segments. Another scenario supporting the choice of a functional organization is the presence of a dominant technology that requires capital
investment or deep expertise. This technology is the center of the business. It may
be hard to duplicate, may require deep technical skills, or may be capital-intensive.
A semiconductor foundry where the cost of manufacturing facilities runs to billions
of dollars is an example. Another is an engineering-intensive, high-technology aerospace business like satellite making.

4.3.2 Product-Centric Organizations

In the product-centric organization, business units are aligned by individual products, product categories, or brands. In Figure 4.8, there is a "minicompany" (what
we call a "sphere") for Product A and another for Product B. Segments 2 and 3,
which buy both A and B, are served by both minicompanies.

For example, automobile companies organize around "platforms" where a single platform is the basis for several branded products. For an auto company, platforms could include minivan, truck, small car, and large car. Each platform group is responsible for design, production, and marketing plus the assets to fulfill these functions. Chrysler came to this arrangement after its "one size fits all" approach, like that in Figure 4.7, proved too slow and unresponsive. A clear case for the product-centric organization is also made when each product demands different process technology. Although this isn't true for a Chrysler-type company, it would be true for a company marketing two product lines like beer and wine.

Also, a new product may justify a product-centric organization through the inception and growth phases of a product's life cycle. This would be the case if current supply chains are unsuitable, and process innovation is needed throughout the supply chain from the suppliers to the distribution channels. This allows these functions to innovate according to the needs of the business. Later, as the product matures and processes stabilize, supply chain processes may be spun off to specialists, leading back to a more functional organization.

Another situation that's perhaps suitable for the product-centered organization occurs when products are distributed across the product life cycle. Separate supply chains might service mature (requires cost-effectiveness) and innovative (requires responsiveness) products, applying the Fisher model described in Section 4.2.1.

4.3.3 Customer-Centric Organizations

Customer-centric organizations are built around targeted segments. Figure 4.9 shows a separate organization for each of the three segments. This arrangement is attractive to the company with well-defined segments that have distinctively different requirements. The customer-centric arrangement also fits when the supply chain is filled with innovative products that change frequently.

Nike, the largest footwear and apparel company in the world, illustrates the importance of organization models. The issue arose because Nike markets 13,000 rapidly changing product styles, and the company used constant product innovation to maintain high margins. As reported in *Forbes*,[9] Nike CEO Mark Parker shifted his company from a product-centric to a customer-centric organization. This paradigm shift moved from a focus on product lines like sneakers and shirts to a market focus defined by individual sports—tennis, golf, basketball, football, hockey, running, and so on. Even a product category like "eyewear" consists of products with designs tailored to the needs of sports like baseball, cycling, golf, and running. The goal of this focus was to maintain the margins that go with product designs that incorporated small differences in design demanded of an individual sport. What was the change driver? It was a social change in the form of sports specialization by end users, particularly young ones. Nike couldn't charge a premium price for products not designed from the ground up to meet the demands of the focused athlete.

Also, tailored extended product features may be important to success. A "grab and go" coffee shop business needs a different supply chain from the coffee house whose customers linger over their espresso. The customer-centric organization is likely to respond to changes in customer preferences faster than other models. With respect to processes, low investment requirements and the need for flexibility in selecting suppliers and distribution channels encourage the customer-centric choice.

An organization doesn't have to pursue any single organization type from end to end. For example, the beer and wine company might allow its product lines to share distribution channels. A car company has an engine unit that serves all its platforms. There are ways to combine types for different steps in the chain. However, one type will likely dominate in any company. Without laying out a structure using the ideas presented here, any attempt at supply chain change may fall short. In the following section, we describe the spheres concept for making decisions regarding organization.

4.4 Task 3: Forging Supply Chain Partnerships

This section describes tools put to work in Section 3 project templates, including "spheres" and a classification methodology for partnerships with outside companies.

4.4.1 Spheres: Businesses Inside the Business

In the preceding section, we encouraged companies to select the best model for their internal organization—process-centric, product-centric, or customer-centric. A concept we call "spheres" is fundamental to decisions on organization and process design at the multicompany level. We describe the concepts here and how to formulate them in Chapter 12. A sphere is a market–product–operation combination that provides a way to "divide and conquer" in developing and implementing the activity systems. The term derives from the fact that a sphere has three dimensions—markets, products, and operations—described in Table 4.5. All but the simplest of organizations are candidates for developing more than one supply chain to serve multiple spheres.

The dimensions in the left-hand column in Table 4.5 are markets, products, and operations. Markets are the segments as defined by the company. Products are those sold to that segment. Operations are the supply chain components (suppliers, manufacturing, and distribution facilities) used to make and deliver the products. Figure 4.10 is one possible result. Using the spheres in the figure, the company will consider one set of initiatives directed at SOURCE to improve processes for obtaining material (Sphere A is characterized as all markets–all products–suppliers and inbound material facilities). Another sphere (B) will integrate MAKE

Table 4.5 Components of a Sphere

Dimension	Basis for Sphere
Markets	Defined by segments where customers and/or end-users have common characteristics and buying behavior.
Products	Should include the base, physical, and extended product services.
Operations	Includes both internal and trading partner operations. The latter can include distribution channels, other company divisions, and key suppliers.

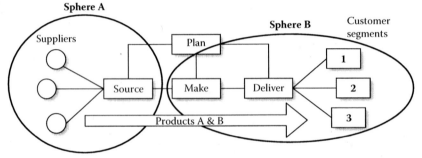

A. All markets-all products-suppliers & inbound material facilities

B. All markets-all products-manufacturing & distribution facilities

Figure 4.10 Spheres for the functionally organized company.

and DELIVER functions for all products. It is characterized as all markets–all products–manufacturing and distribution facilities.

Suppose our functional company is geographically organized with multiple operations serving market segments (1, 2, and 3) that are different regions. Then, those regions might define the spheres. For example, the choice might be Asia, Europe, and the United States, or the East, the Midwest, and the West. Such a division would have Spheres A (for materials) and B (for manufacturing and distribution) for each of the regions, for a total of six.

Spheres for product-centric and customer-centric organizations will also reflect that organization choice. In fact, sphere design should precede staff selection and implementing the organization structure. The supply chain in Figure 4.7 is a "one size fits all" situation. The nomenclature would be "all markets–all products–all operations," the Product A sphere in Figure 4.8 would be "all markets–Product A–Product A operations," and the Market 1 sphere in Figure 4.9 would be "Market 1–all products–Market 1 operations."

Product configuration may also drive sphere definition. A commercial airplane where millions of parts make up one delivered product may shape its spheres around different types of components. On the other hand, a product where a few raw materials make up one base product, like a pill, could identify spheres shaped around multiple distribution channels.

Because they apply to all spheres, a good practice is to create a sphere for ENABLE processes from the SCOR-model and CSCMP's *Process Standards*. These include shared resources, common business rules, and regulatory functions that are justifiably centralized. Sphere A in Figure 4.10 is an enable sphere because it serves all products and all markets. Like the example in Figure 4.10, Wal-Mart has a formidable sourcing capability. This would be captured in the Sphere A definition. Wal-Mart, concerned about having stockouts on frequently purchased staples on its shelves, implemented a "Remix" program. The company set up dedicated distribution and transportation to assure these items are delivered frequently and are shelf-ready. These measures assure the items won't be lost in store backrooms, failing to make the last ninety feet to the shelves in a timely way. Such a sphere would be "all customers–selected fast-moving items–designated remix facilities." In Chapter 12, we differentiate between product-producing spheres and enable spheres. The first has external customers. The latter has internal customers and serves more than one product-producing sphere.

4.4.2 Classifying Partnerships

Many companies pursue collaborative partnerships. Chapter 3 introduced collaboration as a driver of innovation in supply chain change. Like "flexibility," also a driver of supply chain change in Chapter 3, proposals for multicompany partnerships need to describe the fundamental nature of such potential arrangements. A "partnership" can take several forms, bound by agreements ranging from informal to formal, from simple to complex. Examples range from simple forms of information sharing all the way to outright acquisition. In between are shared facilities, shared investments, joint ventures, joint R&D, and many other forms. Here, we describe three partnership dimensions useful for classifying partnerships:

Purpose: Whether the partnership creates new "space" in the supply chain. Space is something unique in the marketplace—a product, extended product, or new service model. A "yes" or "no" defines the purpose. A "yes" almost certainly defines a strategically important partnership.

Direction: Whether the partnership goes up/down (vertical direction) or across (horizontal direction) the supply chain.

Choice: Relative partner power in the relationship. A "many to many," "one to many," "many to one," or a "one to one" relationship.

In the following paragraphs, we briefly explain the three dimensions.

4.4.2.1 Purpose

The term "space" describes the role a company and its selected partners play in its market. This is the niche carved out by the company and could reflect its choices regarding operations, branding, or activity system. A partnership can seek to define new space, perhaps to implement a unique supply chain strategy. An example is the Internet retailer who partners with a brick-and-mortar retailer. For example, Dell has supplemented its direct sales model with partnerships with retail stores. The combined enterprise provides a fuller range of marketing channels for product sales and returns.

The Dell direct model created a new direct channel. Herman Miller created new space with its supply chain design, providing a service level unmatched by its rivals. That model was heavily dependent on both supplier agreements and, at least initially, on a third-party logistics provider. In the service sector, CVS/pharmacy installs MinuteClinics alongside its pharmacies, a process referred to as the "retailization" of health care. The clinics offer no-hassle, 24/7 services with a menu of list prices. Board certified practitioners, not doctors, deliver those services, many of which are covered by medical insurance.

A new partnership creates new space to the degree it's unique among providers in its marketplace. A "yes" in the purpose category signifies an intention to create new space. By definition, this must be a strategic, supply-chain-level endeavor, as defined in Figure 4.4. A "no" in the purpose dimension indicates a partnership for other reasons like achieving economies of scale in an industry consolidation, replacement of a current supplier, or increasing geographic coverage.

4.4.2.2 Direction

With regard to partnership creation, the direction can be either vertical or horizontal. In some cases, both directions may be involved. Figure 4.11 illustrates the direction dimension. In the figure, our supply chain is shown with white circles and our own company is represented by a white diamond. The chain centered on a competitor is shown with black circles and a black diamond represents our direct competitor. We decide to partner with our competitor in a horizontal partnership shown in the figure. If we produce similar products, this partnership is unlikely to create new space. However, it could be seen as creating space if our product lines serve common markets but are complementary. Another horizontal partnership takes place in Figure 4.11 between two suppliers. They provide different products to our immediate supplier, so this partnership creates new space. A vertical partnership, which is also likely to create new space, is shown downstream of our own operation.

4.4.2.3 Choice

Our final dimension, choice, reflects the power held by one partner over another. In some cases, a market is a monopsony, where a single buyer controls demand.

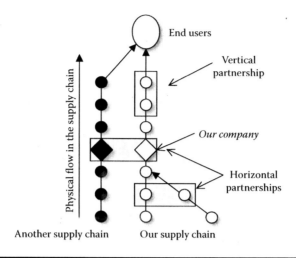

Figure 4.11   Direction dimension in partnerships.

These powerful partners may not seem like partners at all when they dictate the terms of the relationship. The U.S. Department of Defense (DoD), Boeing, and Wal-Mart definitely have rules suppliers must follow to do business with them. These are really not optional in most cases. However, your agreement to provide any of these powerful partners with goods and service implies your willingness, if not your eagerness, to enter into a partnership on their terms.

Figure 4.12 illustrates the "choice" categories. It does this from the perspective of "our company" along the vertical axis on the left-hand side. The company with whom we propose to partner is shown on the horizontal axis. The result is four characterizations of choice in the partnership. If you are one of many suppliers of

	Our Partner	
	One	*Many*
One	Market leaders or larger companies join forces (One-to-one)	Large company chooses small one as a supplier (One-to-many)
Many	Small company chosen by a major one (Many-to-one)	Companies in a competitive market combine forces (Many-to-many)

Figure 4.12   Partnership choice.

your product, you are the weaker partner. This means users of your service or buyers of your goods have many options. A partnership between a weak and a strong partner is a "many to one" partnership (lower left-hand box in Figure 4.12), meaning that a single company in a large field of many is doing business with a powerful customer (the "one"). DoD and Wal-Mart suppliers have many-to-one partnerships with these large customers. These behemoths are quite strategic to you, if you do a lot of business with them.

If our company wanted to team with another "weak" company serving a market, and we are both small fish in a large pool, we might create a "many-to-many" partnership to chase the business (lower right-hand box in Figure 4.12). If we are two large fish, we might create a "one-to-one" partnership to share risk in a large capital project (upper left-hand box in Figure 4.12). Sometimes, size isn't important. The small company holding a patent for unique technology may be in the driver's seat—the "one." Large companies seeking to license or distribute the technology could in fact be the "many."

4.5 Task 4: Managing Supply Chain Information

Figure 3.1 pointed to the emergence of process-centered management as a driver of supply chain change. For many companies, this will change the approach to justifying and implementing information technology (IT). Bensaou and Earl have compared the "mind-sets" that characterize Western and Japanese companies.[10] Motivating their research were the many complaints about system efforts gone awry in Western companies compared to far fewer "disasters" in Japan. (Chapter 9 further explores this theme.)

Table 4.6 summarizes the authors' findings. A principal theme is that Western managers tend to adopt technology for its own sake rather than for what it does for the processes it supports. Too much effort is absorbed in the technical aspects of implementation rather than planning the evolution of the process. A related problem is attempting to modify—rather than configure—the software extensively to make it more acceptable to users. This can result in a high-maintenance system.

No less in importance is the flood of aggressively marketed supply chain management software products. Categories related to SCM include the following:

- MRP/ERP (materials/enterprise resource planning): Back-office systems for fulfilling common functions across the entire company.
- APS (advance planning/scheduling): Planning and scheduling systems that enable faster and more frequent planning of supply chain operations.
- MES (manufacturing execution system): Short-term control applications, including that used in the Miller SQA case (Section 4.2.3.2), aimed at scheduling operations, particularly in applications requiring fast responses.

Table 4.6   Mind-Sets for Framing IT Investments

Issue	Western Mind-Set	Japanese Mind-Set
Match IT with business needs	Align IT with business strategy	Basic way we compete drives IT investments
Return on investment	Capital budgeting process, ROI	Operation performance improvement
Technology and process improvement	Tend to adopt technology—seen as best way to improve	Use the right technology to meet a performance goal
Connections between IT users and specialists	Tech savvy staff and CIOs	Rotation through technical and management roles
Improvement of organization performance	Design elegant system; adapt to it	Design system to use employee knowledge

Source: Adapted from M. Bensaou and M. Earl, "The Right Mind-Set for Managing Information Technology," *Harvard Business Review* (September/October, 1998): 119–28.

- CRM (customer relationship management): Applications that help manage interactions with customers and prospects.
- SRM (supplier relationship management): A "spin-off" application like CRM for suppliers.
- WMS (warehouse management system): Application designed for the particular needs of larger warehouses and distribution centers.
- AIDC (automatic identification and data capture): Encompasses a fast-changing technology area that includes electronic product codes (EPC), radio frequency identification (RFID), and in-transit tracking of goods.

Many of these applications provide a capability to share information among trading partners on the status of material and product inventories in the supply chain as well as forecasts for future consumption. We saw, in the Herman Miller case, the importance of IT in enabling the company's supply chain strategy. Because many companies struggle with new systems, Chapter 9 is dedicated to the project management issues surrounding IT. The chapter describes "complements" like process design that must accompany technology. In Chapter 15, we describe Tasks 4 and 5 project processes addressing the needs for process-centered management.

Information systems requirements for the supply chain logically will occur at the "edges" of the organization—on the upstream and downstream interfaces. This is the observation of John Hagel III and John Seely Brown, who describe the future for "Web services."[11] Getting a major system into place is a formidable, expensive task. Using traditional approaches to system development grows even more complicated when "hooking up" with partners. The advantage to be gained from linking with supply chain partners will spur the growth of Internet protocol software to ease this task. Chapter 9 cites General Electric as an example because it has linked with a half million of its suppliers through an online application.

Acknowledging this movement, James E. Kennedy of CGR Management Consultants recommends structured project management approaches in implementing technology.[12] He points to five disciplines or subprocesses needed to implement enterprise software:

- System governance, including a multicompany organization with decision-making authority.
- IT strategic planning that matches IT development with business objectives and provides IT practitioners that can work with business managers.
- A systems development life cycle (SDLC) for the company and its trading partners. A problem is that trading partners may not employ an SDLC or that it might not be synchronized with one's own company.
- Project management that prevents or mitigates the risks of implementing complex technology.
- Change management that includes constant communication throughout the process, tailored education of participants, and engaged managers who address issues and concerns as they arise.

Kennedy notes that most common obstacles that derail technology projects aren't technological. The problems and opportunities arise in the execution. Technology complexity is a problem. The ability to adapt technology to linked processes that provide barriers to competition is the opportunity. Returning to Herman Miller, one of the largest barriers was not the software but assuring the accuracy of their bill of materials. The tight scheduling in their new operations couldn't tolerate ordering incorrect material. It took years to achieve accurate bills.

Picking the right technology is also daunting. A reaction to proliferation of supply chain software applications is finding ways to sort through available choices. Three managers of major e-Commerce Web sites described their ways of coping with software sales pitches.[13] In a discussion conducted appropriately by e-mail, a reporter queried executives from Lands' End, Eddie Bauer, and Sears. These executives managed their companies' consumer Web sites. The participants reported that they personally or members of their groups received over fifty sales calls a week from software marketers. They make a list of desired features against which to screen the pitches. If a pitch person's software functionality isn't on that list, the vendor is unlikely to get in the door.

The move to Web services and specification of needs in advance are logical approaches for dealing with IT for supply chains. Hagel and Brown, cited earlier, describe the challenges and roles for the corporate IT department:

- IT departments will have to migrate applications to outsourced suppliers of Web services while maintaining existing systems.
- The CIO must be more of a strategist, looking for areas of strategic advantage while building a new IT-based business.
- Nurturing relationships with other companies will become a key IT role as companies become more dependent on their partners for success. This also requires better negotiating skills for CIOs.

Chapter 15 incorporates these concepts into the supply chain project management plan. Section 9.7.3 addresses a method for developing requirements.

4.6 Task 5: Removing Cost from the Supply Chain

Effective supply chain cost reduction must maintain competitive levels of customer service. That said, no other reason comes close to cost reduction as a motivator for supply chain improvement projects. There is good reason for this. If the project requires an investment, cash flow from savings must pay for it. A languishing stock price may also be boosted if the project produces an earnings boost or makes a good story for stock analysts. However, too many cost reduction efforts lash out at the costs themselves, and not their root causes. Therefore, when it comes to identifying projects to lower cost, a first step is uncovering the root causes for the costs. The *Handbook of Supply Chain Management* identified six root causes:

- Lack of clarity: You can't hit the target if you don't see it. Traditional accounting does a poor job of highlighting cost drivers.
- Variability in processes and management behavior: Much cost comes from variation in company processes, a premise that underlies popular lean, Six Sigma, and theory of constraints (TOC) efforts.
- Expensive product design: Much of the cost for manufactured projects is "baked in" during design.
- Information-sharing shortfalls: Observers are right; the cost being "unintegrated" is high.
- Weak links: Links are the glue holding the chain together. They are both intracompany and intercompany. Designing the links is important to achieve needed levels of flexibility in a cost-effective way.
- Unintended consequences: Counterproductive methods of reward and punishment can be a root cause.

Product design as a root cause should be emphasized. Many companies don't include product design as part of their SCM improvement program. "Eighty per cent of the product cost is determined in the first 20 per cent of the product life cycle." This quotation from Steve Church of Avnet applies to electronics.[14] But, it is true for many low-tech products. "Early" refers to design and prototyping phases undertaken by engineering. Once a product moves into production, the supply chain manager's influence on final cost drops significantly.

Chapter 15 describes projects for cost reduction through both non-technology and IT. Templates include the methods for addressing root causes. Exact solutions will call on many technical disciplines. We'll refer to these in our discussion; references to specific techniques are in the Bibliography.

Notes

1. Frank J. Quinn, Morgan L. Swink, and Charles C. Poirer, "The Sixth Annual Global Survey of Supply Chain Progress," *Supply Chain Management Review* (October 2008).
2. Marshall L. Fisher, "What Is the Right Supply Chain for Your Product?" *Harvard Business Review* (March/April 1997): 105–16.
3. Hau L. Lee, "The Right Supply Chain Strategy for Value Creation," Supply-Chain Council executive retreat, February 26, 2003.
4. Peter L. Bolstorff, "From Chaos to Control with SCOR Metrics," *CSCMP Supply Chain Quarterly* (Quarter 2/2008): 65–73.
5. Council of Supply Chain Management Professionals (CSCMP), *Supply Chain Management Process Standards* (six volumes), 2004.
6. Michael E. Porter, "What Is Strategy?" *Harvard Business Review* (November/December 1996): 61–78.
7. Bill Bundy, Art Brown, and Steve Dean, "Changing the Rules of the Game," presentation to the Council of Logistics Management annual meeting, October 1999.
8. Brotherton et al., "The Work Breakdown Structure: A Brief Synopsis," a Project Management Institute white paper. The rule is attributed to Gregory T. Hagan.
9. Monte Burke, "On the Run," *Forbes*, February 11, 2008, 83–7.
10. M. Bensaou and Michael Earl, "The Right Mind-Set for Managing Information Technology," *Harvard Business Review* (September/October 1998): 119–28.
11. John Hagel III and John Seely Brown, "Your Next IT Strategy," *Harvard Business Review* (October 2001): 105–13.
12. James E. Kennedy, Implementing Enterprise Software Toward the Multicompany Environment. In *Handbook of Supply Chain Management*, 2nd ed. (St. Lucie Press, 2006), 441-9.
13. "Making the Sale," *The Wall Street Journal*, January 27, 2003, R9.
14. Steve Church, "The Impact of Globalizing Supply Networks," Supply-Chain Council executive retreat, February 26, 2003.

PROJECT MANAGEMENT AND SCM

Section II turns to structured approaches for project management and supply chain analysis and documentation. The section opens in Chapter 5 with a discussion of "maturity models" for project management. The maturity model is a tool to measure progress in implementing what we preach in the book. Since the first edition, the Project Management Institute (PMI®) and the Council of Supply Chain Management Professionals (CSCMP) have "inundated" the practitioner community with process models and self-evaluation yardsticks that measure maturity in their disciplines. These are on top of previous models from organizations like the Supply-Chain Council, which maintains its SCOR-model™ (Supply-Chain Operations Reference model). We summarize these—for project management knowledge and practice application(Chapter 5 in Section II) and for SCM knowledge and practice application (Chapter 10 in Section III).

Other chapters are devoted to standards promulgated by national organizations for project management and SCM. PMI maintains its *Guide to the Project Management Body of Knowledge* (*PMBOK® Guide*), which is covered in Chapters 6 and 7. The CSCMP has published its Supply Chain Management Process Standards, described in Chapter 8. Chapter 9 uses experience from information technology projects in order to develop a working list of root causes for project failures. Section III project processes seek to address these common project management shortcomings.

Chapter 5

Levels of Project Management Maturity

The chapter covers approaches to measuring project management maturity. The Project Management Institute (PMI) has a comprehensive standard for performing this task, called the Organizational Project Management Maturity Model (OPM3). Harold Kerzner's five-level Project Management Maturity Model (PMMM) provides a simpler framework. Both measure an organization's ability to put project management knowledge and practice to work. Adapting the processes in Section 3 to an organization's business will enable it to reach Level 3 or above in project management maturity in Kerzner's model.

One can argue effectively that improving one's supply chain is impossible without competence in project management. Just ask people at one of the many companies that have difficulties implementing initiatives through lack of planning, focus, patience, skills, or money. What comes first: supply chain competence or project management competence? This is a "chicken and egg" question. Both are required to change supply chains with a minimum of wasted effort. The necessity to move ahead with supply chain change may be all the incentive needed for building its project management capability. Organizations already expert in project management can capitalize on that competence supplementing those skills with the approaches in this book.

The following sections describe the very comprehensive PMI approach and the more intuitive approach from Harold Kerzner. Kerzner provides a top-down intuitive viewpoint, and the PMI viewpoint is more bottom-up, relying on a substantial, detailed evaluation structure. These can be employed separately or together. When used together, an organization would want to start with Kerzner's approach and then rely on PMI resources to "fill in the gaps."

5.1 PMI OPM3® Knowledge Foundation

PMI provides a comprehensive Global Standard called OPM3 (Organization Project Management Maturity Model) that has three elements that constitutes a step-by-step process for sharpening project management capabilities[1]:

- knowledge (a description of what constitutes project management maturity),
- assessment (a methodology for measuring where you are), and
- improvement (a process for moving from a lower level to a higher level of maturity).

OPM3 complements other PMI standards, particularly those in its *Guide to the Project Management Body of Knowledge* (*PMBOK Guide*).[2] The *PMBOK* standards are the best practices in the nine project management knowledge areas introduced in Chapter 1. OPM3 addresses the three "domains" of an organization's project-related efforts: individual projects, groups of related projects called programs, and enterprise-wide portfolios that encompass all the projects and programs. Ideally, this portfolio derives from the enterprise strategic plan. Section 4.2 pointed out that the connection should, but does not always, exist.

Like most products of PMI standard-setting efforts, OPM3 contains an enormous amount of detail. The self-assessment in the OPM3 standard provides over 150 questions that produce a "high-level" view of project management maturity. Its *Best Practices Directory,* also in the OPM3 document, lists over 600 best practices. These are mapped to the domains of organization project management (projects, programs, portfolio) and the four stages of process improvement (SMCI: Standardize, Measure, Control, and Improve). With these dimensions, the *Directory* swells rapidly when nine knowledge areas produce best practices in the three domains and four stages of process improvement.

Tools for a comprehensive analysis (OPM3 Online) are available at extra cost. The licenses provide access to a *Capabilities Directory* and *Improvement Planning Directory.* These match the needed capabilities for each best practice and the plans to put those capabilities into place. Figure 5.1 and Table 5.1 summarize the recommended process.

Figure 5.1 and Table 5.1 explain the OPM3 cycle steps. The Step 2 assessment is divided into the "executive" view (Step 2A) and the "comprehensive" view (Step 2B). The executive view relies on questions from the OPM3 document. The online tool is required for the comprehensive view. PMI naturally recommends using project management practices to implement the changes (Steps 3 and 4). The

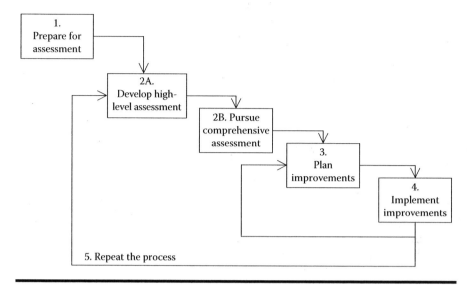

Figure 5.1   OPM3 cycle, summary description.

user should gauge how fast to proceed. Closing the loop by returning to Step 1 or 3 matches PMI's recommendation for progressive elaboration. This means updating project plans based on earlier experience with implementing changes.

5.2 Kerzner's Maturity Model

Dr. Harold Kerzner also offers a vision of how excellence in project management evolves. Kerzner's model is more culture-oriented than the PMI's model. A user pursuing supply chain improvement might employ this tool while implementing the recommended best practices in this book. The description here summarizes Kerzner's PMMM supplemented with comments on its applicability to supply chain management (SCM).[3]

Figure 5.2 displays the five levels of the PMMM beginning with "common language" and progressing to "continuous improvement." The positioning of the levels in Figure 5.2 reflects overlapping in the progression from one level to another. For example, the move from Level 1, common language, to Level 2, common processes, is not necessarily sequential. Migration to common processes can begin even while a common language capability is developing. When Level 3, singular methodology, is implemented, some processes from Level 2, common processes, are likely to be jettisoned in favor of the single "best" way. So, there is little overlap between Levels 2 and 3.

Table 5.2, uses elements from Kerzner's descriptions of different levels for a quick reference to assess maturity. Table 5.2 is slanted toward supply chain needs but should fit most other project types. To place your company, simply find the

Table 5.1 OPM3 Cycle, Description of Steps

#	Step Name	Reference	Description
1	Prepare for Assessment	OPM3,[a] Chapters 1–6	Obtain management support and educate participants.
2A	Develop High-Level Assessment	OPM3, Appendix D	151 questions that highlight best practices that are/are not being performed. Enables the organization to focus its improvement efforts. Also highlights domains and stages that need improvement.
2B	Pursue Comprehensive Assessment	OPM3 Online *Capabilities Directory*	Identifies capabilities that should be implemented to support each needed best practice. Create the *Improvement Planning Directory*.
3	Plan Improvements		Set priorities for acquiring capabilities considering attainability, strategic contribution, benefits, and costs.
4	Implement Improvements		Implement the plan to acquire capabilities over time. Use project management approaches from the *PMBOK Guide*.
5	Repeat the Process		This may involve returning to the start or returning to Step 3.

[a] Organization Project Management Maturity Model Knowledge Foundation, 2005.

description that best fits your situation. Note there is a Level 0 for the organizations without any project management perspective. Unfortunately, the Level 0 company, where the need for formalized project management is not on the radar screen, is not all that rare.

Please note that the PMMM calls for common language and processes in Levels 1 through 3. Chapter 6 and Chapter 7 draw on other resources to suggest the vocabulary and processes for supply chain project management. Section 3 describes specific SCM project management processes for implementation. These offer a "singular methodology," a requisite for Level 3 of the PMMM.

5.2.1 Level 1, Common Language

Use of project management is sporadic at Level 1. At Level 1, an organization has "pockets" of appreciation for project management. Members of the organization

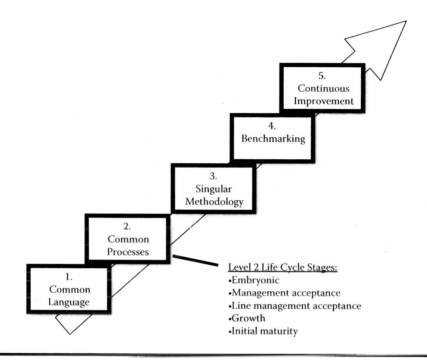

Figure 5.2 Kerzner Project Management Maturity Model (PMMM) levels. This material is adapted from *Strategic Planning for Project Management Using a Project Management Maturity Model*, by Harold Kerzner, Ph.D. Copyright © 2001 by John Wiley & Sons, Inc.

are aware of the need but not competent in execution. Indeed, the level is based more on awareness of what should be done, not what is actually being done. Top management support is lacking or not consistently provided. Any implementation that does occur is bottom-up and varies from project to project.

The organization is also likely to be strongly functional. Managers are protective of their turf and unwilling to join in cross-functional projects or even adopt a common methodology. Supply chain projects, using the terminology shown in Figure 4.4, are "functional" in scope and "non-strategic" in their impact. There is little in the way of project management training and development. To graduate to Level 2, the organization must increase its awareness of project management and its benefits. Moving from Level 1 to 2 can take weeks or years. Resources like OPM3 will help fill in detail about what has to be done.

5.2.2 Level 2, Common Processes

At Level 2, support for project management broadens. It takes the form of support from top to bottom in the organization, training of specialists and other involved

Table 5.2 Assessment Tool for PMMM

	0 *No Project Management Perspective*	*1* *Common Language*	*2* *Common Processes*	*3* *Singular Methodology*	*4* *Benchmarking*	*5* *Continuous Improvement*
Organization awareness	Unaware of the need for project management. Functional orientation.	Awareness exists of need for project management knowledge and language.	Use of project management life cycles (phasing). Scope control. Use of software.	Cultural barriers are eliminated. Individuals can easily shift to "project mode."	Individuals are aware of the need for improving project management processes.	Shared knowledge by project teams. Cultivation of project management talent.
Management support	None. Not on the management agenda.	No investment in project management capability. Little senior management support.	Education provided in project management. Willingness exists to address internal issues.	Support for project management exists throughout the organization. Projects are linked to strategy.	Establishment of a Project Office or Center of Excellence to pursue improvements.	Recognition of continuous improvement as necessary.
Process discipline	No project management processes.	Occasional use of project management methodology initiated at lower levels.	Concerted effort to use project management. Cost and schedule controls are used.	Single, informal approach used on all types of projects.	Company looks outside for upgrading project management processes.	Changes are made to company's own project management processes.
Motivation	Ignorance. No apparent motivators. Overlooked discipline.	Insufficient motivation to take authority away from functional managers.	Company must undertake major important projects to survive.	Project management efficiency perceived to be closely linked to company success.	The company strategy is heavily dependent on projects. Examples include new products, internal improvement, major systems, supply chain design, and capital investments.	

staff, and recognition of the need for processes and methodology. Also, at Level 2, projects are tracked for cost and schedule for project resources and for meeting objectives. This may require changes in the way costs are allocated to supply chain processes. Cost analysis of this type is referred to as "horizontal accounting" or "activity-based costing."

Motivations for moving to Level 2 often come when an organization faces high-risk projects. Examples include major capital expenditures, big systems implementations, new product development, or multicompany supply chain improvements; in fact, the last can involve all the prior examples. Often, the realization that project management will help comes from lower levels in the organization.

Kerzner identifies five "life cycles" at Level 2. These are stepping stones to fully fulfill the requirements at Level 2. Getting through the five phases is not trivial and, like Level 1, can involve an extended period of time. The embryonic phase, the first in the life cycle, is the acceptance of the need for project management. It is often spurred by the need to take on "survival" projects like those listed earlier. By definition, if you fail in executing a survival project, your business fails.

The second life cycle phase, management acceptance, is entered when senior management endorses project management, often at the behest of those performing a major project. This phase is over when senior management becomes willing to change the way it does business. Line management acceptance is gained for project management in the third life-cycle phase. This manifests itself in the willingness to free dedicated people for project management training and for the projects themselves. Level 4, the growth phase, starts to create the project management process. The following achievements mark the end of this phase:

- development of project life cycles;
- formulation of a project management methodology accompanied by training;
- a commitment to planning by executive management;
- resistance to scope changes, usually in the form of scope "creep," by formalizing the change process; and
- implementation of project management software that covers cost and schedule.

Level 5 is the initial maturity phase. A curriculum is available to improve the skills of those working in projects. It includes development and integration of cost/schedule control systems.

5.2.3 Level 3, Singular Methodology

At this level, the organization selects a singular project management methodology. The term "singular" has several meanings: unique, individual, or separate. This infers that the organization takes the best of the methodologies it has found or which it develops and adopts them for all projects. The resulting project management methodology is likely to be unique, hence "singular," to the organization. Another use of the term is as a synonym for "single." That is, having a common process for use through the organization in lieu of multiple versions developed as *ad hoc* approaches to individual projects. Kerzner characterizes a singular methodology as having the following components:

- Integrated processes: There are no separate Six Sigma, product development, information technology systems, or change management projects. The singular project management process covers all. Programs like Six Sigma or lean, because of the discipline required, can be precursors to a singular process.
- Cultural support: The entire organization supports the process. This is a goal of our SCM *Task 2* Implementing Collaborative Relationships where internal resistance to implementing effective supply chains is at a minimum.
- Management support at all levels: Support for the projects and project managers comes from both line and senior management. Line managers, in particular, support the project manager with joint accountability, dedicated staff, alternative plans (if necessary), and implementation. The project manager is empowered by senior management to make decisions. The project team produces recommendations and alternatives, not just restated problems. Status reporting is formalized with regard to timing, distribution, and content.
- Informal project management: The methodology is adapted to the needs of individual projects. Control tools include general guidelines and checklists. An effort is made to minimize paperwork and reinventing the wheel with every project. An example is using red, yellow, and green "traffic lights" to report status on work packages and deliverables. Informality provides the flexibility to adapt the project management methodology to a broad range of project types.
- Return on investment from project management training and education expense: Project management skills development is ongoing. There is a realization that benefits exceed the cost of the training and education. A company at Level 3 will have fewer conflicts rising to senior management because problems are headed off at lower levels.
- Behavior excellence: There is recognition within the organization that project management is different than day-to-day operational management. The needed skills are defined and cultivated.

Kerzner emphasizes that excellence in project management doesn't guarantee the success of the project. However, it does improve chances for success. In fact, if every project is successful, Kerzner observes, the organization probably isn't doing enough projects.

5.2.4 Level 4, Benchmarking

Benchmarking is a popular technique for identifying ways to improve the project management culture. Benchmarking might discover new software or adaptable practices from one's own industry or other industries. The latter might encourage broader use of project management internally. The idea of benchmarking is to take the Level 3 singular methodology to the next level by bringing outside ideas into the organization.

A supporting structure recommended by Kerzner "cements" project management into the company structure. The recommendations begin with a Program Office (PO) or a Center of Excellence (COE) for project management. These differ in that the PO is a permanent line function, and the COE can be a formal or informal committee. Our own experience with SCM indicates that a broad program of supply chain change should have a central project (program) office. This office would assure that each project has similar formats for tracking progress, including the use of verifiable project milestones. A consolidated form of reporting using an accessible project management tool is indispensable in providing progress visibility.

5.2.5 Level 5, Continuous Improvement

At Level 5, the organization puts benchmarking information to work for process improvement. These improvements can occur anywhere in the project management domain. Level 5 lasts "forever." Kerzner cites several examples of continuous improvement:

- Procedural documentation, avoiding re-creating or duplicating of paperwork from project to project.
- Project management methodologies that are tailored to the organization, not "canned."
- Capacity planning that assures the best projects have the resources they need.
- Competency models in which skills, not deliverables or expectations, define the need for project staff.
- Multiple projects managed by single project managers made possible by training and qualification, risk management techniques, project scheduling, and joint accountability with line management.
- End-of-phase reviews that encourage rigorous business-oriented scrutiny and project cancellation if the project is not working.
- Strategic selection of projects that assures that projects align with strategy.
- Portfolio management wherein proposed projects are evaluated based on risk and the benefits from implementation.
- Horizontal accounting where costs of implementation are estimated and closely tracked.

Any of these categories could represent a major effort. Project management skills are a strategic asset. Kerzner's point is to keep one's project management methodology evolving in advance of progress made by competitors.

The remainder of this section and Section 3 project templates are a resource for improving project management processes. The goal of this book is to provide readers at any level of project management maturity workable ideas for improvement. Elements include both necessary vocabulary and project processes directed at the needs of supply chain improvement.

Notes

1. PMI Global Standard: Organizational Project Management Maturity Model Knowledge Foundation (OPM3 Knowledge Foundation), Project Management Institute, 2008. American National Standard ANSI/PMI 08-004-2008.
2. PMI Global Standard: *A Guide to the Project Management Body of Knowledge (PMBOK Guide)*, 4th ed., Project Management Institute, 2008. American National Standard ANSI/PMI 99-001-2008.
3. For more information, see two books by Harold Kerzner: *Strategic Planning for Project Management: Using a Project Management Maturity Model* and *Project Management: A Systems Approach to Planning, Scheduling, and Controlling*, 7th ed., both published by John Wiley & Sons in 2001.

Chapter 6

Project Management Standards

An appropriate tagline for the Project Management Institute (PMI) is "standards are us." Chapter 5 described one of these, measurement of project management maturity. This chapter opens the door to several more.

Project management language described in this chapter primarily comes from PMI's *Guide to the Project Management Body of Knowledge (PMBOK Guide)*.[1] This chapter focuses on the needs for a common project management vocabulary. This will aid users to achieve Level 1, Common Language, of Kerzner's Project Management Maturity Model (PMMM) in Chapter 5. This chapter covers a lot of terms; we list the most important here:

- As described in Chapter 5, there are three "P"s or domains—portfolios, programs, and projects—in the project management space. Chapter 5 described how PMI measures maturity in implementing best practices that support all three. In addition to the Operations Project Management Maturity Model (OPM3), there are three standards documents for the domains—the *PMBOK Guide* for projects and two other separate documents for portfolio and program management.[2,3]
- A portfolio consists of all the enterprise's programs and projects. Section 4.2.2 describes the portfolio landscape as it relates to supply chain projects.
- There's a difference between a program and a project. A project is a temporary and unique effort that has a beginning and an end. A program consists of multiple projects. A program can go on forever, containing a number of projects plus some ongoing operation elements. At some points in its lifetime, a program may not have any active projects.

- Project life cycle phases mark important milestones in the project. A phase usually ends with a major deliverable.
- There are nine project management knowledge areas. Each contains several project processes listed in Figure 7.1. Knowledge and practice in executing these processes will make you a more skilled project leader or team member.
- Each project management process is assigned to a process group. There are five such groups: Initiating, Planning, Executing, Controlling, and Closing.
- A Work Breakdown Structure, or WBS, is a "deliverable-oriented" view of a project. This is useful in communicating expectations in terms of scope and products for the project. It's no surprise that PMI also has a standard covering the WBS.[4]
- All the constituent parts, elements, or pieces are components of the project management environment. These include the three domains, business cases, program management offices, and other ongoing work.

Figure 6.1 shows the relationships between portfolios, programs, and projects in a multicompany, or supply chain, environment. Additional components could include non-project regular work like ongoing operations and maintenance. PMI also refers to business case justifications for projects as components. A business case is likely a needed "feasibility check" before an ambitious project is undertaken.

As shown in Figure 6.1, PMI notes that an enterprise's strategy must drive supply chain designs required to meet its objectives. There are many techniques for strategy formulation, including activity systems (Porter) adapted for supply chain strategic planning in Chapter 4. Others that are widely used include the following:

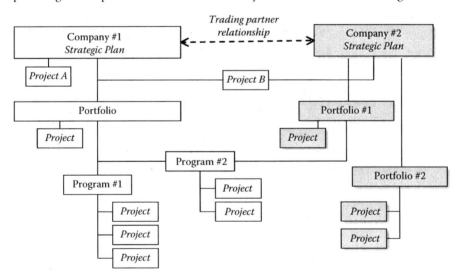

Figure 6.1   Project management components.

- industry analysis using the five competitive forces, choosing between cost leadership and differentiation (Porter);
- core competency identification (Hamel/Prahalad);
- the Blue Ocean approach to defining a totally new capability (Kim/Mauborgne); and
- seeking out disruptive technologies that create whole new markets (Christensen).

Portfolios, as shown in Figure 6.1, are confined to a single supply chain company. Ideally, each trading partner has a portfolio that reflects that company's strategy. On the other hand, programs and projects can be internal, supporting the enterprise-only or joint multicompany efforts. In the figure, Program #2 and its associated projects are an example of a multicompany (Companies #1 and #2) supply chain program. Company #1 also pursues an internal program (Program #1).

Note that a project (like Project A) can be freestanding—not associated with a formally established program or portfolio. So, the project associated with Company 1's strategic planning could be commissioned to study Company #1's market or industry. There is also a jointly sponsored project (Project B) at the strategic level. Figure 6.1 shows that Company 1 is involved in eight projects, Company 2 in four. These portfolios will likely call for multiple business disciplines. The next section describes the interaction of project management with other disciplines.

6.1 Overlapping Disciplines

The *PMBOK Guide* highlights the fact that project management is not a stand-alone discipline. In fact, the need for project management rigor arises because multiple disciplines must work together. Figure 1.1 shows that the four cornerstones of supply chain project management include project management knowledge, project management practice, supply chain management (SCM) knowledge, and SCM practice.

Table 6.1 contains examples of the overlap of project management and SCM disciplines. On the left are possible "events" in the life of an organization. Each event generates work requiring both project management and SCM expertise. Each also requires multicompany efforts to achieve success. For this reason, project management capabilities will be challenged to coordinate the effort. Most organizations delegate the work needed in these examples to functional managers. A company at Level 0 or 1 in the PMMM (Table 5.2) might not even have a project management capability.

Examining the events in Table 6.1 reveals the potential for problems with uncoordinated efforts. For example, you can see the pitfalls in Event E, relocation of a manufacturing plant. Traditionally, this project might be limited to a single function: manufacturing. However, there are several general management tasks associated with Event E that would benefit from project management. For

Table 6.1   Interdisciplinary Examples

	Event	Project Management Challenges	SCM Challenges
A	Partnership with a major supplier	Needed transitions, joint team implementation	Inbound logistics, systems requirements, financial terms, target markets, capital commitments
B	New product introduction	Integration of schedules with R&D, facilities planning	Quality requirements, market development, pricing, distribution channels, sourcing, manufacturing approach, early supplier involvement
C	Horizontal acquisition of a rival company	Integration of products and operations	Design of combined entity supply and distribution networks and processes, product rationalization
D	Implementation of a strategy based on an activity system	Coordinated implementation of new processes, portfolio management	Operational components of the activity system that can require a number of process changes
E	Plant relocation	Construction management, process design, move coordination	Property acquisition, location analysis, plant design, layout, supplier qualification, startup
F	Bill of material cost reduction	Coordination of multiple efforts using different approaches	Supplier interface, value engineering, qualification and testing

example, Marketing must decide what to make and in what quantities. Finance should justify needed changes and determine how to pay for the plant.

In Table 5.2, we described a Level 3 company as having a singular methodology for project management. This methodology should be capable of coping with the complexity inherent in the range of potential projects shown in Table 6.1.

6.2 Project Management Structure and Vocabulary

The *PMBOK Guide* is an impressive and a bit intimidating collection of techniques, procedures, and structures for project management. One would expect no less from a "body of knowledge." Our view is that the *PMBOK Guide* should not be holy writ followed literally but as a set of tools to be shaped to the organization's needs. For those without mature project management, experimentation at Level 2 of the Table 5.2 PMMM will lead to the best solution for any particular organization. The following sections provide a starting point for developing a common vocabulary and methodology.

6.2.1 Basic Definitions

Understanding *PMBOK Guide* terminology begins with the components of a project environment. Figure 6.2 illustrates this environment. At the top are programs, as described earlier. They are groups of linked projects that share common goals, funding, or sponsorship. In addition to projects, a program may have an element of continuous, non-project repetitive activity. A program, for example, can include development of a product (a project) and subsequent manufacturing of the product (a continuous activity).

Whether a company calls its supply chain effort a program or project could depend on its intent. If the SCM effort were to be an ongoing activity that, from time to time, would have no projects, "program" would be a logical label. If the SCM effort is a one-shot affair, then "project" might fit better. Chris Christensen, a

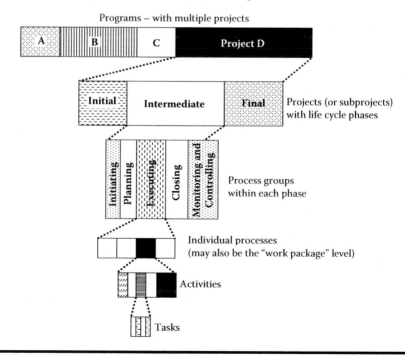

Figure 6.2   Project components.

project management expert, cautions against the use of "program" over "project." He observes that many companies have "programs" where very little is accomplished. There is no real commitment to the effort; it exists more for window dressing than for achieving real results. However, the word "project" is associated with real effort from real people with definite goals for meeting a schedule and producing results.

Examples in Table 6.1 illustrate possible supply chain programs or projects. Event A, partnership with a major supplier, could involve multiple projects, defined by the *PMBOK Guide* as temporary efforts that create something unique in the form of a product, service, or result. In Program A, separate projects might produce new communications links (a product), coordinated transportation (a result), assembly of components at the supplier (a service), development of inventory policies (a service), and so forth. Also Program A is properly a program, not a project, if it involves operations after the partnership starts to operate. Where a project scope is very broad or project components are distinct, subprojects are also appropriate. An example of a "distinct" subproject could be a piece of the project that is farmed out to a third party.

Returning to Figure 6.2, the next level shows how a project decomposes into product life cycle phases. Figure 6.2 shows three generic time-based phases: Initial, Intermediate, and Final. The names and number of phases will depend on the type of project. Construction projects may have life cycle phases like Feasibility, Planning and Design, Construction, and Turnover and Startup. Feasibility and Planning and Design are part of the initial phase. Construction is an intermediate phase. Turnover and Startup is the final phase. Product development might use a stage gate vocabulary with stages being the phases. Examples are Idea Development, Preliminary Investigation, Development, and Launch.

A Level 3 PMMM organization would have guidelines for naming life cycle phases. Actual names will vary with the type of project. In Chapter 11, as an example, we recommend the following life cycle phases for SCM improvement projects:

- Supply Chain Strategy
- Internal Alignment
- Short-Term Improvement
- Long-Term Improvement

Returning to Figure 6.2, each life cycle phase contains processes that are divided into the five process groups. Four process groups (Initiating, Planning, Monitoring and Controlling, and Closing) manage the project. The product-related process group (Executing) produces the output of the project. The *PMBOK Guide* is the domain of the project management groups, while the "application area," SCM in our case, is the domain of the product-related executing group. Section 3 describes SCM processes in all five process groups.

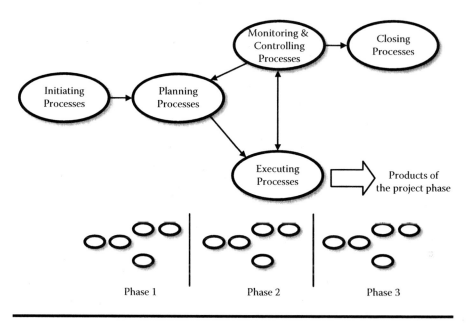

Figure 6.3   Links among process groups in a life cycle phase.

Chapter 7 describes the groups and related processes in greater detail. Figure 6.3 shows information flow among the process groups. Here are short descriptions of each process group:

- Initiating processes authorize the phase.
- Planning processes define and refine objectives and chart the path toward those objectives.
- Executing processes coordinate resources to carry out the plan.
- Monitoring and Controlling processes monitor and measure progress to promote corrective action.
- Closing processes formalize acceptance of the phase or project bringing it to an end.

The bottom of Figure 6.2 symbolizes the presence of each process group within each life cycle phase of the project. Each process has inputs, outputs, and tools and techniques that are described in the *PMBOK Guide.*

Processes consist of multiple activities, as shown in Figure 6.2. Each activity has duration, cost, and resource requirements. Activities may be further broken down into tasks and, if desired, subtasks. In Chapters 12 through 15, we endeavor to accomplish for SCM what the *PMBOK Guide* does for project management. This is to describe the project processes needed to execute an SCM project through the four SCM project phases listed above.

A WBS is a product-oriented view of the program and defines all of its outputs, or scope. This presentation is particularly helpful because deliverables are tangible outputs, useful for getting agreement on the scope, communicating products, and identifying resource requirements. For Event A in Table 6.1, the WBS might list communications links, a redesigned transportation network, subassembly design facility, and inventory policies as project deliverables. This will help the partners in defining requirements, making sure nothing needed to make the partnership work is missing.

6.2.2 Programs, Projects, and WBS Application

PMI acknowledges that the project management discipline is new. As mentioned earlier, it is also a discipline with a great potential for proliferation of terminology from one organization to another. The *PMBOK Guide* seeks to bring consistency in the application of project management terms. A company improving its supply chain must make choices: Is a supply chain improvement initiative a "program" or a "project?" Should supply chain improvement be coupled with other initiatives like strategic planning? Does it make any difference?

An important policy, called the "100% rule," is associated with the WBS.[5] The rule calls for the WBS to contain all the deliverables required by the scope of the project. These include internal, external, and interim deliverables. It also includes the project management components like change orders and schedules. The sum of the work at any level must represent all the requirements, and no more, for the next higher level.

Among project management practitioners, there exists a discussion centered on whether the WBS should contain deliverables ("supply chain strategy") or verb phrases ("create a supply chain strategy"). The 2008 revision to the *PMBOK Guide* uses verb–noun phrases to label project management processes. Formerly, nouns and verb–noun labels were used. Verb–noun phrases enable a user to translate project activities from a schedule into the WBS. Its disadvantage is that it substitutes action for results in the form of work products. This book will adhere to the work-product-deliverable approach.

Flexibility exists in terms of organizing a program or project. In some cases, it may make sense to use a deliverable-oriented phase. For example, an aircraft design program might be broken into WBS components like the wing, fuselage, engines, and so forth. In other situations, particularly where deliverables are highly interdependent, decomposition based on time-based phases fits best. This is generally the case in supply chain development. SCM is a great example of "progressive elaboration" where initial plans are articulated at the beginning of the project and continuously refined as the project proceeds.

The PMI standard, in its Appendices, provides a number of templates for common project types. These can be quite helpful to push ahead a project-centered organization's efforts to establish a standard project management methodology. Example templates are the following:

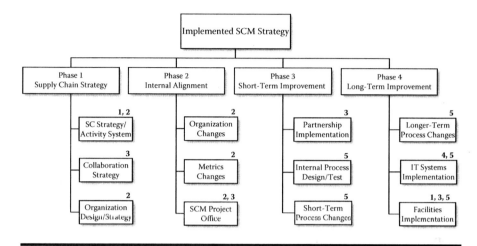

Figure 6.4   WBS or deliverable view, supply chain improvement project. Numbers indicate SCM task/knowledge area(s), as described in Chapter 4.

- Government Design–Bid–Build Construction Project WBS (This author has put this template to work with good results.),
- Service Industry Outsourcing Project WBS,
- Pharmaceutical Product Development Project WBS,
- Telecom Service Infrastructure Development Project WBS.

Figure 6.4 illustrates a time-phased WBS for a supply chain improvement program. The project's ultimate product, shown in Figure 6.4, is Implemented SCM Strategy. The figure relies on the five SCM tasks, our SCM knowledge areas, to develop deliverables with the associated task shown at the upper right corner of each WBS element:

1. Designing Supply Chains for Strategic Advantage,
2. Implementing Collaborative Relationships within the Organization,
3. Forging Supply Chain Partnerships,
4. Managing Supply Chain Information,
5. Removing Cost from the Supply Chain.

Section 3 describes how to develop these deliverables. They require project processes (as described in Chapters 12 through 15) that rely on SCM knowledge and practice.

Notes

1. PMI Global Standard, *A Guide to the Project Management Body of Knowledge (PMBOK Guide)*, 4th ed. (Project Management Institute, 2008).
2. PMI Global Standard, *The Standard for Portfolio Management*, 2nd ed. (Project Management Institute, 2008).
3. *Ibid.*
4. PMI Global Standard, *Practice Standard for Work Breakdown Structures*, 2nd ed. (Project Management Institute, 2006).
5. *Ibid.*, 8.

Chapter 7

Project Management Knowledge Areas

Project management knowledge areas and processes needed to execute projects are the core of project management knowledge and practice. The practitioner must supplement this project management knowledge with supply chain management (SCM) knowledge. Section 3 details the supplemental processes that blend these two knowledge areas.

Chapter 6 introduced the Project Management Body of Knowledge contained in the *Guide to the Project Management Body of Knowledge (PMBOK Guide).*[1] At the time of writing this book, the *PMBOK Guide* was in its fourth edition, published at the end of 2008. In the *PMBOK Guide,* the work of projects is embodied in the five process groups: Initiating, Planning, Executing, Monitoring and Controlling, and Closing. The *PMBOK Guide* also defines the nine project management knowledge areas.

Each of the forty-two project management processes belongs to a knowledge area and a process group. Figure 7.1 depicts the relationships between process groups and knowledge areas. Understanding these ties is important to understanding how project management knowledge supports supply chain projects. Figure 7.1 lists the nine project management knowledge areas down the left column. Along the top row are the five process groups: Initiating, Planning, Executing, Monitoring and Controlling, and Closing. Related processes lie at the intersection of these groups and the knowledge areas.

This chapter summarizes needed *PMBOK Guide* know-how. You should view this as a summary only and no substitute for consulting the *PMBOK Guide* directly. In some knowledge areas, the *PMBOK Guide* provides sufficient expertise to

Process Groups

Knowledge Areas	Initiating	Planning	Executing	Monitoring & Controlling	Closing
Integration Management	Develop project charter	Develop project management plan	Direct & manage project execution	Monitor & control project work perform integrated change control	Close project or phase
Scope Management		Collect requirements Define scope Create WBS		Verify scope Control scope	
Time Management		Define activities Sequence activities Estimate activity resources Estimate activity durations Develop schedule		Control schedule	
Cost Management		Estimate costs Determine budget		Control costs	
Quality Management		Plan quality	Perform quality assurance	Perform quality control	
Human Resources Management		Develop human resources plan	Acquire project team Develop project team Manage project team		
Communications Management	Identify stakeholders	Plan communications	Distribute information Manage stakeholder expectations	Report performance	
Risk Management		Plan risk management Identify risks Perform qualitative analysis Perform quantitative analysis Plan risk responses		Monitor and control risks	
Procurement Management		Plan procurements	Conduct procurements	Administer procurements	Close procurements

Figure 7.1   Project management processes by knowledge area and process group.

navigate a supply chain project with only a little assistance from SCM knowledge. In other knowledge areas, SCM know-how must materially supplement project management knowledge. Section 3 will identify the supply chain project processes and assign them to the appropriate SCM and project management knowledge area and *PMBOK Guide* process group.

7.1 Need for Supplemental SCM Knowledge

A supply chain project, or indeed a project in any other application area, cannot be successful without some application area knowledge. Figure 4.4 illustrates a central reason for supplemental SCM knowledge for supply chain improvement projects. The three levels in Figure 4.4 refer to the breadth of the project in terms of participation by different organization levels. Level 1 involves a single function, often a department. Level 2 broadens the involvement from the department to the business unit level. A business unit might be a division of a large corporation or a stand-alone company. Level 3 is the supply chain level, where more than one company or business unit participates. Increasing levels of implementation bring on the need for more SCM practice skill and knowledge.

Increasing implementation levels also makes formal project management even more critical to successful supply chain change. Most projects in an organization happen at Level 1, the departmental level. This is where sponsorship resides and where clear accountabilities and budget authority support actions to implement change. Control of projects is easiest at this level. However, competitive forces often force organizations to pursue a portfolio of business unit (Level 2) and supply chain (Level 3) projects. For projects that extend to supply chain partners, coordination must cross company boundaries, demanding new integration skills and knowledge. This will tax the capabilities of many.

7.2 SCM Knowledge Requirements by Knowledge Area

Table 7.1 lists the nine *PMBOK Guide* knowledge areas and an estimate of the need for supplemental SCM knowledge for each. The supplement is the need an experienced project manager would have for assistance by someone versed in SCM knowledge areas. The table summarizes—by a "high, medium, low" ranking—the need in the knowledge area for specialized SCM knowledge and practice expertise:

> *High:* High need for tailored SCM-specific processes to support *PMBOK Guide* processes for demanding projects.
>
> *Medium:* Moderate need for tailored SCM-specific processes to support *PMBOK Guide* processes for demanding projects.
>
> *Low: PMBOK Guide* processes are for the most part sufficient for demanding SCM projects.

If a project is demanding in terms of complexity, issues addressed, or the needs for supply chain expertise, then a "high" rating is warranted. A "low" rating is given where *PMBOK Guide* processes should be sufficient for most project managers. Table 7.1 calls attention to "considerations" for projects in the SCM domain. SCM project management considerations stem from one or more of the following factors:

- Aggressive SCM projects are strategic, elevating their visibility and criticality to the business.
- Projects are Level 3, or multicompany, from Figure 4.4. This requires project management coordination across company boundaries. Participants are "partners," not uninvolved buyers and vendors.

Table 7.1 Impact of SCM on Project Management Knowledge Areas

PMBOK Guide Knowledge Area	Need for SCM Expertise	SCM Considerations			
		Strategic	Multicompany	Paradigm Shift	Ambiguous Deliverables
Integration Management	High	●	●		●
Scope Management	High	●	●		●
Time Management	Low				
Cost Management	Medium	●	●		●
Quality Management	Medium	●			●
Human Resources Management	High		●	●	
Communications Management	Medium		●		●
Risk Management	High	●	●	●	●
Procurement Management	High		●	●	

■ A paradigm shift from functional to supply chain thinking is necessary. Other departments, customers, and suppliers are project stakeholders.
■ Ambiguous deliverables require SCM knowledge-based judgment to evaluate completion and proper control response. For example, what form should the deliverable take—a product, a service, or a result?

This chapter identifies sources of complexity and the resulting need for supplemental SCM processes. Section 3 provides the supplemental processes needed to complete demanding SCM projects.

7.3 Knowledge Areas and SCM

This section describes each of the nine knowledge areas and related knowledge requirements for implementing supply chain improvements. Accompanying tables list the *PMBOK Guide* processes for each knowledge area along with the process group to which the process is assigned. The "high, medium, low" rating for required SCM knowledge is given at the top of each table.

7.3.1 Knowledge Area: Project Integration Management

High SCM Knowledge Required

Project Integration Management Processes	Process Group
Develop Project Charter	Initiating
Develop Project Management Plan	Planning
Direct and Manage Project Execution	Executing
Monitor and Control Project Work	Monitoring and Controlling
Perform Integrated Change Control	Monitoring and Controlling
Close Project or Phase	Closing

Processes in the Project Integration Management knowledge area hold the project together and oversee the production of most of its deliverables. As the requirements of a project become increasingly complex, so do the tools and knowledge required. The need for "high" SCM knowledge is inherent because this knowledge area, under the *Develop Project Management Plan* process, assigns all work tasks in the project, most of which require SCM knowledge. In other words, it takes a supply chain "expert" to know what to do and why.

Develop Project Charter can be the most important process in pursuing a project, particularly if scope and charter aren't obvious. An article by Rick Morris points to the importance of this knowledge area.[2] Morris points to estimates of project failure rates ranging between 60 percent and 82 percent. He maintains that those that fail do so in the "first five minutes." This implies the root cause for most failures lies in chartering the project, which is the first step. The charter and scope are mutually dependent. Without some statement on scope, a project manager will have difficulty creating a charter. Table 7.2 lists candidate components of a charter, including a statement regarding scope. The list of charter items is long. However, there is a virtue in keeping charters short, perhaps to as few as two or three pages. The project plan can expand as needed on the charter's intent.

Develop Project Management Plan takes the authorized charter and other planning inputs to produce a project plan. The plan should be modified as the project moves forward, an important *PMBOK Guide* practice called "progressive elaboration." Charter changes should be rare; project plan changes as frequent as needed to respond to new information. The *PMBOK Guide* assumes projects have their genesis from other planning processes, like strategic planning. Chapter 12 describes a process for supply chain design based on company strategy. The *PMBOK Guide* lists elements for the project plan. Among the chief topics are the following:

- project charter;
- inputs to the plan from the company strategy, fit of the project with other programs and projects;
- the strategy for completing the project, including individual tasks, tools, and methodologies from other knowledge areas like SCM;
- a preliminary Work Breakdown Structure (WBS) to the level of control desired plus responsibility for deliverables, project phases;
- added detail for cost and schedule;
- staff required and cost;
- risks, constraints, contingencies, mitigation measures, and responses;
- subsidiary plans for scope, schedule, cost, quality, staffing, communications, risk, and procurement;
- progress tracking, how changes will be monitored and controlled, and performance measure baselines for schedule, cost, quality, and milestones;
- issues faced by the project and required decisions; and
- the needs for methods of communications with stakeholders.

The world would be a better place if all projects had this documentation in place as they kicked off. When several organizations must contribute, a situation common in supply chain projects, a complete plan, is even more important.

Direct and Manage Project Execution oversees performance of the plan and provides needed feedback to change it. Most of the project budget will fund executing

Table 7.2 Elements of a Project Charter

Charter Element	Description
Project name	Project identification
Associated program(s) or related projects	Program of which the project is a component (if any) or other efforts that will affect the project or anticipate outputs from the project
Project sponsor	Executive accountable for success of the project
Project manager	Person assigned responsibility for executing the project
Participants	Supporting staff: full-time and part-time
Background/purpose/ environmental factors	Origins of the project, reasons why it was initiated
Objectives/ deliverables	Products, services, or objectives (tangible outputs)
Project identity	Name of the project (how the project will be identified)
Project description	What the project entails
Purpose and justification	Why the project is necessary
Scope	The sum of products, services, and objectives to be delivered (boundaries of the project or process included, trading partners involved, sphere[s] to be addressed)
Approach/tasks	Brief statement of methodology or required tasks
Project budget	Funds provided for the project
Benefits	Expectations for improvement (competitive position, cost reductions, etc.)
Summary schedule	Milestones, end dates for phases or milestone events
Issues/assumptions	Points in question or matters that should be settled by the project, barriers and constraints faced
Project risks	Uncertainties for the project whether the impact is positive or negative

(continued on next page)

Table 7.2 (continued)   Elements of a Project Charter

Charter Element	Description
Critical success factors	Factors seen as essential to success (examples include agreements with trading partners, successful technology implemented, and availability of project staff)
High-level requirements	Stakeholder desires for the project (delivered as features of the deliverable)
Summary budget	Estimates of major cost components
Executive signatures	Authorization signatures by sponsor and project manager plus other stakeholding executives

processes like those in Section 3 that create project deliverables. According to the *PMBOK Guide,* plan development and execution rely on organizational policies as inputs. Multicompany participation in Level 3 supply chain projects requires agreed-to policies.

Monitor and Control Project Work is the process for assuring that work results meet requirements. It also adjusts the plan accordingly in the case of plan deviations or new information through the Perform Integrated Change Control process.

Change control produces corrective actions, progressive elaboration, that have to be incorporated into project plans. The initial plan provides the baseline for comparing revisions to planning parameters like cost, schedule, and objectives. Chapter 9 examines root causes for project failures. One culprit identified in that chapter is inflexibility in modifying projects as needed, highlighting the importance of this process.

The Close Project or Phase process brings finality to the effort. It assures that the project has met its goals in terms of its scope and deliverables.

7.3.2 Knowledge Area: Project Scope Management

High SCM Knowledge Required

Project Scope Management Processes	Process Group
Collect Requirements	Planning
Define Scope	Planning
Create Work Breakdown Structure (WBS)	Planning
Verify Scope	Monitoring and Control
Control Scope	Monitoring and Control

The need for additional SCM knowledge for the Project Scope Management knowledge area is ranked "high." Scope decisions set the level of the project—whether it's departmental, business unit, or supply chain. Processes in this knowledge area address alternatives for dividing programs into projects or projects into phases. This answers questions like "Do planning and control considerations require us to have five projects in our program, or will three do?" and "How many project phases, which are often centered around major deliverables, do we need to control the effort without bogging down in paperwork?"

A second reason for the "high" rating is of particular importance in supply chain management. This is the issue regarding the supply chain level (function, business unit, or supply chain) for the project. This decision will define project stakeholders who support project execution. Should the project pursue limited scope and only implement at Level 1 or 2, confining the project to one's own company? This strategy may produce faster results but will it sacrifice greater benefits? Or should the project take higher project management risks by collaborating with trading partners?

Collect Requirements is a process addition in the 2008 *PMBOK Guide.* Requirements guide the entire project and provide a way to affirm at the end that each requirement has been fulfilled. Section 8.7.3 describes *A Guide to the Business Analysis Body of Knowledge (BABOK),* modeled on the *PMBOK Guide.*[3] Gathering requirements is no trivial process, particularly if the number of stakeholders is large. Define Scope requires clarity regarding the project's output, or deliverable. Requirements guide this process. In *PMBOK Guide* terminology, the deliverable can be a physical product, a service, or a result. SCM is about designing processes for delivering physical products. So, a supply chain improvement product will likely be framed as a service or a result. An SCM project output/deliverable could be "extend distribution into China" (a service) or "reduce inventory by 30%" (a result).

The product description defining the project comes from company strategic planning, the requirements, or a management steering committee. Driver examples include any of the following:

1. market demand either on a one-time or ongoing basis, such as demand for a new product;
2. business need to increase revenues and profits or improve productivity;
3. customer requests in the normal course of business, like a security alarm company installing a new customer's system;
4. technology advances, driving the need for upgraded or new products or processes;
5. legal requirements such as environmental compliance; and
6. social needs like civil infrastructure or fund-raising.

The first four of these drivers would likely require supply chain change, with the supply chain component an adjunct to another driver. So, that effort, development of a new product for example, might become the "program," as defined in Chapter 6. The supply chain effort can be a project, or a group of projects, within that program.

In Example 1, market demand on a one-time basis might involve a supply chain design to support a construction project in some remote area. In another example, the product life cycle, described in Section 4.2, brings different missions for the supply chain at different stages in a product's evolution—a responsive chain for new, innovative products and an efficient chain for mature, functional products.

In Example 2, companies pursue continuous improvement programs under the mantle of Six Sigma, total quality management, process reengineering, and many local adaptations. Supply chain improvement may have its own continuous improvement effort or it may support other initiatives.

With regard to Example 3, many companies use design-to-order or configure-to-order business models in addition to the more common make-to-stock model. Supply chain design must support these alternatives. This support involves both front-end ordering processes, engineering design for easy assembly, and material delivery requirements, pricing, and fulfillment.

Technology advances, Example 4, include new product technology, new processes for manufacturing or distribution, or advances in supply chain software tools—of which there are many offerings. The supply chain space is fertile ground for new and improved software marketed by a provider multitude. An integrated supply chain project should define supply chain requirements and match those to the universe of candidate solutions.

Perhaps a supply chain project is attached to a new product introduction or seeks to improve the market penetration of an existing product. In this case, it's appropriate to take the view, described earlier in Section 3.3, that supply chains encompass both the base product and the extended product. Figure 3.3 provides examples for an automobile. In the case of a personal computer, the base product is what you carry out of the store. The extended product includes user friendliness, software availability, options, financing, after-sale service, and warranty and repair access. In the case of automobiles and computers, the supply chain program may have all three deliverable types—a product, a service, and a result.

Define Scope is an ongoing process to keep the scope definition current with the progress of the project. Beginning with the project plan developed by the Develop Project Management Plan process, Define Scope involves ongoing analysis of the project along with identifying alternatives and deciding whether to modify the scope or not. In a complex, multicompany supply chain project, there are likely to be a number of triggers for re-evaluating scope. An obvious one is the failure of a supply chain partner to uphold its commitments to deliverables.

Define Scope also subdivides the project. The *PMBOK Guide* calls for application area expertise in identifying and selecting alternative approaches. In particular, the process should use stakeholder requirements to shape the project. Quality

Function Deployment (QFD) is a structured methodology for turning stakeholder requirements into scope definitions. The outputs provide added detail to the charter and plan components. These include objectives, requirements in terms of stakeholder satisfaction, project boundaries, deliverables, assumptions, and constraints.

The Create Work Breakdown Structure (WBS) process produces a detailed WBS down to the "work package" level, the lowest level of the WBS. In Figure 6.2, it is shown at the individual process level in the project component hierarchy. The WBS divides the project into manageable "chunks" or phases, as shown in Figure 6.4. Each phase produces major deliverables, corresponding to the WBS view. Verify Scope confirms with the executive authority like a steering committee confirms the scope. Scope verification is formal acceptance of the product of the project. Control Scope is the ongoing process of reviewing and changing the scope. An SCM challenge may be gaining agreement from partners to changes in scope—changes that might require added staff or funding.

7.3.3 Knowledge Area: Project Time Management

Low SCM Knowledge Required

Project Time Management Processes	Process Group
Define Activities	Planning
Sequence Activities	Planning
Estimate Activity Resources	Planning
Estimate Activity Durations	Planning
Develop Schedule	Planning
Control Schedule	Monitoring and Controlling

The need for supplemental SCM knowledge for this additional knowledge is ranked "low." In fact, the project management discipline has generated many best practices and techniques that enrich this knowledge area. This by no means diminishes the importance of time management in projects. Certainly, poor estimating can sink any project. For supply chain projects, time should be added to account for complications in coordinating across company boundaries. However, time management approaches for SCM projects will be similar to those needed for other types of projects. Figure 7.2 shows the relationship between processes for a systematic approach to time management, along with principal inputs and outputs for each process.

Define Activities requires an understanding of the steps needed to complete a deliverable, as defined in the WBS. The WBS is an output of the Create WBS

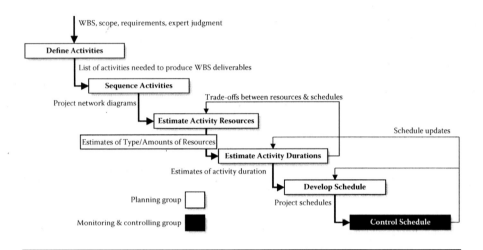

Figure 7.2 Process for time management.

process. An input to the task is expert judgment, which is likely to be drawn from multiple companies in a supply chain project.

Once activities are listed, the Sequence Activities process puts them in the order in which they are performed. This encompasses development of milestones and dependencies. An output is often in the form of a project network diagram. Some companies, at Level 2 or 3 of the Project Management Maturity Matrix (PMMM) described in Chapter 5, may develop templates with activities and associated networks. These templates come in handy when project types repeat. Sequencing becomes critical when different organizations in Level 2 and Level 3 projects are dependent on others for input to their tasks.

Following sequencing are Estimate Activity Resources and Estimate Activity Durations. The duration depends on scope, resources, approvals required, logistics, dependence on other activities, and many other factors. Examples of resources include staff time, money, consultants, teams, equipment, and software. Trade-offs that could extend project duration may be required if resources are limited. Contingencies can also be applied if estimates or their underlying assumptions are uncertain. There are many tools available, some of which are listed in the *PMBOK Guide,* for estimating resources, displaying duration, and testing schedules for ways to reduce duration.

Develop Schedule anchors activities to specific start and stop dates. As a project proceeds, the Control Schedule process generates updates based on actual performance. A schedule baseline, part of the project management plan, should be the standard against which actual progress is marked.

The *PMBOK Guide* describes "rolling wave planning." With this technique, project planners use progressive elaboration to refine their estimates. So, near-term activities are planned in detail to low levels of the WBS. Activities that are further out have estimates at a higher, broader level and are refined to lower levels as the project unfolds. Figure 7.2 shows the rolling wave as a feedback loop between Control Schedule and Develop Schedule, creating a continuous process through the duration of the project. It is also likely to be the best approach in programs with multiple projects and in projects where responsibilities are shared among trading partners.

7.3.4 Knowledge Area: Project Cost Management

Medium SCM Knowledge Required

Project Cost Management Processes	Process Group
Estimate Costs	Planning
Determine Budget	Planning
Control Costs	Monitoring and Controlling

The need for supplemental SCM knowledge for cost management is rated "medium." This is not because the *PMBOK Guide* doesn't describe a complete methodology for cost management of conventional projects. The changes lie in the nature of supply chain programs—particularly multicompany participation. Multicompany participation raises the prospect of joint decisions about conducting the project, including sharing the costs and benefits.

A project, by *PMBOK Guide* definition, produces a product, a service, or a result. Most supply chain projects will have deliverables in the last two categories—services and results. Amazon, the online retailer, is arguably more a service company than a product company. Its innovations have created an alternative channel between product companies and end users. Their contribution is distribution and marketing the products of others that are available through other channels. In another example, a product company may partner with a local distributor to expand into an untapped market. The outcome is a result—penetrating a new market with an existing product. In both examples, the project sets up the businesses that will continue for many years, evolving from a "set up" project into a "sustaining" mode.

Supply chain projects can also be give-and-take affairs with multicompany funding and active participation in the projects. There is less of the buyer–seller role in the traditional sense. An analogy in traditional project management is construction. The buyer owns the asset after the project is completed, and the sellers—the designer, suppliers, the project financers, the construction contractor, and the project manager—reach closure of the project when they turn the building over to the owner. A supply chain project will likely involve partnerships where all participants expect long-range involvement and benefits.

Non-traditional cost management arrangements may come to play in the supply chain project:

- long-term contracting, committing to a supplier or customer;
- tracking cost using innovations like activity-based costing, a version of what Harold Kerzner refers to in Section 5.2 as "horizontal accounting";
- balancing up-front partner capital investments with future profit splits;
- joint investments in information exchange systems to run the supply chain;
- new product development—the contribution of intellectual property (IP), manufacturing capacity, or cash;
- new services or processes—IP and cash contributions;
- penalties for departing from approved practices that add cost or abandoning the effort;
- fixed prices for certain project products;
- innovations in incentives for exceeding the plan; and
- methods for handling changes in scope or products that affect costs and investments.

The cost management planning processes described in the following paragraphs may be done separately or as a continuous process as part of a rolling wave progressive elaboration approach.

Estimate Activity Resources turns WBS and the related activities into resource requirements as part of the Time Management knowledge area. The type of resource and quantity for each WBS element defines resource requirements. Key resources are likely to include expertise, staff for accomplishing work, facilities, systems, tools and equipment, and materials. Identification of resource sources is also a necessary input. Some sources will reside within the participating supply chain organizations; others must be procured from outside the partnership. While planning a supply chain project, partners may or may not have resources. Or one partner can claim to have the resource but other partners may be happier with an alternative source.

Estimate Costs converts resources, resource unit cost, and duration into project costs. Risks should be evaluated for each cost component. Risk arises from uncertainty in any component of cost—resource identification, resource cost, and duration. Contingency estimates can be added to compensate for risk. Bids from vendors might also be an input. The *PMBOK Guide* describes several cost-estimating techniques including the following:

- Analogous estimating: A top-down estimate using actual cost experience from other projects and from expert inputs.
- Parametric modeling: Turning project-related parameters into costs, like using the cost per square foot for estimating home construction cost.
- Bottom-up estimating: Rolling up individual, lower-level components, such as activity-level estimates.

With cost estimates, the Determine Budget process creates the cost baseline necessary to monitor project costs. Ideally, budgeting is done after estimating. However, projects may be budgeted with a top-down approach before formal bottom-up estimates are available.

Control Costs, like other control processes, uses actual experience to update estimates. It also produces an "estimate at completion" to alert managers to the likelihood of final actual cost. In cases of major cost shifts, a "rebaselining" of the project budget may be necessary.

7.3.5 Knowledge Area: Project Quality Management

Medium SCM Knowledge Required

Project Quality Management Processes	Process Group
Plan Quality	Planning
Perform Quality Assurance	Executing
Perform Quality Control	Monitoring and Controlling

As in the Project Time Management knowledge area, the impact of SCM on Project Quality Management is rated "medium." The outputs of a supply chain project are likely to be services and results, not physical products. So, supply chain projects are less amenable to objective measurement against product engineering specifications or drawings. For this reason, quality management of SCM projects is not necessarily easy.

Plan Quality establishes standards relevant to the project and a plan for applying them. The tools vary widely, depending on the needs of the project. Since supply chains are essentially collections of business processes, process cost and service performance standards will measure project quality. Examples include defect rates, first time capability, fill rates for orders, and so forth. The requirements from the Collect Requirements process should help establish quality yardsticks.

In the area of forecasting and inventory control, we suggest using the percentage of planning decisions based on actual demand versus forecasts of that demand. The higher a supply chain ranks on this measure, the more "demand-driven" and the less "forecast-driven" it is. Chapter 15 describes the approach; the technique produces an objective estimate of how demand-driven a supply chain might be. Later, the quality assessment should use the same methodology to measure progress toward the potential.

Perform Quality Assurance is the process that measures quality levels as the project proceeds. It is part of the Executing process group and incorporates execution of the Quality Plan along with periodic audits to assure that the plan is adequate and is being followed. Perform quality control, according to the *PMBOK Guide,* includes not only project products but also the project management outcomes, such as cost and schedule performance.

7.3.6 Knowledge Area: Project Human Resources Management

High SCM Knowledge Required

Project Human Resources Management	Process Group
Develop Human Resources Plan	Planning
Acquire Project Team	Executing
Develop Project Team	Executing
Manage Project Team	Executing

Our assessment need for SCM knowledge is "high." In Chapter 4, we described two tasks for effective supply chain management that center on organization issues: *Task 2 Implementing Collaborative Relationships* inside the organization, and *Task 3 Forging Supply Chain Partnerships* with trading partners. Multicompany supply chain efforts require shared resources and multicompany teams. Also, many supply chain projects will require different mind-sets. While it may be possible to get "bodies" to support a project, integrating these bodies into effective teams is difficult. The term "collaboration" describes processes to overcome these differences.

Develop *Human Resources Plan* establishes roles and responsibilities, an organization structure, and a staff management plan for the project. The management plan profiles requirements as the project plan is executed. The format and formality of the plan are flexible, depending on the needs of the project. When the project depends on partners to staff the project, added detail is justified. The plan should also address what team members will do once they are released from the project.

Roles and responsibilities might be displayed in matrix form. *PMBOK Guide* refers to this as a Responsibility Assignment Matrix (RAM). With phases on one side and participants on the other, the intersection shows the level of participation. These levels can include categories that meet the needs of the project. One supply chain project approach uses Responsible, Accountable, Consulted, and Informed (RACI) or Accountable, Responsible, Consulted, and Informed (ARCI) as categories. The *PMBOK Guide* suggests Participant, Accountable, Review Required, Input Required, and Sign-Off Required.

Confusion regarding terms is easy. Harold Kerzner clarifies the obligations that go with different roles.[4] Authority is granted to those "who make final decisions for others to follow." Responsibility goes with roles in the project as they are assigned to people or groups. Accountability is the "state of being answerable for completion" of the project. This is the highest level of the four categories; hence, the emergence of the ARCI term. Appendix B lists roles and responsibilities for execution of supply chain project processes detailed in Section 3. There can be many variations on RAMs in a project. For example, there may be a RAM assigning communications responsibilities or a RAM delegating responsibilities in the project procurement process.

After requirements are defined, the Acquire Project Team process obtains the identified skills and numbers. Of course, many projects founder for lack of skills, numbers, or both. Even if commitments are made, the need may not be filled in a timely way. This is particularly true when the project is a second priority or regular non-project work is "urgent and unimportant" even though the project work is "non-urgent and very important." It is all too likely that the regular work will take priority over the project work.

Develop Project Team is also an executing process. The *PMBOK Guide* cites tools for team building. Examples are the rewards and recognition for team participation plus collocation of the team. Increasingly, with new technology, teams work at a distance. This is the case for supply chain projects since supply chains tend to spread out over the planet. Training is another tool for team building. It is especially important for teams where individuals represent a number of different disciplines. The Manage Project Team process calls for sustaining the effectiveness of teams once they are in operation. Tools cited in the *PMBOK Guide* include 360-degree evaluations by team members at all levels, creation of issue logs to shape the team's agenda, and facilitation to address conflicts on the team.

7.3.7 Knowledge Area: Project Communications Management

Medium SCM Knowledge Required

Project Communications Management Processes	Process Group
Identify Stakeholders	Initiating
Plan Communications	Planning
Distribute Information	Executing
Manage Stakeholder Expectations	Executing
Report Performance	Monitoring and Controlling

The Communications knowledge area calls for a "medium" level of specialized SCM knowledge. Multicompany participation is the principal reason for added expertise since team members may come from trading partner organizations. Security arising from the potential transfer of proprietary information is an additional factor. This is somewhat mitigated by the fact that supply chain efforts are difficult to hide from an industry's community. Also, building a new capability for a supplier or customer unlocks the possibility that the supplier or customer will pass on the innovation to others.

Identify Stakeholders is necessary to set scope, develop a charter, and to gather requirements from those stakeholders. Stakeholders include employees, department heads, suppliers, technology sources, customers, sources of finance, and company owners. The inability to get all on board or the unwillingness of a key stakeholder to participate will require regeneration of charters and plans, or outright project cancellation.

Plan Communications transforms communications requirements into a Communications Management Plan. The *PMBOK Guide* recommends a stakeholder analysis as the basis for the plan. The WBS in Figure 6.4 calls for a "collaboration strategy" as a Phase 1 deliverable; the Communications Plan can be part of this strategy. The stakeholder analysis addresses information user needs in terms of content, method of delivery, frequency, and support systems. Care should be taken to avoid unnecessary communication. Process templates in Chapters 12 through 15 identify stakeholders.

The Communications Management Plan, according to the *PMBOK Guide*, should cover the following:

- methods of gathering and storing various types of information,
- information distribution and method (report, data, meeting, etc.) that is coordinated with the organization structure,
- publication schedules for each type of communication, and
- updating and refinement of the plan.

Many organizations operating in project environments implement "proactive" systems for project communication. These utilize workflow tools for collaboration where rules provide for automatically forwarding information to designated stakeholders. Many document management and project management software applications provide this capability.

The process for Distribute Information executes the communications plan. Suggested content in *PMBOK Guide* includes lessons learned documentation, project records, reports, presentations, feedback, and stakeholder notifications. The latter covers resolved issues, plan changes, and project status. Manage Stakeholder Expectations calls for "no surprises" for stakeholders. This requires project manager empathy to understand each stakeholder group's needs. Another process, Report Performance, describes what is happening in the project. These reports include both current status and forecasts of future performance based on those results. Performance reporting includes performance review meetings, variance analysis, trends, and earned value analysis.

Earned value analysis has created a vocabulary for reporting progress. Table 7.3 summarizes a few of the measures used for project performance reporting. Again,

Table 7.3   Earned Value Analysis Terms for Project Performance Reporting

Term	Abbreviation	Related Calculation
AC	Actual cost	Measured in accounts
EV	Earned value	Counts, deliverables produced, achievements, expert evaluation
PV	Planned value	What the schedule says
CPI	Cost performance index	$=EV/AC$
CV	Cost variance	$=EV-AC$
SV	Schedule variance	$=EV-PV$

supply chain projects often produce services or results. So, there are challenges in measuring progress in deliverables. In fact, the actual result may not be apparent until the project is over. What is measurable is accomplishment of activities delineated in the project plan.

7.3.8 Knowledge Area: Project Risk Management

High SCM Knowledge Required

Risk Management Project Processes	Process Group
Plan Risk Management	Planning
Identify Risks	Planning
Perform Qualitative Analysis	Planning
Perform Quantitative Analysis	Planning
Plan Risk Responses	Planning
Monitor and Control Risks	Monitoring and Controlling

The *PMBOK Guide* devotes considerable attention to risk associated with project outcomes. In fact, if there is a rationale for the project management discipline, it is as a tool for avoiding negative project outcomes. One could argue that the absence of risk equates to no need at all for *PMBOK Guide*-type disciplined processes. In supply chain project management, there are two types of risk. The first is risk associated with the project itself, the subject of this section. The second is risks associated with the supply chain design. These include reliance on shaky suppliers, market risks, logistics interruptions, product failures, and changes in end-user preferences.

Chris Christensen, a Section 2 reviewer, observes that there are many additional reasons for project management, including communications and increased efficiency in using resources. To a degree, risk is like the flexibility imperative described in Section 3.5. That section described how common supply chain metrics and many of the other drivers of supply chain change demand supply chain flexibility. Being flexible is itself a risk mitigator. Likewise, better communications and use of resources reduce the risk that somebody doesn't do his or her job or that the project doesn't overrun its budget. This applies particularly to supply chain projects that must deliver results, not products or services. A result is more a pass/fail outcome; products and services can be evaluated on a scale from poor to great. Supply chain projects also rely on strategic decisions and the enthusiastic participation of multicompany team members—both "risky" areas fraught with uncertainty.

Risk management, according to the *PMBOK Guide*, maximizes the probability and consequences of positive events and minimizes the probability and consequences of negative ones. Risk management terminology uses "prevention" or "avoidance" to describe strategies that reduce the chances of a negative event and "mitigation" to describe strategies to minimize the impact if an event does occur. Note that risk isn't limited to negative outcomes. Risk management includes capitalizing on good outcomes as well as protecting against poor ones. An example is a supply chain cost reduction project. If a company expects a $50-million annual saving from its effort, each week of delay costs about $1 million. Such a number is useful in making decisions on schedule and resources availability for the project. One might readily add $10,000 in weekly expense to a six-month project, an added cost of about $260,000, to complete the project two months early and save $2 million.

The risk in a supply chain project over that in a conventional project arises from all four "risky" factors inherent in supply chain projects introduced in Section 7.2. These make up the strategic nature of the project, multicompany participation, the need for paradigm shifts, and ambiguous deliverables. So, the risk management knowledge area is ranked "high" in terms of the need for SCM knowledge and processes.

Risks due to strategic projects lie not just in execution, internal risk factors like cost and schedule, or "doing things right." They also lie in "doing the right thing" or external factors beyond the project's control, like sales levels or labor disruptions at a supplier. This means the strategies that the projects generate must be sound and must be soundly implemented. These strategies are themselves a product of the supply chain project, Phase 1 in Figure 6.4. Multicompany risk has been addressed in discussions of other knowledge areas. In particular, the Executing group of processes may be awkwardly coordinated and poorly performed. The same is true for paradigm shifts where participants come from several companies and departments within those companies, each with a different culture, motivations, and values. Ambiguous deliverables apply when the results of the project may not be known for some time.

7.3.8.1 Plan and Identify Risks

The Plan Risk Management process must consider risk tolerances of management. In fact, these risk tolerances will drive the architecture of the supply chain program itself. A risk-intolerant management may limit the program to Level 1 or 2 projects because of perceived difficulties in pursuing Level 3 projects. The risk-adverse managers may also require more reporting and narrower projects done on a slower sequential schedule. The *PMBOK Guide* recommends the following outputs from the risk planning process:

- How risk is to be measured, the tools required, and the type of assessment to use. This includes both quantitative and qualitative risk assessment.
- Roles and responsibilities for risk management, including who is to perform risk-related activities. The *PMBOK Guide* notes that a third party outside the project team may be best for this role.
- The timing of risk assessments during the project life cycle.
- Scoring and interpretation methods for qualitative and quantitative risk analysis.
- Risk thresholds, including criteria for action, who should act, and what response is appropriate.

Identify Risks draws in stakeholders to list areas of uncertainty. Risk categories could include technical, quality, and performance risk. We have mentioned four areas inherent in supply chain projects (strategic projects, multicompany, paradigm shift, and ambiguous deliverables). Additional technical risk comes with dependence on unproven or complex technology. Quality standards and performance goals can also be ambitious if not totally unrealistic. Environmental risks include PESTEL uncertainties, shown in Figure 3.1. The *PMBOK Guide* also recommends developing "triggers" that provide an early warning that a risk event has occurred or might occur.

7.3.8.2 Perform Qualitative Risk Analysis

Supply chain projects will depend heavily on Qualitative Analysis. Many risk factors will be such that a quantitative approach isn't feasible. To score a risk, the *PMBOK Guide* recommends an approach that multiplies the impact of an event by the probability that event will occur. The scores are displayed in a probability-impact matrix. Following is the procedure for constructing a matrix, which we use in an example later in this section:

1. Prepare a list of objectives for the project. Stakeholder requirements will be helpful. A *PMBOK Guide* example consists of internal project performance measures: cost, schedule, and quality. Such a list should also include external factors.
2. Prepare descriptions of each outcome classified by the impact of that outcome from best to worst.

3. Use tolerance for risk to set a scale for each level of impact. Such a scale can be linear or non-linear. Non-linear scales reflect risk aversion because bad outcomes carry a heavy penalty.
4. Prepare a table of risk scores that multiply the probabilities of occurrence by the impact of the result. Designate which areas of qualitative risk will be low, medium, and high.
5. Provide relative risk factors for each outcome using the risk score table. Use the scores to set priorities for risk reduction efforts.

A risk-associated issue with supply chain projects arises from the nature of the product. In many cases, as mentioned earlier, the project product is often a service or a result. So, one can have a successful project from the viewpoint of internal project measures, like cost and schedule, but fail because the environment needed for success failed to materialize. Also, success can't be measured until results are known. This can be later in the project life cycle after the solution is installed and has operated long enough to measure results.

As an example, consider a project whose mission is "to extend distribution into China." The project team may be successful in setting up the distribution system. The cost, schedule, and quality goals may be met. However, the strategy that set sights on China may be flawed. The Chinese hate the product, returns are flooding in, and retailers won't pay. Is such a project a failure? In a construction project, this is analogous to the office tower built on speculation that there was a market for the space. But, the market didn't materialize, bankrupting the project. In other words, "the operation was a success but the patient died."

Ambitious supply chain projects will challenge managers to decide where risk should be assessed and accounted for. In Table 7.4 and Table 7.5, we've adapted the five-step approach to risk assessment described earlier to include both external (strategy-related) and internal (cost, schedule, quality) risk factors for a project. We next apply the five-step procedure to develop qualitative risk scoring for a supply chain project:

1. Prepare a list of project objectives. Table 7.4 lists four objectives. Two are "internal" project performance measures. The other two are "external," measuring the result the project is designed to accomplish. These are business goals for sales (volume sold multiplied by average price) and operating profit.
2. Prepare descriptions of potential outcomes from best to worst. These outcomes populate Table 7.4. The organization believes that project expectations can be exceeded if things go well. This can bring the benefit of early implementation, increasing sales and profits plus beating the competition into a new market. These outcomes are shown in the "Favorable" column. The "High" column contains outcomes that are the most negative in their impact.
3. Use tolerance for risk to set a scale for each level of impact. The scores (–1, 3, 5, 9) are a non-linear scale, meaning higher impact penalties for really awful

Table 7.4   Impact of Risks on Project Objectives

Project Objectives	Impact			
	Favorable −1	Low 3	Medium 5	High 9
Internal Risk Factors				
Implementation project cost	Below budget	<10% over budget	10–30% over budget	>30%over budget
Implementation project schedule	>1 month ahead of schedule	<1 month late	1–3 months late	>3 months late
External Risk Factors				
Unit sales	>10% over plan	>90% of plan	70–90% of plan	<70% of plan
Operating profit	>10% over plan	>90% of plan	70–90% of plan	<70% of plan

Table 7.5   Scoring a Risk: Impact Multiplied by Probability

Probability (%)	Outcomes and Their Impact (from Table 7.3)			
	Favorable −1	Low 3	Medium 5	High 9
80–100	−1.0	3.0	5.0	9.0
60–80	−0.8	2.4	4.0	7.2
40–60	−0.6	1.8	3.0	5.4
20–40	−0.4	1.2	2.0	3.6
0–20	−0.2	0.6	1.0	1.8
Low risk				
Medium risk				
High risk				

outcomes. So, being more than 30 percent over budget earns a "9" impact. A "–1" is used for favorable outcomes so that poorer outcomes produce higher risk scores than favorable ones in this particular matrix.

4. Score the risk for probabilities of occurrence resulting in a matrix of risk scores. Table 7.5 is a "lookup" table that shows risk scoring. The table is a tool for classifying specific risks contained in Table 7.4. Scores are the product of the Impact rating and the Probability shown in the left-hand column of Table 7.5. The probability used is at the high end of the range (e.g., the probabilities in the 60%–80% range use 80%).

5. Designate which areas of qualitative risk will be low, medium, and high. Estimating the probabilities of outcomes in Table 7.4 does this. Shaded areas in Table 7.5 show areas of risk. Outcomes with scores of "4.0" or greater are high risk. Medium risk scores are between 2.0 and 3.9. Low risk scores are 1.9 or below.

If the probability of being greater than 30 percent over budget is 40 percent, reference to Table 7.5 produces a risk score of 5.4. Of course, the probabilities of outcomes for any risk factor cannot exceed 100 percent. The *PMBOK Guide* notes that this process can be adapted to the needs of any project. Most supply chain projects will likely need both internal and external risk measures, and measures will probably extend past initial implementation into the operating period of the project life cycle.

In application, project risks are identified through interviewing, brainstorming, and analysis of the project activities. If our program is to "extend distribution into China," an important project or subproject could be to "establish a transportation network." If this is a critical path item, lateness in this project can make our project late. Suppose we have allowed six months for setting up the network but think it could easily take ten months because we are uncertain about the problems we might encounter. These potential problems are called "threats." The threat is that "the transportation network is late in becoming established." This shouldn't be confused with what the cause of the delay. Potential causes might be bureaucracy, lack of local contacts, bad weather, the death of an important agent, or difficulty in coming to terms with trading partners. If we assume there is a probability of 50 percent of taking ten months to establish the network, we assign a "9" score for impact since that is greater than three months late. Our risk score, taken from Table 7.5, is 5.4, a high-risk project component due to schedule uncertainty.

Once risks are collected and scored, according to the *PMBOK Guide*, the outputs of the task should include the following:

■ Overall risk of the project: A project risk profile can be based on the highest risk score for each project objective.
■ List of risks grouped in different ways: Examples include risk scores, priorities for addressing the risks, time-phased risks, and related objectives.

- Risks requiring further analysis: High and medium risks may be served by performing a quantitative risk analysis.
- Trends in qualitative risk analysis: The trend in risk can be tracked over time as the project proceeds.

7.3.8.3 Perform Quantitative Risk Analysis

As needed, the Perform Quantitative Analysis process follows qualitative analysis when risks are screened qualitatively and deemed to merit further analysis. Quantitative analysis can take several forms, which are mentioned briefly here:

- Interviewing to develop ranges for outcomes instead of single, most-likely planning outcomes.
- Sensitivity analysis to understand the impact of a risk item on the overall project. For example, schedule uncertainty for an activity that's not on the project's critical path may not present that much risk to the project. The analysis approach is to vary the risk item event's outcome while holding other factors at their baseline levels.
- Decision trees, described later, structure anticipated outcomes to lead to a decision that reduces overall risk.
- Simulation uses computer models to translate uncertainties from multiple factors into expected outcomes. The display shows the range and distribution of outcomes.

Figure 7.3 illustrates the use of a decision tree. The example assumes that, in conjunction with our move into the Chinese market, we have a choice of using the existing transportation network or developing our own new network. Logistics are problematic in China so we believe having our own network will lead to increased sales. However, a proprietary network increases costs of market entry to $10 million from $5 million for using the existing network.

On the left, we begin with the decision required, whether to develop or outsource our transportation requirements. At the next level are our two alternatives: to develop our own network or use the existing one. The Probability/Payoff level captures assumptions about demand and profit. It shows the units sold and profit, assumed to be $2 per unit sold. Different sales levels reflect uncertainties about the market plus the capabilities of the chosen transportation network to get our products to those markets. Developing our own network is expected to enable us to reach more customers but there is a risk that it won't.

So, in the case of strong demand, our forecast is that the dedicated network will push 15 million units into targeted markets. Using the existing network, with its limitations, would enable us to sell only 10 million units, despite strong demand from the market. "Net Path Value" captures the profit from each outcome. So, the new network, with strong demand, produces the best outcome—a profit of

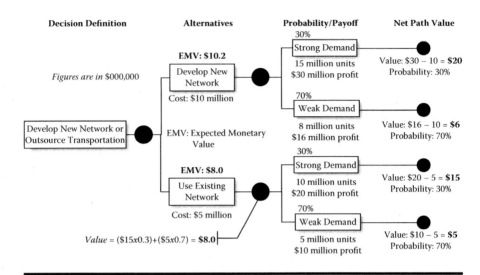

Figure 7.3   Use of a decision tree to analyze risk.

$20 million. This includes the profit ($30 million) less the initial cost needed to set up the network ($10 million).

Weak demand, with the existing network, means a profit of only $5 million. Applying the probabilities of each outcome, we value the new network at $10.2 million, use of the existing network at $8.0. Assuming we have access to the additional capital and trust our analysis, we should develop our own transportation network. The *PMBOK Guide* recommends as outputs of Perform Quantitative Analysis a prioritized list of quantified risks, forecast distributions of cost and schedule, probabilities of achieving objectives, and trends as quantitative analysis is repeated throughout the project.

7.3.8.4 Plan Risk Responses and Monitor and Control Risks

Plan Risk Responses devises options for dealing with identified risk events. This is a planning process, not a reaction to an actual outcome. Of course, the level of advanced planning should be in proportion to the risk involved. A feature of the *PMBOK Guide*'s recommended approach, one that has excellent potential in SCM projects, is selection of "risk owners." These are the responsible stakeholders to be involved in developing risk responses. Following are measures recommended by the *PMBOK Guide*:

■ Avoidance of the risk by changing the project plan: This could eliminate the risk by reducing the project scope, adding resources, extending the schedule, or using more tested methodologies and approaches.

- Transference involves shifting risk consequences to third parties: Such a move may not eliminate the risk but could reduce the consequences. An example is an insurance policy, where the issuer of the policy is paid for assuming the risk. Another transference device is the fixed-price contract for services needed to execute the project.
- Mitigation reduces the probability of suffering the consequences of the risk: This is a prevention measure where extra effort is justified before the event occurs rather than responding afterward. From our China case, this might involve more market research to determine whether demand will be strong or weak.
- Acceptance means that no preventive action will be taken. A "contingency plan" plots what will happen if the risk event occurs. For a high-impact event, a "fallback plan" may be prepared to reset direction of the project. A "contingency allowance" is an acceptance response if a project cost overrun is a risk.

The principal output is a Risk Response Plan specifying what risks remain after the plan is in place. Secondary risks may exist. These are new risks that arise because a risk response is in place. Other outputs include needed contractual arrangements and contingency reserves.

Monitor and Control Risks is a process for reviewing known risks and identifying new ones. Part of this process is developing earned value, a measure of progress in executing the project plan. Table 7.3 contains a vocabulary for earned value. Another output is the "work-around plan." These are responses to emerging risks that should be incorporated into the project plan.

7.3.9 Knowledge Area: Project Procurement Management

High SCM Knowledge Required

Project Procurement Management Processes	Process Group
Plan Procurements	Planning
Conduct Procurements	Executing
Administer Procurements	Monitoring and Controls
Close Procurements	Closing

Because supply chain efforts will be multicompany and partnerships with suppliers and customers will require new ways of thinking, the need for SCM knowledge is ranked "high." There are two contexts for "project procurement management" for supply chain projects. The first context, around which the *PMBOK Guide* processes are developed, is the procurement of goods and services for the project itself. Choice of a contractor to build your new house is an illustration. Your criteria are probably price, delivery, and reputation for quality. However, you are not likely to build a house more than once or twice in your lifetime, so your criteria are straightforward.

However, if you are a developer who plans to build many houses, you'll look at the contractor decision differently. Certainly, you will want to be an important customer. You will want financial stability in the organization you select. You will also seek favorable financial consideration in exchange for the volume of business you'll give your selected organization.

SCM procurement is often performed in an environment like the developer's. In a supply chain effort, a frequent project activity is selecting partners or being selected as a partner not only for setting up the supply chain but also for running it for the long run. If you are doing the procuring, those who are selected will be those you may work with after the supply chain is established and operating. In this case, the provider of project management services and the provider of materials for running your business are the same entity.

Procurement responsibilities in supply chain projects may reside with a single party or they may be shared. To the extent several companies will use the procured product or service, there is need for collaboration and joint decision making in supplier selection. Partnerships in many companies are "unnatural" acts. This is particularly true if the pathway to partnerships goes through the purchasing function. Transforming one's mind-set from a "buyer" to a "collaborator" can be difficult. This is especially true because few partnerships are developed among true equals. One partner is usually dominant. Slipping back into the arm's-length paradigm is easy.

Procurement in a supply chain context is a two-step process. The first step is often referred to as "strategic sourcing." If you provide major components to your customers, you want to be a partner to your customers. The second step is "procurement," day-to-day purchases of goods from the suppliers selected during the sourcing process. Because so many supply chain projects depend on collaboration with suppliers, procurement processes are key to a successful effort. Likewise, customers may seek out one's company as a partner. Not being selected because you are an unattractive partner jeopardizes your future.

Plan Procurements begins with deciding what to buy and when during the project. The process includes deciding whether to make or buy the purchased product or service. It also requires a decision on the type of contract needed. Options include fixed price, cost-reimbursable, and time and material contracts. The risk analysis may assist in contract-type decisions. The result is a procurement management plan. The procurement planning process also includes what won't be bought by the organization. Responsibility for procuring some items can be assigned to suppliers.

Another output is the Statement of Work (SOW). At the outset, these should be as complete as possible. The SOW can be revised as needed throughout the project. A Statement of Objectives (SOO) covers procurement items where specific products or services are difficult to define. Contract planning develops procurement documents and evaluation criteria. Conduct Procurements, which entails actual solicitation, gathers responses, often through bidders conferences and advertising. A formal solicitation process makes sense to solidify a partnership arrangement. This requires reviews of supplier responses and selection of the supplier, resulting in a contract for the goods and services.

Administer Procurements is ongoing and needed to see that contract terms related to the project are fulfilled and to administer changes to the contract. Close Procurements brings a formal close to each of these procurements. There may be many procurement actions over a project's life cycle. So, there will likely be multiple closeouts.

Notes

1. PMI Global Standard: *A Guide to the Project Management Body of Knowledge* (*PMBOK Guide*), 4th ed., Project Management Institute, 2008. American National Standard ANSI/PMI 99-001-2008.
2. Rick A. Morris, "Stop the Insanity of Failing Projects," Industrial Management (November/December 2008): 20–4.
3. International Institute of Business Analysis (IIBA), *A Guide to the Business Analysis Body of Knowledge (BABOK)*, Release 1.6, 2006.
4. Harold Kerzner, *Project Management: A Systems Approach to Planning, Scheduling, and Controlling*, 7th ed. (New York: John Wiley and Sons, 2001), 100, 243.

Chapter 8

Supply Chain Process Standards and Reference Models

This chapter summarizes two tools available to support supply chain projects: the Supply-Chain Operations Reference-model (SCOR-model or SCOR) from the Supply-Chain Council and the Council of Supply Chain Management Professionals' (CSCMP) six-volume Supply Chain Management Process Standards (Process Standards). *Each volume is about fifty pages. The chapter also explains the author's view regarding the role of models in supply chain projects. Despite the value they offer, over-reliance on models is a potential trap.*

Chapter 5 described maturity models related to project management. Level 1 of that model is a "common language" for project management; Level 2 is "common processes," which evolves to Level 3, "a singular process." Chapter 6 and Chapter 7 described approaches for honing a singular process using PMI's *Guide to the Project Management Body of Knowledge* (*PMBOK Guide*). Judiciously applied, the Supply-Chain's SCOR-model and the CSCMP's *Process Standards*, maintained by each organization's members, supplement other procedures in this book. CSCMP boasts of participation by over 50 subject management experts in developing its *Process Standards*. A larger number of participants, myself included, have labored over the years on behalf of SCOR.

You should note that there are other models available. These include the Supply Chain Management Institute's SCM Global Supply Chain Forum, APQC's (American Productivity and Quality Center) Process Classification Framework, and the Supply Chain Consortium's Best Practice Framework. These have been described and evaluated for strengths and weaknesses along with the SCOR-model.[1]

8.1 SCOR and the CSCMP's Process Standards

Table 8.1 summarizes and compares the two models. You will note that they have identical top-level process architectures. These include Level 1 processes called PLAN, SOURCE, MAKE, DELIVER, and RETURN.* This is a compliment to SCOR, which was the first model published. In its own words, CSCMP copied the structure to "aid in the use of the *Process Standards* as a companion to the SCOR-model."

The Supply-Chain Council has published a handy twenty-five-page SCOR Overview for interested parties.[2] The document is available at no cost from the Supply-Chain Council's Web site (www.supply-chain.org). Version 9.0 was released in 2008. The SCOR-model incorporates supply chain architectures, performance measures, and best practices for a wide range of supply chain activities. It omits the following:

- sales and marketing—demand generation,
- research and technology development,
- product development, and
- some elements of post-delivery support.

Some of these gaps are filled by "sister" models, the Design-Chain Operations Reference-model and the Customer-Chain Operations Reference-model. These aren't covered in this book. However, our definition of "supply chain" in Section 2.4 included these functions and all others that are essential to delivering products and services to customers and end users. Having to go outside SCOR for modeling "non-supply" processes calls attention to the limited scope of SCOR.

SCOR Execution processes recognize three supply chain business models: make-to-stock (MTS), make-to-order (MTO), and engineer-to-order (ETO). In the MTS company, forecasts drive production requirements and customer shipments are made from a finished goods inventory. An MTO company has an order in hand before it produces. Boeing's commercial aircraft business and Dell direct sales model for computers are examples. An ETO company must design components or software according to customer requirements. Each delivered product to a

---

* Model processes are shown in CAPS; for example, "PLAN."

Table 8.1   SCOR-Model and the CSCMP's Process Standards

Points of Comparison	*SCOR-model*	*CSCMP's Process Standards*
Availability	Access to SCOR is limited to members of the Supply-Chain Council. Annual fees vary by member category.	Standards may be purchased directly from the CSCMP (www.cscmp.org).
Types of processes	Planning Execution Enable	Not formally divided into groups.
Level 1	***Core Management Processes***: PLAN SOURCE MAKE DELIVER SOURCE RETURN DELIVER RETURN	***Main Processes***: PLAN SOURCE MAKE DELIVER RETURN
Level 2	***Configuration Level Process Categories (refer to Figure 8.1)***: 5 Plan Categories 3 Source Categories 3 Make Categories 4 Deliver Categories 3 Source Return Categories 3 Deliver Return Categories 10 Enable Categories ***Examples***: • P1 PLAN SUPPLY CHAIN • M2 MAKE-TO-ORDER • SR3 RETURN EXCESS PRODUCT	***Process Subcategories***: 3 Plan Attributes 4 Source Attributes 7 Make Attributes 9 Deliver Attributes 5 Return Attributes 11 Enable Attributes ***Examples***: 1.1 SUPPLY CHAIN PLANNING 3.3 PRODUCT or SERVICE CUSTOMIZATION 5.3 REPAIR and REFURBISHMENT

(continued on next page)

Table 8.1 (continued)   SCOR-Model and the CSCMP's Process Standards

Points of Comparison	SCOR-model	CSCMP's Process Standards
Level 3	***Process Element Level***: Level 2 subprocesses including the following for each process element: • Definition • Inputs and Outputs • Performance Metrics • Best Practice Definitions Process elements are labeled in order by Level 2 Process Category. For example P1.3 is BALANCE SUPPLY-CHAIN RESOURCES WITH SUPPLY-CHAIN REQUIREMENTS.	***Process Attributes***: Structured to facilitate self-assessment. Each attribute has two elements: Suggested Minimum Process Standard and Typical Best Practice Process. Standards users can rank their organizations on a 1–5 scale from Below Minimum (#1 above) to Best Practice (#2 above).
Levels 4, 5, 6 implementation level	Not included in SCOR. These are company-specific processes.	
Enable processes	Provides processes for each type of planning and executing process. Establish and Manage Rules Assess Performance Manage Data Manage Inventory Manage Capital Assets Manage Transportation Manage Supply Chain Configuration Manage Regulatory Compliance Manage Supply Chain Risk Process Specific Elements	Provides a single set of processes. Strategy and Leadership Competitive Benchmarking Product/Service Innovation Product/Service Data Management Process Visibility and Control Measurement Technology Business Management Quality Security Industry Standards

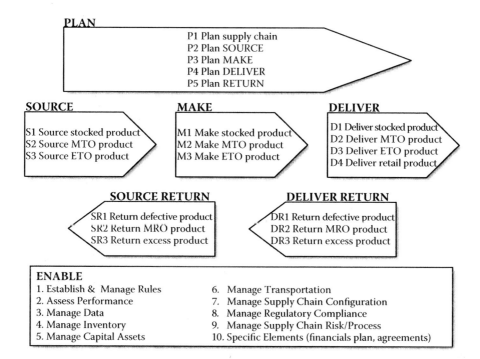

Figure 8.1 SCOR Version 9.0 Level 2. (Adapted from *SCOR Overview, Version 9.0*, published by the Supply-Chain Council.)

customer could be unique. A configure-to-order company, not specifically addressed in SCOR, is a hybrid of the MTO and the ETO models. The sandwich shop used to define flexibility criteria in Section 3.5.2 is a CTO example.

SCOR Level 2 is called the Configuration Level. This level is useful for creating "thread" flowcharts and geographic maps. A thread of three companies might use the following models (refer to the Level 2 execution steps in Figure 8.1): an S1, M1, D1 manufacturer (Company 1) has a ready inventory, with levels established by forecasting production requirements to meet demand for an S2, M2, D2 manufacturer (Company 2) that replenishes according to actual demand communicated by pull signals from customers, and supplies an S1, D3 distributor (Company 3) that assembles one-of-a-kind engineered products for its customers from stock replenished according to forecasts. Figure 8.2 depicts this thread in two formats recommended in the SCOR-model. Company 1 is a traditional build-to-stock (BTS) manufacturer. It serves its customers by forecasting and producing to these forecasts for finished goods inventory. One of its customers, Company 2, is a specialized firm that only replenishes stock and builds to order (S2, M2, D2). Company 2 also orders stock only when it has such an order (S2). Herman Miller shifted from the Company 1 to the Company 2 model in the

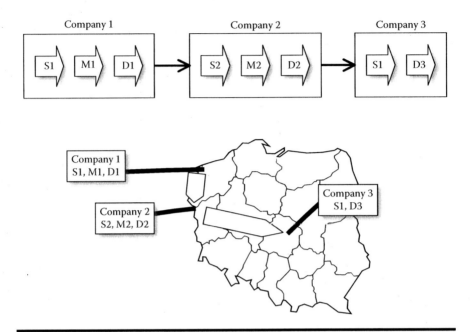

Figure 8.2   Thread examples.

case described in Section 4.2.3. The final link in the supply chain is Company 3, an engineering company that does light assembly, including the addition of customized software to the product. It must do some customization (D3) to deliver its products that are one-of-a-kind in their final configuration. Company 3 does maintain a components inventory (S1) to meet its customer service goals. Because its "manufacturing" is limited to assembly, its modeling team doesn't use the MAKE component.

The presence of multicompany threads in the supply chain evokes the need for collaboration to set them up. Section 4.4.1 described "spheres" as a tool for dissecting the supply chain. For terminology clarification, "spheres" and "threads," are not synonymous. Spheres are broader definitions covering customer–product–operation combinations. Companies needing multiple threads to serve different markets might create separate spheres for each market.

SCOR also proposes performance attributes and "strategic metrics." Table 8.2 lists ten Level 1 metrics in five attribute categories: reliability, responsiveness, agility, cost effectiveness, and asset utilization. Changes since Version 5.0 have increased emphasis on "flexibility" and "adaptability." This emphasis is consistent with the raised awareness of the "flexibility imperative" described in Section 3.5. The Level 1 metrics are supported by dozens of additional metrics at Levels 2 and 3.

SCOR and the CSCMP's *Process Standards* are intended to apply across industries, flexible enough to be used in any company that is part of a supply chain. An obstacle to the success of multicompany efforts can be the lack of a common

Table 8.2 SCOR Level 1 Strategic Metrics

Attribute	Customer-Facing			Internal-Facing	
	Reliability	Responsiveness	Agility	Cost	Assets
Perfect Order Fulfillment	●				
Order Fulfillment Cycle Time		●			
Upside Supply Chain Flexibility			●		
Upside Supply Chain Adaptability			●		
Downside Supply Chain Adaptability			●		
Supply Chain Management Cost				●	
Cost of Goods Sold				●	
Cash-to-Cash Cycle Time					●
Return on Supply Chain Fixed Assets					●
Return on Working Capital					●

vocabulary to facilitate communications among companies linked in the chain. Supply chain design is intrinsically a complex process. So, it is no accident that navigation through the models is not particularly easy for the neophyte. However, those that stick with it report good success.

8.2 Model Contributions to Project Management

Figure 8.3 suggests how SCOR and the CSCMP's *Process Standards* components fit in terms of producing the supply chain project deliverables introduced in the Work Breakdown Structure (WBS) in Figure 6.4. The boxes under each phase suggest focus points in the two frameworks for each project phase. For Phase 1, Supply Chain Strategy, the CSCMP's *Process Standards* explicitly address high-level strategy development

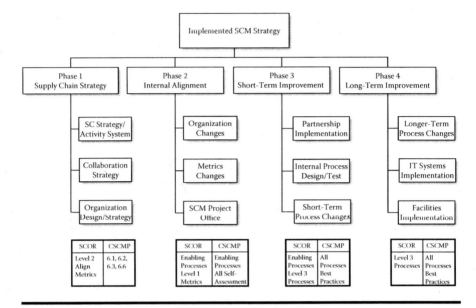

Figure 8.3   WBS view with model support roles.

through its Enable processes (6.1, 6.2, 6.3). In Phase 2, Internal Alignment, practitioners can turn to the models for Enable processes and metrics. Internal Alignment could also employ benchmarking and aligning supply chain metrics with the strategy. Phases 3 and 4 will turn to the models for best practices in processes selected for improvement. SCOR-model Enable processes could also support Phase 3.

8.3 Putting the Models to Work

This section offers advice on deploying the models based on personal experience. It also seeks to aid you in adapting the models to other methodologies proposed in this book.

8.3.1 Standard Processes Aren't the Path to Competitive Advantage

Section 4.2.3 described two approaches using the supply chain as a way to advance company strategy. The first way was the industry best practice approach. A case study there described how SCOR and the CSCMP's *Process Standards* support this approach. An alternative recommended in this book is the use of Michael Porter's activity system approach. This should be coupled with defining spheres that deserve supply chain designs of their own, which could lead an organization to developing multiple supply chains. The activity system approach is an effective tool for defining what processes are needed to support a strategy. Unique activity systems that are hard to duplicate are the best way to fend off competition. The SCOR-model and the *Process Standards* strive to define the processes that match supply and demand in a supply chain. They also list best practices and rely on benchmarking in their methodologies. By definition, these don't assure uniqueness. That doesn't mean they don't have a role in logistics process design to optimize processes inside the activity system. As such, they may find more use for tuning an existing supply chain rather than in creating a new one.

8.3.2 Enabling Processes Pave the Way

ENABLE processes may be the most important of the processes. ENABLE processes are ongoing, providing a platform for supply chain projects. They address resources that can be shared among multiple supply chain spheres, as defined in Section 4.4.1. Example enabling processes address facilities, the transportation network, distribution centers, contracted service providers, metrics, information systems, and preferred suppliers. Figure 8.3 records their prominence in the early stages of a supply chain project. Many supply chain failures can be traced to the absence of one or more of these processes. ENABLE processes are the backbone of any supply chain. Without an adequate backbone, supply chain performance can go only so far. Such processes turn a path in the woods into a superhighway.

ENABLE processes are good candidates for oversight by the SCM Project Office, shown as a Phase 2 deliverable in Figure 8.3. The alternative is to assign enabling work to functional departments, like distribution, transportation, or facilities. However, functional groups may lack visibility over all supply chain requirements.

One approach calls for planners to create an "Enable Sphere." This sphere would include activities supporting "product-producing" spheres. In short, if multiple spheres rely on common business rules, systems, and other supply chain components, they could be included in the Enable Sphere.

When starting a project, a team could undertake a self-assessment like the one shown in Figure 8.4. The example used ENABLE processes from an earlier SCOR version. Each team member evaluated the degree to which enable processes supported each of the five Level 1 product-producing plan and execution processes: PLAN, SOURCE, MAKE, DELIVER, and RETURN. Scoring was on a 1–4 scale with "4" being best. Scores at 2.0 or lower are highlighted in bold. The exercise raised much discussion regarding the organization's process support backbone. Scores along the bottom gave an overall evaluation of the need for bolstering a particular enabling process.

8.3.3 Broaden Your Horizons

The article in *Supply Chain Quarterly* cited at the opening of this chapter[3] came with a warning. The authors found current models lacking in the following areas:

	1	2	3	4	5	6	7	8	9	
	Maintain business rules	Assess performance	Manage data	Manage inventory	Manage capital assets	Manage transportation	Manage supply chain configuration	Manage regulatory compliance	Align supply chain & financials	
Performed?										
Yes	5	5	6	6	4	6	5	5	4	
No		1			1				1	
Unsure	1				1		1	1	1	
PLAN	2.0	1.4	1.6	2.6	2.5	3.3	1.4	3.0	1.8	2.2
SOURCE	2.2	2.4	1.5	1.8	2.5	3.5	2.4	2.8	1.5	2.3
MAKE	2.0	2.3	2.6	2.0	2.0	3.0	1.7	2.3	2.0	2.2
DELIVER	2.6	3.0	2.3	2.3	3.5	2.8	2.4	3.2	2.8	2.8
RETURN	2.6	2.4	2.0	1.8	2.0	3.3	1.0	2.3	1.5	2.1
	2.3	2.3	2.0	2.1	2.5	3.2	1.8	2.7	1.9	

Figure 8.4   Self-assessment of ENABLE processes.

- They don't support a common definition of SCM.
- They lack common definitions for key supply chain processes.
- They lack formats that are easy to understand, implement, and practice as modeling and improvement tools.
- They don't facilitate a cross-functional, multicompany view of the organization and their partners.

We've already cautioned against taking a narrow approach—limiting the organization's definition of SCM to logistics activities while ignoring the importance of extended product features. The models have allure to some because they appear to be broad, covering many processes in considerable detail. But, competitive improvement may require an even broader scope. This is particularly true in cases where the organization is looking to the supply chain for competitive improvement, not just cost reduction opportunities.

8.4 Shortcut to Better Project Management

Despite their limitations, the SCOR-model and the CSCMP's *Process Standards* are important contributions to supply chain practice, as shown in Figure 1.1. These tools will help an organization "jump start" its supply chain improvement projects. There is no reason to duplicate what others have already done. To illustrate, Table 8.3 contains examples of how the tools supplement each of the *PMBOK Guide* knowledge areas described in Chapter 7. The table shows the need for supplemental SCM knowledge—high, medium, or low—in each area.

Table 8.3   Using SCOR in Supply Chain Improvement Projects

PMBOK Guide Knowledge Area	Need for SCM Expertise	SCOR and CSCMP Standards Contribution
Integration Management	High	The models cover many of the activities involved in a supply chain, making it an important integration tool.
Scope Management	High	The models contain several types of activities: planning, executing, and enabling. This provides a checklist of items that might be included in any supply chain improvement project.
Time Management	Low	The metrics of SCOR and the CSCMP Best Practices relative to industry standards can aid priority setting.
Cost Management	Medium	SCOR and the CSCMP's *Process Standards* can justify or not justify expenditure for supply chain improvements. Enabling processes in both models describe how to achieve alignment of supply chain and company financial goals.
Quality Management	Medium	SCOR contains many metrics at Level 3 process elements for measuring supply chain service and cost performance.
Human Resources	High	By defining activities an organization should undertake, that organization can better identify the skills it needs. Threads will help identify the capabilities needed in partner organizations.
Communications Management	Medium	Both models provide a vocabulary for better communications between supply chain partners. New collaboration approaches also provide a framework for ongoing communication processes.
Risk Management	High	Enable processes should lower the risk in planning and execution on a variety of fronts. The models' content should reduce the risk that a technology or approach to operating a supply chain is not overlooked in the design process.

(continued on next page)

Table 8.3 (continued)   Using SCOR in Supply Chain Improvement Projects

PMBOK Guide Knowledge Area	Need for SCM Expertise	SCOR and CSCMP Standards Contribution
Procurement Management	High	The models will aid partner selection by defining what is needed in a partner and how to structure a framework for partnership agreements.

Notes

1. Christopher Moberg, Kate Vitasek, Theodore L. Stank, and Abré Pienaar, "Time to Remodel," *CSCMP Supply Chain Quarterly* (Quarter 3/2008): 36–48.
2. Supply-Chain Council, *Supply-Chain Operations Reference-model, SCOR Overview*, Version 9.0, 2008.
3. Christopher Moberg et al., "Time to Remodel."

Chapter 9

IT Projects—
Lessons for SCM

Information technology (IT) is an important enabler of supply chain change. IT project successes and failures are more widely assessed and documented than other types of supply chain projects. As a response, the IT industry has formulated valuable standards designed to avoid or mitigate project management failures.

9.1 Why Look at IT Projects?

There is little doubt that IT is an important enabler of supply chain improvement. The experience of others with IT projects provides broader lessons for supply chain project management. And, there is certainly a great deal written on the subject. In addition, the IT industry has been proactive by creating standards that list best practices and the knowledge required to execute projects more successfully. Section 9.7 summarizes three of these standards: the Information Technology Infrastructure Library (ITIL), Skills for the Information Age (SFIA), and the *Business Analysis Body of Knowledge (BABOK)*.

Prior chapters contain a foundation of knowledge and practice applicable to supply chain management (SCM) projects. Knowledge is what is known about the field. Practice refers to actions that build on that knowledge. Chapters 2 through 4 addressed knowledge areas and practices for SCM. Chapters 5 through 8 covered both SCM and project management knowledge and practice. These include the Project Management Maturity Model (PMMM), the Supply-Chain Council's

Supply-Chain Operations Reference-model (SCOR-model), *Supply Chain Management Process Standards (Process Standards)* from the Council of Supply Chain Management Professionals (CSCMP) and project management knowledge areas embodied in *A Guide to the Project Management Body of Knowledge (PMBOK Guide)* from the Project Management Institute (PMI).

Sources in this chapter report shortfalls in IT projects that implemented supply chain technology. Documenting these is a worthy exercise for two reasons. First, the reported experiences identify the types of project failures, allowing us to tailor our project templates in Section 3. Second, the findings provide solid guidance to those setting up their own projects. This should decrease the chances that project planners will overlook an area of vulnerability.

Each of the following five sections describes a project failure root cause. Following the five sections addressing these root causes is a section dedicated to the industry tools to mitigate these root causes. A summary at the end of the chapter describes the conclusions we reach from reviewing these root causes and the industry's response. Our five root causes are the following:

- rigidity, insufficient flexibility;
- organization roadblocks;
- top management abrogation;
- inadequate technical capability; and
- misunderstood technology.

9.2 Rigidity, Insufficient Flexibility

Chapter 3 described the need for flexibility in our supply chain designs. Flexibility enables the supply chain to better match supply and demand in the face of fluctuations in either. Flexibility is also needed in our project management approach to avoid project failures.[1] Robert Austin and Richard Nolan of the Harvard Business School conducted the study of enterprise resource planning (ERP) projects that led to this conclusion. Their survey, reported in the *Harvard Business Review*, reports that 65 percent of executives surveyed reported that "ERP systems have at least a moderate chance of hurting their businesses" because of implementation problems.

9.2.1 Root Cause

The researchers observe that most ERP systems as they are ultimately implemented are different from what was envisioned in their original requirements. Austin and Nolan reach a counterintuitive conclusion. They recommend that ERP implementation not be viewed as a "project" structured by traditional project management paradigms. Instead of the project model, they recommend a new business venture model. The venture model is preferable because a growing organization must continually adjust its plan as the business changes due to unforeseen demands by financers, customers, or trading partners. Austin and Nolan observe that the same kinds of changes are likely during an extended ERP implementation.

Following are Austin and Nolan's specific recommendations:

- Divide the effort into stages and invest accordingly. Change plans frequently; don't be "locked in" on requirements and priorities throughout the project. In other words, it's the planning that's important, not the plan.
- Appoint an "unsnowable" executive leader to screen proposals made by vendors and team members. (This person obviously has to know his stuff, and people like this may be in short supply.)
- Assign strong, solidly qualified team members. Austin and Nolan note that most investors in new enterprises base their investment choices on the executives running the company, not on the plan. (The SFIA framework described in Section 9.7 supports this need.)
- Use incremental funding to trigger periodic reviews and adjustments to the plan.
- Share risks for success, including outside vendors who have to make complex decisions during the project.
- Big projects are risky; pay for information that lowers risk, even though it doesn't produce a deliverable. This might take the form of market research, as described in Section 7.3.8.

The *PMBOK Guide* describes the "progressive elaboration" property of projects. As new information becomes available, project plans are "elaborated" to take this information into account. This root cause calls on project managers to build appropriate mechanisms for managing changes to the project.

9.2.2 Links with Knowledge and Practice Areas

The lessons cited by Austin and Nolan apply as well to the technology and non-technology components of large-scale SCM programs. In particular, correction will be facilitated by attention to the following knowledge and practice areas:

Project management knowledge	Project Integration Management and Project Scope Management knowledge areas will be challenged by the need to change frequently. This is counter to the idea that project plans should be unchanging through the product life cycle. Sophistication is required to incorporate this flexibility. Dr. Andrew McAfee points to the need for "organizational complements" to be present to achieve success (see Section 9.7). A company also might consider the supply chain improvement as a major project with a series of short subprojects.

(continued on next page)

	Procurement Management may require risk-sharing contracts with suppliers for both IT and supply chain services. Risk Management encourages the use of project phasing to reduce risk as well as information-gathering where justified.
Project management practice	At Level 3, Singular Methodology, of Kerzner's PMMM, the company has a structured approach for project management. But, that approach is broad enough to accommodate a number of project types. A feature of Level 3 is "informal project management," a flexible approach, requiring trust in the project team to apply the singular approach.
SCM knowledge	Execution of Task 1 Designing Supply Chains for Strategic Advantage will design the new supply chain. Little advanced planning likely means more changes during the project; more planning should result in fewer changes.
	Work associated with Task 3 Forging Supply Chain Partnerships will spin off supplier and customer agreements. These agreements could produce a systems design to support interconnections with suppliers and customers.
SCM practice	Task 2 Implementing Collaborative Relationships requires assignment of high-level staff to projects. "High-level" refers to both talent and status in the organization. This includes both team members and project leadership. The task must also address which functional departments, suppliers, and customers that should be on the team. The SFIA framework (Section 9.7) provides "job descriptions" for a variety of related roles.

9.3 Organization Roadblocks

One of our SCM tasks, described in Section 4.3, is to align internal departments to implement changes in supply chain design. John Bermudez of AMR Research reinforces this need.[2] His firm, like the Harvard researchers cited in the previous section, also researched success rates for companies implementing supply chain software. The success rate was less than 15 percent in terms of implementing "more than a few of the applications they had purchased." Bermudez doesn't fault the software companies but blames organization complexity and lack of understanding of how supply chains actually work.

9.3.1 Root Cause

Supply chain processes cross many functional silos in the organization. Bermudez cites the problem of department-sponsored software projects. Each silo often has its own procedures and makeshift systems using tools like Excel spreadsheets on local hard drives as data repositories and e-mail for communication. Goals also vary across silos and often conflict. For example, the customer service department's objectives for high levels of customer service may conflict with the distribution department's objective for low inventory. If the distribution center is the function charged with implementing supply chain software, it has three basic choices:

- Tailor the application to the existing needs of both organizations, an added expense that could "hardwire" existing organization conflicts.
- Implement the application within its own function, which limits its potential.
- Fight for changing processes, including the conflicting performance measures, in both departments.

Which option would you take if you were running the distribution center? Neither of the first two approaches will produce the sought-after "bang for the buck" from the software. The best option from the company viewpoint is the third option, moving to a cross-functional supply chain process before implementing new technology. This requires the organizational complements described in Section 9.7, namely, enterprise-level processes. Too often, however, this isn't politically feasible or is not a company priority.

9.3.2 Links with Knowledge and Practice Areas

The problems raised are often the result of sponsorship of projects at the departmental level. This idea was first introduced in the discussion of Figure 4.4, which shows three levels of supply chain project—department, business unit, and supply chain. Companies faced with organization roadblocks must raise the level of project planning at least to the business unit level. Without sufficient cross-department collaboration, this is a necessary step to resolve conflicts like those between the distribution and customer service functions cited earlier.

Project management knowledge	Project Scope Management is challenged by organization boundaries. Boundaries are an obstacle to changing cross-department processes. Lack of awareness of the consequences is often the barrier that must be addressed in project management planning.
Project management practice	A situation like that described would be typical of a Level 1 company (Figure 5.2) on the PMMM. It demonstrates that project management thinking hasn't permeated the organization. The company isn't capable of effectively implementing a multidepartment change.

(continued on next page)

SCM knowledge	Task 1 Designing Supply Chains for Strategic Advantage calls for identifying "spheres" before designing supply chains. This tool helps align the organization before designing systems and procedures.
	Task 2 Implementing Collaborative Relationships calls for elevating performance measures to the company or supply chain levels and away from parochial departments.
SCM practice	The SCOR-model and the CSCMP's *Process Standards* recommend ENABLE processes that address methods to align supply chain design with company strategy. The SCOR-model also uses "threads" to define supply chain configurations for different products or markets. The tool communicates the shape of different types of supply chain. Figure 8.2 illustrates.
	Classifying projects, as shown in Figure 4.4, will identify the types of projects an organization is pursuing. Too few supply chain projects (Level 3) signals that the efforts may not be broad enough.

9.4 Top Management Abrogation

Management support from the top is a requisite for success in implementing any change endeavor. This is no less important for supply chain and IT efforts, which are often wrapped together. Too often, management classifies the overall effort as a "systems" initiative and then relegates critical decisions to IT professionals that they should retain.

9.4.1 Root Causes

Jeanne Ross and Pete Weill, affiliated with MIT's Center for Information Systems Research, have identified six decisions that fall into the category of decisions not to be delegated.[3] Their research shows that companies that retain these decisions achieve returns 40 percent higher than in companies that do not. The six, divided into strategy and execution categories, include the following:

Strategy
1. How much to spend overall on IT.
2. What business processes should receive IT funds.
3. What company-wide IT capabilities are required to be competitive.

Execution

4. Required information systems service levels.
5. Acceptable security and privacy risks.
6. Who should be held responsible for IT failures?

Their message was reinforced by a report from Forrester Research.[4] The report covered 291 companies and compared financial performance with IT spending expressed as a percentage of revenue. Financial performance measures were growth in cash flow and sales as well as return on assets. To account for industry differences, Forrester compared the companies to others within their industry group.

The result showed that throwing money at technology is not the road to financial success. Top-quartile companies spent 3.3 percent of revenue on IT; second- and third-quartile companies spent 4.5 percent and 4.2 percent, respectively, and fourth-quartile companies spent 2.6 percent. Ross and Weill concluded that getting a return on investment requires strategic alignment, process alignment, and change management. Sometimes, less spending produces more results. All these issues are the purview of top management. The study leads to another question any company might ask of itself: If our management abrogates decisions in important areas related to IT, what other important decisions are relegated to functional managers?

9.4.2 Links with Knowledge and Practice Areas

So much here depends on the willingness and ability of senior managers to be involved in "nuts and bolts" issues. Project management and SCM disciplines assure that the right organization level addresses the right issues. Project templates in Chapters 12 through 15 recommend senior management roles for each project process.

Project management knowledge	Scope Management is challenged by the need to draw lines where projects start and end. A determining issue could be the organization's risk exposure as changes are implemented. This calls for use of Risk Management knowledge to identify and analyze these risks.
Project management practice	The behavior noted here, abrogation of decisions, is typical of a Level 1 PMMM organization. A motivation for company's moving to Level 2 of the PMMM is the survival stake the company has in its major supply chain projects. Components at Level 2 include financial accountability in projects and disciplined project management policies and procedures. Of particular importance are project charters and plans.

(continued on next page)

SCM knowledge	A company needs a tool like spheres to design customer-focused processes. Each sphere will have different process requirements, avoiding a "one size fits all" supply chain and the risk of lost market share. Limited funding should address spheres that provide the best market opportunities.
SCM practice	SCOR-model Level 3 processes are useful for process characterization to support planning for projects. Companies should review their enabling processes to determine whether they have sufficient infrastructure to support new processes. Better metrics, along the lines of those in the SCOR-model (Table 8.2), aid measurement of process performance.

9.5 Inadequate Technical Capability

A company should not pursue technology for its own operations without necessary technical talents. Supply chain systems raise the bar even further. Not only must one's own company possess needed capabilities but also its trading partners may have to match it. So, risks rising from weak technical capabilities apply to both our own and our partners' competence in SCM, project management, and technology domains.

9.5.1 Our Own Capability

Key to this is an effective IT function—whether it is comprised of internal staff or acquired through a contracted external capability. Two resources identify questions to ask and issues to address regarding the readiness of the IT function. One expert[5] recommends asking the following questions about the company's development function before launching a new project:

- Is the development organization aligned to company business needs?
- Are users satisfied with current products of the developers?
- Are managers and users satisfied with the development organization's schedule and cost performance?
- Are development processes adequate to the task?
- Are development people's skills, training, and morale adequate to the task?

If the answer to any of these is no, the company should correct the shortcoming before beginning to mitigate project risk. The ITIL framework described in Section 9.7.1 provides a model for IT services in the organization. The SFIA framework (Section 9.7.2) details qualifications needed for specific roles.

However, many companies have no choice about when they must move ahead with change. David Ritter of the Boston Consulting Group encourages IT managers to "be prepared" for the call to implement new systems. His twelve-step process, summarized here, specifically addresses processes and systems for material acquisition that are an important supply chain element:

1. Understand your existing process. Don't automate it if it's a mess. Re-engineer it first.
2. Coordinate with suppliers. Make sure your solution will fit.
3. Examine your internal network. If you need to change, consider moving from electronic data interchange (EDI) to the Internet. Also consider a virtual private network for sharing with your suppliers. General Electric set an example by enlisting online software to manage 500,000 suppliers.[7] This is an example of "cloud" computing where an outside vendor provides the software and hardware. The vendor's customers train and populate the application with data.
4. Understand technical challenges for extracting data from legacy systems. ERP system data to support forecasting is a good example of a supply chain application.
5. Adopt existing standards where possible. Examples include XML and data exchange initiatives in your industry.
6. Survey application vendors. Understand what different applications can or cannot do.
7. Determine what product information you must pass on to suppliers; identify the form it's in and its accessibility. Is it accurate? Are formats appropriate? Is it accessible to suppliers?
8. Survey electronic markets. Understand what role they should play, if any.
9. Automate processes with workflow to standardize the way work is performed and tracked.
10. Consider needs for different kinds of tendering, particularly short-term spot buying versus long-term contracts. What is being done now? What should the future look like?
11. Re-evaluate current legacy systems. Should they be extended? What has to be done to get ready for the new technology?
12. Have your purchasing managers select suppliers who have appropriate SCM capabilities.

These steps provide a blueprint for project planning before committing to a course of action. Another consideration is the ability of partners along the chain to respond technically to your initiatives. In particular, actions resulting from Step 1 in the twelve-step list will call for a joint supply chain and IT effort.

9.5.2 Partner Capabilities

"A chain is no stronger than its weakest link" is a saying that applies to real chains—the kind attached to anchors. To a degree, the statement is also true of supply chains. Certainly, an important element in SCM is reducing risk in the supply chain. Figure 9.1 illustrates the nature of the risks. With respect to IT, there are two types of partner limitations faced by a company leading an initiative. The first limitation is differences between partners in technical capability. This disparity is a common complaint, particularly when the initiating company is more sophisticated than its trading partner. Figure 9.1 shows this separation with the difference between capabilities increasing further up the vertical axis. A wide gulf in capabilities is likely to increase project risk. General Electric, cited earlier, addressed this situation with a Web-based solution.

The second limitation is differences due mostly to geography and takes the form of "infrastructure" disparities, shown along the horizontal axis in Figure 9.1. Infrastructure is the network capability along with logistics capabilities in the regions where the companies are located. In this context, a company in a country with a strong infrastructure must deal with partners in "have not" areas with weak infrastructures. Infrastructure in this sense can include communications and transportation.

Steven Morris and Denise Johnson McManus describe this situation as a barrier to constructing the virtual enterprise—one that's a network of companies brought together quickly in response to a business opportunity.[8] In particular, they

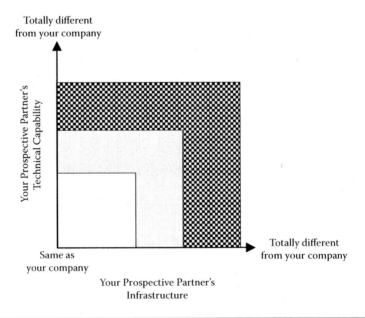

Figure 9.1 Capability and infrastructure disparities.

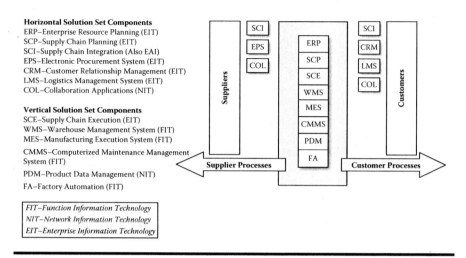

Figure 9.2   Supply chain applications. (Adapted from Beaver, Alex N. Jr., *Roadmap to the e-Factory*, Boca Raton, FL: Auerbach Publications, 2001.)

warn that development of internal technology reliant on a first-world infrastructure limits options for expansion to places where that infrastructure doesn't exist. Figure 9.2 shows the broad spectrum of supply chain applications that might reside within a single organization or along a supply chain. These are the "vertical solutions set components." One way that partners can gain links is with SCI (supply chain integration) applications, shown at the intersection of the companies. These are in the category of horizontal solutions that enable disparate systems and processes to interact with each other. In each case, a company may want to temper its choice of supply chain technologies. This would provide added flexibility to take on less IT-enabled but otherwise capable partners.

9.5.3 Links with Knowledge and Practice Areas

Most of the previously mentioned root causes of project failure have focused on "management," not "technical" issues. This root cause encompasses risk due to technical limitations. The risks involved are compounded by the need to work with trading partners and in parts of the world with undeveloped or unfamiliar enabling infrastructure.

Project management knowledge	Addressing the cited issues lies in the Risk Management knowledge area. Risk may be mitigated through application of Procurement Management knowledge. Mind-sets for implementing IT (Table 4.6) are also important considerations in formulating projects. The proper mind-sets put practical process improvement ahead of technology "elegance."

(continued on next page)

Project management practice	A Level 2 company in the PMMM may be reluctant to move from its disciplined processes at that level to informal processes at Level 3. And maybe it shouldn't. It is likely that a company must reach Level 2 before seriously considering complex supply chain projects.
SCM knowledge	Task 3 Forging Supply Chain Partnerships uses frameworks for characterizing partnerships. Task 4 Managing Supply Chain Information addresses needs for internal competence in supply chain technology tools. The idea that the enterprise has multiple supply chains whose boundaries are defined in spheres will lead system developers away from "one size fits all" solutions. Poorly performing existing processes should be reinvented before undertaking automation.
SCM practice	Process mapping tools, which Chapter 15 describes, for both cost and cycle time will prove useful, particularly if they track information and material movement in the entire supply chain. They can also be used to search out weak links for strengthening with appropriate technology tools.

9.6 Misunderstood Technology

Figure 9.2 provides a picture of the potential for confusion about technology choices. The application types referred to would confuse even the most sophisticated. What does each application do? When should it be used? How much effort is involved in implementing the application? Is a particular package a good fit for my industry? These and other questions are natural. A trap is trying to correct basic process flaws with complex software. The same confusion applies to highly visible non-IT efforts like Six Sigma, lean, and theory of constraints. The consequences of the confusion can be seen in the implementation of one popular IT application: customer relationship management (CRM). CRM is certainly a supply chain application, shown in Figure 9.2 at the interface between the company and its customers.

9.6.1 Root Causes

In the late 1990s, many companies rushed to implement CRM applications. Three consultants from Bain and Company described their research into outcomes from these efforts.[9] Their decision to pursue this line of research came from low CRM ratings in Bain's survey of management tools: third from the bottom of twenty-five tools evaluated. As an example, they note one manufacturer who scrapped a

$30 million investment in the technology. The researchers attribute the failure of CRM installations to one central factor: the assumption on the part of management that the software would manage the customer relationship.

The reality is that CRM is a "bundling of customer strategy and processes," supported by software. The authors recommend avoiding the following four perils in implementing CRM, pitfalls applicable to many supply chain projects and technologies:

- No customer strategy: According to the Bain consultants, strategy starts with identifying attractive customer segments and determining what it takes to acquire and retain customers in those segments. Less attractive segments will have alternative strategies depending on the prospects for making them profitable to serve. At this point, it is possible that a company will conclude that it doesn't need CRM software to woo attractive segments. They could better pursue other measures like reducing cost, building a focused supply chain, or tailoring the product line.
- Implementing CRM without the environment needed to make it work: Noting that this may be the most dangerous pitfall, the authors draw on a survey by the CRM Forum that attributed 87 percent of CRM failures to inadequate change management. Such change management requires new organization structures, policies, training, metrics, and processes—oriented to the attractive segments. This problem is discussed in Section 9.7 in the description of the need for organizational complements.
- Assuming more technology is better: CRM, in its management context, doesn't require technology to be implemented. Proper responses can range from low tech to high tech, depending on the needs and wants of the targeted segment. One can also ramp technology use as the change process proceeds, starting with low-tech, easy-to-implement CRM measures for short-term gains and proceeding to hard-to-implement, higher-technology solutions.
- Stalking customers: "Just because managers can contact a customer doesn't mean they should." This quote from the authors demonstrates the fine line between zealous customer care and stalking. Any investment in CRM techniques should reflect what that customer would like to see, and that may not be—and most likely will not be—pestering from salespeople. CRM technology has sometimes been pursued for the wrong reasons. In the supply chain technology space, there are many other examples where the promise fell short of the reality. A key is a requirement for the purchaser to know their business need well enough to evaluate a solution. The *PMBOK Guide* scope management planning process (Collect Requirements) makes a similar recommendation. The *BABOK*, described in Section 9.7.3, addresses the role of requirements. If the solution still looks attractive, the next step is to prepare the organization for the technology. This is the strategy of the e-Commerce Web site managers described in Section 4.5.

9.6.2 Links with Knowledge and Practice Areas

Many organizations place huge bets on technology and other supply chain projects with little understanding of the payoff and the risks. The software supply is abundant, and vendors constantly produce new products. The manager is on his or her own in evaluating candidate solutions in the form of software and other management techniques.

Project management knowledge	Overcoming this root cause requires competencies in structuring programs and then phasing the projects that make up those programs. This will challenge processes in the Scope Management knowledge area.
Project management practice	Level 2 and 3 organizations in the Kerzner PMMM will be leery of "quick fix" technology solutions. They will understand the large stakes involved in expensive software efforts.
SCM knowledge	General business knowledge and its implications for SCM are essential building blocks. Chapter 4 mentioned the product life cycle, functional/innovative products, and differing customer requirements. Awareness of all of these is needed to understand how a technology will support a business.
	Task 4 Managing Supply Chain Information includes the need to stay current with technology advances and retain the practical know-how to apply technology to business requirements. Task 5 Removing Cost from the Supply Chain may bring non-technical process change that is better than an ambitious systems effort like CRM. At a minimum, existing processes should be redesigned to satisfy the strategy as completely as possible before automating.
SCM practice	A principal theme of Chapter 4 was that supply chain and customer strategies should be aligned. Tools like activity systems designed for targeted spheres make this possible. Developing such activity systems will help produce finely tuned, rifle-shot requirements for supply chain processes.

9.7 Information Technology Industry Best Practice Tools

The lessons learned described earlier call for skills and processes to capture advantages from technology. Andrew McAfee has framed the challenge.[10] McAfee, an associate professor at the Harvard Business School, describes IT as a general-purpose technology (GPT). Historically, GPTs accelerate the normal progress in the way an industry operates. Past GPT examples include electricity, the transistor, and the laser. McAfee notes that, after the technology is introduced, innovators develop "organizational complements" to take advantage of the GPT. An example is deploying fiber-optic cable so lasers, a prior GPT, could be employed to transmit data.

Dr. McAfee points toward four organizational complements to arise with the availability of a new GPT:

- better skilled workers,
- higher levels of teamwork,
- redesigned processes, and
- new decision rights.

An example is the impact of electric motors, another GPT, on factories. Early factories located by rivers and streams were supported by water wheels that powered drive shafts. The drive shafts served machines throughout the entire factory. At first, a single electric motor simply displaced the drive shafts. Later, smaller, cheaper motors were attached to each machine; this drove the need for the four organizational complements. Better-skilled workers were empowered to operate and maintain the machines, making decisions needed to keep the process flowing smoothly. New factories were built on a single floor and were far more flexible since machines were no longer linked to one drive shaft.

McAfee notes that the importance of complements varies with the category of the IT implementation: Function IT (FIT), Network IT (NIT), or Enterprise IT (EIT). Figure 9.2 associates each of the applications with one of these categories. Function IT supports the execution of a discrete task. It would be at the Function level (Level 1) in Table 4.4. Examples include personal spreadsheets and computer-aided design (CAD) supporting the engineering department. Presence of complements isn't necessary but is helpful in exploiting Function IT.

The Network IT category includes e-mail, messaging, and blogs. Such technologies speed the distribution of information. Complements emerge over time but aren't imposed at the beginning. No tasks or workflows are specified, and data may come in many formats. Enterprise IT, unlike Function and Network IT, does specify business processes. This level imposes complements throughout the organization by defining tasks and sequences. Data formats and the use of the technology are mandatory. Examples are ERP, CRM, and supply chain management applications like EDI. The author notes that FIT delivers productivity and optimization, NIT assists collaboration, and EIT standardizes and monitors work.

McAfee recommends that selecting IT applications be an "inside-out" process. This requires the organization to define its requirements before committing to a "solution." The reason for failures, the author notes, is that the needed complements aren't developed in the organization. In particular, this makes implementing EIT much more difficult than implementing FIT or NIT. For example, one reason

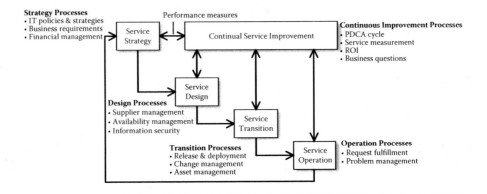

Figure 9.3   ITIL overview.

is that employees rebel at having the process associated with the EIT imposed on them. The following sections point to sources that are available to assist in cultivating needed organizational complements.

9.7.1 ITIL

ITIL provides a set of best practices for IT service delivery. The Office of Government Commerce (OGC) in the United Kingdom maintains the standard. ITIL is recognized globally and supports ISO standards and certification of practitioners designing IT services. Figure 9.3 shows the ITIL service delivery life cycle in the form of a flowchart. (The official ITIL version uses a wheel.) The cycle begins with strategy and proceeds to service design, transition, and operation stages. The loop closes with performance measurement and continuous improvement processes. The figure lists a few of the processes for fulfilling the role of each stage.

ITIL publishes its standards in the form of separate books for each life cycle stage. These are directed at company management and IT staffs seeking to develop a capability in the organization. In the supply chain process models described in Chapter 8, this infrastructure would support the development of multiple Enable and Executing processes. A separate, briefer publication contains articles targeted at senior management.[11] The book's mission is "to explain to IT service suppliers how to engage more effectively with their business customers." A major theme is how components of the ITIL service life cycle support business objectives.

9.7.2 SFIA

The SFIA Foundation provides its Skills Framework for the Information Age.[12] Like the CSCMP's *Process Standards*, the framework describes different competency levels for over seventy skills needed to manage technology. These skills are also aligned to the ITIL life cycle. The framework applies to both IT product (software and hardware) and service providers (IT staff, system integrators) as well as the business users. A seven-level spectrum ranging from "least" to "fully developed" provides a yardstick for assessing the organization's capability. In a self-assessment, the organization uses the spectrum to establish its current level and set goals and action plans for attaining higher levels. Most skill profiles don't use all seven levels.

Table 9.1 shows the structure for just one skill, business process improvement, (BPRE). This is defined as "the identification of new and alternative approaches to performing business activities." This mission corresponds to that of practitioners seeking to create or restructure supply chains. Only three of the seven levels (Levels 5, 6, and 7) are defined for this skill. Table 9.1 contains brief descriptions of all seven levels.

9.7.3 Business Analysis Body of Knowledge (BABOK)

The International Institute of Business Analysis (IIBA) is an organization based in Canada with roots in the IT industry. Formed in 2003, it maintains its *Guide to the Business Analysis Body of Knowledge* (*BABOK*).[13] The organization offers a certification program for Certified Business Analysis Professional (CBAP). A draft update available at the time of writing this book runs to over 300 pages. The organization seeks to establish business analysis as a profession distinct from other professions like project management, financial analysis, and organization development. The role of the business analyst, according to the *BABOK,* is "to elicit, analyze, communicate, and validate 'requirements' for changes to business processes, policies, and information systems."[14] The business analyst will need to understand business problems and the opportunities available to help the organization meet its goals. The *BABOK* is a road map to fulfilling this need and provides a comprehensive methodology for a project that involves developing a list of requirements for information technology solutions as well as the accompanying process improvements. The *BABOK* also recognizes the need for domain knowledge in disciplines like SCM.

The *BABOK* focuses on requirements gathering and incorporation into processes and systems. Following is its definition of "requirements":

1. A condition or capability needed to solve a problem or achieve an objective.
2. A condition or capability needed to satisfy a contract, standard, or specification, or other document.
3. A documented representation of a condition or capability as in #1 or #2.

Requirements, according to the *BABOK,* are the foundations of systems or their components. As the term "requirements" implies, they are obligatory and are "foundation elements" for systems. They can be defined as a condition or a capability. A condition might be "the system has to be available at all times." A capability is that "the system must display the status of all work orders." Most of the *BABOK*

Table 9.1   Example SFIA Framework Example; Business Process Improvement (BPRE)

1	2	3	4	5	6	7
Follow	*Assist*	*Apply*	*Enable*	*Ensure, Advise*	*Initiate, Influence*	*Set Strategy, Inspire, Mobilize*
Closely supervised Little discretion	Routine supervision Minor discretion	General supervision Minor discretion	Clear responsibility Plans own work	Full accountability Provided objectives	Establishes objectives Delegates work	Authority and responsibility for area of work
These levels are not ranked for the BPRE skill				Analyzes processes Identifies alternatives Assesses feasibility and recommends changes	Same as 5 plus evaluates financial, cultural, technological, organizational, and environmental factors	Identifies and leads significant improvement programs taking responsibility for the work performed

is dedicated to tools and methodologies for uncovering requirements. Structured like the *PMBOK Guide,* the *BABOK* has its own knowledge areas centered on process requirements:

- Enterprise Analysis,
- Requirements Planning and Management,
- Requirements Elicitation,
- Requirements Communication,
- Requirements Analysis and Documentation, and
- Solution Assessment and Validation.

Table 9.2 summarizes *BABOK* content for each knowledge area. Figure 9.4 is a *BABOK* overview showing the relationship between the knowledge areas. The figure also has a summary of the content in *BABOK* chapter covering each knowledge area. The Enterprise Analysis that kicks off requirements development can be folded into the planning process that Chapter 12 describes.

9.8 Conclusions: Lessons Learned

All four SCM and project management knowledge and practice components are necessary to successfully complete a project. This is just like having all the parts of a car—the engine, various fasteners, the steering wheel, etc.—needed to drive that car. However, that doesn't mean that some knowledge and practice components shouldn't receive special attention. Table 9.3 summarizes what the five project shortcomings described in this chapter suggest for special attention. The bold items are the most important in addressing a particular risk in supply chain projects.

9.8.1 Project Management Knowledge

Of the nine project management knowledge areas, just three are mentioned more than once as corrections for project shortcomings: Project Scope Management is mentioned four out of five times. Project Risk Management is mentioned in three. Project Cost Management and Project Human Resource Management are mentioned in two. A reasonable conclusion is that if an organization focuses on getting these project processes right, chances for success increase significantly.

9.8.2 Project Management Practice

Many project shortcomings would likely be addressed by moving the organization to higher levels of the PMMM. This requires a level of awareness that's absent in many organizations. At least, Level 2 maturity is required in four of five situations. Level 3 is likely to be required to avoid rigidity since Level 3 calls for an "informal

Table 9.2 *BABOK* Knowledge Areas

1	Enterprise Analysis	Early project or pre-project activities. Can be a separate project. Establishes scope of the project. Defines business issues. Referred to as investigative, feasibility, or business architecture. Establishing spheres and employing SCOR and the CSCMP's *Process Standards* would be appropriate for this stage. So would business case justification. Conducting an initial risk analysis is also recommended.
2	Requirements Planning and Management	This knowledge area plans the requirements-gathering process. The plan should coordinate with other activities, assure resources are available for the effort, and provide a means for monitoring the progress of the effort.
3	Requirements Elicitation	The knowledge area describes methods to gather the requirements. The knowledge area includes what *BABOK* refers to as the "business system" that consists of the processes that go with the technology. Among the tools covered are brainstorming, document analysis, focus groups, interface analysis, interviews, observation, prototyping, workshops, reverse engineering the code in an existing system, and surveys.
4	Requirements Communication	Communication is ongoing throughout the elicitation process. The business analyst must understand the audience and select the communications methods appropriate to the situation. These can also be defined in the Enterprise Analysis.
5	Requirements Analysis and Documentation	This knowledge area is structured as a set of tasks, many of which are more "art" than "science" and require expertise in process improvement methods like those in this book. The tasks include the following: • Structure requirements packages so that solutions are matched with problems or issues that have been identified. • Create business domain model that describes the current and future state. • Analyze user requirements for individual users and user groups. • Analyze functional requirements that describe the capabilities of the system.

Table 9.2 (continued) ***BABOK* Knowledge Areas**

		• Analyze quality of service requirements not directly related to the functionality of the system but describe environmental conditions under which the solution must be effective.
		• Determine assumptions and constraints that will affect or limit the solution. Assumptions are unknowns that have to be identified; constraints limit what we can do and can't be changed.
		• Determine requirements attributes that can include "metadata" like priority, source, processes affected, and so forth.
		• Document, validate, and verify requirements to assure that they meet the needs of stakeholders.
6	Solution Assessment and Validation	The knowledge area structures the path from requirements to the design and implementation of a solution. For systems and processes, the product is a description of the solution capabilities. This will provide estimates of resources for implementation and alternatives. The knowledge area covers solution implementation and post-implementation review and assessment.

process" that is flexible enough for a variety of projects. Structuring project phases into shorter periods will also increase agility in adjusting to change. These changes are likely in dynamic business environments.

9.8.3 SCM Knowledge

All five SCM tasks are represented in Table 9.3. *Task 1 Designing Supply Chains for Strategic Advantage* is mentioned as a solution four times. Not having a strategy is a frequent complaint when projects go bad. Kerzner's PMMM is designed to provide a competitive advantage from better project management. *Tasks 2 and 3, internal and external collaboration*, are mentioned twice. Our observation, confirmed by a 2008 CSCMP survey, is that companies still struggle with internal alignment. Aligning several companies in a supply chain is a relatively new challenge.[15]

Task 4 Managing Supply Chain Information also appears twice. The lesson to draw is that shortcomings in IT projects are less about technology and more about management. *Task 5 Removing Cost from the Supply Chain* appears twice, as the knowledge area contains tools for analyzing operations. However, few processes should be automated without improvements in current processes. Perhaps the automation won't be needed at all. So, this task will likely accompany any major system improvement.

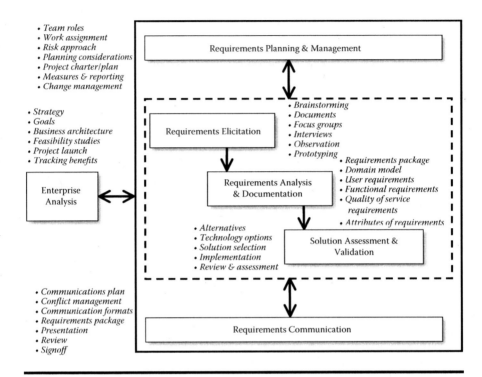

Figure 9.4 *BABOK* overview.

9.8.4 SCM Practice

Knowledge of several SCOR-model and the CSCMP's *Process Standards* elements will help address risk areas. The idea of "threads" that cross organization boundaries communicates supply chain missions to departments and partners. Metrics play a role in preventing conflicts between functions. All the SCOR elements—processes, metrics, and collaboration—provide a decision tool for top management to define which responsibilities to delegate and which to retain.

Table 9.3 Summary of IT Project Shortcomings

	Rigidity	Organization Roadblocks	Management Abrogation	Technical Capability	Misunderstood Technology
Project management knowledge	Integration **Scope** Cost Human resources Risk	Scope	Scope Cost Risk	Human resources Risk	Scope
Project management practice	PMMM Level 3 **Project structure (phasing)**		PMMM Level 2	PMMM Level 2	PMMM Levels 2 and 3
SCM knowledge	Task 1, Strategy Task 2, Collaborative relationships Task 3, Partnerships	Task 1, Strategy **Task 2, Collaborative relationships**	Task 1, Strategy	Task 3, Partnerships Task 4, Information Task 5, Cost removal	Task 1, Strategy Task 4, Information Task 5, Cost removal
SCM practice		SCOR threads SCOR metrics Types of SCM projects	SCOR Level 3 processes, metrics, collaboration		

Note: **Bold** items are likely to be the most important.

Notes

1. Sarah Cliffe, "ERP Implementation: How to Avoid $100 Million Write-Offs" (*Harvard Business Review*, January/February 1999): 16–7.
2. John Bermudez, "Supply Chain Management: More Than Just Technology" (*Supply Chain Management Review*, March/April 2002): 15–16.
3. Jeanne W. Ross and Peter Weill, "Six IT Decisions Your IT People Shouldn't Make" (*Harvard Business Review*, November 2002): 85–91.
4. "Technology Spending Offers No Guarantee of Better Performance," *Wall Street Journal*, November 1, 2002, B2.
5. Paul C. Tinnirello, *Project Management* (Boca Raton, FL: Auerbach Publications, 2000), 464.
6. David Ritter, "We Must Never Break the Chain," in *The Supply Chain Yearbook* (New York: McGraw-Hill, 2001), 199–200.
7. Ben Worthen, "GE May Set Example in Online Software Trend," *Wall Street Journal*, November 6, 2008, B1.
8. Steven A. Morris and Denise Johnson McManus, "Information Infrastructure Centrality in the Agile Organization" (*Information Systems Management*, Fall 2002): 8–12.
9. Darrell K. Rigby, Frederick F. Reichheld, and Phil Schefter, "Avoid the Four Perils of CRM" (*Harvard Business Review*, February 2002): 101–9.
10. Andrew McAfee, "Mastering the Three Worlds of Information Technology" (*Harvard Business Review*, November 2006): 141–9.
11. Office of Government Commerce, The Business View on Successful IT Service Delivery, OGC, 2006.
12. SFIA Foundation, Skills Framework for the Information Age, Version 3.0, 2005.
13. International Institute of Business Analysis (IIBA), *A Guide to the Business Analysis Body of Knowledge (BABOK)*, Release 1.6, 2006.
14. *Ibid.*, 9.
15. Frank J. Quinn, Morgan L. Swink, and Charles C. Poirer, "The Sixth Annual Global Survey of Supply Chain Progress," *Supply Chain Management Review* (October 2008).

SCM PROJECT PROCESSES

This section contains templates for an expansive supply chain project. It borrows *PMBOK Guide* process standards for the recommended project structure. The section is designed to help practitioners shape their own efforts, particularly those who want cross-functional and multicompany participation.

Chapter 10

SCM Maturity Models

Maturity models track progress in the organization's supply chain management (SCM) capability and progress toward improving its supply chains. As supply chain projects are implemented, managers should confirm progress by quantitative measures for customer service, market share, and financial performance.

Measurable SCM improvement requires models that help define levels of performance. Section 5.2 describes a maturity model that tracks deployment of project management processes. The Council of Supply Chain Management Professionals' (CSCMP) *Supply Chain Management Process Standards (Process Standards)* described in Section 8.2 are another tool that fits the maturity model category. The *Process Standards* are notable for the extensiveness of their model—six volumes and hundreds of best practices for assessing the organization's supply chain processes.

However, like a potent pharmaceutical, reliance on these models should come with a huge warning label. An article quoted in earlier chapters warned of model shortcomings.[1] It called attention to the fact that most models emphasize operating excellence and are silent on measuring strategic contributions. The models also are "quiet," if not entirely silent, regarding ways to measure the presence of necessary skills. The Skills for the Information Age (SFIA) framework (Section 9.7.2) provides such a method for information technology (IT) and process improvement roles.

This book aspires to fill these gaps by providing tools like spheres and activity systems, explained in Chapter 4. Also, Section 9.7 described how indispensable organizational "complements" are to success at implementing new technology. A "complement" supports (i.e., "complements") technology implementation. Complements include increased skills, greater teamwork, redesigned processes, and

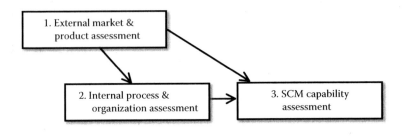

Figure 10.1 SCM maturity assessment requirements.

new decision rights delegated to process participants. These "soft," hard-to-measure attributes are also missing in popular SCM maturity models.

The two SCM maturity models that this chapter describes provide higher-level, single page approaches. One measures the state of the company's supply chain; the other addresses the presence of necessary SCM skills. The models enable users to quickly define Point A on the maturity matrix, where they are now, and track their progress to Point B, where they want to be. Different organizations are unlikely to start from the same place nor will they necessarily seek the same destination. Figure 10.1 explains interactions between the factors to consider in assessing both a supply chain and an SCM capability[2]:

1. external market and product assessment—market structure, product positions in the market, position of products in the product life cycle (see Section 4.2);
2. internal process and organization assessment—whether our processes, systems, and organization structure match the challenges presented by our market and product positions (addressed in this chapter); and
3. SCM capability assessment—the capabilities of our people in terms of responding to supply chain challenges (also addressed in this chapter).

An assessment is complete only if the organization begins by starting with an understanding of its market and product position. Figure 10.1 pictures external market and product assessment (#1) driving the other two (#2 and #3). Internal process and organization assessment (#2) also drives SCM capability assessment (#3).

10.1 External Market and Product Assessment

Chapter 4 was dedicated to discussing market dynamics and the process of defining spheres, or businesses inside the business, for focused supply chains. Each sphere calls for a dedicated supply chain designed around the unique demands of a particular market or product. So, measuring maturity requires the organization to identify the spheres and create, at least in a "rough-cut" fashion, the activity system required to successfully execute the strategy. This rough-cut supply chain design becomes the standard for measurement of SCM skills and existing supply chains.

10.1.1 Supply Chain Types

Such an effort should recognize that different market environments have evolved competitive models for supply chains for serving that market. Joseph L. Cavinato represents the Center for Strategic Supply Leadership at the Institute for Supply Management and teaches SCM courses at Arizona State University. The Institute is the former National Association of Purchasing Management—another example of displacing "purchasing" and "logistics" in favor of "supply" in organization names. Cavinato maintains that there is no "one size fits all" supply chain design.[3] In fact, because of current fashion, many use the term "supply chain" in describing their operations. Yet, these companies have little or no supply chain at all. In reality, they are a loose-knit group of specialized functions or departments. Cavinato's research concludes that there are many "generic" supply chain types and that the chosen supply chain model must be aligned with company goals for competing. He also notes that most companies have or need to have not just one but multiple supply chains—a proposition this book supports.

Based on strategy, a company may choose any number of levels of integration internally or with its partners. After a two-year study, Cavinato's organization identified sixteen supply chain types, a "spectrum" of possible models. Table 10.1 summarizes each of the sixteen types. The table also has a column describing the "complexity" of operating a supply chain of a particular type along with a name assigned by Cavinato's team. The need for complements contributes to this complexity and drives the need for advanced SCM skills. Also shown is the level of support for achieving competitive advantage and profit, using a four-level scale.

At the first level—the traditional supply chains—chains 1 through 3 have a negative impact on the company's fortunes. Their chains are "anchors" holding the company back. Chains 4 through 8 are neutral with regard to longer-term strategic benefits. However, their implementation produces benefits in cost savings. Chains 9 and 10 begin to produce not only savings but also competitive advantage on the supplier and customer side. Chain 11, which may be illegal in some places, through Chain 16 offer increasing long-term benefits in terms of market share and revenue. Chain 11 is the least complex to implement; chain 16, information networks, is the most complex.

The sixteen models capture variations that are common in different industries. Auto manufacturing is a much different environment than that in a technology or food distribution industry. These environments place constraints on how far one should or can go in implementing generic supply chain solutions. The recommended approach described later is to reframe maturity models in terms of the

Table 10.1 Supply Chain Types

	Type of Chain/ Network	Description/Characteristics	Relative Complexity	Maturity Model Stage
1	No chain	Functions act freely, no strategic advantage from supply chain.	Low	1
2	Don't know	Mostly outsourced supply chain operations. No strategic advantage. "Blank check to outsiders" such as third-party logistics providers or systems consultants.	Low	1
3	Chains that tie down the firm	Internally focused. Lagging competitors, catch-up mode. Logistics-centered with measures focused on warehousing and transportation cost.	High	1
4	Nano-chain	Internally focused on manufacturing efficiencies in plants requiring high utilization. Inbound and outbound processes are secondary. Examples include automobiles and aircraft manufacturing.	Low	2
5	Micro-chain	Logistics model with integrated physical and information flows. Balances inbound, production, and outbound distribution.	Low	2
6	Project logistics chain	Efficient at project supply and execution. Integrates multiple suppliers to the project. Like the nano-chain except it's a project environment.	Medium	2

Table 10.1 (continued) Supply Chain Types

	Type of Chain/ Network	*Description/Characteristics*	*Relative Complexity*	*Maturity Model Stage*
7	Cash-to-cash cycle chain	Focused on cash flow, perhaps to detriment of suppliers. The starting point is a cash flow goal, with operations structured accordingly.	High	2
8	Synergistic chain	Eliminates duplication. No competitive advantage. Seeks to leverage buying power. Common in large companies with multiple independent divisions. Focus on common commodity purchases.	High	2
9	Demand chain	High collaboration often dictated by dominant customers like Wal-Mart. Interdisciplinary with sales and operations. Tailored arrangements by customer. Flexible company. Uses technology.	Medium	2
10	Extended supply chain	Has a supply chain mind-set. Managers developed in the supply chain role. Good processes for new products and production of existing ones.	Medium	2
11	Market dominance and blocking	Enjoys a monopoly with control over market and pricing. Illegal in some countries.	Low	3

(continued on next page)

Table 10.1 (continued)   Supply Chain Types

	Type of Chain/ Network	Description/Characteristics	Relative Complexity	Maturity Model Stage
12	Supply integration	Highly interdisciplinary, evolving from process-oriented cost reduction efforts. Complete supply chain view, platform for competitive initiatives.	Medium	3
13	Speed-to-market	Emphasizes new product development. Flexible. Uses time as a metric. Seeks to tap unused capacity in the supply chain to speed product rollouts.	Medium	3
14	Innovation	Network of manufacturing and logistics suppliers organized to provide flexibility. Focuses on product creation, launch, and growth phases of product life cycle. Examples are high-tech electronics and seasonal toys.	Medium	4
15	Value chain	Chain-to-chain competition, seeking innovation throughout the chain. Shared outcome arrangements are common. Procurement coordinates. Partners invest to develop capabilities needed for their part of the chain.	High	4
16	Information networks	Flexible networks with few physical assets processing a flow of innovations. Supply chain managers are network creators and leaders. Data is accessed and converted into information, knowledge, and intelligence.	High	4

desired activity system and the five competencies that comprise our SCM knowledge areas, not the advanced state of the technology a company employs.

Another reality in Cavinato's model is that, although supply chain designs in an organization can be a source of operating efficiencies and competitive advantage, they can also hold a company back. That is, they can be dysfunctional when it comes to reaching goals for growth and profits. The dysfunctional level also appears in our model of SCM capability maturity since such situations are common.

10.1.2 Assessing the Project Portfolio

Figure 10.2 depicts a framework for characterizing current and desired supply chain-related efforts. Its purpose is to confirm the value of these projects by asking questions about our plans. It can also point to gaps in the organization's pursuit of a particular supply chain type from Table 10.1. The questions answered include the following:

- Does a project change the basis for competition moving in a direction we desire? That is, is it strategic?
- What level is the project—function/department, company or strategic business unit (SBU), or supply chain?
- Is our portfolio of projects aggressive enough given our market and product challenges?

The result is the grid in Figure 10.2 that characterizes existing projects using the framework introduced as Figure 4.4. The grid has six categories covering the strategic or non-strategic nature of each project on one dimension and the level

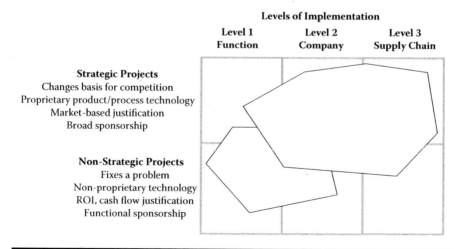

Levels of Implementation

| Level 1 Function | Level 2 Company | Level 3 Supply Chain |

Strategic Projects
Changes basis for competition
Proprietary product/process technology
Market-based justification
Broad sponsorship

Non-Strategic Projects
Fixes a problem
Non-proprietary technology
ROI, cash flow justification
Functional sponsorship

Figure 10.2   Gap between supply chain planning and execution.

of the project on the other. The criteria for strategic and non-strategic projects are listed in the figure. The level corresponds to the organization level where the project is focused and sponsored: the function or department (usually a cost center), the company/business unit (a profit center—often a division or an independent company), and the supply chain (multicompany level that includes trading partners).

Figure 10.2 shows the boundaries of a supply chain project portfolio in the lower left-hand corner of the grid that is typical of many companies. Most projects, sponsored by functional managers, are non-strategic and offer only a local impact at the department or company level. Should a company's external assessment indicate their current portfolio isn't aggressive enough, the company should push their portfolio toward the upper right-hand corner, as shown by the shaded area. This will likely require dropping some projects and adding others because of limited resources.

Table 10.2 applies the model to a few examples of supply chain projects. Just because a project extends beyond the immediate company, it doesn't mean it is strategic. It could be "catch-up" to reach parity with a more aggressive competitor or of little relevance to competitive position. So, venturing outside the company to do a supply chain project alone is not a prerequisite for a strategic project. Likewise, a project at the function level could be strategic if the supply chain model, like #5 (micro-chain) and #6 (project logistics chain) in Table 10.1, demands it. Two famous supply chains—those of Toyota and Dell—grew out companies striving to decrease their cash-to-cash cycles (model #7). These companies are noted for implementing demand-driven supply chains, replenishing stock based on pull signals from end users.

Section 9.7 described the need for organizational complements for implementing technology at three levels: function, network, and enterprise. As mentioned earlier in this chapter, broader projects call for complements in terms of skills, process design, teamwork, and decision rights. For example, sharing information between trading partners requires processes on both sides to put the data to work. Lack of these complements is a barrier to implementing broader projects.

Table 10.2 Application of the Supply Chain Project Grid

Changes Competition	S1: Function	S2: Business Unit	S3: Supply Chain
Yes	Proprietary factory floor process	New product introduction process	Offering to take over field maintenance from customers
No	Skills training for sales force	A 10% across-the-board budget cut	Direct marketing over the Internet

10.2 Maturity Matrix for Organization, Process, and Systems

Table 10.3 is a maturity matrix for three operational dimensions of importance to SCM: organization, process, and systems. Dave Malmberg of CGR Management Consultants, a supply chain expert, devised the categories. The well-received tool asks evaluators to place the supply chain operations being examined at the current as-is stage of maturity. Practitioners should employ this tool when kicking off a supply chain initiative. Descriptions on the matrix guide the assessment. Evaluators should use their knowledge of markets and products from the external evaluation, the content of any activity systems they've designed, and documentation of their current project portfolio to make their assessments.

The term "demand-driven supply chain" defines our process dimension. Like Dell and Toyota, many managers pursue the goal of being demand-driven rather than forecast driven. In a startup operation short on cash, like these companies at an early age, this minimizes the cash-to-cash cycle. The degree to which a supply chain is "demand-driven" is measured by how many decisions along the supply chain are based on actual end-user demand rather than forecasts. Being demand-driven has also become shorthand for the lean, synchronized supply chain. The demand-driven supply chain has closely connected links through whatever tool best communicates end-user demand to trading partners. It is thus able to operate with a minimum of inventory, expediting, price write-downs, and other supply chain waste.

Companies have a number of strategies they can follow to make this happen, as described in detailed maturity models in this and other publications. Examples include information technology, collocating operations, or physical signals like the *kanban* or two-bin signals. Chapter 15 describes project management processes for implementing the demand-driven supply chain. Supply chain managers can assess how demand-driven they might become. The assessment examines each decision in the supply chain, documenting whether the information used at that step derives from actual demand or a forecast, and an assessment of the possibility to convert a forecast-driven decision to a demand-driven one. This assessment results in the "potential" to be demand-driven. For example, a supply chain has ten production-related decisions and eight are forecast-driven. It is thus 20 percent demand-driven. However, if an assessment identifies four forecast-driven decisions that can be converted to demand-driven, the demand-driven potential is 60 percent.

10.3 Stages of SCM Maturity

Table 10.4 briefly summarizes the SCM five knowledge area tasks described in Chapter 4. The descriptions in the table point to the problems in achieving

Table 10.3 Maturity Matrix For Organization, Process, and Systems Evaluation

	Stages of Evolution			
	1. Infrastructure	2. Cost Reduction	3. Collaboration	4. Strategic Contribution
Supply chain organization	Capability building Execution of basic tasks	Root cause analysis Item stratification "Optimal" buys	Multicompany improvement programs Financial sharing arrangements	Customer-focused organization structures along supply chain Supply chain level steering committees
Demand-driven supply chain	Supplier reduction Negotiations Mostly forecast driven; backorder and simple service-level indicators	Quality systems Outsourcing Supplier ratings Lead-time reduction (cells, small batches) Modest JIT/pull arrangements; 25% of demand-driven potential	Design changes Postponement strategies Information exchange (inventories, forecasts, demand) 50% application of demand-driven potential	Segment strategies New product involvement 80% to 100% implementation of demand-driven potential
Supply chain systems	Basic capabilities (e.g. Bills of Material) Data timeliness and accuracy Paper-based or rudimentary computer procurement systems	Mature technology deployment (ERP, EDI, forecasting tools) Stratified forecasting and inventory practices	Web-based technology for information exchange Partner system integration	Increased use of customized transaction and planning tools integrated with supply chain operations
Stage challenges	People, skills, discipline, time	Systems support, knowledge Inertia, unwillingness to change supply chain partners and their roles	Procurement paradigms, willingness and/or ability to be creative	Barriers between operations, engineering, and marketing functions Difficulties in coordination Amenability of trading partners for such collaboration Weakness in organizational complements Weak links in chain

Table 10.4   Five Tasks for Better SCM

	SCM Task	Description
1	Designing Supply Chains for Strategic Advantage	Success in the marketplace requires supply chain innovation. A supply chain strategy that supports company strategies for competing should guide the design.
2	Implementing Collaborative Relationships	Internal organization form, responsibilities, and measures enable supply chain innovation. The task covers relationships inside the organization and has been identified in surveys as the most difficult area to change.
3	Forging Supply Chain Partnerships	Outside partners are needed to be successful. Old paradigms must be discarded. Implementation requires an organized, multicompany project approach.
4	Managing Supply Chain Information	Opportunities to succeed wildly or fail miserably abound. Supply chain systems must support supply chain processes. Particular attention should be paid to the areas where complements are needed.
5	Removing Cost from the Supply Chain	Effective change to improve service and reduce cost requires understanding and managing root causes of cost in supply chain processes.

excellence at each of the tasks. The typical organizational mind-set lags far behind what is needed to build great supply chains. First, the supply chain is not seen as a source of strategic advantage. The functions that comprise the supply chain like procurement, manufacturing, and distribution do contribute their pieces to their strategic plans; however, they do so as functions and not with an integrated, supply chain viewpoint (supply chains #1 through #3 in Table 10.1).

Second, most companies rely on budgets built on traditional accounting practices to measure their performance; these do a poor job of identifying "horizontal" process costs. For example, Section 4.2.1 described market mediation costs that arise from mismatches between supply and demand. Assigning accountability for these real costs is not done, mostly due to ignorance of their presence and the difficulty of capturing them.

Third, a preference for arm's-length relationships also stands in the way of multicompany efforts. Few in traditional departments like procurement, manufacturing, and distribution are prepared, either by education, training, or inclination, to work strategically with other departments or suppliers. In fact, performance measures may discourage such activity. When the need for process improvement arises, few are undertaking processes that cross company boundaries, despite the fact that one's own company, through the way it operates or the design of its products, determines the cost of operations up and down the chain. So, process engineers can only achieve small improvements; larger opportunities are overlooked entirely.

Table 10.5 uses the five SCM tasks for the points of capability evaluation. Figure 10.1 indicates that a user should have an appreciation of the company strategy and have performed the assessment in Table 10.3's maturity matrix. The first two columns are our five SCM tasks described in Chapter 4. Along the top are maturity Stages I through V, ranging from dysfunctional to strategic contribution. You should note that the levels in this matrix use Roman numerals and those in SCM matrix are regular numbers. At each stage for each task, there is a short description of what it takes to achieve that stage. These descriptions are framed in terms of management's use of SCM knowledge and practice. Note that this presentation steers clear of measuring maturity by the amount of technology implemented. Other maturity matrices use a technology yardstick. Like the SCM maturity matrix, this matrix should be used two ways. The first is to establish where we are, the second is to assess our current capability. For example, a company's processes, perhaps determined using the maturity model in Table 10.3, may be at Stage I but the management team feels it is capable of implementing Stage IV processes. With regard to Task 1 Designing Supply Chains for Strategic Advantage, a company may have no strategy equivalent to Stage I, Dysfunctional. A new management team, a reading of this book, or some other stimulus may cause the company to seek immediate strategic contributions, a Stage V condition. For such companies to actually be Stage V, however, they must implement the activity systems they design. In fact, many organizations are like chains 1, 2, and 3 in Cavinato's sixteen supply chain spectrum. They are in a "deep hole" with a need to overhaul processes, systems, and organizations, including those inside department boundaries, before they can inch forward. However, the awareness of the need to do so also exists.

As an example, departments may do well against traditional functional measures or even against best practices published in the Supply-Chain Operations Reference-model (SCOR-model) and the CSCMP's *Process Standards*. But, the practices being measured are downright counterproductive where supply chain excellence is required. For example, a company expects its transportation manager to minimize transportation costs. But, a tight-fisted policy can hurt customer service. The functional measures produce unintended circumstances and present a barrier to moving to the next SCM level.

The Stage I "dysfunctional" organization really struggles with basic processes that cross functional boundaries. A number of factors cause this, including high turnover, poor leadership, fast changing markets and products, misguided functional measures, unabsorbed acquisitions, or lack of basic information technology. Such companies are often a "mess," and working in one is chaotic. A company at

Stage I needs to get its own house in order. It must cease counterproductive practices to be ready for Stage II. Having the sharpest, most finely tuned departmental functions as described in supply chain best practice models may cause you to flop as a company since your measures are too narrow and ambitions too limited.

At Stage II, called "Infrastructure" in Table 10.5, the company remains functionally focused. Internal efforts concentrate on department budgets, squeezing the organization for cost reduction. The Stage II company is in a position, however, to put together basic systems and procedures, talent, organization, and measures. A Stage II company should be at Level 1 in Kerzner's Project Management Maturity Model (PMMM) described in Section 5.2. At least, managers may be talking about project management as a discipline.

Stage III is labeled "Cost Reduction." At this level, the company optimizes its own cost and profits. It does so with both internally and externally directed cross-functional efforts. Six Sigma and lean process improvement initiatives for internal process improvement would be a typical Stage III activity. In terms of the PMMM, the Stage III company might be at Level 2, using disciplined project management tools. Cross-functional cost reduction efforts are underway in a Stage III company, likely targeting bill of material and service provider costs. Supplier cost reduction at Stage III usually focuses on price negotiations of a "zero-sum game" nature. This is often the case when the company has power over its suppliers and is able to dictate the terms of engagement. Supply chain types 4 through 10 in Table 10.1 would be typical of this stage. Able competitors can readily copy most initiatives, so little in the way of sustainable advantage is produced by the effort.

Stage IV in Table 10.5 is "Collaboration." Supply chain partners adopt collaboration models appropriate to process needs. Section 3.7 defined the following modes of collaboration:

- Data exchange collaboration where partners (internal or external) exchange information for transactions as required. Data exchange can be one-way or two-way.
- Cooperative collaboration where partners (internal or external) share systems and tools so that partners have access to information simultaneously.
- Cognitive collaboration is the highest level requiring "joint, concurrent intellectual and cognitive activity between partners." This includes information-sharing of all types, leading to mutual decisions.

Collaboration at Stage IV is shaped by efforts to reduce cost and speed supply chain processes. This is admirable. However, the overriding collaboration goal is improvement in market position, customer service, or operating effectiveness. Collaboration takes forms like sharing end sales data, working together on new products, optimizing competencies with outsourcing, and rationalization of products and production resources. Chain types 12 and 13 in Cavinato's spectrum fit Stage IV.

Table 10.5 Stages of SCM Capability

Task	Name	Stages of SCM Capability				
		I. Dysfunctional	II. Infrastructure	III. Cost Reduction	IV. Collaboration	V. Strategic Contribution
1	Designing Supply Chains for Strategic Advantage	No strategy exists around which to create supply chain designs	Supply chain awareness takes hold; however, managers still view the company as stand-alone	Supply chain is viewed as a non-strategic "cost center" for internal cost reduction	Joint strategic initiatives are pursued on a limited basis with suppliers and customers	Activity systems are implemented for strategic advantage
2	Implementing Collaborative Relationships	Internal department measures, goals, and objectives conflict with supply chain excellence	The organization is functionally focused; initiatives are departmental	Cross-functional initiatives begin, limited to the company and focused on cost reduction	Supply chain has moved into a single function, which manages multicompany relationships	The organization has established multicompany infrastructure for important chains

3	Forging Supply Chain Partnerships	Relationships with suppliers and customers are arm's-length at best, antagonistic at worst	Collaboration up and down the supply chain is limited to transaction data	Efforts are limited to supplier initiatives focused on cost reduction, not revenue increases	Upstream and downstream partners collaborate but roles are static; partners pursue sphere strategies	Trading partners in the supply chain expand their value contributions guided by activity system designs
4	Managing Supply Chain Information	Basic information needed for decision making is missing; all replenishment is forecast-driven	Technology improvements focus on individual departments and maintenance	Systems efforts support cost reduction within the organization; may or may not be process justified	Two-way information exchange supports transactions and mutual decision making	Technology is integrated into supply chain activity systems; organizational complements are present
5	Removing Cost from the Supply Chain	Cost reduction and process improvement is a "hit and miss" affair; efforts often hurt more than they help	Reductions are internal and measured through department budgets; service isn't an issue	Cost reduction efforts cross departments but are limited to internal efforts	Supply chain cost reduction is limited to logistics and other operating costs	Cost reduction across the supply chain is the target; benefits are shared among partners

A maturity model shouldn't view deployment of technology solutions as the end game. Of course, technology can be an important enabler; but the company that measures progress in terms of the technology it installs runs the risk of missing the mark competitively—an important lesson from Chapter 9. Michael Porter supported this view in an award-winning article.[4] His view is that the Internet and related technology should "complement" the strategy. This calls to mind the organizational complements (skills, teamwork, empowerment, process improvements) described in Section 9.7. Your strategy should define the source of your company's competitive advantage. This advantage arises because somehow you are different from your competitors. And that difference makes you the logical choice by the customer you have targeted. Technology alone doesn't bestow this difference but it can be an important element in its delivery.

Porter also notes that the Internet will change the structure of many industries, and most readers have witnessed this in buying books and music, courting the opposite sex, and job searching. This will make some industries more attractive and some less so. This openness of the Internet means that the technology is available to all competitors, perhaps wiping out an industry leader's advantage. The Internet also enables companies to bypass traditional channels and appeal directly to end users.

For these reasons, we define Stage V as "Strategic Contribution." At this stage, the outputs of our tasks are measured not by technology but by their support of strategies for improving its competitiveness. These strategies derive from the business model, strategy, and the activity system that makes the organization different from competitors. In the Stage V company, the supply chain is no longer a "cost" of doing business but a clear component in its strategy to survive and prosper. Cavinato's chain types 14 through 16 in particular correspond to this stage.

The assumption is that pursuing ever more expansive and complex SCM projects also requires ever greater maturity in project management plus the appropriate organizational complements. This chapter is intended to help you establish your current position as well as select a model that best fits your destination. Chapter 11 introduces a process template for the processes required to move from lower to higher stages of SCM maturity.

Notes

1. Christopher Moberg, Kate Vitasek, Theodore L. Stank, and Abré Pienaar, "Time to Remodel," *CSCMP Supply Chain Quarterly* (Quarter 3/2008): 36–48.
2. James B. Ayers, *Handbook of Supply Chain Management*, 2nd ed. (Boca Raton: St. Lucie Press, 2006), Chapter 5.
3. Joseph L. Cavinato, "What's Your Supply Chain Type?" *Supply Chain Management Review* (May/June 2002): 60–6.
4. Porter, Michael E., "Strategy and the Internet," *Harvard Business Review* (March 2001): 62–78.

Chapter 11

Introduction to SCM Executing Processes

Here we describe the process for translating supply chain management (SCM) knowledge and practice into processes for executing supply chain projects. The format is a template modeled on the A Guide to the Project Management Body of Knowledge (PMBOK Guide).

Section 2 describes best practices in project management from the Project Management Institute's (PMI) *PMBOK Guide.* Our recap in Chapter 7 included descriptions of the *PMBOK Guide*'s project management processes. As shown in Figure 7.1, these were sorted into nine project management knowledge areas and five process groups, listed here for reference:

PMBOK Guide *Knowledge Areas*	PMBOK Guide *Process Groups*
Integration Management (H)	
Project Scope Management (H)	
Project Time Management (L)	Initiating
Project Cost Management (M)	Planning
Project Quality Management (M)	Executing
Project Human Resource Management (H)	Controlling

(continued on next page)

PMBOK Guide Knowledge Areas	PMBOK Guide Process Groups
Project Communication Management (M)	Closing
Risk Project Management (H)	
Project Procurement Management (M)	

Note: (L), (M), (H) indicate the relative need (low, medium, or high) for SCM expertise, described in Chapter 7.

The *PMBOK Guide* "executing" process group is the domain of application areas like SCM. In the remaining chapters, we provide *PMBOK Guide*-style descriptions of these executing processes, plus a few in other process groups, for supply chain improvement projects. The chapter also addresses project management processes requiring "supplemental" SCM expertise to perform them effectively. The previous table indicates our rating (high, medium, or low) for each knowledge area from Chapter 7.

Our purpose is to fill a gap in the project management practices of most companies; that is, the gap between planning and execution, between strategy setting and implementing that strategy. The gap is illustrated in Figure 10.2. Most projects are functional and non-strategic, as shown by the shape in the lower left-hand corner of the figure. If SCM is performed effectively as measured by SCM capability stages in Table 10.5, the project portfolio should migrate to the upper right-hand corner of the figure. This is the domain of strategic, enterprise-wide and supply chain level projects.

In Chapter 9, we traced root causes of project failures by examining reported shortcomings in projects that are closely related to SCM. Our list of root causes includes the following:

■ rigidity, insufficient flexibility—project management straitjackets and an inability to adapt to external changes during the project;
■ organization roadblocks—goal conflicts between departments and trading partners;
■ top management abrogation—overdelegation to lower levels of what should be executive decisions;
■ inadequate technical capability—inside the organization and at supply chain partners; and
■ misunderstood technology—what the technology will and will not accomplish and whether it is the right solution to satisfy the organization's requirements.

To be complete, we also must also address these shortcomings in the design of our SCM project processes. Concepts from Kerzner and the *PMBOK Guide* facilitate the effort. Kerzner, at Level 3 of his Project Management Maturity Model (PMMM), recommends a "singular methodology" for managing projects. So, our processes comprise a single but flexible structure despite the fact that programs and projects covered can differ substantially. We hope you will find value in adapting these elements as their own singular methodologies. Or, if you have such a singular methodology, you can use ideas here as part of a continuous improvement effort, reflective of Level 5 maturity in Kerzner's model.

The Supply-Chain Operations Reference-model (SCOR-model) and the CSCMP's *Supply Chain Management Process Standards* contain structures and best practices that aid implementation of our processes. These include both supply chain operating processes and enabling processes that assure an organization has its infrastructure in order. The SCOR-model is also a top-down model. This means it can only go so far, in SCOR's case Level 3, in recommending processes. Beyond that, Level 4, processes are tailored to the organization. You can consult these models when assistance is needed.

Chapter 7 described the *PMBOK Guide*'s nine knowledge areas and their related processes. Chapter 4 described five knowledge areas for SCM, which we employ as a backbone for our executing process descriptions. The chapter listing below describes the content of each:

	Chapter	Description
12	SCM Task 1 Developing a Supply Chain Strategy	Covers strategies to achieve supply chain excellence. Includes the strategy and supporting organization.
13	SCM Task 2 Implementing Collaborative Relationships	Develops internal collaboration among departments and dedicates staff to improvement efforts.
14	SCM Task 3 Forging Supply Chain Partnerships	Develops relationships up and down the chain with outside suppliers and customers.
15	SCM Task 4 Managing Supply Chain Information and Task 5 Removing Cost from the Supply Chain	Covers strategies to improve supply chain processes and systems.

Table 11.1 is the process template to be employed in Chapters 12 through 15. Inputs, outputs, and tools and techniques are also covered in *PMBOK Guide*'s process descriptions. Where appropriate, we will provide additional elements—process definition, project management shortcomings addressed, SCM maturity, terminology, stakeholders, and process model support—as shown in Table 11.1. In some cases, a template element is not included because it doesn't apply or has been covered elsewhere.

Table 11.2 lists the twenty-six processes we cover. They represent all the *PMBOK Guide* process groups but are naturally weighted to the executing processes in the

Table 11.1   Process Template

Inputs		Process Name (Process from Table 11.2)	Process Group
		Process Element	Outputs
Inputs to the process from other processes or external sources (source of the input[a])	Process definition	Includes scope and objectives of the process	Outputs from the process to other processes or external users
	Approaches and techniques	Concepts and tools useful in executing the process	
	PM shortcomings addressed	Shortcomings in project management addressed (Chapter 9)	
		PMMM status (Chapter 5)	
		Project management knowledge areas and processes (Chapter 7)	
	SCM maturity	Relevant stages in the supply chain maturity model (Chapter 10)	
	Terminology	Supply chain terms applicable to the process (Glossary)	
	Stakeholders	Those who execute the process, influence its outcome, or are affected by its outcome (Chapter 7)	

[a] For documents generated inside the project, the source is the process that generated it. "External" refers to company documents generated outside the project or outside the process. External inputs are shown in regular type; internal inputs are shown in italics.

Table 11.2 Mapping of SCM Processes to Process Groups and Knowledge Areas

SCM Knowledge Area	Process Groups				
	Initiating	Planning	Executing	Controlling	Closing
1. Developing a Supply Chain Strategy	Charter the Supply Chain Effort	Develop Project Plan	Define Spheres Design Activity Systems Align Organization Develop Collaboration Strategy	Control Changes	Close Phase
2. Implementing Collaborative Relationships		Plan Organization Acquire Staff	Organize for Activity System Implementation Implement Metrics	Control Schedule	
3. Forging Supply Chain Partnerships		Plan Communications	Implement Supplier Base Plan Implement Customer Base Plan Install Multicompany Organization Plan Risk Sharing	Acquire Multicompany Staff Resources Verify Partner Scope	
4. Managing Supply Chain Information			Define Linkages		
5. Removing Cost from the Supply Chain	Plan Process Improvements		Map Supply Chain Processes Identify Root Causes for Cost Reduce Material Cost Implement Demand-Driven Supply Chain		

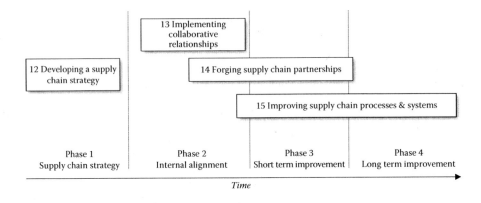

Figure 11.1 Interrelationships between SCM project life cycle phases.

SCM application area. There are two processes in the Initiating group, four in the Planning group, fifteen in the Executing group, four in the Monitoring and Controlling group, and one in the Closing group. The process numbering system uses the SCM tasks (1 through 5) shown previously, which define SCM knowledge areas. The processes are at the second level, 1.1, 1.2, and so forth. The third level covers inputs (1.1.1), process elements (1.1.2), and outputs (1.1.3).

Chapters 12 through 15 are organized by process. The process numbering approach shown in Table 11.2 will be carried through Chapters 12 through 15. So, *1.1, Chartering the Supply Chain Effort*, is the first process to be covered in Chapter 12. *Inputs* for the process are 1.1.1; *process elements* are 1.1.2; *outputs* are 1.1.3. These appear in Sections 12.1.1, 12.1.2, and 12.1.3, respectively.

Users have flexibility in determining which components they want in which project phases. We suggest beginning with the arrangement shown in Figure 11.1. The figure shows four generic life cycle phases for a supply chain improvement project:

- supply chain strategy,
- internal alignment,
- short-term improvement, and
- long-term improvement.

Table 11.3 describes when each life cycle phase starts and ends. Note that SCM knowledge area processes can occur in more than one phase. This is due to the nature of the work involved. For example, Forging Supply Chain Partnerships can begin in Phase 2 and carry over to Stages 3 and 4.

An important element in keeping the "players" straight is a Responsibility Assignment Matrix (RAM). The RAM is a project management tool that summarizes who is accountable for the success of the project, who is responsible for producing work products, who participates or is consulted, or who is informed.

Table 11.3   Descriptions of SCM Project Life Cycle Phases

	Life Cycle Phase	Start	End
1	Supply Chain Strategy	Upon initiation	When the strategy is accepted and implementation plans are developed; includes conceptual design for organization
2	Internal Alignment	On completion of strategy and related organization design	When the organization design is implemented and defined improvement projects are staffed and funded
3	Short-Term Improvement	When service and cost improvement projects are started	When short-term projects (those that require no large systems and/or facility changes) are completed
4	Long-Term Improvement	When long-term projects are started (not just approved or funded)	When long-term projects (those requiring major systems and/or facilities) are completed

Appendix A is a RAM for supply chain project processes. The labels use the ARCI format (accountable, responsible, consulted, and informed) for the responsibility assignment categories. The roles of various players are also described throughout the process descriptions. The players identified in Appendix A include the following:

Company Steering Committee	A single group of senior managers in our company. Responsible for the overall project.
Multicompany Steering Committee	One or more senior-level groups convened as needed to oversee collaboration between our company and one or more partners. There could be several of these to fit the type and number of collaborations.
Project Manager or Project Office	The person or group responsible for executing the project. The project could proceed through Phase 1 with a manager and be expanded to a project office, depending on the strategy developed.
Supply Chain Design Team	A single group from supply chain and related functions charged with execution of the project.
Sphere Design Team	Multiple teams who design supply chains in each identified sphere.

(continued on next page)

Process Design Team	Multiple teams selected to improve an assigned process or multiple processes.
Company Internal Departments	The supply chain and supporting functions within our organization.
Partner Internal Departments	The supply chain and supporting functions in our partners' organizations.

Chapter 12

Developing a Supply Chain Strategy

This chapter describes processes for creating a supply chain strategy, referred to here as the "how," that is consistent with the company's strategic direction, the "what." Activity systems define the supply chain processes needed to fulfill the strategy.

The supply chain strategy defines the role for operations shaped by corporate strategies. Section 4.2 described tools and techniques for developing a supply chain strategy; this chapter describes how to use those tools. The strategy should set clear objectives for supply chain operations. However, the strategy needed to guide supply chain design may not be fully defined. The absence of a formal strategy need not impede a supply chain effort if managers choose to move ahead. However, best practice demands that a project team gather as much information about the desired direction as possible.

Figure 12.1 is a flowchart for *Task 1 Develop a Supply Chain Strategy*, showing eight project processes for developing the supply chain strategy. This edition, like the latest *Guide to the Project Management Body of Knowledge (PMBOK Guide)*, has adopted verb–noun formats for process names; for example, "develop a strategy" has replaced "strategy development." This chapter describes the inputs, process elements, and outputs for the processes in Figure 12.1, following the format described in Table 11.1. The following sections list each process by section number. The number in parenthesis is the process number that follows our process numbering convention shown in Table 11.2. Appendix A contains summaries of all SCM project processes with their outputs and Appendix B gives recommendations for organization assignments for each project process.

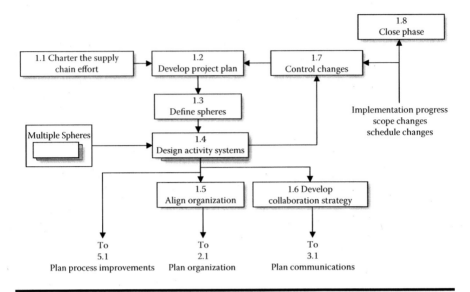

Figure 12.1 Develop a supply chain strategy.

12.1 Charter the Supply Chain Effort (1.1)
12.2 Develop Project Plan (1.2)
12.3 Define Spheres (1.3)
12.4 Design Activity Systems (1.4)
12.5 Align Organization (1.5)
12.6 Develop Collaboration Strategy (1.6)
12.7 Control Changes (1.7)
12.8 Close Phase (1.8)

Processes 1.1 through 1.6 lie in the domain of SCM knowledge and practice. *1.7 Control Changes* is a *PMBOK Guide* monitoring and controlling process. *1.8 Close Phase* is in the *PMBOK Guide*'s closing process group and applies to each phase as well as project closure after the last phase is complete. These two processes will be covered in this chapter because they are logically associated with the necessary strategy setting that guides the total project.

12.1 Charter the Supply Chain Effort (1.1)

Table 12.1 summarizes the chartering process that sets expectations for the entire supply chain project. In fact, many consider chartering to be the most important project process. The "Inputs" columns in Table 12.1 lists documents and other substantive items that guide chartering the project. Insights provided by these inputs best assure alignment of the supply chain project with the organization's strategic initiatives. The process definition also includes gathering the inputs needed to define the issues that the project should address. A running list of project issues is valuable for establishing project scope and keeping track of progress. One measure of project completion is progress in addressing these issues. When the issues are all addressed, the project is near completion.

12.1.1 *Inputs to* 1.1 Charter the Supply Chain Effort *(1.1.1)*

The purpose of inputs is to understand what strategic planning (the "what") requires of supply chain features (the "how"). If documentation is lacking, ideas may be lodged in the minds of managers representing a number of functions. Examples include executive management (chief executive officer [CEO], chief operating officer [COO]), marketing and sales, engineering, and operations. A supply chain project team should elicit as much participation as possible in chartering the project. The following inputs are suggestions that may be delivered in document, presentation, or brainstorming formats. The fastest way, in the absence of formal documents, could be an off-site session to surface issues and expectations for the role of supply chain design in addressing those issues.

12.1.1.1 *Customer and Product Briefing*

This input defines for planners what customer/product combinations are in the project scope. Section 4.2.1 describes ways to portray these combinations. These include the position of products within their life cycle—inception, growth, maturity, or decline. Each phase makes different demands on supply chain design. Another concept described in Section 4.2.1 is the idea of innovative and functional products. Innovative products require a responsive supply chain. Functional products require a cost-effective one. Mismatching the type of supply chain with the product is a common mistake. Also, the customers and products in the project scope need not be limited to the current ones. New products and targeted segments should also be addressed.

Desired information includes sales by major product or product group to each identified market segment. Ideally, it should also include market share, key success factors in the market, and strengths and weaknesses of competitors. In the sections that follow, "external" indicates that the input comes from documentation and other sources outside the supply chain project; these inputs are shown in plain type. "Internal" inputs, shown in italics, come from other tasks inside the project.

12.1.1.2 *Strategy (External)*

The external strategy covers formal or informal plans for becoming a more effective competitor. Understanding the plan will go a long way toward identifying initiatives that can be supported by better supply chains. If the strategy requires supply chain projects, the requirements should also be listed and documented to

Table 12.1 Charter the Supply Chain Effort (1.1)

1.1.1 Inputs		1.1 Charter the Supply Chain Effort	Initiating
		1.1.2 Process Elements	1.1.3 Outputs
Customer and Product Briefing (external) • Business forecasts • Customer requirements • Profitability • Relative competitive performance Strategy (external) • New product plans • Product sought/desired deliverables • Strategic plan and objectives (the "what")	**Process definition**	Authorizes the project. Links the supply chain project with other efforts. Start the process of listing issues.	*SCM Charter Elements* • Assumptions • Change management considerations • Constraints • Project authorization • Updated issues list *Project Management Charter Elements* • Project management assignments (project management, PMO, project team members) • Project change procedures
	Approaches and techniques	Group meetings to discuss the potential role SCM (the "how") can play in strategy (the "what") execution.	
	PM shortcomings addressed	Well-designed charters should mitigate the consequences of rigidity, organization roadblocks, and top management abrogation. Linkage of projects to strategy is key to higher levels on the PMMM. In particular, Level 3 calls for reliance on project management to implement strategy. Chartering addresses the initiation process in *PMBOK Guide*'s Project Scope Management knowledge area.	
	SCM maturity	Narrow charters lead to Stage II or III. Broader charters lead to Stage IV or V (Table 10.5)	

Environmental Briefing (external)	**Terminology**	Business model	Charter	
• Change drivers		Economic value added	Manufacturing strategy	• Decision-making authority
• Governance structure		Issue, issues list	Steering committee	• Deliverables required
• Historical perspective		Target costing	Trigger events	• Responsibilities
• Product/process technology background		Value chain	Voice of the customer	• Schedule objectives
• Issues (internal)	**Stakeholders**	Senior management, through the company steering committee, should be responsible for the charter. A project manager could be assigned to speed the process. Functional managers/department heads should provide viewpoints on the charter.		• Steering committee assignments
• Initial list of issues				

the extent possible, according to the model described in Section 4.2.2 and shown in Figure 4.4. That figure shows six types of projects based on whether they are strategic or non-strategic and at what level they are—functional, business unit, or supply chain. Of course, it is quite possible that there's no mention of the supply chain in the company strategy. This is not an unusual situation but missions for the supply chain must be developed as part of the project if it's to support the strategy. Development of activity systems is the recommended way to fill this hole.

12.1.1.3 Environmental Briefing (External)

The environmental briefing should define other outside issues. These can be from key functions. For example, an engineering vice president can speak on product and process technology. A marketing vice president can address plans for penetrating a new overseas market. The chief financial officer (CFO) can describe financial constraints and opportunities. Drivers for supply chain change, described in Chapter 3, should also be addressed. This input might come from the CEO or COO.

12.1.1.4 Issues (Internal)

An effective way to achieve focus on a project's scope is to maintain a running list of issues. Issues are defined by questions that arise at any point in the project. The list can grow to dozens, even hundreds, of issues. Theoretically, when all the scope questions posed through the issues have been addressed, supply chain project planning is complete. By selecting or rejecting questions as "in scope" or "out of scope," the project team, particularly the project manager and the company steering committee, is expanding or shrinking the project's boundary.

Each issue should receive a name and include three parts: the issue stated as a question or questions, background on the issue needed to explain how it surfaced, and any decisions related to the issue as they are made. Those decisions can resolve the issue or identify further steps to achieve resolution. The following example, from the risk analysis case in Section 7.3.8, illustrates.

Issue Name: Transportation Network in China	
Question(s)	Is the existing network suitable for distributing our products? Should we develop a new network? How much would developing a new network cost?
Background	Profitability of our products in the Chinese market will depend on our effectiveness in reaching targeted customers. Existing transportation is problematic in China for our type of product. A risk analysis shows that developing a new network is attractive, but our board of directors will be reluctant to make the required investment.

Decision	We need to strengthen the case for investing in the transportation network by doing further studies of the market potential and identifying supply chain partners that can provide the needed transportation services.

Because the issues list can be a long one, issue categories are useful. Consider the following alphabetical list of candidate categories:

- Customers/markets: Customer requirements that affect product and supply chain design.
- Decision making: Availability and accuracy of information.
- External constraints: Conditions that limit supply chain options for the company.
- Finance: Financing and cash flow considerations. Includes justification processes.
- Infrastructure/capacity: Physical plant—buildings and equipment, locations.
- Internal relations: The role of the supply chain organization with respect to other company divisions.
- Organization: Operating functions performed by the supply chain organization and its business partners and their assignment.
- Processes: Supply chain processes required to provide base and extended products.
- Staff: Questions regarding the number and/or skill levels of staff members.
- Technology: Product and process technology and its capability, cost, and reliability in service.

Supply chain planners should choose categories that fit their situations and add others as needed. A database tool is useful for updating issues, making changes, and issuing reports that communicate status. Periodically, the project manager should update the issues list. This will close some issues that are resolved and will open others for creation of new project tasks.

12.1.2 Process Elements for 1.1 Charter the Supply Chain Effort (1.1.2)

This section describes aspects of chartering that recognize the special characteristics of a supply chain improvement project. Section 7.3.1 identified integration, the project management knowledge area, as being one requiring high levels of supplemental SCM knowledge and practice. This is due to the strategic nature of SCM projects and the fact that supply chain projects can cross company boundaries.

12.1.2.1 Process Definition for 1.1 Charter the Supply Chain Effort

The chartering process, as shown in Table 12.1, should gain approval of the project, link the supply chain project with other projects, and define initial issues for project coverage. Section 7.3.1 and Section 7.3.2 list integration and planning elements. Project drivers listed in Section 7.3.2 include market demand, an internal requirement to improve performance, a specific customer request, or a product or process technology advance. The charter should document the motivators for the project. The list in Table 7.2 and the supply chain driving forces described in Chapter 3 support this documentation.

12.1.2.2 Approaches and Techniques for 1.1 Charter the Supply Chain Effort

The charter is an essential first step. Gaining such a charter can be painful or relatively easy, often depending on the level of management issuing the charter. A group meeting of key stakeholders is sometimes sufficient to start a project. At other times, getting off the ground can take months. The charter is complete when the planning team that includes the steering committee and the project manager/office has the input they need to plan the project (*Process 1.2 Develop Project Plan*). The business-unit executive and company steering committee members should sign the charter.

12.1.2.3 Project Management Shortcomings Addressed by 1.1 Charter the Supply Chain Effort

A strong charter decreases the chances of encountering "showstoppers" like those listed in Chapter 9 that jeopardize project success. These include lack of flexibility in changing the direction of the project, organization roadblocks, top management abrogation, inadequate technical capability, and misunderstood technology. Flexibility is introduced if the charter calls for periodically synchronizing the project with changes in the environment. Organization clout counts; the charter from an executive in a strong position will reduce the chances of organization roadblocks. Of course, not getting a charter from that level is a signal that the project must be narrowly focused or does not have executive backing.

12.1.2.4 SCM Maturity for 1.1 Charter the Supply Chain Effort

The charter should be explicit regarding the reach of the supply chain project. Section 4.2.2 described the three possible levels: functional, business unit, and supply chain. The broader the project, the more complex it becomes. Counteracting that, there may be an advantage in pursuing a broader project as long as the scope doesn't exceed the project team's capabilities. Broader scopes correspond with higher levels, Level III and above, of SCM maturity, as defined in Section 10.3 and shown in Table 10.3.

12.1.2.5 Terminology for 1.1 Charter the Supply Chain Effort

Glossary terms for the chartering process focus on strategic planning. The supply chain project is an extension of the organization's overall strategy. In fact, it may be the centerpiece of that strategy if the company requires operational excellence to be competitive.

12.1.2.6 Stakeholders for 1.1 Charter the Supply Chain Effort

Chartering should involve top management in the sponsoring organization, the project manager, the project team if assigned, and functional managers. The charter is an announcement of the project. Internal stakeholders and involved partners should comprehend and accept, if not support, the charter. Appendix B recommends that the company steering committee approve the charter; the project manager should supervise its development.

12.1.3 Outputs from 1.1 Charter the Supply Chain Effort (1.1.3)

The charter should include two deliverables. The first deals with the supply chain aspects of the project; the second with the project management elements. Table 12.1 lists components of the deliverables. These two deliverables need not be separate documents. However, they might be prepared by different people in the project office—one with supply chain expertise and another with project management expertise.

12.1.3.1 SCM Charter Elements

Suggestions for the supply chain portion of the charter include assumptions, change management considerations, constraints, an updated issues list, and the project charter. This package should contain any inputs to the project management team that the authorizing authority wants conveyed. Changes to *SCM Charter Elements* may occur during the course of the project. *Change Management Considerations* contain guidance regarding anticipated ways of communicating and gaining acceptance of changes from the internal organization and supply chain partners.

12.1.3.2 Project Management Charter Elements

The listing of project management charter elements in Table 12.1 should signal management expectations for the project. This includes assignment of a company steering committee to oversee progress, be responsible for key decisions, and retain responsibility for project success. This steering committee, at the strategy-setting stage, is internal. Later, a multicompany steering committee should address cross-company issues. If it hasn't been decided, another important structural output is identification of the project manager or the project office.

12.2 Develop Project Plan (1.2)

Table 12.2 summarizes the project plan development processes. This process takes chartering inputs (Process 1.1) and converts them into concrete plans for proceeding. This process corresponds with the *PMBOK Guide's Develop Project Management Plan* process in the *Project Integration Management* knowledge area. The project plan is the document containing project scope and needed resources. As such, it draws on several project management knowledge areas:

- *Project Scope Management* including Collect Requirements, Define Scope, Verify Scope, and Control Scope. Scope changes are addressed in *1.7 Control Changes*.
- *Project Time Management* including the processes of Define Activities, Sequence Activities, Estimate Durations, Estimate Resources, and Develop Schedules. We also address schedule changes in *1.7 Control Changes*.
- *Project Cost Management* including Estimate Costs and Determine Budgets. Control Costs is also part of *1.7 Control Changes*.
- *Project Quality Management* including Plan Quality and Perform Quality Assurance. Quality control is also part of *1.7 Control Changes*.
- *Project Human Resource Management* including Develop Human Resource Plan, Acquire Team, Manage Team, and Develop Team. The process templates suggest roles for SCM management and project teams throughout the processes.
- *Project Communications Management* including Identify Communications, Plan Communications, Distribute Information, Manage Stakeholder Expectations, and Report Performance. Administrative Closure is part of *1.8 Close Phase*.
- *Project Risk Management* including Plan Risk Management, Identify Risks, Perform Qualitative Analysis, Perform Quantitative Analysis, Plan Risk Responses, and Monitor and Control Risk.
- *Project Procurement Management* including Plan Procurements, Conduct Procurements, Administer Procurements, and Close Procurements.

If you want to supplement the SCM executing process described in this chapter and Chapters 13 through 15, you should draw on the *PMBOK Guide* and Chapter 6 and Chapter 7 for more information on approaches to address these knowledge areas.

12.2.1 Inputs for 1.2 Develop Project Plan *(1.2.1)*

The outputs of *1.1 Charter the Supply Chain Effort* are the inputs for this process. These include the SCM and Project Management Charter Elements described in the last section. These documents are primarily views external to the project, taking into account the organization's goals for success in its markets with the products it delivers. Careful scope planning should match the needs presented in the external view with a view of the company's supply chain. This supply chain view should include an honest assessment of how well one's supply chains are doing the job they need to do. The gap between these views defines the SCM project's scope.

12.2.2 Process Elements for 1.2 Develop Project Plan *(1.2.2)*

In this section, we assume our effort is a single SCM project. Chapter 6 observed that the SCM effort could be a "program" instead of a project. This is best if SCM is expected to go on for a long time with multiple intermittent projects. Alternatively, a project with several components may use "subprojects" to make the job more manageable. This process should address this structural issue—whether SCM is a "program" or a "project." As we proceed, we will call it a "project."

The core of our project plan is scope definition. The *PMBOK Guide* makes two distinctions regarding the definition of "scope." Product scope constitutes the products, services, or results produced by the project. A Work Breakdown Structure (WBS) is a way of displaying the products or deliverables of the project. Project scope is the work to be done to produce the products. The term "scope" encompasses both components.

12.2.2.1 Process Definition for 1.2 Develop Project Plan

There are many possible paths when defining the scope and content of a supply chain project. Supply chain projects can be defined in terms of any of the three definitions for the output of a project, a product, a service, or a result. The same SCM project can be defined as a product ("implement a distribution system in China") or as a service ("make sure our stores in China have our product") or as a result ("maximize our profitability in China"). Note that each level is broader in terms of scope and produces a product that will take longer to evaluate as a success or failure.

This insight reinforces the idea first presented in Section 9.2.1. That section pointed to lack of flexibility as a principal reason for project failures. The proposed solution was to treat projects like a new business venture rather than as a traditional project. Supporting recommendations, listed in Section 9.2.1, include dividing the project into short phases, providing incremental funding, making sure your best people are on the project, sharing risk and reward with partners, and paying for more information to lower risk.

Table 12.2   Develop Project Plan (1.2)

1.2.1 Inputs		1.2 Develop Project Plan	Planning
		1.2.2 Process Elements	1.2.3 Outputs
SCM Charter Elements (1.1)	**Process definition**	Develop operations and WBS to be included in the supply chain project. Produce activities, budgets, schedules, and assignments. Create additional issues. Develop a project vocabulary.	SCM Plan • Benefits expected
Project Management Charter Elements (1.1)	**Approaches and techniques**	Alternatives identification Communications with supply chain partners Cost–benefit and risk analysis Decomposition Modeling of supply chain operations Project selection and justification processes Work breakdown structure	• Enabling process evaluation • Functions covered • Partner policies
	PM shortcomings addressed	Rigidity, organization roadblocks are targets of better planning. Project plan development is fundamental to achieving Level 1 of PMMM. No project plan development is indicative of Level 0 maturity.	• Project vocabulary • Updated issues list
	SCM maturity	Willingness to define supply chain project broadly will lead to higher levels (IV and V) of the maturity model.	Project Management Plan • Activity list • Activity sequencing

Terminology	Activity	Cost baseline	• Approval to proceed
	Critical path	Decomposition	• Cost baseline
	Design team	IDEF	• Resource requirements
	Network diagram	Partner	
	Phase	Program	• Project phasing
	Progressive elaboration	Project	• Project schedule
	Project life cycle	Project office	
	Scope	Subproject	• Scope management plan
	Task	Work breakdown structure (WBS)	• WBS
Stakeholders	The company steering committee should oversee the project plan development. Candidates for the supply chain design team can support effort. Users of supply chain processes and key operating managers should be consulted		

12.2.2.2 Approaches and Techniques for 1.2 Develop Project Plan

Project plan development should consider the organization's level of maturity in terms of the Project Management Maturity Model (PMMM). It should also understand its business plan and the importance of the supply chain in fulfilling that plan. If SCM is vital and needs are urgent, the organization may have no choice but to pursue broader supply chain programs, Stage 3 and above in Table 10.3. Time may also be limited, affecting the schedule and level of resources required. Often, there is a range of choices available. In these cases, the tools described here will be useful.

A good start is identifying the alternatives. How do we frame the project—as a product, a service, or a result? How much discretion do we give to the project team? What phasing do we see? This will determine how frequently the project team returns for progress reviews and renewal of their charter. Alternative WBSs like that in Figure 6.4 can represent different product alternatives. This defines the deliverables of the project and can mirror project phases. Operations coverage could rely on Supply-Chain Operations Reference-model (SCOR-model) or the Council of Supply Chain Management Professionals' (CSCMP) *Supply Chain Management Process Standards (Process Standards)* process elements including planning, execution, and enable processes. Threads, a SCOR tool, can tie these processes together in high-level flowcharts. Because scoping is "top-down," decomposition can provide added levels of detail as necessary.

Talking to partners is a way of communicating intent and gaining commitments to broader scope projects. If partners are unable or unwilling to work with you, then your scope will be limited to your own organization. Modeling, cost–benefit analysis, and risk analysis are other tools to analyze alternatives. Section 7.3.8 provided an example of risk analysis. Activity-based costs can be quickly constructed for the purpose of scope planning and project justification.

12.2.2.3 Project Management Shortcomings Addressed by 1.2 Develop Project Plan

Project management failures due to rigidity and organization roadblocks can be anticipated by project plan development. Too broad a scope may exceed the organization's capability to implement the project. The fact that project scope is planned at all is indicative of Level 1 in the PMMM, shown in Table 5.2. If the project is to go beyond the organization's boundary, Level 3, a singular methodology, is necessary.

12.2.2.4 SCM Maturity for 1.2 Develop Project Plan

The scope definition directly reflects the maturity level reached by the organization's management team, as shown in Table 10.5. Stage III is indicative of a company ready to undertake cross-functional projects inside its own walls, even if those projects are limited in scope. At Stages IV and V, a multicompany group might make, review, or approve scope decisions.

12.2.2.5 Terminology for 1.2 Develop Project Plan

Terms listed in Table 12.2 describe project management terms encountered in project plan development. The scope will also indicate how the project might be completed, what it will take in resources, and how ambitious its effort will be.

12.2.2.6 Stakeholders for 1.2 Develop Project Plan

Senior management, represented on the company steering committee, has an important stake in scope development. As the example of the China distribution issue in Section 12.2.2.1 indicates, alternative scope definitions will produce vastly different projects. Different scenarios call for a wide range of staff resources, technical skills, money for the project, and time to complete the effort. The company steering committee should also include operations managers who will operate the redesigned processes; of course, those charged with carrying out the project are key stakeholders as well. The project manager or office will be charged with executing the project. A strategy design team from inside the company will be in charge of identifying and designing new supply chain processes. Scope definition may be an appropriate time to enlist partners in the project. This interaction will likely provide important insights about how to proceed and how far the project can go in implementing changes.

12.2.3 Outputs from 1.2 Develop Project Plan *(1.2.3)*

The outputs, SCM and project management plans, correspond to the input charters, as shown in Table 12.2. An essential element is whether the supply chain coverage will be functional, business unit, or supply chain in scope. From the project management point of view, the output should define the products and, to the extent possible, the traditional project planning and control elements common to any project. This includes phasing, participation, and governance. These will call on the project management knowledge areas listed at the beginning of this process description. Examples are Project Time Management for the *Project Schedule* and Project Cost Control for the *Resource Requirements* section of the *Project Management Plan.*

The process of project plan development should raise more issues to be addressed by the project. The running list should document these. In the cases of issues that are resolved in the process, project planners should document the resolution.

12.3 Define Spheres (1.3)

Table 12.3 summarizes the *Define Spheres* process. The rationale for spheres was introduced in Section 4.4.1. In summary, many organizations operate a "one size

Table 12.3 Define Spheres (1.3)

1.3.1 Inputs		1.3 Define Spheres	Executing
		1.3.2 Process Elements	*1.3.3 Outputs*
Customers and Products Briefing Strategy Environmental Briefing Issues SCM Plan (1.2)	**Process definition**	Define spheres, market–product–operations combinations, which warrant separate supply chain designs. Determine the enabling processes needed to support product-producing spheres.	*Enabling Process Definition* • Enabling processes needed
	Approaches and techniques	Market segmentation. Functional (sales, marketing, manufacturing, procurement, distribution) expertise. Group meetings.	*Supply Chain Sphere Definition* • Sphere definition
	PM shortcomings addressed	The use of spheres targets rigidity, organization conflicts, inadequate technical capability, and misunderstood technology. Spheres break down an overall supply chain project into "subprojects" where different designs suited to the sphere's business needs are implemented. A singular methodology (Level 3) supports multiple efforts.	• Nomination of sphere design teams for activity system development • Updated issues by enabling and product-producing sphere

SCM maturity	Using spheres as a basis for strategy moves the organization to Stage IV for Task 1 in the supply chain maturity model.	
Terminology	Branding	Business model
	Channel	Collaboration
	Customer-centric supply chain	Early manufacturing and supplier involvement
	Enable sphere	Extended product
	Focused factory	Functional product
	Innovative product	Integration
	Kano model	Manufacturing strategy
	Product-centric supply chain	Product-producing sphere
	Project life cycle	Representative product
	Segmentation	Sphere
Stakeholders	The supply chain design team should be responsible. The company steering committee should approve the choices. Users of supply chain processes and key operating managers can support the definition. Support functions like IT, finance, and facilities should also provide guidance.	

fits all" supply chain. Supply chain design takes the form of functions like procurement, manufacturing, and distribution working in departmental "silos." The design is seldom the result of a conscious decision but one born of long-time habits like striving for cost reductions in each of the functions.

If the supply chain designer took a "clean sheet" approach, it is doubtful that the present supply chain structure, including processes and organization, would be the result. Except in the smallest organizations, it is unlikely the ideal situation would be a single supply chain for all the company's product–market combinations. This process, *Define Spheres*, is necessary to either validate the current single supply chain or identify the need for multiple supply chains, each with a separate design, that can include activities and processes, organization, information systems, and measures.

A supply chain "sphere" is a three dimensional market/product/operations combination. The market can be specific customers or a customer segment. A segment, for our purposes, is a group of customers with the same preferences and buying behavior. The product is a single product category or a group of products consumed by the market. Operations include the factories, suppliers, distributors, retail outlets, warehouses, support organizations, and transportation links needed to produce the product or products for the markets.

Sphere design entails making choices about serving customer segments. A company that pursues too many spheres (likely more than four to six) is spread too thin. That company should combine the spheres or drop some low-profit customer segments, reducing the number of spheres. This is a difficult choice in a company driven by sales growth.

There are two types of sphere. An enable sphere serves other product-producing spheres that are centered on customer segment or products. Figure 12.2 shows the relationships between these two types of spheres. Product-producing spheres can be customer-centric or product-centric, depending on their focus. An example is Nike's shift from an organization based on products (apparel, shoes, etc.) to one based on individual sports (golf, tennis, running, etc.), a market focus.

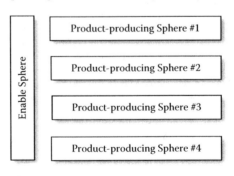

Figure 12.2   Relationship between product-producing and enable spheres.

12.3.1 Inputs for 1.3 Define Spheres *(1.3.1)*

Table 12.3 shows the inputs for *Define Spheres*. These should identify segments served and provide an understanding of their needs. The *SCM Plan* from Process 1.2 is also important to this process. It provides a mission statement for the project and defines what parts of the supply chain are in scope and out of scope. Also important is an understanding of market position and needs for improvement in supply chain operations. Documents developed for *1.1 Charter the Supply Chain Effort* are useful here. The running list of issues will help in defining spheres.

12.3.2 Process Elements for 1.3 Define Spheres *(1.3.2)*

Consulting experience indicates that this process, or its equivalent, is seldom performed. This is a direct result of a Stage I and Stage II SCM maturity (Table 10.5). Companies make major investments in facilities, systems, new businesses, and equipment with too little attention to their fit in the overall supply chain. Also absent is any thought that the SCM project might change the organization's structure. The consequence is an effort that fails for lack of support from its own people. So, this process is vital in creating a new way of thinking about the business, leading to better decisions and avoiding disappointment, if not catastrophe.

12.3.2.1 Process Definition for 1.3 Define Spheres

The process takes what is probably a single supply chain and divides it into customer-centric, product-centric, or enable spheres. These spheres are distinct enough to warrant customized activity systems developed in the next process. A likely outcome is definition of two to seven product-delivery spheres and a single enable sphere. The enable sphere contains activities that are shared among the product-delivery spheres. Table 12.4 provides examples of spheres. Note that operations aren't limited to those inside the organization. Upstream and downstream partners' operations should also be included the definitions.

12.3.2.2 Approaches and Techniques for 1.3 Define Spheres

Developing spheres is an art. A team, identified in Appendix B as a sphere design team, is best when team members have an understanding of the markets, products, and operations within the project's scope. Asking a series of questions about the company's business is a logical approach. In addition to knowledge of the business, access to data on operations and profitability will certainly help. The following paragraphs provide examples of questions that might be asked in the process of defining spheres.

Table 12.4 Sphere Examples

Company	Markets	Products	Operations
Car company	Affluent customers	SUVs, luxury sedans	Flexible plants for SUVs and large cars, high-end dealers.
Contract machine shop	Customers desiring one day lead times	High volume products	Short cycle manufacturing cell, finished goods inventory, WIP buffer inventory, customer service center.
Personal computer products firm	Customers desiring the latest technology whatever the price	Stage 2 life cycle products (new microprocessor, premium price, latest features)	Flexible manufacturing cells designed to be responsive to changes in demand, lots of inventory in the distribution network, and supplier contracts calling for fast response.
	Customers wanting a "capable" machine at a lower price	Stage 3 life cycle products (older technology, heavily discounted price, value-seeking customers)	Functional manufacturing cells focused on efficiency, low-cost distribution network, supplier contracts emphasizing cost.
Capital equipment aftermarket parts distributor	All markets/customers	All products supported	Selection and business arrangement negotiation with suppliers for high-value commodity groups, supplier certification, and supplier performance measurement.

Markets

1. Does your company serve different market segments? If yes, list the segments. (If no, then the supply chain design will not depend on market segmentation. Skip to Question #4.)
2. Do the segments make different demands on supply chain design? (If yes, then your segments require different market-centric supply chain designs.)
3. Do segments differ in profitability or have the potential to be profitable? (If some aren't profitable or produce very little profit, they might be ignored in terms of catering to them with a specialized supply chain.)

In general, a segment has to pass two tests: have different needs (#2) and be profitable or have the potential to be profitable (#3) to justify a market-centric supply chain design. An exception is the case of a project mission to turn an unprofitable product into a profitable one.

Products

4. Do products or product lines differ in terms of profitability? If so, why is one product more profitable? Note that Question #3 assesses market, not product, profitability. Group products by profitability. Profitability is measured by either gross margin per unit sold or by total gross margin produced (unit profit margin multiplied by the number sold).
5. Do products or product lines require different production capabilities? If so, group the products by the production capabilities they require.

The questions yield four categories of products based on high/low profit and unique/common processes. A product or product group must be either more profitable or have different production requirements to be considered for a distinct market-centric or product-centric sphere.

Operations

6. Do different operations (including key suppliers and distribution channels as well as your own operations) specialize in producing specific products? (If so, group the operations by the products they produce.)
7. What is the capacity and current utilization of each of the operations? (Allocate the utilized capacity to the product groups.)

To consider dedicating an operation (e.g., facility, work cell, distribution channel, or supplier capability) to a market-centric or product-centric sphere, operations must be specialized; capacity considerations must make it attractive; and market segment and/or product requirements must make it necessary.

Sphere definition for product-producing spheres will likely reflect one of three themes: functional, product-centric, or customer-centric, depending on the answers to the questions posed here. An enable sphere should capture important activities like ENABLE process elements in the SCOR-model or the CSCMP's *Process Standards* addressed in Section 8.3.2.

12.3.2.3 Project Management Shortcomings Addressed by 1.3 Define Spheres

Sphere definition adds flexibility to the project since supply chain solutions are tailored to market–product groups with different needs. A sphere acts as a "firewall" reducing the risk of being "whipsawed" by changing requirements during the project. Problems in developing one sphere need not affect progress in another. A program for enabling elements also assures that the backbone structure is available to serve product-producing spheres. Organization design is a by-product of sphere definition. The sphere approach to organization substitutes the sphere's goals for those of functional departments. One of the lessons of failed projects, described in Section 9.3, is that organization goal misalignment is a major pitfall.

Technology solutions can also match a particular sphere's requirements. The whole supply chain project need not be held hostage to a technology needed in one sphere. One basis for sphere identification can even center on a technology capability. Thus, one sphere might embrace Internet channels where business is conducted online. Another sphere might comprise traditional brick-and-mortar channels. Examples in the personal computer markets include Dell's turning to stores alongside its famed direct model. Lenovo, who purchased IBM's ThinkPad line, has global market-centric supply chains dedicated to large institutional buyers, small retailers in less developed countries, and large retailers in slower growth mature markets.

Breaking the supply chain into spheres does increase project complexity. In a way, if there are three spheres, there may be triple the amount of project management activity and other work required. However, spheres help assure that the right things are being done but there will be more project activity to assure they are done right. At this stage, project managers may want to spin off subprojects to control implementation in individual spheres.

12.3.2.4 SCM Maturity for 1.3 Define Spheres

Differentiating one's supply chain to achieve competitive advantage is characteristic of Stages IV and V (Table 10.5) of SCM maturity for building strategic supply chains (Task 1). The spheres are also the foundation for the execution of the other tasks: Organization alignment through internal collaborative relationships (Task 2) is based on the demands of specific spheres. Collaboration with partners (Task 3) follows as well; suppliers and customers may be engaged for overall improvement. The activity systems for each sphere will define the processes that need to be done well, many of which will employ information technology (Tasks 4 and 5).

12.3.2.5 Terminology for 1.3 Define Spheres

Terms shown in Table 12.3 refer to different ways to create spheres. For example, separate spheres might be created for innovative and functional products (Section 4.2.1). This is consistent with the idea that innovative products require responsive supply chains and functional products require cost-effective ones. Another basis for spheres is making splits based on the product life cycle. New products might have one sphere, growth products another, and mature products another still. Material sources and internal operations are also possible foundations for spheres. Extended product features are a driver of supply chain change. The activity system should identify what processes are needed to provide extended product features that accompany a product line or serve a market segment.

12.2.2.6 Stakeholders for 1.3 Define Spheres

Since spheres are likely to play an important role in reorganizing the reporting structure, all managers have an interest in the outcome of the sphere definition process. A common result is the broadening of responsibilities for some and narrowing of responsibilities for others. The company steering committee, which is ultimately responsible, will have to reassign people and perhaps their own members based on sphere decisions.

The supply chain design team is also an important stakeholder because it develops the sphere design for approval by the company steering committee. Creation of spheres raises project management complexity and may force the company steering committee to make choices for moving ahead, focusing on high-priority efforts and delaying low-priority ones. Support functions that provide enabling services will see their roles change. This is due to different demands from managers in product-producing spheres. In essence, support activities that catered to functional departments will now provide services to managers in spheres that look at the world differently than functional department managers.

12.3.3 Outputs from 1.3 Define Spheres (1.3.3)

Outputs consist of sphere definitions for both enabling and product-producing spheres. Table 12.4 provides examples of the format. The top four are product-producing spheres. The last is an enable sphere. In this case, the enable sphere is a central sourcing function that identifies and negotiates agreements with top-tier suppliers. The activity focuses on top commodities where such arrangements have the greatest impact on the company's material spend. Another deliverable of the process is an update of the issues list. The update should show the resolutions of issues as they occur and the additions of others that have emerged from sphere definition.

12.4 Design Activity Systems (1.4)

Section 4.2.3.2 provided background on activity systems and how a design team develops them. Summarizing, activity systems are "networks" of operating processes, including those we associate with the supply chain. Competitive advantage increases when multiple activities and their associated processes support each other. For example, in Figure 4.5, an expert scheduling application supports a build-to-order activity. The impact of linked activities is greater than the sum of its parts. Although a competitor might replicate individual activities, they will find it much more difficult to copy a network of activities.

Activity systems for each sphere identified in Process 1.3 will enhance the job of project planning for implementation. Enhancement comes because, through spheres, the total SCM effort carries on in smaller pieces that are more easily prioritized. The organization is less likely to be dragged into a major, "world peace"-type project, one of the root causes for project failure described in Chapter 9. This process may also produce changes in the SCM project scope, managed through *1.7 Control Changes*.

The activity system tool is particularly amenable to group design. The concepts behind the tool are easy to understand, and experts knowledgeable of sphere issues can best conceive the activity and processes for that sphere. In Appendix B, the sphere design team is chartered with design of an activity system in a sphere. These teams are distinguished from the supply chain design team.

12.4.1 Inputs for 1.4 Design Activity Systems (1.4.1)

The principal input for *1.4 Design Activity Systems*, as shown in Table 12.5, is the sphere definition from Process 1.3. There will be two types of spheres: product-producing and enable. Product-producing spheres have external customers. Enable processes have internal customers, the product-producing spheres. Enable spheres provide the infrastructure for ENABLE processes like those in the SCOR-model and the CSCMP's *Process Standards* as well as other shared processes defined in the project. The last example in Table 12.4 is an enable sphere.

12.4.2 Process Elements for 1.4 Design Activity Systems (1.4.2)

Activity systems constitute a vision for future operations. The sphere design teams should ignore any perceived constraints like political acceptability, the cost, current organization assignments, and the need for special skills. A good model is the "green-field" vision unconstrained by existing operations. Also, activity systems—in the supply chain spirit—should not be confined to one's own company. Encompassing the "supply chain," not just the business unit or single department, should release creative juices. Appropriate consultation with partners will be necessary as well.

12.4.2.1 Process Definition for 1.4 Design Activity Systems

1.4 Design Activity Systems should cover all the spheres produced in Process 1.3. A project team may be tempted to pick only one or two of these spheres for initial design, believing that the company can't handle all the spheres at once. This should be discouraged. Designing the requirements for all the spheres provides a complete vision of what needs to be done. With assembled requirements, priorities can be set for subprojects or high priority activities that warrant immediate attention; so, scope changes may be required, as indicated in Figure 12.1. After that, the company steering committee could decide to implement in selected spheres.

12.4.2.2 Approaches and Techniques for 1.4 Design Activity Systems

The process for developing activity systems, outlined in Section 4.2.3.2, is straight-forward and includes the following steps:

1. Pick attractive market segments for your products. This is done in *1.3 Define Spheres.*
2. Choose how to compete for attractive segments. For enable spheres, consider the "customer" to be the product-producing spheres.
3. Develop themes that require choices of how to compete to support each choice from Step #2. The themes are foundations for the activity system.
4. Design activities to support each theme. Activities define needed supply chain processes, which should also be listed. These will be the basis for process development or improvement.
5. Link the activities into the activity system. The links provide a difficult-to-duplicate barrier to competitors.

Supporting tools for the process include an understanding of customer requirements. The Quality Function Deployment (QFD) tool can capture and display these requirements. Benchmarking one's own processes against "best practice" companies or competitors is also helpful. This is where models like the SCOR-model and the CSCMP's *Process Standards* can contribute. Section 4.2.3.1 described how supply chain model metrics also support this approach by showing gaps in company performance that need to be filled.

Table 12.5 Design Activity Systems (1.4)

1.4.1 Inputs	1.4 Design Activity Systems		Executing
	1.4.2 Process Elements		1.4.3 Outputs
Supply Chain Sphere Definition (1.3)	**Process definition**	Develop a vision for operations to be conducted in each sphere. This involves choices on ways to compete and identifying relationships between activities.	*Activity System Designs* • Activity diagram • As-is understanding
Enabling Process Definition (1.3)	**Approaches and techniques**	Use of customer requirements in design. Activity systems. Benchmarking.	• Conceptual designs – Processes
Environmental Briefing	**PM shortcomings addressed**	Activity systems enable closer control of project scope (Level 2 in the PMMM) through the ability to set implementation priorities in spheres. They also enable short-cycle project implementation tasks that can be sequenced to produce fast results.	– Organization • Strategic themes/choices
Issues	**SCM maturity**	Activity systems that produce cross-functional projects and closer bonds with partners lead to higher levels of SCM maturity.	• Operational gaps • Processes related to activities

Terminology			• Subproject definition and priority • Sphere measures • Collaboration points *SCM Change Requests*
Activity system	Benchmarking	Category management	
Cellular manufacturing	Channel	Channel master	
Collaborative execution systems	Customer	Demand-driven supply chain	
Echelon	End user	Flexibility	
Functional organization	Greenfield vision	Order penetration point	
Partnership classification	Performance-based pricing	Price-taker	
Product tree	Quality Function Deployment (QFD)	Re-engineering	
Reverse logistics	Strategic sourcing	Supply chain strategy	
Stakeholders			
Sphere design teams should develop activity systems. Support functions needed to implement the activity systems should be represented on the teams.			

Table 12.6   Example Project Portfolio

Projects	Sphere	High Priority	Medium Priority	Low Priority
#1	•			
#2		•		
#3			•	
#4 (Enable)	•	•	•	

12.4.2.3 Project Management Shortcomings Addressed by 1.4 Design Activity Systems

An important by-product of defining spheres and developing activity systems is identification of competitive gaps and the efforts required to fill those gaps. This enables priority setting for implementing where resources are limited. Table 12.6 is a simple example of how project selection is facilitated where it is impossible to do everything at once. The table shows four projects, one for each of three product-producing spheres and one enabling project that applies to all three.

If the organization can only do two of the four projects in the near term, the two most viable alternatives appear to be the following:

Option #1: Project #1 and Project #4
Option #2: Project #1 and Project #2

Selection of Option #1 over Option #2 would depend on the benefits expected for Project #4 in all three spheres compared with the benefits from Project #2 in one sphere. The enable sphere implementation may also provide important infrastructure. Also to be considered are the cost of the projects, the timing of benefits, and the availability of resources. However, without spheres and the ability to define focused projects, the company might commit to too many projects or to a huge single project. The ability to make choices addresses the flexibility shortcoming described in Section 9.2. The recommended solution calls for project managers and steering committees to be "fast on their feet" by funding incremental improvements with measurable benefits.

12.4.2.4 SCM Maturity for 1.4 Design Activity Systems

A focused project portfolio will move the organization to higher levels of SCM maturity. By definition, efforts to fill gaps in activity system processes should move process improvement out of the Level 2 functional level into, at a minimum, the Level 3 business-unit level shown in Figure 4.4.

12.4.2.5 Terminology for 1.4 Design Activity Systems

Terms listed in Table 12.5 are likely to arise during activity systems design.

12.4.2.6 Stakeholders for 1.4 Design Activity Systems

The supply chain design team that defined the spheres should add to its ranks in developing the activity systems. The purpose is to gather the expertise needed in what goes on in a sphere. If resources are limited, the company steering committee may have to choose which projects it wants to pursue. Its job is more complex since the total supply chain effort has more components. Moving ahead isn't a "one-shot" chunk of work. Top management must stay involved since the total supply chain effort is more "granular" with many options available for picking and choosing projects. Since the activity systems define how the organization intends to operate, the work of most employees in those processes will change.

12.4.3 Outputs from 1.4 Design Activity Systems (1.4.3)

The principal outputs are activity systems designs. These should contain the items listed in Table 12.5.

- *Strategic themes/choices:* The foundations for the activity system design and why they were selected.
- *As-is understanding:* How current processes work and how well.
- *Activity diagrams:* Activities supporting the themes and their interrelationships. Figure 4.5 is an example. A list of existing or needed processes that support performance of an activity.
- *"Greenfield" conceptual (high-level) designs for processes and organizations:* What's expected of the processes and their inputs and outputs. Conceptual (high-level) organization design.
- *Sphere measures:* Measures of performance that should improve by implementing the projects.
- *Operational gaps:* Differences between where we are and where we want to be. A recommended format lists processes that are in place and operating satisfactorily, processes that are in place that aren't operating satisfactorily, and processes that need to be added.
- *Project definition and priority:* Initiatives in the form of separate projects or subprojects needed to close the gaps.

These outputs are the basis for all subsequent SCM tasks. Figure 12.1 reflects this by showing the flow of outputs to process improvement planning, organization planning, and communications planning. Communications planning addresses the information needs of partners and other stakeholders who must support the strategy. In addition, *1.4 Design Activity Systems* is likely to produce scope changes for the overall supply chain project. This output will return to *1.7 Control Changes*.

12.5 Align Organization (1.5)

1.5 Align Organization, summarized in Table 12.7, requires decisions to implement the conceptual organization design from *1.4 Design Activity Systems*. *1.5 Align Organization*'s purpose is to weigh alternatives, evaluate the current organization's capability, and produce a deliverable, *Organization Design*. This is a plan to be implemented as part of supply chain knowledge area Task 2 Implementing Collaborative Relationships.

12.5.1 Inputs for 1.5 Align Organization *(1.5.1)*

The principal input *is 1.4 Design Activity Systems* that contains high-level, conceptual designs of sphere processes and organizations. These cover both product-producing and enable spheres. The activity system will be accompanied by as much information as the sphere design teams are capable of producing. Items listed in Table 12.5 include processes, organization, metrics, gaps between the need and the current reality, and a tentative definition of subprojects needed to develop the capability. This process is not part of *1.4 Design Activity Systems* because it requires decisions from the senior management steering committee. These decisions address people-sensitive issues and require many trade-offs.

12.5.2 Process Elements for 1.5 Align Organization *(1.5.2)*

The Organization Design process is crucial to the success of the project. Should the organization structure be lacking or the people in it not committed, successfully implementing new processes will be impossible. To address this reality, in *2.1 Plan Organization* we recommend implementing organization changes before proceeding with process changes. This sequencing gives managers who must run the new processes a role in their design and implementation.

12.5.2.1 Process Definition for 1.5 Align Organization

This process produces an organization structure designed around the activity systems and their related processes. Each of those activity systems will contain one or more processes that need people to make them work. These people may be in product-producing sphere activities and processes. They may also be in enable-sphere processes serving the product-producing spheres. The company may also decide to

Table 12.7 Align Organization (1.5)

1.5.1 Inputs		1.5 Align Organization	Executing
		1.5.2 Process Elements	1.5.3 Outputs
Activity Systems Design (including organization conceptual design) (1.4) Issues	**Process definition**	Define the organization structure to support sphere activity systems. This includes both supply chain and supply chain enabling process execution. Confirm metrics to measure performance in each sphere.	Organization Design • Activity responsibilities— planning, execution, and enable processes from SCOR • Metrics • Skills needed • Structure
	Approaches and techniques	Organization design. Use of functional, product-centric, or customer-centric structure. Approaches such as the Balanced Scorecard. Benchmarking.	
	PM shortcomings addressed	Assigning implementation tasks to those who will run the processes leads to at least PMMM Level 1 in which the organization is aware of the need for project management. A new organization structure should remove organization roadblocks. Also, focused efforts to develop enabling processes should address shortcomings in technical capability and misunderstanding technology.	

(continued on next page)

Table 12.7 (continued)   Align Organization (1.5)

1.5.1 Inputs		1.5 Align Organization		Executing
		1.5.2 Process Elements		1.5.3 Outputs
	SCM maturity	This process will enable the organization to move to Stage III (cross-functional projects) and beyond to Stages IV or V.		
	Terminology	Balanced Scorecard	Customer-centric organization	
		Enable process	Functional organization	
		Focused factory	Product-centric organization	
		Supply chain orientation (SCO)		
	Stakeholders	This is a senior management process, executed by the supply chain design team under direction from the company steering committee. Most employees will be affected if the strategy changes roles and reporting relationships.		

outsource some staff capabilities. Confirmation of metrics, done in this process, will define organization roles more clearly. Since organization design in this process is a long-term "end state" structure, it is unlikely to be implemented all at once. Deciding just how implementation is phased is done in *2.1 Plan Organization*.

12.5.2.2 *Approaches and Techniques for* 1.5 Align Organization

The *1.3 Define Spheres* process produces conceptual designs for both future processes, in the form of activity descriptions, and organizations to support those processes. There will likely be different organizations and employee functions in each product-producing and enable sphere, depending on the needs of the processes. The design, at this stage, is a "clean sheet" or greenfield vision, including both structure and performance measures. Perhaps the most difficult aspect is deciding whether processes will be in the product-producing sphere, an enable support organization, or outsourced. Those functions in enable organizations will serve all product-producing spheres, as shown in Figure 12.2.

Where to place a responsibility is a decision driven by an assessment of how unique a requirement is to a product-producing sphere. Uniqueness argues for assigning the function to that product-producing sphere. Commonality among spheres argues for a supporting enable function. Supply chain capabilities available from third parties are candidates for outsourcing. To illustrate: A company providing aftermarket support for capital equipment chose the following enable functions; these supported several product-producing spheres serving different channels for aftermarket parts:

Enable Function	Reason
Continuous improvement/ Six Sigma	A consistent process for the whole business was desired.
Customer interfacing systems	A common interface solution for customer ordering was seen as efficient regardless of the channel.
Human resources	The parent corporation required standard practices.
Organization planning	This function resided with the business-unit executive.
Product configuration	All product spheres relied on similar configuration data. Product-producing spheres set priorities for documentation.

(continued on next page)

Enable Function	Reason
Replenishment order processing	A common system covered ordering of replacement parts from suppliers. Delivery of those parts to customers was assigned to product-producing spheres.
Return part refurbishment	Used parts for recycling from any sphere were handled by a common supply chain.
Sourcing/key supplier interface	All product spheres used common sources of supply.
Supplier quality	Material for all product-producing spheres came into the same facility where it was inspected and supplier performance (quality, delivery) was recorded.
Warehousing for incoming material	Central warehousing was more economical. The product-producing spheres did not have the volume to justify separate facilities. This was also considered an outsourcing candidate.

The same organization chose to assign the following functions to the product-producing spheres' delivery functions:

Product Delivery Function	Reason
Common parts requisitioning	The functions were in direct touch with customers. Equipment needs and country languages varied from customer to customer.
Custom parts purchasing	Items, unique to a sphere, were sourced and procured in the sphere.
Customer logistics	Part replenishment triggers and delivery service expectations varied among customer segments.
Customer service warehousing	Each customer contract had tailored requirements for staging parts for consumption.
Project management	Specialists were required to serve customer technical needs and maintenance needs.
Sales, customer requirements definition, bidding	Each service product provided by the organization required different customer logistics.
Warehousing for outgoing material	Each large contract had unique requirements with regard to location, parts carried, and service level requirements.

The two tables illustrate the thinking that must go into organization design. The most important point is to start with processes and activities and then build the organization chart. With basic decisions on where a function is to be performed, measures developed in *1.3 Define Spheres* should be confirmed.

12.5.2.3 Project Management Shortcomings Addressed by 1.5 Align Organization

Translating strategy into organization responsibilities should energize those who will play roles in new supply chains. This "wake-up call" should be an incentive to turn to formal project management techniques if not yet used. This is a criterion for PMMM Level 1 (Figure 5.2). This process addresses several of our project shortcomings described in Chapter 9. Aligning the organization with supply chain designs is fundamental to removing misaligned departmental goals. The need for enabling technologies like information systems are likely to be better understood by defining what holes the enable processes must fill. This could result in going outside for skills or altering plans or priorities to proceed with the skills available internally. Finally, because top management must be involved in organization alignment decisions, members of the steering committee will likely have personal stakes in supply chain project outcomes.

12.5.2.4 SCM Maturity for 1.5 Align Organization

Alignment of the organization, particularly into product-producing spheres, enables cross-functional efforts. It also creates a climate for exploring outside partnerships with customers and suppliers to implement strategy. This is characteristic of Stage III SCM maturity (Table 10.5) at least, establishing a basis for partnerships and multi-company process improvement initiatives.

12.5.2.5 Terminology for 1.5 Align Organization

Terms for this process characterize different ways of thinking about and structuring an organization.

12.5.2.6 Stakeholders for 1.5 Align Organization

The steering committee and the human resources function will actively perform this process, assisted by the supply chain design team. Most employees will be affected by an aggressive reorganization. At this stage, the most important stakeholders are those who will lead the spheres or "businesses inside the business." They will have to assemble teams from inside and outside the organization to staff their functions.

12.5.3 Outputs from 1.5 Align Organization (1.5.3)

The principal output, *Organization Design*, advances the conceptual design developed in *1.4 Design Activity Systems*. The product should be sufficient to draw an organization chart and a table mapping activities to these organization entities. Supply chain metrics will confirm objectives for the organization functions. This product will be handed off to the *2.1 Plan Organization* process to begin the organization transition.

12.6 Develop Collaboration Strategy (1.6)

Table 12.8 summarizes this process. A plan for implementing collaboration relies on *1.4 Design Activity Systems*. The strategy also calls for identifying a role for multicompany, or Stage III, steering committees. These multicompany steering committees are separate from the company steering committee that oversees the supply chain project inside the company. These steering committees are formed with senior management at one or more trading partners to facilitate joint collaborative decision making.

12.6.1 Inputs for 1.6 Develop Collaboration Strategy (1.6.1)

Sphere definition and activity system designs are the principal inputs to this process. There are likely to be several activity systems, one for each sphere. Candidate departments and trading partners for internal and external collaboration should be identified in the design.

12.6.2 Process Elements for 1.6 Develop Collaboration Strategy (1.6.2)

This process engages top management in the process of partnership development. To the extent the organization will rely on partnerships for strategy implementation, it will need the output of this process to guide its efforts. The supply chain design team will consult with sphere design teams in the preparation of the strategy.

12.6.2.1 Process Definition for 1.6 Develop Collaboration Strategy

Like *1.5 Align Organization*, this process defines the "rules of engagement" for collaboration during the supply chain project. Elements include necessary internal and trading partner collaboration. Internal collaboration covers department-to-department efforts as well as collaboration with other business units in the same corporation. Upstream partnerships are with suppliers; downstream partnerships are with distribution partners, customers, and end users. The basics of the collaboration strategy include the following:

What: Where is internal and external collaboration authorized, based on needs from the activity system designs?

Who: Which partners or partner groups—internal or external—require a collaborative effort? Is a multicompany steering committee needed? If so, how many—one for each partner or only one with several partners?

When: What are the priorities for collaboration and expectations for completing arrangements? Should there be both short- and long-term plans for collaboration efforts?

Where: Which internal organizations are responsible for executing the collaborations?

How: What is the shape of the effort in each case where collaboration is needed? This includes technology requirements, business arrangements, and products and services covered.

12.6.2.2 Approaches and Techniques for 1.6 Develop Collaboration Strategy

Section 4.3 described a classification methodology that addresses the "how" on the previous list. This "vocabulary" characterizes a partnership in terms of its purpose, direction, and choice. Purpose asks whether the partnership creates new "space" in the supply chain. If the answer is yes, roles along the supply chain will change. Bypassing a level of distribution is an example. Having a supplier provide assemblies rather than components is another.

Direction is either horizontal or vertical, or both. Vertical is a partnership in the direction of product flow in the supply chain. For a typical manufacturer, these partnerships are usually with suppliers, distributors, or customers. A horizontal partnership is with like functions. A consolidating industry "rollup" of organizations with like products and services is an example.

Choice reflects relative power in the partnership. A "one-to-many" choice reflects a strong partner, the "one," making a relationship where "many" choices were available. Figure 4.12 illustrated the concept. The form of interaction in the partnership can include four types. These range from simple exchanges of information to joint decision making, as shown in Figure 3.5.

12.6.2.3 Project Management Shortcomings Addressed by 1.6 Develop Collaboration Strategy

The process addresses most of the project management shortcomings described in Chapter 9. Definition of collaboration actions is a vehicle for organization

Table 12.8 Develop Collaboration Strategy (1.6)

1.6.1 Inputs	1.6 Develop Collaboration Strategy		Executing
	1.6.2 Process Elements		1.6.3 Outputs
Activity Systems Design (1.4)	**Process definition**	Develop the goals and objectives for collaborating with upstream and downstream partners. Define "space" to be created, process needs, and technology requirements.	Collaboration Strategy • Characterization of the supply and customer base
Issues	**Approaches and techniques**	Partnership classification (Section 4.3) and SCOR-model collaboration approaches (Section 8.4).	• Information requirements • New upstream and downstream roles
	PM shortcomings addressed	The strategy defines expectations for partner technical capability. It also develops the "how" for consideration in making supply chain links, reducing the risk of ineffective links.	• Technology requirements
	SCM maturity	The strategy will identify Stage III, IV, and V (Table 10.5) efforts involving partners. It communicates the need for outside-the-organization projects.	• Multicompany steering committee plan

Terminology		
	Core competence	Customer
	Demand chain	Downstream
	Early manufacturing and supplier involvement	Echelon
		Independent, dependent demand
	Extended product	Lean enterprise
	Integrated supply	Product-centric supply chain
	Price-taker	Strategic sourcing
	Stage 3 supply chain organization	Synchronized supply chain
	Supplier clustering	Upstream
	Target costing	
	Virtual enterprise	
Stakeholders	The supply chain design team, at the direction of the company steering committee, executes this senior management task. Major players in the supply chain will be affected. Those trading partners not selected may not receive long-term commitments.	

communication. Complex collaboration efforts, pulling in multiple departments and partners, will build the case for formal project management. A strategy for a multicompany steering committee captures the need for formal oversight of the joint project. Top management, represented by the company steering committee, must ratify the strategy, so it has their stamp of approval. Early development of the strategy should help remove organization roadblocks. A well-developed strategy includes consideration of alternatives, identification of appropriate technology, and timing of implementation. Communication with partners provides an early start in making sure the technology used matches process needs and partner technical capabilities.

12.6.2.4 SCM Maturity for 1.6 Develop Collaboration Strategy

The collaboration strategy bridges the space between the strategy, a Task 1 product, and Tasks 2 and 3 covering internal collaboration and external partnerships. For Task 2, this corresponds multicompany-level actions. The strategy is likely to contain a range of collaborative links best described as Stage II, III, IV, or V in Table 10.5, depending on the level of the link.

12.6.2.5 Terminology for 1.6 Develop Collaboration Strategy

Terms are those that might arise in developing and communicating the strategy internally and externally.

12.6.2.6 Stakeholders for 1.6 Develop Collaboration Strategy

The company steering committee will ratify the collaboration strategy. It need not develop it, however. This can be the role of the supply chain design team, assisted by the sphere design team that developed the activity system.

12.6.3 Outputs from 1.6 Develop Collaboration Strategy (1.6.3)

The strategy should communicate as much of the organization's collaboration intent as possible. Characterization of the supply and customer bases will frame recommended upstream and downstream collaboration. New roles may be planned for one's own company with or without the support of partners. Organization of the strategy report should be by activity system. If two or more activity systems have similar collaboration needs, the strategy should integrate these.

Linkages should recognize the information requirements of processes served by the collaborative arrangement. Much money is spent on collaboration technology tools. Some, if not most, as described in Chapter 9, are wasted. The strategy should address risk reduction in the development of these technology links. The best approach is to define closely the requirements for these technology links.

12.6.3.1 Characterization of the Supply and Customer Base

This portion of the collaboration strategy defines the "as-is" of the upstream and downstream components of the supply chain. The characterization should include summary information like the following:

- flowcharts of the supply chain within the sphere;
- numbers of suppliers/customers, amount of business done with each;
- type of current partnership using the framework described in Section 4.4.2;
- profitability of products and downstream markets;
- supplier ratings; and
- constraints and issues.

12.6.3.2 Information Requirements

This component should describe requirements up or down the supply chain. The format should describe the data, not the applications for delivering it. Examples of data requirements include the following:

- actual sales to end users;
- forecasts;
- product technical information;
- customer complaints/suggestions for improvement;
- financial information including cost and investment data;
- suggestions for improvement (those received to date/possibilities);
- test data and other quality information;
- performance targets (cost, quality, delivery, flexibility); and
- new or modified business rules.

12.6.3.3 New Upstream and Downstream Roles

Activity systems designs should produce ideas for new "space" in the supply chain. New space means new roles in the chain. The new roles may be assumed by one's own company, by an upstream or downstream partner, or a combination.

12.6.3.4 Technology

Technology refers to both product and process and includes information technology. Process technology could point to the need for investment by one's own company or a partner. Also, it can include manual or automated linkages. Alternatives should be identified, like a choice between sophisticated or simpler technology.

12.7 Control Changes (1.7)

Table 12.9 describes this process. It corresponds with the *PMBOK Guide's Perform Integrated Change Control* process. *PMBOK Guide,* in its integration knowledge area, pulls together all monitoring and control and the associated change management processes from other knowledge areas. These include scope, schedule, cost, quality, risk, and contract administration. This process takes change requests of any of the types from many sources and translates them into changes to the project plans developed in Process 1.2. If you want to supplement the control elements in this description, you should refer to the *PMBOK Guide.*

12.7.1 Inputs for 1.7 Control Changes (1.7.1)

Many circumstances in a supply chain project will generate change requests. For example, progress tracking and review meetings can show when the project is falling behind or moving ahead of schedule. Such a situation can generate a change in scope or schedule, or both. A change in the environment, or external situation, can also generate needs for change. Another source of change can be actual supply chain operating performance, a factor outside the execution of the project. An example is a quality problem at a supplier or a competitor's announcement of a new product or service. The situation may indicate a need to do something different, increase the focus on an issue needing attention, or change deliverables in the Work Breakdown Structure.

Trading partner relationships can also produce suggestions for scope changes. These can be explicit or implicit. Explicit changes take the form of written or spoken requests. Implicit changes lie in the ability or lack thereof of a partner to support a supply chain design. For example, if our own company seeks an elaborate technology solution but the partner can't support that technology, then a change is called for. The change can take the form of switching partners—if possible—or reducing the technology challenges called for in the plan.

12.7.2 Process Elements for 1.7 Control Changes (1.7.2)

This process sits at a major "crossroads" in the flow of project control information. It receives inputs from a variety of sources, generated for many reasons. Changes that are generated by the process affect many elements of the project, including scope, schedule, cost, and quality of project work.

12.7.2.1 Process Definition for 1.7 Control Changes

In these templates, changes can occur to either of two documents, the SCM Plan or the Project Management Plan. Both are generated in Process 1.2 and rely on many SCM and project management knowledge areas. Any single change request can deal with one or more of the project's aspects, including all SCM knowledge areas and project management concerns like those dealing with risk, schedule, and cost.

12.7.2.2 Approaches and Techniques for 1.7 Control Changes

1.7 Control Changes uses *PMBOK Guide* tools and techniques. These include a change control system, configuration management, performance measurement, and project management information systems. The need for formality will depend on the organization and its project management practices. The broad scope for most SCM projects highlights the need for more formal processes, characteristic of Level 3 maturity as defined in the PMMM (Section 5.2).

12.7.2.3 Project Management Shortcomings Addressed by 1.7 Control Changes

In Chapter 9, lessons learned pointed to rigidity in projects as a root cause for failure. The recommended solution is to be ready to change frequently. A company can't launch a project and forget it. A well-oiled change control process is needed to make ongoing adjustments. Such a process requires at least Level 2 maturity on the PMMM. Supply chain projects, where many spheres have been identified, also calls for responsiveness in processing changes. This is a strong motivation for Level 3 informal processes common to all projects.

12.7.2.4 SCM Maturity for 1.7 Control Changes

Supply chain trading partners will have valuable inputs for project changes. Changes at partners may also make the company more susceptible to changes because such changes are less controllable. This requires enhanced collaboration along the chain, characterized as Stages IV and V for Task 3 Forging Supply Chain Partnerships in SCM maturity (Table 10.5).

12.7.2.5 Terminology for 1.7 Control Changes

Terms listed in Table 12.8 are related to areas where project changes are likely to occur.

12.7.2.6 Stakeholders for 1.7 Control Changes

A project manager or the project office should administer this change process. The company steering committee should ratify important changes. Project planning should identify authority for making changes. Project participants—internal and external—will generate the change requests.

Table 12.9 Control Changes (1.7)

1.7.1 Inputs	1.7 Control Changes		Monitoring and Controlling
		1.7.2 Process Elements£	1.7.3 Outputs
Change Requests (1.4, 2.5 3.5, 3.7)	Process definition	The process incorporates both internally and externally generated changes. The changes can be to project products or the project work needed to produce them. SCM projects are expected to be dynamic with "progressive elaboration" causing ongoing changes in scope, phasing, and schedules.	Project Management and SCM Changes
Environmental Updates			• Corrective actions
Implementation Progress			• Project planning document updates
Partner Inputs	Approaches and techniques	Performance reporting using project management reporting techniques will indicate when the project is off plan. Special studies into root cause of variances may also accompany changes.	• Supply chain configuration changes
Performance Reports	PM shortcomings addressed	The process specifically addresses rigidity in project management. Integrated Change Control is necessary at Level 2 of the PMMM.	• WBS changes
Project Management Plan (1.2)	SCM maturity	To the extent partner inputs of project changes are considered, Stages IV and V are achieved.	
Review Meetings			
SCM Plan (1.2)			
Supply Chain Performance Measures			

Terminology	Cause and effect diagram	Certified supplier
	Charter	Cost baseline
	CPIO	Critical path
	Milestone	Optimization
	Process owner	Progressive elaboration
	Project life cycle	Project office
	Schedule baseline	Specification
	Steering committee	Work package
Stakeholders	The project manager/office oversees this process. All participants (internal and external) should be able to instigate and review project modifications.	

12.7.3 Outputs from 1.7 Control Changes *(1.7.3)*

The output of the process consists of changes to the project management and SCM plans developed in Process 1.2. Likely updates to other documents encompass the WBS, supply chain configuration, other project documents, and corrective actions. The latter are measures that will prevent a recurrence of a problem, assuring that future actions will be in line with the project plan.

12.8 Close Phase (1.8)

Project discipline calls for formal closure of a phase of the project and the entire project when all phases are completed or the project terminates. Table 12.10 summarizes the process involved in closing a phase or the project itself. This process corresponds to *Close Project or Phase* in the *PMBOK Guide.*

12.8.1 Inputs for 1.8 Close Phase

There is flexibility in deciding what phases are appropriate for a supply chain project. *1.2 Develop Project Plan* defines project phasing. Chapter 11 recommended the following phasing for initial consideration:

1. Supply Chain Strategy
2. Internal Alignment
3. Short-Term Improvement
4. Long-Term Improvement

The milestones that mark key points using this phasing arrangement are in Table 11.3.

12.8.2 Process Elements for 1.8 Close Phase (1.8.2)

The company steering committee should monitor deliverables and progress toward phase completion. This is one way to communicate and obtain stakeholder agreement that deliverables are complete. The project manager/office should administer the process and assure compliance with the project plan.

12.8.3 Outputs from 1.8 Close Phase (1.8.3)

Phase closure is the principal output. This includes the last phase when the project is declared at an end. It also includes shutdown of the project in progress for whatever circumstance warrants it. The *PMBOK Guide* calls for archiving documentation and cataloging lessons learned from the project experience.

Table 12.10 Close Phase (1.8)

1.8.1 Inputs		1.8 Close Phase	Closing
		1.8.2 Process Elements	1.8.3 Outputs
Deliverables Project Management Plan (1.2)	**Process definition**	Each project phase is formally closed. This involves confirmation that deliverables for that phase are complete.	*Phase Closure*
	Approaches and techniques	Deliverables review.	
	PM shortcomings addressed	Formal reviews of deliverables addresses top management abrogation. Phases and reviews are also a fundamental building block of a singular process, Level 3 of the PMMM.	
	SCM maturity	This process facilitates internal and external communication of progress – needed for Stage II and above.	
	Stakeholders	The project management manager/office oversees this process. Any participant, particularly those who are responsible for completing a phase, will be a stakeholder. Top management in the company, the company steering committee, and multicompany steering committees that review progress should review and confirm phase closures.	

Chapter 13

Implementing Collaborative Relationships

This chapter describes processes to achieve alignment of functions inside the company with the supply chain strategy. The processes in this chapter focus on enlisting internal cooperation and staffing improvement projects. Because management must capture employees' hearts and minds, implementing collaborative relationships is a high-risk endeavor. In fact, it is the most difficult of the five SCM tasks.

Success in project implementation depends on the people tasked to do the job—their availability, numbers, skills, and motivation. Filling permanent organization and temporary project roles is critical. This task calls for "collaborative" relationships because cooperation will be necessary among functions with different measures, culture, and mind-sets. Figure 13.1 is a flowchart of five processes that implement collaborative relationships to support strategy implementation.

Harold Kerzner points out that the likelihood of success depends on the people's comfort level in working on projects.[1] If people have been accustomed to working autonomously, they will have difficulty with the project environment, particularly broad projects using market–product–operations combinations, spheres, as domains for improvement. Lars Rosqvist, who reviewed Section 2, also warns that many employees don't view their companies as project-delivering organizations. They do not want to be involved because they are more comfortable "plugging along" in a routine work environment.

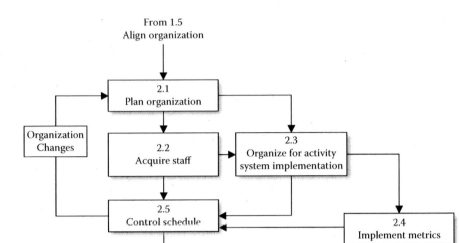

Figure 13.1   Implementing collaborative relationships.

13.1 Plan Organization (2.1)

This process takes the Organization Design, which is a vision produced by the company steering committee, and converts that vision into a short-term "pathway" transition plan. Table 13.1 is a summary of the process.

13.1.1 Inputs to 2.1 Plan Organization (2.1.1)

The principal input to this process is the *Organization Design,* a product of Process 1.5 described in Section 12.5. The *Organization Design* shows how activities and processes are to be assigned to organization units. These reflect the needs of spheres, or "businesses within the business," that have unique activity systems. The activity systems, prepared by sphere design teams, reflect management decisions on how to compete. Required implementation skills are set by the activity structure design to be implemented. As time passes, updates in the form of *Organization Changes* from process *2.5 Control Schedule* should modify the *Organization Implementation Plan,* the output of this process. These changes will reflect actual progress made in finding people and integrating them into their organization roles.

Table 13.1 Plan Organization (2.1)

2.1 Plan Organization			Planning
2.1.1 Inputs		2.1.2 Process Elements	2.1.3 Outputs
Organization Design (1.5) Organization Changes (2.5)	**Process definition**	Use the *Organization Design* to plan implementation of organization changes. Implementation encompasses the skills, numbers, structure, and metrics needed to implement activity systems. The plan reflects staff availability and project priorities.	Organization Implementation Plan • Detailed, time-phased organization structure • Justification for choices • Required documentation (e.g., titles, position descriptions, compensation, etc.) • Sources of people for identified positions • Timing of implementation
	Approaches and techniques	Sequencing organization and process change. Portfolio management.	
	PM shortcomings addressed	The planned organization seeks to minimize conflicts between functions. This process requires top management participation to authorize staff additions and organization changes, so it counters abrogation by senior managers. The process supports organization awareness and management support elements on the PMMM. Changing one's title or position gets attention.	
	SCM maturity	Task 2 maturity, at least at Stage II, is supported. This process responds to the strategy and the organization structure needed to implement it.	

(continued on next page)

Table 13.1 (continued)   Plan Organization (2.1)

2.1.1 Inputs	2.1 Plan Organization		Planning
	2.1.2 Process Elements		2.1.3 Outputs
	Terminology	Activity system	Core competence
		Customer-centric organization	Customer-centric supply chain
		Demand-driven supply chain	Functional organization
		Greenfield vision	Project portfolio
		Product-centric organization	Product-centric supply chain
	Stakeholders	Stakeholders are internal, including all those who work in supply chain positions or functions whose mission and structure will change. The company steering committee will have provided its vision in the *Organization Design*. The supply chain design team can complete this process with staff assistance from the Human Resources function.	

13.1.2 *Process Elements for* 2.1 Plan Organization *(2.1.2)*

The process converts a long-term vision for the organization into a time-phased plan. The *Organization Design* from process 1.5 is the end game and the organization plan from this process charts the pathway to that vision. This plan reflects constraints and other realities like current capabilities and priorities for implementing the supply chain strategy.

13.1.2.1 *Process Definition for* 2.1 Plan Organization

The process is a foundation for moving ahead with strategy implementation. A company can take different approaches to implementing a strategic activity. So, the skills component is particularly critical. For example, implementing links with suppliers could rely on pull signal methods that require little automation. An alternative would be to pursue information technology to meet the same end. Each of these alternatives demands different skill sets to implement. A decision on the path to take has broad ramifications for acquiring skills.

13.1.2.2 *Approaches and Techniques for* 2.1 Plan Organization

The organization planning process must juggle priorities and constraints. Appendix B recommends that the assignment be given to the supply chain design team. An example of a constraint is the availability of needed skills. A big hurdle is passed if the skills are already on board and need only be deployed to improvement projects or subprojects. If the skills are not present, then they must be acquired. Priorities are related to the urgency for improving operations. Greater urgency, particularly where added skills are needed, also makes skills and numbers a constraint. Consultants or temporary employees are often the best solution.

To justify added expense, the company steering committee should weigh the benefits and costs. A sound approach is to estimate the monthly benefits as measured by increased profits and/or cost savings. This monthly benefits figure puts a value on timely implementation. For example, if full implementation will produce a $1,000,000 monthly improvement in cash flow, planners can better gauge the value of speeding up the process. Too often, only costs are considered when making decisions regarding the timing of a project's implementation.

Ideally, the people who will run a new process should supervise its design. Figure 13.2 illustrates the ideal sequence for implementing organization and process changes. A conceptual design of activities and processes is item #1 in Figure 13.2. The conceptual organization design, item #2, follows the process conceptual design. For implementation (items #3 and #4), the sequence should be reversed. To assure the involvement and commitment of people in the organization, organization implementation precedes process change implementation.

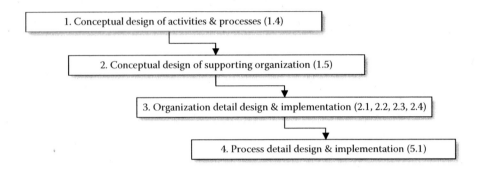

Figure 13.2 Sequencing organization and process change.

Constraints from limitations on staff additions require portfolio management decisions. This means that the staff shortages will necessitate changes to the Project Management Plan. Figure 13.1 shows this flow from the *2.5 Schedule Control* process back to *2.1 Plan Organization*.

13.1.2.3 Project Management Shortcomings Addressed by 2.1 Plan Organization

There is nothing like organization restructuring to engage people whose jobs and responsibilities are about to change. This is why this task is so difficult if changes are "radical." Top management involvement is inevitable if organization changes range over multiple functions, which is likely. Top management, represented by the company steering committee, will necessarily make trade-offs regarding elements of the plan. This requires using available resources for the highest priority strategy elements. The resulting structures should be more closely aligned with the strategy, addressing project failures due to unaligned objectives.

With respect to the Project Management Maturity Matrix, or PMMM, organization shifts reinforce the need for top management support for the program. If the strategy leads to organization shifts, the "corner office" must be serious. This is a planning process, so it disciplines downstream processes setting goals and enabling measurement of progress.

13.1.2.4 SCM Maturity for 2.1 Plan Organization

The organization changes facilitate cross-functional initiatives. This is characteristic of Stage III of SCM maturity (Table 10.5) for Task 2 Implementing Collaborative Relationships. In the recommended phasing of the supply chain project introduced in Chapter 11 and documented in Table 11.3, internal alignment is a precursor to broader collaboration with partners and implementing multicompany process improvements.

13.2.2.5 *Terminology for* 2.1 Plan Organization

The terms listed in Table 13.1 relate to issues described in this process and are likely to arise in its execution. They include the types of organization and supply chains that might result from the strategy. This process requires often difficult trade-offs in terms of implementing parts of the supply chain project and subproject portfolio.

13.2.2.6 *Stakeholders for* 2.1 Plan Organization

The project management function, whether it is a single project manager or a project management office (PMO), should oversee the organization transition. Assistance from the Human Resources staff should support the effort. The supply chain design team is a good candidate to execute the process, and the company steering committee should ratify the plan. Functional departments inside the company and at partner organizations should be consulted. The consultation can include availability of skills, priorities, and preferred technical approaches. Comprehensive programs will touch many employees through changes in assignments, shifts in their responsibilities, or new methods for doing their work.

13.1.3 Outputs from 2.1 Plan Organization *(2.1.3)*

The *Organization Implementation Plan* is the principal output. The plan includes a time-phased organization structure, a road map for moving from where the organization is to where it needs to be. The plan's format can include six-month "slices" showing where the organization expects to be at the end of each period. *Justification for choices* should contain analysis needed to authenticate decisions. Supporting information includes *required documentation* matching the organization's policies for defining employee positions. It should also identify *sources of people* that are internal or recruited from outside the company. *Timing of implementation* summarizes milestones in the implementation for easy reporting of progress.

13.2 Acquire Staff (2.2)

Acquisition of staff can easily be a critical path activity in project implementation. The plan developed in process *2.1 Plan Organization* guides the effort. Table 13.2 summarizes the staff acquisition process.

13.2.1 Inputs to Acquire Staff *(2.2.1)*

The *Organization Implementation Plan* (from 2.1) to change the organization through additions, reductions, or transfers should be backed by the resources to implement that plan. *Staff Acquisition Resources* include internal personnel staff, budgets for recruiting, and dedication of employee time to the recruiting process.

Table 13.2 Acquire Staff (2.2)

2.2.1 Inputs	2.2 Acquire Staff		Executing
		2.2.2 Process Elements	2.2.3 Outputs
Organization Implementation Plan (2.1)	**Process definition**	This process is central to success at implementing supply chain change. It populates the organization with those who must execute the supply chain strategy.	Staff Resources • Internal transfers • New recruits • Temporary resources
Staff Acquisition Resources	**Approaches and techniques**	Employee evaluation. Staff identification and recruiting.	
	PM shortcomings addressed	Excellence in this process is central to execution of the overall plan.	
	SCM maturity	Placing the right people in the right slots in a timely way improves the chances of having an organization aligned to the strategy. This corresponds to Task 2 Levels IV and V of SCM maturity.	
	Stakeholders	Managers of departments undergoing change are stakeholders as are managers with new assignments. The Human Resources staff, assisted by recruiters, will pursue the plan. The project manager/office should track progress.	

13.2.2 Process Elements for Acquire Staff *(2.2.2)*

The process includes traditional ways to obtain, retain, and manage staff resources. *Employee evaluations* can help decide whether to transfer an existing employee to a new role or to recruit a new employee. Supply chain project success is limited by the capabilities of people executing the plan. These include people who both implement and run new processes. Building the organization will engage many stakeholders, as shown in Table 13.2. Knowledge of supply chain technology and process models like the Supply-Chain Operations Reference-model (SCOR-model) and the Council of Supply Chain Management Professionals' (CSCMP) Supply Chain Management *Process Standards* can be positive factors in staff selection.

13.2.3 Outputs from Acquire Staff *(2.2.3)*

The *Acquire Staff* process output takes several forms. *Internal transfers, new recruits,* and *temporary resources* are all sources of specified skills.

13.3 Organize for Activity System Implementation (2.3)

Having a great plan and great people is insufficient for successful implementation. The two must be meshed in a way that implements the intent of the supply chain strategy and, where necessary, generates changes to the strategy. So, this process is a "make or break" one for the supply chain project. People in the project management and operating roles are the source of the "progressive elaboration" property in the project environment. This property of projects means that the "car must be steered," not neglected to find its own way down the road.

13.3.1 Inputs to 2.3 Organize for Activity System Implementation *(2.3.1)*

This process matches people with positions. The people come from the *2.2 Acquire Staff* process. The position definitions are output from the *2.1 Plan Organization* process. This process, summarized in Table 13.3, integrates the staff plan with the strategy, creating an environment for success. The structure is aligned with the needs of the business. Measures are consistent, and skills match the demands of new processes. The implementation plan and staff resources are the central inputs. However, many other documents like the strategy, issues list, and the environmental briefing will add value in mobilizing people.

Table 13.3   Organize for Activity System Implementation (2.3)

2.3.1 Inputs	2.3 Organize for Activity System Implementation		Executing
		2.3.2 Process Elements	2.3.3 Outputs
Organization Implementation Plan (2.1)	**Process definition**	This process integrates people and a time-phased organization plan. It implements the new internal organization over time.	Implemented Organization Plan
Staff Resources (2.2)	**Approaches and techniques**	*Employee oriented:* Orientation. Team building. Process design training (e.g., lean, Six Sigma, theory of constraints). Technical skills development. Leadership skills training. Process owners. Design teams. Front line teams. Chief process improvement officer. Facilitation.	Organization Plan Implementation Progress Reports
		Structural: Recognition and reward systems. Design Teams. Front line teams. Information System Requirements. Chief Process Improvement Officer. Facilitation.	
	PM shortcomings addressed	The process addresses top management abrogation, organization roadblocks, and internal technical capability.	
		In terms of the PMMM, the process is essential to organization awareness, management support, and process discipline.	

SCM maturity	The process moves the organization to higher levels of Task 2 maturity (Stages III, IV, and V) and sets the stage for higher levels of Task 3 maturity.	
Terminology	Center of Excellence	Channel
	Channel master	Chief process improvement officer (CPIO)
	Design team	Process owner
	Project office	Sponsor
	Steering committee	Third-party logistics provider
Stakeholders	Internally, senior managers are involved, particularly those responsible for coordination with supply chain partners like procurement, sales, and distribution. The project management function, a manager or project office, should implement the process in a coordinated effort with the Human Resources function.	

13.3.2 *Process Elements for* 2.3 **Organize for Activity System Implementation** *(2.3.2)*

Table 13.3 lists the process elements. The process covers an extended time and requires attention to countless details. Employee-oriented approaches and techniques list ways to communicate to operating and project employees about the project. Other techniques are structural in nature, including teams and roles in process change. Many companies enjoy the process of planning much more than the job of implementing. Ease of implementation will depend on whether the roles designed for an individual are operating or project management, or both. The following are questions about the realism of implementation plans:

■ Will a new person assigned to an operating role design the new job or the process? Or will design be the responsibility of a dedicated project team? Can dedicated people be made available?

■ How much time will operating managers have for the project? How much is sufficient to gain their commitment?

■ Is implementation of new supply chain processes a "bootstrap" operation? That is, will operating managers have to design and make changes to processes at the same time they operate them? Many organizations do just this.

The "right" answers depend on the amount of change, the degree of difficulty, requirements for specialist knowledge, and available funds for dedicated project staff. Project implementation often calls for people in the organization to take on roles described earlier and illustrated in Figure 13.3. The first role is the operating role, gray in the figure. If you spend 100 percent of your time running the business, there is no time for the project role to change the business. On the other hand, a

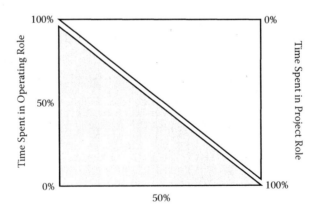

Figure 13.3 Split responsibility for implementation.

dedicated project person will spend 100 percent of his or her time on a project role. If so, will that person have sufficient input and acceptance by operating people?

Our experience is that split roles usually don't work. In general, the operating role dominates since operating jobs create necessary, urgent tasks that demand immediate decisions and actions. There is no time to focus on needed intermediate or long-term changes. Therefore, dedicated people are needed for the project. However, operating people have to have a role. A practical limit to the amount of time spent by operating managers is about 20 percent. A possible solution is to add facilitation skills to the project team. This makes it possible for operating managers to spend non-disruptive time on the project. Facilitation may be from process improvement staff, consultants, or the project management team.

Many supply chain initiatives unravel at this point in the project. Putting resources to work on implementation is confirmation that the project is real. A company that forsakes bootstrapping implementation is at least demonstrating Level 2 maturity as measured by the PMMM.

With regard to SCM maturity, failure at this process is likely to cause a regression from the intent to be a Stage III company back to Stage II, as shown on Table 10.5. This is akin to the rubber band that, after stretching, returns to its natural state. The use of spheres and their related activity systems is a risk-mitigating approach. Failure to find staff or implement change in one part of the business need not slow implementation in another where the people are available to implement the strategy. The project management team should oversee this process. However, it requires close coordination with operating managers, particularly those in key new roles. The company steering committee should monitor the process continuously.

13.3.3 Outputs from 2.3 Organize for Activity System Implementation (2.3.3)

The output is an *Implemented Organization Plan*. The plan will call for staffing the organization over time. Needed skills aren't likely to be needed or available all at once. So, the deliverable unfolds as the process proceeds. *Organization Plan Implementation Progress Reports* will communicate progress in staffing positions. Whether faster or slower than called for in the *Organization Implementation Plan*, implementation progress will set the pace for strategy implementation. For this reason, Figure 13.1 calls for inputs to *2.5 Control Schedule*. This process, described later in this chapter, generates schedule, scope, and additional organization changes.

13.4 Implement Metrics (2.4)

This process, described in Table 13.4, takes earlier inputs and solidifies measures for both project and supply chain performance. Placing this process at this point in

Table 13.4 Implement Metrics (2.4)

		2.4 Implement Metrics	Executing
2.4.1 Inputs		2.4.2 Process Elements	2.4.3 Outputs
Activity Systems Design (1.4) Collaboration Strategy (1.6)	**Process definition**	Develop or confirm metrics for supply chain operations tailored to each key position as it is filled, including those that supply chain partners can use in monitoring their own supply chain performance.	Project Control Metrics Supply Chain Metrics
Organization Design (1.5)	**Approaches and techniques**	Balanced Scorecard (refer to Glossary). SCOR metrics (refer to Section 4.2.3.1 and Table 4.2).	
Organization Plan Implementation Progress Reports (2.3)	**PM shortcomings addressed**	Project Control Metrics measure the effectiveness of the implementation effort. In fact, the PMMM is itself one such metric. With respect to the root causes for project failure, metrics alert us when plans go awry.	
	SCM maturity	Metrics measure the ability of the organization to execute in all the SCM knowledge areas. The SCM maturity matrix is a metric measuring internal capabilities to use the supply chain to improve competitiveness. Supply Chain Metrics will monitor the health of new processes.	

Terminology		
Activity-based costing	Balanced Scorecard	Benchmarking
Business model	Cash-to-cash cycle time	Cost baseline
Cost of quality	C_p, C_{pk}	Cycle time
Discounted cash flow	Economic value added	Forecast error
Key characteristic	Mean absolute deviation	Mixed-model product
P:D ratio	Quality threshold	Six Sigma
Statistical process control	Synchronized supply chain	Target costing
Total cost of ownership (TCO)	Velocity	Yield management
Stakeholders	All supply chain members will be measured and guided by selected metrics. Initial stakeholders will be those in the organization responsible for operations in various spheres. The project manager/office should oversee execution by the supply chain design team.	

the overall project gives employees responsible for the process the opportunity to set goals for process measurements.

13.4.1 Inputs to 2.4 Implement Metrics (2.4.1)

Candidate measures for new supply chain processes are developed along with the process. *Activity Systems Design* (from 1.4) contains metrics developed by the sphere design team. These transmit the design team views regarding the objectives of their activity system designs. *1.5 Align Organization* goes one step further. It makes assignments of metrics to specific organizations or functions. *1.6 Develop Collaboration Strategy* should signal opportunities and constraints for dealing with partners. There is no reason that internal metrics shouldn't be considered for use outside our organization up and down the supply chain.

Organization Plan Implementation Progress Reports from process 2.3 reflect the pace of metrics confirmation and development. At a minimum, new functions should reaffirm metrics proposed earlier in the project. If employees taking up roles need new metrics, these should be added to those developed by the sphere design team.

13.4.2 Process Elements for 2.4 Implement Metrics (2.4.2)

The process doesn't start from scratch. Metrics development has been a part of prior processes, particularly *1.4 Design Activity Systems* and *1.5 Align Organization*. This process confirms some metrics, deletes some, and adds some. In measurement, more is not necessarily better. So, pruning metrics is perfectly acceptable. The metrics address two needs. The first is measuring performance for the balance of the project; the second is performance measurement for supply chain operations in the future. Project-related metrics would result in changes to the project's scope and schedule. These are handled through process *2.5 Control Schedule*. The supply chain metrics will confirm or modify metrics for supply chain performance. They are an input to process *5.1 Plan Process Improvements*. Supply chain scope should not be limited to one's own organization but should also include upstream and downstream partners.

Table 13.4 terminology refers to Glossary terms relating to supply chain performance. The Balanced Scorecard and supply chain process models provide approaches useful for this process. Table 13.4 points out that the PMMM and the SCM Maturity Model are essentially ways to measure the effectiveness of the process of creating more competitive supply chains. Embracing higher levels of maturity does not guarantee success in creating a high-performance supply chain. It is, however, a necessary prerequisite to achieve that end.

Managers, as they take up new operating or project management roles, should confirm the metrics on which they will be measured. Those filling operating roles should be responsible for achieving improvements measured by supply chain metrics. They can develop these with the assistance of project staff. Project managers will address project control metrics. Those with split responsibility, as illustrated in Figure 13.3, should produce both.

13.4.3 Outputs from 2.4 Implement Metrics (2.4.3)

Project Control Metrics are those to be used to complete the process implementation phase of the project. Using the phasing suggested in Chapter 11 and summarized in Table 11.3, these can be for both short-term and long-term efforts. These are inputs into *2.5 Control Schedule. Supply Chain Metrics* are those that measure expected performance of the supply chain once new processes are implemented. To the extent possible, managers should document current performance.

13.5 Control Schedule (2.5)

A schedule control process, described in Table 13.5, is inserted here to transmit change requests to process *1.7 Control Changes.* These change requests result in modifications to the project plan. Changes arise from variations in the plan for finding staff (process 2.2), variations in integrating people into project management and operation functions (process 2.3), and changes generated by the need to move people into new positions (process 2.4).

13.5.1 Inputs to 2.5 Control Schedule (2.5.1)

The inputs to the process, listed in Table 13.5, are outputs of other tasks described in this chapter.

13.5.2 Process Elements for 2.5 Control Schedule (2.5.2)

Table 13.5 describes project elements. The project management staff should manage the process. The environment is likely to be complex, particularly in larger organizations. There can be several "spheres" in some phase of the development process. Places where there is activity can be scattered geographically. There may also be language barriers in companies operating in several countries or with trading partners abroad. The pace of change will vary from sphere to sphere. The project management team will have to be proactive in soliciting change and assuring that the project plan is up to date.

Table 13.5 Control Schedule (2.5)

		2.5 Control Schedule	Monitoring and Controlling
2.5.1 Inputs		2.5.2 Process Elements	2.5.3 Outputs
Organization Plan Implementation Progress Reports (2.3) Project Control Metrics (2.4)	**Process definition**	Responsibility for implementation will reside inside the organization. So, a control process is placed here that recognizes that the addition of people and their inputs will produce modification to the supply chain design and the schedule.	Organization Changes SCM Change Requests Project Change Requests
Supply Chain Metrics (2.4)	**Approaches and techniques**	Time estimating. Project network diagrams. Project management software.	
	PM shortcomings addressed	Control of scope, time, and cost elements is fundamental to project success. Placed here it is tied to responsibility centers in the initiating organization. Rigidity was also a root cause of poor project outcomes described in Chapter 9. This process provides for making adjustments to the project as it proceeds.	
	SCM maturity	Metrics that control multicompany efforts characterize Stage III and IV organizations.	

Terminology	Activity	Cost baseline
	Critical path	Decomposition
	Deliverable	Level of effort
	Network diagram	Phase
	Process, process group	Program
	Progressive elaboration	Project
	Project life cycle	Project office
	Risk	Schedule baseline
	Subproject	Task
	Template	Work package
Stakeholders	Internal functions must react to needs for changes. The company steering committee should ratify changes; the project manager/office should execute the process.	

13.5.3 Outputs from 2.5 **Control Schedule** *(2.5.3)*

The process produces *Organization Changes*. These can be changes to the *1.2 Plan Project*, that is, the overall plan for the strategy, or *2.1 Plan Organization*, which sets the timing of staff changes. *SCM Change Requests* recommend modification to the design of the supply chain. *Project Change Requests* recommend changes to the project management plan.

Note

1. Harold Kerzner, *Project Management: A Systems Approach to Planning, Scheduling, and Controlling*, 7th ed. (New York: John Wiley & Sons, Inc., 2001), 26–32.

Chapter 14

Forging Supply Chain Partnerships

A "supply chain" project won't fulfill its potential unless the project involves upstream and downstream partners. This chapter describes project processes to plan multicompany efforts.

Figure 14.1 is a flowchart of seven project processes associated with our *SCM Task 3 Forging Supply Chain Partnerships*. Chapter 13 described processes for alignment of internal functions. This chapter moves outside the four walls of the organization. The project property "progressive elaboration" works with a vengeance in the processes that will be covered in this chapter. Arguably, one has a greater control over its own operations. However, it may have little or no influence over what partners will do, won't do, or are even able to do. A whole lot depends on the degree to which the company and its trading partners have embraced the seven core SCM principles described in Section 2.1. This chapter takes the perspective of a sponsoring company along the chain who has initiated the supply chain project. Until the sponsoring company presents its upstream and downstream partners with a proposal, it won't know for sure what it can or cannot accomplish if their cooperation is required.

So, Figure 14.1 recommends two control processes. The first, *3.6 Acquire Multicompany Staff Resources,* occurs when the partnership calls for a multicompany staff to projects. The second, *3.7 Verify Partner Scope,* calls for feedback to *1.7 Control Changes* that results in changes to the project plan. Performance at these control points will expand or limit the scope of the supply chain project. Principal features of the Figure 14.1 processes include the following:

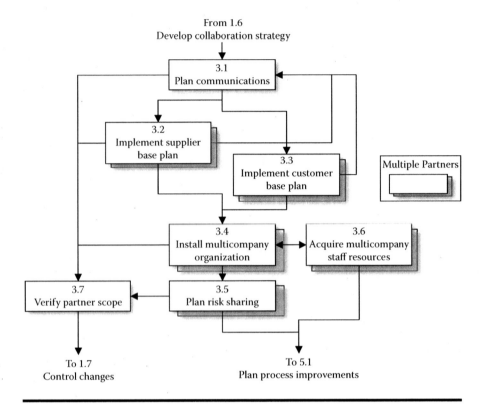

Figure 14.1 Forging supply chain partnerships.

- Process *3.1 Plan Communications* to elicit participation from partners.
- Separate processes for upstream and downstream partners. These include two executing processes (3.2 for the upstream supplier base and 3.3 for the downstream customer base) with similar steps tailored to individual partners or partner groups.
- The use of a multicompany organization to guide collaborations and staff improvement efforts founded process *3.4 Install Multicompany Organization*. Components could include a multicompany steering committee and project office.
- Risk sharing through win–win arrangements developed in *3.5 Plan Risk Sharing*.
- A process for defining the scope of partner participation, *3.7 Verify Partner Scope.*

The importance of these processes will vary enormously among companies pursing supply chain improvements. Variables include the following:

- number of significant trading partners;
- location of our own company in the chain (how many upstream and downstream partners?);
- relative power and influence of our company over our trading partners; and
- supply chain complexity as measured by the number of spheres, or "businesses inside the business."

The project team has flexibility in applying the processes that will be described in this chapter. For example, the processes here treat upstream and downstream partners separately. However, in Chapter 4 we described "vertical" spheres that include our company, upstream, and downstream partners. In this case, the planning may include both types of partner in a single effort.

14.1 Plan Communications (3.1)

This process translates outputs of strategy processes into a plan or plans for communicating the organization's intent for modifying its existing partnerships. The process takes what are essentially internal planning documents and turns them into instruments for communications.

14.1.1 *Inputs to* 3.1 Plan Communications (3.1.1)

The *Collaboration Strategy* (described in Section 12.6.3) defines what the project plan seeks from trading partner contributions to strategy fulfillment. This input is developed in process *1.6 Develop Collaboration Strategy.* Elements described in Section 12.6.3 include the following:

- characterization of the supply and customer base,
- information requirements,
- new upstream and downstream roles, and
- technology.

Another input to the process is *Collaboration Plan Change Suggestions* from upstream suppliers and downstream customers. These external inputs result from dialog during processes 3.2 and 3.3. Partner suggestions lead to changes in the *External Communications Plan.*

14.1.2 *Process Elements for* 3.1 Plan Communications

Communications planning, summarized in Table 14.1, launches collaboration initiatives along the supply chain. It is a "selling" document, or series of documents. If

Table 14.1 Plan Communications (3.1)

3.1 Plan Communications		Planning
3.1.1 Inputs	3.1.2 Process Elements	3.1.3 Outputs
Collaboration Strategy (1.6) *Collaboration Plan Change Suggestions (3.2, 3.3)*	**Process definition** Develop a plan addressing goals, staffing, oversight, projects, contracting, and process integration. Include all spheres. The process provides external communications to upstream and downstream partners. It also communicates company direction for collaboration to internal stakeholders.	**External Communications Plan** Objectives Description and Scope Timetable Technology Business Rules Risk Sharing Enabling Processes Participation
	Approaches and techniques Drivers of supply chain change (Chapter 3). Cross-company process documentation. External stakeholder needs analysis. Contracting. Activity-based costing. Risk analysis techniques.	
	PM shortcomings addressed Since several companies who may have bargained at arm's length must support the broadest implementations, this is especially challenging. Success requires Level 3 PMMM performance for multiple organizations. This requires embracing supply chain principles among these parties. (See Section 2.1) The resulting plan should address senior management abrogation, technology, and organization roadblocks.	

SCM maturity	The willingness to communicate externally implies at least a Stage II organization with regard to Task 3. The depth of collaboration will determine whether a company is reaching Stage III, IV, or V.		
Terminology	Activity-based costing	Certified supplier	Continuous replenishment planning
	Customer relationship management (CRM)	Disintermediation	Drumbeat
	Echelon	E-commerce	Electronic Data Interchange (EDI)
	Extended product	Independent, dependent demand	Just in Time
	Kaizen	*Kanban*	Lean enterprise
	Milk run	PDCA	Point of sale
	Postponement	Process owner	Product pipeline, product funnel
	Push and pull systems	Replenishment cycle time	Reverse logistics
	Risk pooling	Safety stock	Target costing
Stakeholders	The company steering committee should be accountable; the supply chain design team should execute the process. Any upstream or downstream contact person, important supply chain partners, and internal functions that must collaborate are stakeholders.		

it isn't persuasive to partners, those elements of the strategy are in jeopardy. In cases where partners can't be compelled to collaborate by virtue of the organization's influence in the chain, planning must address the "what's in it for me" question.

14.1.2.1 Process Definition for 3.1 Plan Communications

The process should screen the inputs provided by the *Collaboration Strategy* to determine what is available for "public consumption." Also, the plan can have separate parts for each partner or group of partners. For example, on the upstream side, one part may address smaller suppliers of commodities. Another may address large suppliers of components engineered for the company. On the downstream side, separate communications may be tailored to the needs of a few large customers or major distribution channels. Of course, multiple tailored communications will take longer to produce. So, priorities for communications should guide document release.

14.1.2.2 Approaches and Techniques for 3.1 Plan Communications

Collaboration can cover a broad range of issues and topics. Examples include negotiation of prices, service levels, risk distribution, extended product features, and investments for mutual benefit. The document should recognize the industry drivers behind the need for collaboration. Chapter 3 listed six:

- PESTEL, the political, economic, social, technological, environmental, and legislative changes that occur external to the supply chain;
- the need for extended products with additional services accompanying the physical product;
- globalization of markets and sources of supply;
- the flexibility imperative that defines supply chain responses in dynamic environments;
- process-centered management that addresses multicompany processes rather than local, functional improvement; and
- collaboration requirements that generate further supply chain improvements.

The communication plan should translate these drivers into requirements for supply chain process changes. The plan might use the many process documentation tools available including several that will be covered in Chapter 15. Activity-based costing is a powerful way to establish a cost model to facilitate communications and provide a negotiation tool. Risk analysis, a topic introduced in Section 7.3.8, adds structure to conversations about risk sharing along the chain. An example is carrying extra inventory to ensure against disruptions and to respond quickly to changes in end-user demand.

14.1.2.3 Project Management Shortcomings Addressed by 3.1 Plan Communications

The *External Communications Plan*, because it goes outside the company to important partners, should be subject to top management approval. The company steering committee is the logical forum. This is a signal of commitment to the project's direction. The plan calls for a section on technology requirements. This should trigger a dialog with partners regarding their readiness to participate at the plan-defined technology level. Organization roadblocks inside and in partner organizations should be addressed by the plan. Communication should raise partner comments and feedback that the company steering committee and supply chain design team should address.

14.1.2.4 SCM Maturity for 3.1 Plan Communications

Maturity in Task 3 Forging Supply Chain Partnerships depends on the type of collaboration planned. Stage II in the SCM maturity model (Table 10.5) is simple data exchange. Stage III is characterized by cost reduction with suppliers where the organization has most of its leverage. Stage IV begins upstream and downstream partnerships but roles of partners in the supply chain remain static. This is typical of incremental efforts addressing cost and service. No new space is created by the planned partnerships through value-adding services. Stage V brings role changes and characterizes major change in the chain.

The company steering committee is responsible for oversight of the project internally. A multicompany steering committee is an additional governance group to coordinate the effort among partners. Multicompany steering committees, formulated in process 3.4, are needed for higher levels of maturity, particularly Stages IV or V. There may be several multicompany steering committees. Some will have just two members, our own company and a single partner. An example is the case of a major supplier who works with our companies to develop a key technology. Others may have more than two members, with representatives from a group of upstream or downstream trading partners. Many companies already have "supplier conferences" and "user groups." The multicompany steering committee will have a more intense agenda than that typical of these forums.

14.1.2.5 Terminology for 3.1 Plan Communications

Terms in Table 14.1 support a multicompany interaction. Multicompany teams should direct particular attention at several topics: cost accounting, flexibility definition, risk sharing, postponement, appropriate technology, reverse logistics, and push and pull systems. Adoption of any one of these could be a considerable undertaking requiring much of the communications activity.

14.1.2.6 Stakeholders for 3.1 Plan Communications

The process is intended to draw key partners into the project. The ones selected will be those who are most important to the company's future, those partners one wants to transform from an arm's-length negotiating relationship into a collaborative one. This will not be all suppliers or all customers. Appendix B recommends that the supply chain design team should execute the process, under close monitoring from the company steering committee. If they exist at this point, multicompany steering committees and internal and partner functions should be consulted.

14.1.3 Outputs from 3.1 Plan Communications (3.1.3)

The *External Communications Plan* should, at a minimum, have the following components:

- objectives, including financial objectives both for customer service, market share, and cost reduction;
- description and scope, products and processes included;
- timetable (desired implementation schedule);
- technology (process requirements, including information technology, facilities, and equipment);
- ground rules (guidelines and policies for the partnership), rules covering operations, planning, and partner contributions;
- risk sharing (how risks and rewards might be measured and distributed);
- enable processes (required processes listed in the Supply-Chain Operations Reference-model (SCOR-model) and the Council of Supply Chain Management Professionals' (CSCMP) *Supply Chain Management Process Standards* on both sides of the partnership needed to make collaborative processes work); and
- participation (anticipated trading partner contributions to a multicompany steering committee and project staff).

14.2 Implement Supplier Base Plan (3.2)

This executing process, shown in Table 14.2, takes the collaboration plan and, through a joint effort with a partner or several partners, turns it into an organization design for supplier and company implementation. One result is the identification of a process design team. A similar process takes place with the downstream side in process *3.3 Implement Customer Base Plan*. The organization, once the design developed in this process is implemented, will prepare partners for improvements to supply chain processes that will be covered in Chapter 15. The sequence is also consistent with Figure 13.2 that shows the organization going into place before new processes are implemented.

Table 14.2 Implement Supplier Base Plan (3.2)

3.2.1 Inputs		3.2 Implement Supplier Base Plan	Executing
		3.2.2 Process Elements	3.2.3 Outputs
Activity System Design (1.4) Collaboration Strategy (1.6) External Communications Plan (3.1)	**Process definition**	Execute the plan for upstream (supplier-side) collaboration. Include all spheres. Address goals, staffing, oversight, projects, contracting, and process integration.	Multicompany Organization Design: Supplier Base Implementation
	Approaches and techniques	Regular meetings. Feedback from partners.	
	PM shortcomings addressed	The process engages upstream partners. The presence of Level 3 singular processes in the PMMM will facilitate the effort, particularly if the several suppliers are engaged in the effort. A well-executed process will reduce risks from mismatched technical capability and misunderstood technology. It also engages top management across the companies involved.	
	SCM maturity	Such a plan is needed for moving beyond Stage I of SCM maturity. The scope of initiatives in the plan will determine which level (II, III, IV, or V).	
	Stakeholders	Internal functions facing upstream in the supply chain. These include commodity managers, buyers, quality engineering, warehousing, engineers, and sourcing managers. Principal upstream supply chain partners, of course, are also key stakeholders. The company steering committee is accountable for the process; the supply chain design team should execute the process.	

The process is limited to upstream partners where collaboration is desired. These are expected to be the few largest suppliers, probably the 20 percent of suppliers that supply 80 percent of the materials and services purchased by the company. Priorities for spheres as well as resources from one's company and the supplier's organization will dictate the order and pace of design development.

14.2.1 *Inputs to* 3.2 Implement Supplier Base Plan *(3.2.1)*

The principal inputs are the *Activity System Design, Collaboration Strategy,* and the *External Communications Plan.* The project team, assisted by functional staff, should coordinate partnership design with the supplier, including the organization to support it. Organization requirements may entail new staff and functions for one's own company and the supplier. However, it may be possible to execute the plan without such additions. This process is an important first action of that partnership.

14.2.2 *Process Elements for* 3.2 Implement Supplier Base Plan *(3.2.2)*

Table 14.2 lists the process elements that produce an organization design based on input planning documents. This is the point in the process where suppliers provide input regarding what they can or can't do. It reinforces the need for progressive elaboration of project plans since the desired cooperation of partners may not materialize. This interaction will be a test of our own willingness and ability to collaborate with the trading partner. Suppliers will be different in their capability. Reactions can vary from complete willingness to support the partnership to downright hostility. Much will depend on our own company's tradition with regard to supplier relations. If our company has been antagonistic and a "price taker," suppliers will be wary of any new initiative described as "collaboration." Also not resolved at this time is risk sharing in the partnership. The supplier has a right to ask, "What's in it for me if I collaborate?" The going-forward plan should list the alternatives and plan negotiation of risks and rewards.

14.2.3 *Outputs from* 3.2 Implement Supplier Base Plan *(3.2.3)*

The design will reflect the upstream supplier's commitment to the company's supply chain initiative. The deliverable is the plan for placement of functions within its organization. It is unlikely that both parties will get all they want. So, changes will have to made to the project plan. These changes are funneled through process *1.7 Control Changes.* There are many examples of supplier organization responses to a supply chain initiative:

- providing engineering support for new products or value engineering for existing products;
- establishing manufacturing cells dedicated to your product to support a sphere strategy;
- establishing a customer service function tailored to your organization's need;
- agreeing to just-in-time deliveries, tailored packaging, or buffer inventories;
- adding capacity through purchases of equipment and/or facilities;
- commitment to linkages and production control approaches; agreeing to information technology investments to support collaboration;
- sharing of quality data and joint efforts to improve quality; these can include changes to your part or subsystem specifications;
- selection of second tier suppliers; and
- changes to return processes.

Commitments made in this process pave the way for process improvements; Chapter 15 will cover these: service improvements, cost reductions, and changes that improve supply chain flexibility.

14.3 Implement Customer Base Plan (3.3)

This executing process, shown in Table 14.3, takes the collaboration plan and turns it into a design for downstream implementation. This includes channels from our own company to end users. These channels cover downstream manufacturers, distributors, retail outlets, customers for our product, and end users. As described in the previous section, a similar process takes place with the upstream side in process *3.2 Implement Suppler Base Plan.* The organization, once the design developed in this process is implemented, will prepare partners for improvements to supply chain processes that will be covered in Chapter 15. The sequence is also consistent with Figure 13.2 with organization design commitments made before embarking on process improvements.

The process is limited to downstream partners where collaboration is desired. These are expected to be the few largest distributors or customers, probably the 20 percent of downstream partners that handle 80 percent of a company's sales. Priorities for spheres, as well as resources from your company and the targeted partner, should dictate the sequence of design development.

14.3.1 *Inputs to* 3.3 Implement Customer Base Plan *(3.3.1)*

The principal inputs are the *Activity System Design, Collaboration Strategy,* and the *External Communications Plan.* The project team, assisted by functional staff, should coordinate the design of the partnership with the downstream partner,

Table 14.3   Implement Customer Base Plan (3.3)

3.3.1 Inputs	3.3 Implement Customer Base Plan		Executing
		3.3.2 Process Elements	*3.3.3 Outputs*
Activity System Design (1.4) Collaboration Strategy (1.6) External Communications Plan (3.1)	**Process definition**	Execute the plan for downstream (customer-side) collaboration. Include all spheres. Address goals, staffing, oversight, projects, contracting, and process integration.	Multicompany Organization Design: Customer Base Implementation
	Approaches and techniques	Regular meetings. Feedback from partners. Priority setting.	
	PM shortcomings addressed	The process engages downstream partners. It is facilitated by Level III singular processes in the PMMM. A well-executed process will reduce risks from mismatched technical capability and misunderstood technology. It also engages top management across the companies involved.	
	SCM maturity	Such a plan is needed for moving beyond Stage I of SCM maturity. The scope of initiatives in the plan will determine which level (II, III, IV, or V).	
	Stakeholders	Internal functions facing upstream in the supply chain and principal downstream supply chain partners are stakeholders. The company steering committee is accountable; the supply chain design team should execute the process.	

including the organization to support it. This process is an important first action of that partnership.

14.3.2 *Process Elements for* 3.3 Implement Customer Base Plan *(3.3.2)*

Table 14.3 lists the process elements. It produces an organization design for downstream operations based on the input planning documents. This is the point in the process where each downstream partner provides input regarding what they can or can't do. This interaction is a test of both parties' willingness and ability to collaborate. Downstream companies with whom we deal will be different in their willingness and ability to enter into a new relationship. Reactions will vary from complete willingness to downright hostility to our company's overtures. Much will depend on our own company's tradition with regard to the targeted partners. If our company has been antagonistic and hard to work with, potential partners will likely be wary of a new initiative. Also not resolved at this time is risk sharing in the partnership. The partner has a right to ask, " What's in it for me if I collaborate?" The going-forward plan should list the alternatives and plan negotiation of risks and rewards.

14.3.3 *Outputs from* 3.3 Implement Customer Base Plan *(3.3.3)*

The design will reflect the downstream partners' commitment to the company's supply chain initiative. The deliverable is the plan for placement of functions within its organization. It is unlikely that both parties will get all they want. So, changes will have to made to the project plan. These change are funneled through process *1.7 Control Changes*. There are many examples of downstream organization responses to a supply chain initiative. Examples include the following:

- shifting assembly operations to a downstream partner as part of a postponement plan;
- providing demand data for end product sales to assist our planning;
- establishing a liaison function that uses an S&OP (sales and operations planning) process with periodic meetings of decision makers in both companies;
- adding capacity through purchases of equipment and/or facilities;
- commitment to linkages and production control approaches (agreeing to consider information technology investments to support collaboration);
- sharing of quality data and joint efforts to improve quality (these can include changes to downstream partner specifications that our company must meet);
- changes in our supply base imposed by our downstream customer; and
- establishing or changing a return process.

Commitments made in this process pave the way for process improvements; Chapter 15 covers these: service improvements, cost reductions, and changes that introduce flexibility to the supply chain.

14.4 Install Multicompany Organization (3.4)

This executing process takes upstream and downstream plans and builds the corresponding multicompany infrastructure. Table 14.4 summarizes the process. As shown in Figure 4.4, "Level 3" refers to multicompany efforts; Level 1 is departmental; Level 2 is the business unit level. Key features include the following:

- a focused goal for the effort including strategic positioning, increased revenue, and profit improvement;
- multicompany groups supporting and funding the effort;
- if needed, a third party "honest broker" to facilitate the effort;
- a steering committee, manned by senior managers, to guide the effort;
- a project or group of projects that generate financial returns for all the partners;
- contracting that distributes costs and rewards based on achieving measures of performance; and
- balanced deployment of technology with judicious use of legacy systems, new technology, and "low tech" linkages.

This process integrates plans from processes 3.2 and 3.3 to put these elements into place. One can't ignore the timing issue with this process. An aggressive supply chain plan will cover many partners. Not all can be addressed at once. So, the multicompany organization will have evolving membership, reflecting the partner involved at any point. Also, multiple multicompany steering committees can serve different parts of the strategy.

14.4.1 Inputs to 3.4 Install Multicompany Organization (3.4.1)

The *Activity Systems Design* (1.4) and the *Collaboration Strategy* (1.6) are internal documents. Level 3 plans from processes 3.3 and 3.4 are the result of partner collaboration. This process takes these inputs from paper to reality.

14.4.2 Process Elements for 3.4 Install Multicompany Organization (3.4.2)

The goal is to staff project positions, then identify and possibly fill operating positions needed to start implementation of process improvements. As mentioned earlier, this corresponds to the sequence of implementation described in Figure 13.2. Implementing the sequence results in assigning design responsibility to people who will operate the process.

Table 14.4 Install Multicompany Organization (3.4)

3.4.1 Inputs	3.4 Install Multicompany Organization		Executing
		3.4.2 Process Elements	3.4.3 Outputs
Activity System Design (1.4) Collaboration Strategy (1.6) Multicompany Organization Design: Supplier Base Implementation (3.3) Multicompany Organization Design: Customer Base Implementation (3.4)	**Process definition**	The process puts in place the logistics required to maintain communications links and decision-making procedures for ongoing collaboration. Elements include project staff leadership at partners and appointments to steering committees.	SCM Subprojects Multicompany Project Staffing Requirements Multicompany Risk Sharing Plan
	Approaches and techniques	Organization meetings. Joint decision making in activity system implementation. Partnership classification.	
	PM shortcomings addressed	A continuing organization will provide ongoing multicompany awareness, management support, and process discipline.	
	SCM maturity	Forums are needed for reaching Stage IV and V levels of SCM maturity.	
	Stakeholders	Important upstream and downstream partners are key stakeholders; so are company employees in functions that must support the plans. The company's supply chain project team should be responsible for executing the process. The multicompany steering committee should be accountable.	

In Table 5.2, project management maturity is measured by organization awareness, management support, and process discipline. This process requires partner commitments, which are confirmed by their making staff commitments to the project. An output is SCM subprojects or, if it's the preference of the project team, separate projects for implementation.

Higher levels of SCM maturity are hampered by the lack of a "governance" structure beyond the immediate company's boundaries. This is a major obstacle in achieving supply chain improvements. The structure put in place in this process will promote communications and formal decision making. Again, partners will vary in the level of SCM maturity. An organization should be prepared for different levels of cooperation, leading to decisions to change partners or to make modifications in project goals or plans.

14.4.3 *Outputs from* 3.4 Install Multicompany Organization *(3.4.3)*

The process has three principal outputs. *SCM Subprojects* represent efforts that the multicompany steering committee has ratified. The term "subprojects" is used since these are components of the overall supply chain project. You have choices in nomenclature. These efforts can be "activities" within the supply chain project, project extensions, or stand-alone projects. The choice will depend on the effort's scope and relationship with parallel efforts. This deliverable is used in processes *3.5 Plan Risk Sharing, 3.6 Acquire Multicompany Staff Resources,* and *3.7 Verify Partner Scope.*

Multicompany Project Staffing Requirements are needs for project and operating staff to support the plan approved by the multicompany steering committee. The output is to a control process, *3.6 Acquire Multicompany Staff.* The plan should include positions, numbers, skills, and timing for each staffing requirement.

A *Multicompany Risk Sharing Plan* establishes business arrangements between the partners regarding assumption of risk for supply chain performance. This plan might be considered a memorandum of understanding, or MOU, to be later supplanted by formal contracts, if necessary. This could include the following:

- agreements/contracts needed to solidify the relationship;
- duration of the collaboration;
- contacts between the collaborating companies, which can include a variety of functions (engineering, tech support, and so forth) beyond procurement staff;
- metrics for service and cost;
- requirements including service guarantees, staffing, and investments; and
- rewards/penalties for meeting or not meeting requirements.

The *Multicompany Risk Sharing Plan* should identify which risks are important in each partner relationship. It should then define expectations for each party.

For example, delivery performance and cost might be an important metric for a particular supplier. The plan should define expectations for performance and the premiums and penalties that go with exception or substandard performance.

14.5 Plan Risk Sharing (3.5)

This executing process, summarized in Table 14.5, formalizes collaborative agreements to share risk in the supply chain relationship. Risk sharing defines the rewards and liabilities when things go right or things go wrong in a supply chain process. Collaboration in process *3.4 Install Multicompany Organization* has produced a "handshake" agreement to risk sharing. However, this is a signal of overall intent worked out a high level. This process formalizes it with agreements and contracts, as detailed as necessary, with each supplier. The agreement is a necessary step to planning and designing supply chain processes.

14.5.1 Inputs to 3.5 Plan Risk Sharing (3.5.1)

The *Multicompany Risk Sharing Plan* is the principal input. This executing process turns the plan into reality. It involves negotiations with each major partner within the framework provided by the plan.

14.5.2 Process Elements for 3.5 Plan Risk Sharing (3.5.2)

Table 14.6 lists some topics to address while forging agreements and contracts. Of course, the need will vary from partner to partner. Working with a third-party transportation company for downstream distribution of products certainly would require it.

14.5.3 Outputs from 3.5 Plan Risk Sharing (3.5.3)

Partner Business Arrangements are the resulting deliverable. The business arrangement goes beyond the normal arm's-length transaction. In fact, it may not even specify normal purchase order terms like price and delivery terms if these are spelled out in alternative documents. A principal goal is to gain agreements to pursue supply chain level process improvements and define participation in those efforts.

14.6 Acquire Multicompany Staff Resources (3.6)

This monitoring and controlling process, summarized in Table 14.7, monitors the readiness of partners and the company to make supply chain process improvements.

Table 14.5 Plan Risk Sharing (3.5)

3.5.1 Inputs		3.5.2 Process Elements	3.5.3 Outputs
		3.5 Plan Risk Sharing	Executing
Multicompany Risk Sharing Plan (3.4)	Process definition	Collaboration between upstream and downstream partners leads to formal and understood arrangements for operating supply chain processes. Risks can be external (such as natural disasters) and internal (related to partner performance).	Partner Business Arrangements
	Approaches and techniques	Contingency planning. Risk identification and analysis. Financial analysis. Capital investment analysis.	
	PM shortcomings addressed	Most agreements to share risk will require top management participation. Larger risks will involve correspondingly higher levels of approval.	
	SCM maturity	Risk sharing will likely be key in achieving Stage V of SCM maturity for Task 3. Risk sharing is also a component of aggressive (Level IV and V) supply chain process improvements (Chapter 15).	
	Stakeholders	The process is the responsibility of the multicompany steering committee. All participating companies are stakeholders. Normal partner contacts—procurement on the upstream side and sales/customer service on the downstream side—are stakeholders as principal contacts with trading partners.	

Table 14.6 Multicompany Business Arrangement Checklist

Partnership Article	Description
Purpose	Establishes the need for the partnership.
Parties to the agreement	Provides the legal names involved in the partnership.
Basis of the agreement	The shared value proposition. Partner expectations.
Organizational process boundaries	Areas of primary supply chain process responsibility.
Interface response time	Response expectations over time and space (geography).
Decision escalation	Individuals on both sides who will resolve issues.
Face-to-face meetings	The parties involved in the meetings and the frequency.
Performance measurement	Shared performance measures to track partnership effectiveness.
Intellectual property	Rights to partnership trade secrets, trademarks, copyrights, and patents.
Investment decision making	Each party's share of investments and returns.
Mediation and conflict resolution	Defined process for conflict resolution.
Non-exclusive provision	Rights of either party to participate in other supply chain networks, even if they compete.
Renewal	Term of the partnership, whether renewal is automatic or not.
Signatures	Senior executive commitment from each organization.

Methods to implement these improvements constitute Chapter 15. This process is considered a monitoring controlling, not an executing, process. This is because it tracks "compliance" with agreed-to staffing plans. The staffing plans encompass needs for both project and operating staff. Project staff includes people assigned for the duration of the project extension or subproject. Operating staff is also likely to be needed for new functions identified as part of the supply chain strategy. Key people may have to be recruited from external sources.

Table 14.7 Project Staffing (3.6)

3.6.1 Inputs	3.6 Project Staffing		Monitoring and Controlling
		3.6.2 Process Elements	3.6.3 Outputs
Multicompany Project Staffing Requirements (3.4)	**Process definition**	This process monitors partner company commitments of staff to multicompany SCM projects on both the upstream and downstream sides. It includes activities to confirm the suitability of people nominated for certain positions. Exception reporting causes modifications to project plans.	Staffed SCM Projects, Subprojects, or Project Extensions. Staff Plan Exceptions
	Approaches and techniques	Planning for scope changes, subprojects or new stand-alone SCM projects. Reporting of readiness to proceed on process improvements.	
	PM shortcomings addressed	Staffing is a sign of commitment from top management (to counter abrogation) and should include the skills necessary to make new processes work. Process methodology at Level 3 of the PMMM will communicate project needs to partners.	
	SCM maturity	Staff commitments reflect willingness to commit to process improvements that cross company boundaries, Levels IV and V of the SCM maturity model for Tasks 4 and 5.	
	Stakeholders	All participating companies and particularly the assigned employees are stakeholders. The project staff should monitor the process.	

14.6.1 *Inputs to* 3.6 Acquire Multicompany Staff Resources *(3.6.1)*

Multicompany project staffing requirements from process 3.4 are the principal input. The requirements, as described in the previous process, include the position, number of people, the skills needed for the position, and the timing of the requirement.

14.6.2 *Process Elements for* 3.6 Acquire Multicompany Staff Resources *(3.6.2)*

The process is not complicated in concept. However, if staffing requirements are ambitious and complicated, acquiring staff will be difficult. It is assumed this is to be done outside the project by partner human resource functions. Often, a person nominated for a project or operating position is a "near fit." In these cases, the process should include confirmation of the near-fit selections by examining what risks might be involved and how missing skills will be provided. Filling the gaps could include training the candidate, consultants, or creating another position. The arrow between processes 3.4 and 3.6 in Figure 14.1 is two-headed. This reflects the need for the multicompany steering committee to deal with variances to the plan.

14.6.3 *Outputs from* 3.6 Acquire Multicompany Staff Resources *(3.6.3)*

Outputs include exception tracking of the pace of staffing the plan. The output is reported as *Staffed SCM Projects, Subprojects, or Project Extensions. Staff Plan Exceptions* are reported to *1.7 Control Changes;* the exceptions could cause changes to the project plan. Such changes might only affect the implementation schedule. If the changes reflect a serious shortcoming in finding people to get the work done, then the scope of the supply chain project will change.

14.7 Verify Partner Scope (3.7)

This monitoring and controlling process, summarized in Table 14.8, takes various change suggestions and processes them into *change requests*. These are of two types: changes in the SCM elements and changes in the project management elements of the overall supply chain project plan.

14.7.1 *Inputs to* 3.7 Verify Partner Scope *(3.7.1)*

Table 14.9 lists examples of the types of changes that arise in the process of developing partnerships with other companies.

Table 14.8 Verify Partner Scope (3.7)

	3.7 Verify Partner Scope		*Monitoring and Controlling*
3.7.1 Inputs	*3.7.2 Process Elements*		*3.7.3 Outputs*
Changes (3.1–3.6) SCM Subprojects (3.4)	**Process definition**	Collaboration with partners is likely to produce many changes to the project plan.	SCM and Project Management Change Requests
	Approaches and techniques	Project and scope plan reviews.	
	PM shortcomings addressed	Scope changes formalize an important project management element.	
	SCM maturity	Scope changes formalize an important SCM collaboration element.	
	Stakeholders	Project office. Project steering committee.	

Table 14.9 Typical Changes Associated with Partnership Formulation

Process #	*Process Name*	*Examples*
3.1	Plan Communications	Development of the external communications plan turns up the need for changes. An example is disclosure of company-confidential information.
3.2	Implement Supplier Base Plan	Feedback from suppliers reflecting their willingness to participate and suggestions for the shape of the partnership.
3.3	Implement Customer Base Plan	Feedback from downstream partners reflecting their willingness to participate and suggestions for the shape of the partnership.
3.4	Install Multicompany Organization	Meetings with partner executives and staff will lead to more suggestions for changing the project plan.
3.6	Plan Risk Sharing	The actual shape of partner business agreements may differ from the original collaboration plan's intent.

14.7.2 *Process Elements for* 3.7 Verify Partner Scope *(3.7.2)*

The naming of the process reflects the need in a supply chain project to get trading partner "buy in." An organization can conceive of a plan to suit its need. But, to the extent the organization depends on its partners, they must come aboard as well.

14.7.3 *Outputs from* 3.7 Verify Partner Scope *(3.7.3)*

Outputs from the process are inputs to process *1.7 Control Changes.* Accepted changes will make their way into project planning documents.

Chapter 15

Improving Supply Chain Processes and Systems

Ultimately, all supply chain project efforts either develop or improve pro-cesses. Traditionally, these efforts target performance metrics; cost, inventory, and defects are common targets. Many of these efforts will fall short. The most effective projects will support strategy, involve partners, take a process-centered approach, and address root causes, not symptoms.

Many, if not most, companies pursuing supply chain improvement make a huge mistake. That is, they start their efforts at this point in the overall process, omitting processes described in Chapters 12 through 14. These efforts call to mind the "whack a mole" game. In this game, the furry animal appears at one of several holes. The player must whack it on the head before it disappears to reappear at another hole. Projects like this ignore, explicitly or out of sheer ignorance, several important questions: What is our strategy? Does what we do in the supply chain affect our ability to compete? Is our organization aligned across its departments to make changes? Can "vendors" help the effort? Why involve customers (they want to beat us up)?

Without executing processes from earlier chapters, disappointment should be expected. That said, a quick payback—even a local one—could spark and sustain interest in a longer project. To move the process forward quickly, conceptual design in Chapter 12, internal alignment in Chapter 13, and enlistment of partners in Chapter 14 can proceed on a fast track for high priority or obviously broken processes.

Figure 15.1 is a flowchart of the six processes covered in this chapter. The processes cover two of our five supply chain management (SCM) tasks: Task 4

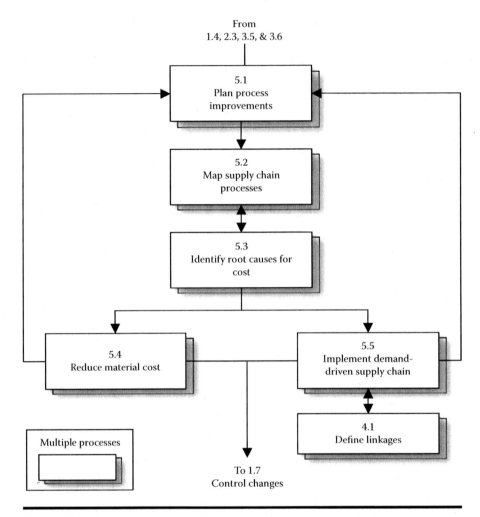

Figure 15.1 Improving supply chain processes and systems.

Managing Supply Chain Information and Task 5 Removing Cost from the Supply Chain. The underlying principle for addressing them in a single chapter is that information exchange through links between partners is integral to process design. This is consistent with a "process-centered" philosophy, described in Section 3.6. Labeling SCM Task 5 as "removing cost" should not be misinterpreted. The intent is not only to remove cost but also to make more money by improving delivery and quality.

Section 4.2.1 described the market and product nuances that need to be considered. Considerations include the position of the product in its life cycle and whether the product is innovative, requiring a responsive supply chain, or functional, requiring a cost-effective supply chain. You should also note that the emphasis on identification and elimination of root causes for cost. With the root cause gone, the costs also vanish. Not addressing root causes brings on unintended consequences. An example is hard negotiations with suppliers to lower prices, when actions from our own company, like changing a design or specification, is the best way to lower supplier costs and the prices we pay those suppliers. Another common mistake is using "benchmarking" to set budgets. A typical method is employment of ratios like dollars of procurement cost per dollar of material spend. This approach is generally too broad-brush to account for differences between companies and between our own company's "businesses within the business" or spheres.

The processes described here apply to both establishing new processes and improving existing ones. In many cases, the strategy for a sphere calls for brand new processes—activities that aren't currently performed in the organization or even elsewhere in the supply chain. In other cases, a process may be in place but is deemed inconsistent with the direction demanded by the supply chain strategy. Also, some processes are acknowledged by all to be broken and in need of repair. The motivators for new or improved processes can also be higher performance in any measure—service, cost, quality, flexibility, or a combination thereof.

Process improvement is an expansive topic. There are many management and software tools available to conduct needed analysis of the process and implement improvements. As an example, the Supply-Chain Council's Supply-Chain Operations Reference-model (SCOR-model) and the Council of Supply Chain Management Professionals' (CSCMP) *Supply Chain Management Process Standards*, described in Chapter 8, document in great detail higher-level supply chain processes. Both include many best practices for employment in these processes. This book describes what we believe to be the most indispensable approaches to improve supply chain performance. As mentioned earlier, when it comes to process improvement, the greatest errors are those of omission because Chapters 12 through 14 processes are ignored, not because of an absence of motivation, analytical tools, or software.

Process improvement efforts are likely to be "subprojects" within the overall supply chain project. Referring to Figure 15.1, process *5.1 Plan Process Improvements* launches individual process improvement efforts, which can focus on improving an existing process or creating a new one; *5.2 Map Supply Chain Processes* follows this process, collecting information that puts the process under a microscope.

Process *5.3 Identify Root Causes for Cost* seeks out the real cost drivers based on information from the process mapping. This approach is recommended because too few efforts really address root causes. Too many companies pursue "results," not causes—the "whack a mole" approach. Examples of pursuing results include reduction in costs categories like inventory or labor. Such fixes become Band-Aids, only effective for a short time. Failure to address root causes will result in futility.

From root causes, the processes then branch into *5.4 Reduce Material Cost* and *5.5 Implement Demand-Driven Supply Chain*. These processes implement actions that evolve from root cause identification. As its name implies, *5.4 Reduce Material*

Cost looks for solutions related to material cost like design specification, material used, lack of commonality in components, and tolerances. These interventions require support from our own company's engineering function.

Process 5.5, addressing the demand-driven supply chain, covers operating activities including manufacturing, distribution, production control, procurement, and inventory management. The "demand-driven" name embodies what has become a universal vision—to make supply chain replenishment decisions with "perfect," actual end-user consumption data. Visually, the demand-driven supply chain is the tightly linked chain where demand signals from end users are instantly transmitted throughout the chain. Most supply chains fall far short of the ideal. In many supply chains, a "bullwhip effect" occurs where level end-user demand, when transmitted upstream, produces wide swings in production.

We give this process the "demand-driven" label since such a chain is a safe goal for supply chain designers. Other labels include the "synchronized" or lean supply chain and reflect the same intent. The supply chain process design teams should examine the potential of each supply chain to be demand-driven, determine the gap in the current operations, and then systematically close the gap.

Abetting the demand-driven supply chain are links among partners along the chain. Process *4.1 Define Linkages* characterizes those links for any particular chain. The links invariably involve the passing of data, so linkages are necessary for handling information. This process is tied to our SCM Task 4 Managing Supply Chain Information. However, other features of the linkage should be captured in the process. Examples include transportation, forms of collaboration, face-to-face meetings, and planning for supply chain exceptions called "events." Supply chain practitioners are awash in sales pitches for linkage "solutions." Task 4.1 should define linkage requirements before embarking on the search for software.

The Glossary and the tables in this chapter list terms that have proliferated around information technology (IT) links. Most of these solutions are expensive. More perniciously, however, they can bring on complacency through the illusion that "something is being done" to improve the process. But, without a strategy or knowledge of root causes, that "something" may not be the right something. Chapter 9 recounted root causes for technology failures. It is fervently hoped that those who employ disciplines in this book will sidestep lurking disasters.

Chapter 11, as illustrated in Figure 11.1, described four phases for a SCM project. Process improvements covered by this process fall chiefly into the last two of the four phases: short-term improvement and long-term improvement. Processes described in this chapter will note this division in anticipation that some process improvements will be achieved in the short term and some will require more time. It is often the short-term improvements that managements look to for financing the longer-term ones. In applying the concept of process-centered management, cleaning up the existing process and organization can be a short-term measure. A system to further enhance the processes might be long term.

15.1 Plan Process Improvements (5.1)

Table 15.1 summarizes this process. There will likely be multiple process improvements in a single supply chain effort. Many will justify their own project or subproject label. That is, they are significant enough to warrant being managed as independent efforts using project management knowledge and practice. Since we are considering our overall supply chain effort to be a project, we will refer to each separate process improvement effort as a subproject. Departing from the conventions of *A Guide to the Project Management Body of Knowledge (PMBOK Guide)*, we identify this process with three project management process groups: initiating, monitoring and controlling, and planning. In other words, it is an "integrated" process incorporating several elements. Process 5.1 plays the role of "traffic cop" at a busy intersection when the traffic lights don't work. The traffic cop must decide when to initiate, or turn on, traffic movement in any particular direction. He or she must also decide when to stop flow in that direction or divert the flow, being mindful of the build up in traffic at the intersection. This requires decisions in all three areas—initiating, monitoring and controlling, and planning—to balance the workload with the organization's ability to handle it. This is an important function, needed to avoid taking on too many projects or the wrong projects. Appendix B recommends assigning execution of this process to the project manager or project office.

15.1.1 Inputs to Process 5.1 Plan Process Improvements (5.1.1)

This process assures that the company manages process improvement in a disciplined way. The approach urges project managers to make no distinction between technology projects and other operational improvement initiatives. This philosophy was introduced in Section 3.6 describing process-centered management and reinforced in Chapter 9. Inputs to the process, as shown in Table 15.1, should provide the following needs for a go-ahead:

- *Activity Systems Design (1.4)* identifies conceptual designs of needed processes.
- *Implemented Organization Plan (2.3)* puts key people in place that will operate new processes. Sponsors for the effort and the process design team should come from this group.
- *Multicompany Project Staffing Requirements (3.4)* brings needed resources from outside the company. In particular, this assures there is assigned partner staff, where needed, to support the effort.
- *Partner Business Arrangements (3.5)* define business rules for the partnership. Agreements should be in place to govern the process improvement.
- *Staffed SCM Projects, Subprojects, or Project Extensions (3.6)* is a deliverable that tracks progress in making assignments. Its outputs signal when partners are ready to proceed.

Table 15.1   Plan Process Improvements (5.1)

5.1.1 Inputs	5.1 Plan Process Improvements		Initiating/Planning/Monitoring and Controlling
	5.1.2 Process Elements		5.1.3 Outputs
Activity Systems Design (1.4) Implemented Organization Plan (2.3) Multicompany Project Staffing Requirements (3.4) Partner Business Arrangements (3.5) Staffed SCM Projects, Subprojects, or Project Extensions (3.6) Progress Reports from Process Improvement Subprojects (5.4 and 5.5)	**Process definition**	Initiate and plan supply chain process implementation and improvements by sphere. Set priorities for implementation. Confirm staff deployment for improvement projects. Coordinate efforts with project phasing from *1.2 Develop Project Plan* (Table 12.2).	Process Improvement Initiation Charter Elements (Table 12.1) Project Plan Elements (Table 12.2) Subproject Plan Changes Change Requests
	Approaches and techniques	Cost analysis. Customer priorities. Competitive analysis. Project management knowledge and practice. Project progress reporting. Earned value measures (see Section 7.3.7 and Table 7.2).	
	PM shortcomings addressed	This multicompany commitment requires top management support for the effort. It will also deploy needed skills to projects, reducing the cost of failure. Process improvement planning will test the "process discipline" component of project management maturity. There will be multiple projects that must be coordinated across departments and companies.	

SCM maturity	Broader scope process projects are indicative of Stages IV and V of the SCM maturity model (Table 10.5).	
Terminology	Business process re-engineering Chief process improvement officer (CPIO) Portfolio, project portfolio management (PPM)	Category management Discounted cash flow Process owner
Stakeholders	Participating internal departments and partners are stakeholders. Any department can participate in multiple projects. The ability of partnerships to implement may be the limiting factor in the improvement achieved. The supply chain project team should administer the process. The company steering committee should have the ultimate responsibility for process success.	

The process synthesizes these inputs into a *Process Improvement Initiation* document that charters and plans the effort. The process also takes feedback from ongoing process improvement subprojects. This input will cause adjustments in plans for the portfolio of process development and improvement subprojects.

15.1.2 Process Elements for 5.1 Plan Process Improvements (5.1.2)

The process will be continuous while process improvements continue, tracking the portfolio of ongoing subprojects. It will also have an intermittent element each time a process improvement is kicked off. Each supply chain project will be different. The number of discrete subprojects will depend on the number of spheres, requirements for enabling processes, subproject priorities, and management's desires for overall control. An organization desiring close control would tend to have many smaller, narrower subprojects. Looser control would produce fewer, larger projects.

15.1.2.1 Process Definition for 5.1 Plan Process Improvements

Principal responsibilities for executing the process include the following:

- Track progress made in developing deliverables, inputs in Table 15.1, needed to charter the improvement subproject.
- Monitor the workload generated by subprojects and their progress. Avoid overloading the company and their partners. Don't "under-load" them either.
- When incoming deliverable "packages" for a process are complete, develop the charter and project plan for the subproject. Cluster like projects together.
- Launch projects at the appropriate time. Timing will avoid conflicts between projects for staff, budgets, and management attention.
- Provide inputs to process *1.7 Control Changes* regarding needed changes.
- Confirm budgets for implementation. Use the company approval process to gain budget approvals. Budgets can be quite large if major expenditures for IT or large assets are planned.

15.1.2.2 Approaches and Techniques for 5.1 Plan Process Improvements

Techniques listed in Table 15.1 address the need to coordinate several subprojects and play the role as "dispatcher" for a complex undertaking. Work described in prior chapters should assure that resources are available. However, plan changes are inevitable. Cost–benefit analysis will help set priorities. Similarly, customer priorities may make a project that saves less more important. Intelligence on competitors' initiatives may also cause priorities to shift. Feedback of progress toward milestones and achievement of results will also lead to changes in plans. Project management measurements, such as earned value, can measure progress toward goals.

15.1.2.3 Project Management Shortcomings Addressed by 5.1 Plan Process Improvements

Any project that reaches this stage should have internal senior management support and, to the extent partners are involved, multicompany support. Combining IT and process improvement should also address both misunderstood technology and partner technology capabilities, as described in Chapter 9. The first downfall can be sidestepped by closely weaving the technology requirement into process improvement. By signing off on the project, one's own company and its partners are confirming that the technology choices match their capabilities. Project management maturity is advanced by the process discipline provided by this step. To the extent there are many subprojects, central control enforces a singular methodology. In fact, without such a singular methodology, it may be impossible to manage the complexity involved in executing the subproject portfolio.

15.1.2.4 SCM Maturity for 5.1 Plan Process Improvements

Achieving Stages IV and V SCM maturity, as described in Table 10.5, for Tasks 4 and 5 requires multicompany efforts. In particular, working jointly to reduce material costs is a signal of Stage V maturity. The presence of several multicompany subprojects signals achievement of this level.

15.1.2.5 Terminology for 5.1 Plan Process Improvements

Terms in Table 15.1 relate to methods for sorting and selecting subprojects for implementation. The chief process improvement officer (CPIO) term is relatively new. The process owner is another position recommended in information management standards like ITIL (Information Technology Infrastructure Library). If there were ever a road map for such a position, the overall process described in this book would be a good place to start.

15.1.2.6 Stakeholders for 5.1 Plan Process Improvements

The supply chain project manager or project office should administer the process. Any function involved in the project—whether in our company or that of a partner—is a stakeholder. Other stakeholders include outsiders like software vendors, system integrators, and consultants. These parties may constitute the process design team. The company steering committee should retain ultimate responsibility for the process. Some processes may require outsourcing service provider companies for contracting out supply chain activities.

15.1.3 Outputs from 5.1 **Plan Process Improvements** *(5.1.3)*

The outputs include a charter and subproject plan to move ahead. This plan, like the supply chain project plan developed in process 1.2, should include both supply chain and project management elements. The following is a list of project management elements, including several from Table 12.2 that lists components of a project plan:

- role of the subproject within the overall supply chain project,
- approval to proceed with the subproject,
- Work Breakdown Structure listing deliverables,
- activities that must be done in the project and their sequencing,
- subproject phasing and schedule—a particularly important component when large expenditures are required,
- network diagrams showing interrelationships of activities,
- cost baseline for project budgeting,
- design team assignments from one's own company and participating partners, and
- scope management plan including controlling processes.

Two control outputs from this process are changes to the overall supply chain project and to process improvement subprojects that are already underway. The former goes back to process *1.7 Control Changes.*

15.2 Map Supply Chain Processes (5.2)

After initiation, a logical next step is to "map" the process. We've said that the process under consideration can be either a new process or one that's already in place. Mapping in the first case is a design effort, describing in detail how the process should operate. In the case of an existing process, we seek process changes to meet new requirements or to improve old ones to be more competitive. In either event, mapping provides the detail needed to make design decisions. Some prefer not to map the "as-is," in the case of existing processes. Those recommending "as-is" mapping cite the need to understand why a process has shortcomings, to help plan the transition to a new process, and to identify aspects of the current process worth keeping. We strongly recommend "as-is" documentation.

5.2 Map Supply Chain Processes, summarized in Table 15.2, documents the process and focuses attention on areas for further action. Here, mapping is broadly defined. We include documentation of customer requirements, product structure, and all elements of outbound and return flow, including the physical, information, and financial components. The deliverables for process mapping described here are not exhaustive. Practitioners should add as needed or subtract items that aren't needed for a particular effort.

Also, many of the suggested flowcharting components assume some degree of partner cooperation. In the event that cooperation isn't forthcoming, it may be impossible to gather or estimate needed information. This could include partner costs, technology employed, lead times, and quality parameters as warranted. In Figure 15.1, the link between the mapping and root cause identification is two-headed. This means the project team should augment initial documentation if initial mapping doesn't uncover root causes, only symptoms.

15.2.1 Inputs to 5.2 Map Supply Chain Processes *(5.2.1)*

The charter and project plan from *5.1 Plan Process Improvements* define the scope of the process for mapping and lay down goals for completing the mapping. Each process will support an activity that in turn supports a sphere-centered strategy for competing. Section 4.2.3.2 describes the activity system approach for developing these strategies.

15.2.2 Process Elements for 5.2 Map Supply Chain Processes *(5.2.2)*

This process gathers information about the process. The elements suggested here enable an organization to identify the process improvements available by applying a number of technical approaches. These include process streamlining by removing low-value activities, value engineering, changes in product specifications and design, information links between partners, new performance metrics, and organization changes.

15.2.2.1 Process Definition for 5.2 Map Supply Chain Processes

This process sets the vision for new or re-engineered processes based on information gained through mapping. Its purpose is to gather sufficient information to determine root causes for deficiencies in an existing process or for a new process design. This work doesn't design the solution; that is done in downstream project processes. However, the ability to come up with the best solution will depend on the understanding gained here. An important element is multicompany participation. Too often, a company pursues its initiatives with blinders on. Perspectives are limited to what's going on inside the organization, not what is happening elsewhere in the supply chain. In the case of non-existing processes, partner participation is even more vital, providing technical support to the team. For new, complex manufacturing processes or information systems, equipment suppliers and consultants will be important contributors.

Table 15.2 Map Supply Chain Processes (5.2)

		5.2 Map Supply Chain Processes		Executing
5.2.1 Inputs		5.2.2 Process Elements		5.2.3 Outputs
Process Improvement Initiation (5.1)	Process definition	Characterize each authorized process as defined in the process improvement strategy.		*Process Analysis* Markets: • Customers served • Distribution channels • Customer requirements/ performance gaps Products: • Product descriptions/ structure
	Approaches and techniques	Cost and lead-time tracking. Functional flowcharts ("swim lane" format). Activity-based costing. ABC inventory analysis. Constraint analysis. Product structure (VAT). Supply chain surveys. Benchmarking.		
	PM shortcomings addressed	Developing a "standard" for characterizing a process and its effectiveness should be a component of Level 3 "singular methodology" for project management.		
	SCM maturity	Skill in assessing processes is fundamental to success in creating new value (SCM Task 1) and reducing the cost of supply chain processes (SCM Tasks 4 and 5).		

Terminology			
Activity-based costing	Assemble-to-order	Capacity strategy	• Product profitability
Batch-and-queue system	Cash-to-cash cycle time	Cellular manufacturing	• Materials consumed
Channel	Configuration	Constraint	• SKU ABC analysis
Control points	Cost driver	Cost of quality (COQ)	Operations:
C_p, C_{pk}	Customer service ratio	Cycle time	• Flowcharts
Deficiency, discrepancy	Drumbeat	Engineer-to-order	• Cost/cycle time map
Extended product	Five focusing steps	GMROI	• Cost categories
Implosion	Inventory turns	Just in Time (JIT)	• Quality performance
Key process parameter	Lead time	Make-to-order	• Facilities/assets employed
Make-to-stock	MRP, MRP II	Order penetration point	• Information systems support
Process owner	Quality standard	Representative product	
Reverse logistics	Seven wastes	Six Sigma	
Specification	Stock-keeping unit (SKU)	Statistical process control	
Theory of constraints	Throughput	Transfer pricing	
VAT analysis	Velocity	Wall-to-wall inventory	
Stakeholders	Process design teams for each process from functions and companies involved in the process map the supply chain. Employees who contribute to the assessment of the process are also stakeholders.		

15.2.2.2 Approaches and Techniques for 5.2 Map Supply Chain Processes

The following tools will document the processes and analyze their potential for improvement. As stated above, a project team should add to this list or delete approaches based on the issues they face.

15.2.2.2.1 Activity-Based Costing (abc[1])

This tool is particularly useful for multicompany process analysis. It moves away from compliance-driven accounting systems that vary from partner to partner and aren't particularly helpful for process design. The technique should capture the resources required by a process whether they are represented by traditional "direct" or "indirect" cost. The former includes costs like labor and material, the latter costs like capital recovery, maintenance, engineering, support, scrap and rework, and administrative overhead. In essence, abc turns as many indirect and overhead costs created by a process into direct costs that vary with changes in the activity volume. The volume variable is called a cost driver. Examples include labor or machine hours, number of transactions, or cost per time period (hour, day, month).

15.2.2.2.2 Constraint Analysis

In the theory of constraints (TOC), bottleneck operations determine the capacity of the process of which they are a part, in this case the supply chain. A bottleneck operation warrants special attention. Expanding capacity there raises the capacity of the whole chain to produce profits for its partners. So, the potential benefits, assuming the products produced by the added capacity can be sold, are magnified. This is because the operation itself may not only be more efficient but also the added capacity produces more profitable revenue. Increasing capacity elsewhere will have little effect since these operations are not bottlenecks. Improving them produces no more supply chain capacity.

At this point, the process team should identify supply chain constraints. The constraints may be in one's own company or at a partner's operation. A good indicator is to look at lead times throughout the process. Long lead time for a component is indicative of a bottleneck in the production of that component.

15.2.2.2.3 Cost Improvement Categories

Different cost categories are amenable to different techniques for performance improvement. Table 15.3 lists categories for cataloging activity-based costs. The broad categories include labor, capital, and material components. Labor comes in four forms, as shown in the table. Each requires a different approach for improvement. Without knowing how much activity cost there is in each category, it is difficult to set priorities and identify root causes in the next process.

Table 15.3 Cost Improvement Categories

Workforce costs	Direct labor	Labor that "touches" the product. Often has assigned work measurement standards.
	Indirect labor	Labor that doesn't have a work measurement standard but supports the direct labor component.
	Clerical/ administrative/ sales	Secretaries, accounting staff, receptionists, clerks, and sales administration.
	Technical/ professional	Design engineers, system engineers, procurement staff, and "white collar" functions.
Fixed costs	Annualized costs of capacity including depreciation and capital cost, generally plant and equipment. Other fixed expenses.	
Purchased item costs	Services	Includes accounting, consulting, and engineering support.
	Subcontracted material	Material made to the company's specification. This category is normally susceptible to cost reduction.
	Commodity material	Material bought by many companies. There is normally a "market" price for this category and it is not considered susceptible to cost reduction. Cost reduction can focus on the administrative and inventory-related costs.

Fixed costs include both real-life depreciation and required return on investment. "Real life" is not the accounting life span of the asset but the period that the asset will be productive. This is often much shorter than the physical life, due to obsolescence of the asset. Even though your four-year-old computer still works as well as it did when new, it may be obsolete because it's too slow for modern software.

Purchased material items are another example where approaches must differ. We have much more control over subcontracted material that we design ourselves or with a partner than we do over commodity material that is widely available. We might turn to bidding in exchanges for commodities. On the other hand, we may want to limit the number of suppliers for subcontracted material to collaborate with a few key partners to reduce cost.

15.2.2.2.4 Flowcharts

Flowcharts are always useful for displaying a process. Figure 15.2 is an example. The figure uses a "swim lane" format familiar to many practitioners. There are many

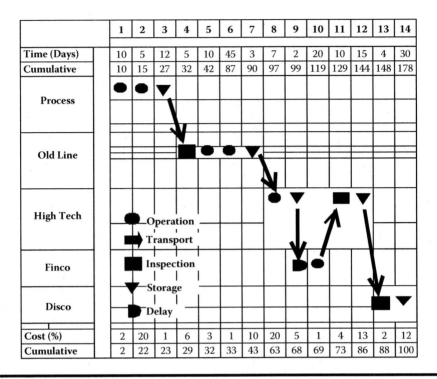

	1	2	3	4	5	6	7	8	9	10	11	12	13	14
Time (Days)	10	5	12	5	10	45	3	7	2	20	10	15	4	30
Cumulative	10	15	27	32	42	87	90	97	99	119	129	144	148	178
Process														
Old Line														
High Tech														
Finco														
Disco														
Cost (%)	2	20	1	6	3	1	10	20	5	1	4	13	2	12
Cumulative	2	22	23	29	32	33	43	63	68	69	73	86	88	100

Figure 15.2   Flowcharting the supply chain.

other formats for flowcharting. The Business Process Modeling Notation (BPMN) is a swim lane approach that has become an international standard. Figure 15.2 shows the path of a component or product along a supply chain with five companies and fourteen process steps. At the top of the flowchart is the lead time in weeks, with individual work center and cumulative figures. Along the bottom is similar information for costs. Note that the figures on the top are for lead time, not cycle time. Cycle time, as defined in this book, is the actual time an operation takes. The lead time is the amount of time between the replenishment order and the delivery of the order. The "velocity" of the process is the percentage of cumulative cycle time to cumulative lead time and is often less than 5 percent.

Such a display focuses one's attention on high cost and long lead time steps. Can one avoid the side trip to Finco for a process that takes over twenty days? Why does Old Line take so long—fifty-five days—to process our work? Note the operations are only 4 percent of cost. Herman Miller used this approach to design its supply chain, as described in Section 4.2.3.2. Their approach recognized that much of the lead time and cost occurred outside manufacturing. A project team may face a decision regarding the level of detail required to document their processes. A process that produces over 100 components using a common process doesn't require 100 flow-charts. The use of a "representative part" chosen from the 100 should be sufficient.

15.2.2.2.5 Product Structures (VAT)

The product structure is also important to the analysis of root causes for cost. Another model from the TOC, called VAT analysis, reflects the relationship between components and their final products. A "V" product has a few component materials (at the bottom of the "V") that can be turned into many end products (at the top of the "V"). A pharmaceutical company manufacturing a pill could have multiple end-item SKUs (stock-keeping units). For a single tablet, these SKUs could include different bottle sizes and country-specific labeling for global distribution. Some companies also incorporate storage locations into their SKU numbering, leading to even more numbers for the same physical product.

An "A" structure is the opposite of the "V" structure. With the "A" structure, many components are assembled into a single product. Aircraft and automobiles are good examples; thousands of SKUs and millions of individual parts make up one deliverable product. The "T" product line uses common components or assemblies to make a few finished products. A Mexican restaurant is an example. Beans, rice, tacos, tortillas, chicken, shrimp, pork, and beef combine to make many menu items.

The VAT approach should cause the process design team to look downstream for "V" product improvements and upstream for "A" and "T" products. For example, product structure is at the heart of postponement strategies. Postponement, for a "V" structure, delays production commitments to more closely track production to actual demand, a goal of the demand-driven supply chain. A company may also have products with "A" structures that can be transitioned into "T" products by standardizing parts or modules.

15.2.2.2.6 Surveys and Benchmarking

Surveys and benchmarking are ways to assess supply chain process effectiveness. Surveys can target respondents upstream or downstream in the chain. If partner participation hasn't been sought or hasn't been forthcoming after requests, there may be no choice but to use surveys outside the partner base to gather information. Benchmarking looks for best practices for targeted operations from companies in any industry. Insights provided include the following:

- What you do well and what you don't do well as a supplier or a customer.
- How you stack up to your peers and/or competitors.
- Where you might add more value for your customers.
- Methods your partners are using for collaboration.
- Actions you should take to make your suppliers' lives easier and lower your cost.
- "Best practice" objectives for process performance that you might adopt.

15.2.2.2.7 Supplier/SKU ABC Analysis

The previous section recommended activity-based costing, or "abc." This acronym is popular; "ABC," defined further in the Glossary, is also a term used in inventory analysis. From a manufacturer's or distributor's perspective, "A" inventory items, or SKUs, are the top few (10–20 percent) that make up the largest share of material spend (in the range of 50–70 percent). "C" items are reversed—the many items that account for a small share of material spend. "B" items are in between. "C" items, for the fact they are missing at critical times, frequently cause the biggest headaches. Although they are purchased for low prices, they can stop a production line or hold up an order.

Dave Malmberg of CGR Management Consultants recommends applying ABC simultaneously to both SKUs and suppliers. Figure 15.3 illustrates the approach and suggests strategies for different categories. For example, for "A" suppliers providing A SKUs (upper left-hand corner), Figure 15.3 suggests partnering and other collaborative efforts leading to a demand-driven supply chain. The partnering recommendation is in plain type, indicating it's a supplier strategy that applies to all the SKUs provided by that supplier. The three other recommendations—instituting a demand-driven supply chain, lead time reduction, and cost reductions—are in italics to indicate they are SKU strategies to be applied on an item-by-item or category-by-category basis.

Key:
- *SKU strategy*
- Supplier strategy

		Suppliers		
		A	B	C
Products/SKUs	A	Develop partnerships *Engineer synchronized demand-driven supply chain for key SKUs* *Reduce lead times* *Pursue cost reduction with incentives*	Add business *Negotiate consigned/demand-driven supply chain* *Reduce lead times*	Focus on "A" SKUs *Move B & C items to other suppliers* *Reduce lead times*
	B	Develop partnerships Pursue supplier-managed inventory	Add business Move to distributor	Find A or B supplier *Eliminate SKU*
	C	Consolidate demand Apply activity costing Buy more "C" SKUs from the supplier	Move business to distributor *Eliminate/substitute SKUs* *Consolidate demand*	Move business to distributor *Eliminate/substitute SKUs* *Consolidate demand*

Figure 15.3   Supplier/SKU ABC analysis.

At the other end of the spectrum, the box for "C" suppliers and SKUs, a SKU strategy might seek elimination of the SKU or substitution of one SKU for another. A corresponding supplier strategy could shift that business to a distributor who supplies a portfolio of similar purchased items, in effect outsourcing the costs of administering and stocking these SKUs.

15.2.2.3 Project Management Shortcomings Addressed by 5.2 Map Supply Chain Processes

In the event there are multiple processes for development or improvement over multiple companies, using common methods of process documentation is consistent with a singular methodology for project management. "Erratic" and inconsistent methods will create confusion, blunting the ability to achieve objectives. The standard for Business Process Modeling Notation (BPMN) is useful for creating flowcharts.

15.2.2.4 SCM Maturity for 5.2 Map Supply Chain Processes

With regard to SCM maturity, mapping is an important opportunity to test the strength of collaborative relationships described in Chapter 10. Such relationships represent Stage III and above for Task 3 Forging Supply Chain Partnerships. For Task 5 Making Money from the Supply Chain, such collaboration is indicative of Stage V.

15.2.2.5 Terminology for 5.2 Map Supply Chain Processes

Terms selected for the process, defined in the Glossary, are useful for process documentation. They include performance measures, techniques for documentation, and common features found in supply chain processes.

15.2.2.6 Stakeholders for 5.2 Map Supply Chain Processes

A multicompany design team should map the processes under the direction of the multicompany steering committee. Stakeholders in the process include any involved function. These stakeholders, to the degree possible, should contribute to mapping and review its results. Stakeholders are also a rich source of commentary on the effectiveness of processes.

15.2.3 Outputs from 5.2 Map Supply Chain Processes (5.2.3)

The output format, it is suggested here, can follow the markets–products–operations approach used to define spheres. This is a useful way to collect and present a large amount of information for determining root causes for cost—whether the process is an existing or a new one.

15.2.3.1 Customer Documentation

A beginning should address the customers or customer segments served. This effort should indicate the distribution of sales by customer or segment. This level should be expressed in terms of revenue and unit volume. Documentation should also identify end-user distribution channels. From documentation gathered earlier in the project, customer requirements should be documented and performance gaps estimated. Quality Function Deployment (QFD) provides a user-friendly approach. A robust description of QFD is available in *The QFD Handbook*.[2] Chapter 6 of the *Handbook of Supply Chain Management*, Second Edition, describes its application in a supply chain improvement case.

15.2.3.2 Product Documentation

Each sphere represents a product, several products, or one or more product groups. These products include both the physical and extended product. For cost reduction, the information gathered about products will yield opportunities to improve the design of the physical, or base, product, potential postponement strategies, and other measures like material substitution.

- Product descriptions/structure: This deliverable should describe products in the sphere's portfolio. That description should include the VAT structure.
- Product profitability: This information identifies priorities for improvement. "Profitability" is defined here as the product of unit margin and volume. Under this definition, a high-volume product with a low profit-contribution margin would still be "profitable." High-profitability products might be high priority for implementing new capabilities; low profitability might indicate the need for operating improvements or dropping the product. Profitability data also indicates whether the product is innovative or functional, using terms introduced in Section 4.2.
- Materials consumed: Material documentation should include the ABC analysis for purchased items. Surveys may also uncover other opportunities to reduce cost in the bill of materials.

15.2.3.3 Operations Documentation

Table 15.2 lists some deliverables in this category. Flowcharts, a cost/lead time map (Figure 15.2), and cost categories were described earlier. Quality performance can include the cost of quality, first pass yields on processes, and individual yields along the supply chain. Low yields at a supply chain capacity constraint deserve special attention. Also, an upstream process may be a bottleneck by virtue of low yields downstream. In other words, to produce one pound of product for sale we have to launch two pounds into the front end of the supply chain. The root cause for a bottleneck at the front end is not necessarily lack of capacity but poor yields downstream.

Perhaps the solution is improving those yields, reducing capital investment for more equipment, and saving money from wasted materials lost to scrap. Facilities/assets employed is an inventory of investments supporting the process. Information systems support should list the hardware and software in use by the process. Particularly germane to this process are the computerized links between partners.

15.3 Identify Root Causes for Cost (5.3)

This process, summarized in Table 15.4, is separated from the collection of data about the process (5.2) and execution of changes to the process (processes 5.4 and 5.5). The reason for this separation is to stress the value gained by agreeing to root causes for process shortfalls. As Chapter 9 indicated, things aren't always what they seem, and we have to dig deep to uproot the real reasons. The process uses documentation from process *5.2 Map Supply Chain Processes.* The two-headed arrow in Figure 15.1 symbolizes the potential for "back-and-forth" movement of information between the processes 5.2 and 5.3. If initial mapping data isn't sufficient to identify root causes, more mapping-type investigation may be necessary.

The process output is root cause identification and a "to-be" design. This may not be a perfect, ultimate design—a version we call the greenfield, or start from scratch, vision. However, it will be something that is capable of achievement, and it will address root causes. The to-be often has two components: short-term changes without major systems and facility changes, and a long-term version with those system and facility features. These correspond to Phases 3 and 4 in our generic phases for the supply chain project introduced in Figure 11.1.

15.3.1 *Inputs to* 5.3 Identify Root Causes for Cost *(5.3.1)*

The *Process Analysis* from process 5.2 is the principal input. An exhaustive documentation should contain plenty of clues pointing toward root causes. However, it's important to get agreement from supply chain partners that these are problems worth solving. The approach is just as applicable to new processes at a startup or as it is to processes that are in place. For processes that are totally new to the company or supply chain, the organization must understand the critical drivers for a successful process.

15.3.2 *Process Elements for* 5.3 Identify Root Causes for Cost *(5.3.2)*

Identifying root causes and getting agreement is a mixture of art and science. It requires analytical skills, process design ability, and persuasion. Analytical skill—that is, "science"—is needed to dissect information provided by the process mapping. Process design skills are needed to translate specifications into short-term and

Table 15.4   Identify Root Causes for Cost (5.3)

		5.3 Identify Root Causes for Cost	Executing
5.3.1 Inputs		*5.3.2 Process Elements*	*5.3.3 Outputs*
Process Analysis (5.2)	**Process definition**	Identify the root cause for costs inherent in each process examined. "Cost" here is interpreted broadly. Reducing cost by diminishing service to uncompetitive levels isn't a legitimate cost reduction.	**Process Root Cause Identification and To-Be Process Design**
		Root causes, listed in Section 4.6, include lack of clarity over costs, process variability, product design, poorly executed or nonexistent information sharing, weak links, and unintended circumstances.	Root Causes Addressed To-Be (Short-Term) To-Be (Long-Term) Action Steps
	Approaches and techniques	Ask "why" five times. Spend analysis. Partner meeting/task forces. Gap analysis. Demand-driven potential assessment.	
	PM shortcomings addressed	Analysis of root causes will reduce the risk of applying the wrong solution to improve the process.	

SCM maturity	Understanding root causes will help preserve the collaborative relationship in the supply chain. This is particularly important if one's own company holds economic power over the partner.	
Terminology	5S	ABCD analysis
	Cause and effect diagram	Economic order quantity
	Operational excellence (OE)	Optimization
	Safety factor, safety stock	Total cost of ownership (TCO)
	Total productive maintenance	Total quality management
	Toyota Production System (TPS)	Variable costing
Stakeholders	A process design team should identify root causes. Process improvements involve considerable investments in time and money. Executives approving these efforts will need assurances that the correct solution is being proposed. The multicompany steering committee should agree to the identified root causes and the to-be design.	

long-term process designs. Persuasion—that is, "art"—is required to enlist stake-holders in the effort to make sure the recommended changes will work.

15.3.2.1 Process Definition for 5.3 Identify Root Causes for Cost

The process begins with data on the process from *5.2 Map Supply Chain Processes.* The same people, presumably in the process design team, that collect the information should also draw out the root causes. Once root causes are identified and agreed to, a "specification" should set criteria for the new process design. There are two downstream processes: *5.4 Material Cost* and *5.5 Demand-Driven Supply Chain.* There are two processes identified because the remedies for the two categories—materials and operations—require different approaches.

15.3.2.2 Approaches and Techniques for 5.3 Identify Root Causes for Cost

Approaches and techniques are geared to getting approval for moving ahead with implementation. This requires laying out the path to implementation.

15.3.2.2.1 Gap Analysis

Figure 15.4 shows the relationship between elements in a gap analysis. The gap referred to is between today's existing situation and where one would like the process to be. Step 1 in Figure 15.4 documents the as-is processes. The project process *5.2 Map Supply Chain Processes* supports this step. Step 2 evaluates how well these processes work, a product of process *5.3 Identify Root Causes for Cost* supports this step. Step 3 creates a vision called a "greenfield" or "destination" for processes, organization, and systems, also supported in process 5.3. The greenfield should be thought of as what you would do if you could start from scratch. Step 4 creates subproject plans for advancing from where we are to where we want to be. Processes 5.4, 5.5, and 4.1 provide blueprints for moving along the path to the destination. These plans must account for barriers. Some projects, particularly initial ones, will be internal to the organization; later, more aggressive projects will be multicompany and longer-term measures. If you are really starting from scratch, then Steps 1 and 2 in Figure 15.4 can be skipped. Elements of the destination greenfield vision (Step 3) include the following:

- a new or revised process flow,
- organization structure to support the process,
- required information systems,
- other infrastructure support (facilities, equipment, and systems),
- performance measures for the redesigned process, and
- implementation cost and benefit estimates.

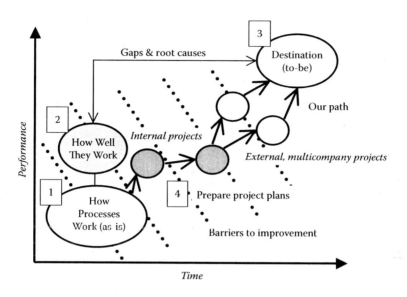

Figure 15.4   Gap analysis.

15.3.2.2.2 Demand-Driven Supply Chain Assessment

The technique establishes the design team's assessment of the potential for a supply chain to be demand-driven. Figure 15.5 and Table 15.5 illustrate the technique. Such a presentation could be an output of *5.2 Map the Supply Chain* or this process. Figure 15.5 shows points along the supply chain where decisions are made to

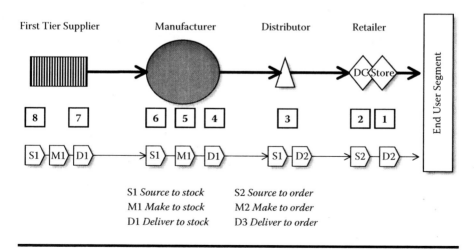

Figure 15.5   Demand-driven assessment.

Table 15.5 Assessing Demand-Driven Potential

#	Entities	Step and Action (Order or Produce)	Decision/ Action(s) Required	Frequency	Lead Time (weeks)	Basis of Decision	Responsibility	Forecast- or Demand-Driven
1	Retail chain	Order: Store level replenishment	Refill stock to target levels	Daily	1	Point of sale system data	Automatic, set by chain replenishment system	Demand-driven
2		Order: Chain distribution center replenishment	Reorder predetermined batch quantity	Weekly	2	Reorder point set in system by SKU	Automated system, buyer reviews by exception	Demand-driven
3	Distributor	Order: Manufacturer warehouse replenishment	Order predetermined batch quantity	Every two weeks	4	Reorder point and forecast	Demand manager using forecast, review exceptions	Forecast-driven
4	Manufacturer (OEM)	Produce: Manufacturer	To make or not to make a batch on fixed schedule	Monthly	2	Orders from warehouse	Factory production planner, manufacturing manager	Forecast-driven

5		Order: Manufacturer raw material	Order predetermined batch quantity	Quarterly	4	Sales forecast	Commodity manager/ buyer, sales department	Forecast-driven
6	Manufacturer's supplier	Order: Supplier warehouse replenishment	Batch size based on forecast	Quarterly	4	Manufacturer forecast	Commodity planner	Forecast-driven
7		Produce: Supplier	Batch size based on forecast	Quarterly	1	Sales forecast and production plan	Factory production planner, manufacturing manager	Forecast-driven
8		Order: Supplier material replenishment	Batch size based on forecast	Quarterly	3	Sales forecast	Commodity manager	Forecast-driven

replenish end-user stock, manufacture product, and order raw materials. It also displays the corresponding SCOR-model threads described in Section 8.2. Table 15.5 documents the basis for each decision, identifying whether the basis for the decision is actual demand or a forecast of actual demand. For the example in Table 15.5, there are eight decisions points. Only two—the closest to the end user—are demand-driven, making the existing demand-driven percentage 25 percent. Note that the table captures lead times and the frequency replenishment decisions are made along the chain. One collaborative approach to becoming more demand-driven is synchronizing decisions, having the same decision-making frequency—hourly, daily, monthly, or even annually—for each decision point. This approach results in constant cycle, variable quantity business rules. The 3C approach described later is such a methodology.

The second step in assessing demand-driven potential is to whether a decision based on forecasts can be converted to a decision based on actual demand at other steps in the chain. Once this is done, we know the potential for our supply chain to be demand-driven. From there, we can create project action plans to convert forecast-driven steps to demand-driven ones. The analysis might begin at the end user and result in a plan to convert decision points 3, 4, and 5. This would raise the demand-driven percentage in the supply chain to 62 percent (five of eight replenishment decisions). This is the potential for the chain to be demand-driven. The analyst should recognize that demand-driven decisions could supply forecast-driven ones. The fact that a manufacturer's customer is ordering on the basis of forecasts doesn't mean the manufacturer can't plan and schedule for "pull"-driven production based on that demand.

15.3.2.2.3 Spend Analysis

The name pretty much explains what has to be done. This analysis can be a by-product of the *Supplier/SKU ABC Inventory Analysis* conducted in *5.2 Map Supply Chain Processes*. The spend analysis should profile spending by both supplier and commodity or SKU. Other categories might include country, lead time and delivery reliability, a measure of engineering content, and a history of prices paid. It should include the purchased item categories shown in Table 15.3.

15.3.2.3 *Project Management Shortcomings Addressed by 5.3 Identify Root Causes for Cost*

Misunderstood technology, as described in Chapter 9, is the most important project management shortcoming addressed. Unless the entire project team, including key partners, accurately identifies root causes, new systems may be implemented that solve the wrong problem. Identifying root cause is an important step to achieving Level 3 on the Project Management Maturity Model (PMMM). Organization communication that seeks employee support is more credible if the audience knows the "homework has been done." Few want to expend precious time and other resources on a wild goose chase. Such efforts sap an organization's ability to respond to real threats and opportunities.

15.3.2.4 SCM Maturity for 5.3 Identify Root Causes for Cost

The ability to jointly reach conclusions on root causes is mark of high-level SCM maturity for Tasks 3 through 5 in Table 10.5. Since the effort will likely enlist marketing and engineering functions inside the company, Task 2 skills must also be well developed.

15.3.2.5 Terminology for 5.3 Identify Root Causes for Cost

The terms listed in Table 15.4 point to methodologies for analyzing root causes for cost.

15.3.2.6 Stakeholders for 5.3 Identify Root Causes for Cost

Few executives on the company and multicompany steering committees will authorize an effort unless they are confident that the proposed solutions address root causes. The design team assigned to the process should identify the root causes and present the case to the multicompany steering committee.

15.3.3 Outputs from 5.3 Identify Root Causes for Cost (5.3.3)

The output is called *Process Root Cause Identification and To-Be Process Design.* That documentation provides a plan for implementation going forward. Elements include the following:

- Root causes addressed: These will fall in the categories identified in Section 4.6. Those related to processes are lack of clarity over costs, process variability, poorly executed or nonexistent information sharing, weak links, and unintended circumstances. Product design, another root cause, is related to manufacturability and relative ease of material acquisition.
- "To-be" scenarios for the short and long term: Short-term improvements are implemented in whatever time horizon, probably less than two years, has been defined as "short term." These are improvements that can be achieved inside the current systems environment and facilities configuration. Long-term changes require systems and facilities changes.
- Action steps answer the question "what's next" for implementation: Measures related to material constitute work done in process *5.4 Material Cost.* Measures related to operational improvements constitute work for process *5.5 Demand-Driven Supply Chain.*

15.4 Reduce Material Cost (5.4)

This process focuses on work with upstream partners to improve service and quality and, if possible, lower costs. Table 15.6 summarizes the process. In many companies, such activity requires a radical mind-set change. Many people are not at all willing or even able to work in cooperative fashion with suppliers. An article in the *Journal of Business Logistics* describes two models attributed to Wal-Mart founder Sam Walton for collaboration between supply chain partners.[3] In a "diamond" relationship, partners are connected across a broad front. The interface is at the middle of the diamond where the bases of two triangles meet. The broad front includes procurement as well as engineering, finance, marketing, production, and other functions. The reverse is the "bowtie." In this model, partners are connected at a single point, probably purchasing.

Relative power between partners is another factor setting the stage for partner collaboration. If one partner is more powerful than the other, collaboration can turn to dictation. Relatively equal partners may find collaboration an economic necessity, and probably easier to establish. Our process description assumes that both sides of the link are motivated toward mutual benefits and follow the diamond model.

15.4.1 Inputs to 5.4 Reduce Material Cost (5.4.1)

Process 5.3 produces a deliverable, *Process Root Cause Identification and To-Be Process Design*, which includes action items. The short- and long-term to-be environments describe what is hoped for in terms of improvement. Identified root causes will shape the implementation. Table 15.7 lists some symptoms, root causes, and their indicated actions. Symptoms become apparent in process *5.2 Map Supply Chain Processes*; root causes are identified in process *5.3 Identify Root Causes for Cost*.

15.4.2 Process Elements for 5.4 Reduce Material Cost (5.4.2)

This process reserves a window in the supply chain project for a broad range of subprojects. As the examples in Table 15.7 illustrate, there are a number of initiatives that could be brought to the table with a supplier. This is particularly true if the company buys or makes engineered products designed to our specification.

15.4.2.1 Process Definition for 5.4 Reduce Material Cost

Table 15.6, under "Process definition," lists some of the solutions to pursue reduced material cost. Solution selection will depend on accurate identification of root causes for cost. That is assisted by supplier cooperation in mapping processes and identifying root causes.

15.4.2.2 Approaches and Techniques for 5.4 Reduce Material Cost

The choice of technique will likely depend on relative partner power. For equal partners, joint teams and cost–benefit sharing are more likely. Unilateral actions include dropping a supplier through supplier base consolidation and dropping unprofitable products to avoid related headaches. Engineering changes address key characteristics, value engineering, and design for manufacturing or assembly (DFM/DFA). If the supplier is responsible for design, then an inducement may be needed to encourage a redesign. If our company is responsible, the ball will be in our court. Not infrequently, a recurring defect will receive a "use as is" disposition. If this happens, a specification change may be in order. In some cases, our company's design may impose a poorly performing second tier supplier on our first-tier supplier. Dropping the poor supplier may require a design change.

15.4.2.3 Project Management Shortcomings Addressed by 5.4 Reduce Material Cost

This effort doesn't directly fix any of the project management shortcomings described in Chapter 9. Its success, however, does depend on an absence of those shortcomings. Top management support should enlist suppliers in the effort. Especially if one's company is "weak" and heavily dependent on partners, top management will want this involvement. Organization roadblocks are also obstacles to successful implementation. If your organization has a bowtie approach to partnering, not much will get done. Rigidity in its approach to supply chain improvement will also be a roadblock. The variety of solutions available calls for "give and take" with supply chain partners to reach mutually agreeable solutions.

15.4.2.4 SCM Maturity for 5.4 Reduce Material Cost

This process lies in the heart of Stage V for SCM maturity. For companies where non-commodity materials are key for product and financial success, effective execution of activities in this process is vital. A major barrier can be the lack of "strategic sourcing" skills in procurement functions. Strategic sourcing establishes relationships with upstream trading partners. The willingness to collaborate should be a criterion for selecting these partners. This obstacle, if it exists, should be addressed to achieve Stage V maturity. Chapter 14 described ways to get partners on board. In this, partners must commit to actions likely to require staff commitments, added expense, or investments on their part.

Table 15.6 Reduce Material Cost (5.4)

5.4.1 Inputs		5.4 Reduce Material Cost	Executing
		5.4.2 Process Elements	5.4.3 Outputs
Process Root Cause Identification and To-Be Process Design (5.3)	**Process definition**	Pursue improvement efforts to reduce material costs over the product's life cycle. These include design changes, quality control, value engineering, altering specified materials, standardization of components, supplier base changes, product rationalization, and other measures.	Reduced Material Costs Project Plan Change Requests
	Approaches and techniques	Joint teams representing engineering, marketing, and operations. Design for assembly (DFA). Key characteristic analysis. Capital investment analysis. Cost/benefit sharing. Supplier base consolidation. Partnership classification (Section 4.4.2). Product line rationalization.	
	PM shortcomings addressed	Efforts to reduce material cost may require subprojects or entirely new projects using the singular project management methodology. Depending on their scope the efforts may be included in the overall supply chain improvement project. Multiple material cost reduction efforts increase the need for singular methodologies that benchmark best practices in the varied technical areas that can come into play in reducing material cost.	

SCM maturity	Stage V of the SCM maturity model for Task 5 requires new behaviors in most companies. However, achieving this level offers the best opportunity for achieving material cost savings in the supply chain.	
Terminology	ABC inventory classification	Auctions or line
	Certified supplier	Consignment
	Integrated supply	Price-taker
	Strategic sourcing	Supplier clustering
Stakeholders	Suppliers representing the highest spend areas are stakeholders. If one's own organization is a key material supplier and a major customer has targeted you for cost reduction, your senior management will be fully engaged. This includes top management, finance, sales and marketing, procurement, and operations.	

Table 15.7 Example Material-Related Symptoms, Root Causes, and Indicated Actions

Symptom	Root Cause	Indicated Actions
Material costs are too high	"Overspecification" leading to low supplier yields	Change specification, requalify products. Substitute alternate products. Redesign product. Invest in new processes.
	Volumes are too low	Cancel the product through product line rationalization.
Product too hard to assemble	Too many parts	Combine part functionality reducing the number of parts.
Supplier has proprietary technology	Supplier's technology is designed into product	Find an alternative technology (if possible). Collaborate with supplier on technology advances, share benefits.
Supplier has large aftermarket share	Your company has a poor aftermarket supply chain	Create aftermarket supply chain and business arrangement that is attractive to supplier.
Incoming inspection failure rates are high but supplier quality processes are adequate	Testing process doesn't yield consistent results	Remove variability in testing procedure. Redesign product features that cause variable test results.

15.4.2.5 Terminology for 5.4 Reduce Material Cost

The terms represent some of the efforts used by companies to execute their material cost reduction efforts.

15.4.2.6 Stakeholders for 5.4 Reduce Material Cost

Major suppliers and interfacing organizations are stakeholders. The process design team that identified root causes will likely be augmented for this process. Example skill augmentations include product, quality, and process design engineers.

5.4.3 Outputs from 5.4 Reduce Material Cost *(5.4.3)*

The principal output of this process is a result, *Reduced Material Costs*. These may not be directly measured in contract prices. The savings may show up in a savings in our own operation. This is because the incoming material has more consistent quality, is easier to assemble, is reliably available when needed, or contains lower-cost materials or subcomponents. Accompanying the deliverable may be commitments to the supplier for future business or financial support to justify capital investments. The outputs are likely to be implemented in Phases 3 and 4 in the project life cycle recommended in Chapter 11.

15.5 Implement Demand-Driven Supply Chain (5.5)

Implementation of the demand-driven supply chain is the purpose of this process. We cover two of the processes shown in Figure 15.1 in this section: *5.5 Implement Demand-Driven Supply Chain* and *4.1 Define Linkages*. Becoming demand-driven requires an assessment of the potential made in root cause analysis (process 5.3). This assessment can be in two parts: short-term and long-term. Short-term improvements implement non-technical, low capital investment changes. Long-term improvements might include new systems for supply chain visibility, supplier network changes, and new facilities.

Table 15.8 and Table 15.9 summarize the processes for developing the demand-driven supply chain. Table 15.8 summarizes the framework for reaching the demand-driven supply chain. Table 15.9 points to the information systems and other means to create linkages between partners. The two processes should go hand in hand.

15.5.1 Inputs to 5.5 Implement Demand-Driven Supply Chain *(5.5.1)*

Inputs include the demand-driven potential described in *5.3 Identify Root Causes for Cost*. This should set short-term and long-term visions for how demand-driven the chain should and might be. Root cause analysis should indicate how the increased demand-driven level should be achieved. It is likely that several techniques, described in the following section, will play a role in fulfilling the vision.

15.5.2 Process Elements for 5.5 Implement Demand-Driven Supply Chain *(5.5.2)*

This process is likely to have the longest duration and require the most resources among all in the supply chain project processes. Process improvement, along with material cost, are the "bottom line" of the overall effort. The process uses inputs from root cause definition and linkage assessment to create the new supply chain design.

Table 15.8   Implement Demand-Driven Supply Chain (5.5)

		5.5 Implement Demand-Driven Supply Chain		Executing
5.5.1 Inputs		5.5.2 Process Elements		5.5.3 Outputs
Demand-Driven Potential Assessment (5.3) Process Root Cause Identification (5.3) Linkage Requirements (4.1)	**Process definition**	Pursue improvements to supply chain operating processes. These will generally support achievement of a supply chain where decisions are based increasingly on actual demand rather than forecasts. The demand-driven supply chain is enabled by changes to the process and information sharing.		Implemented Supply Chain Operations Project Plan Change Requests
	Approaches and techniques	Decision support: • Supply chain decision analysis (5.3). • Activity-based costing including accounting for inventory and assets. • Flexibility framework (Section 3.5.2). Long to short lead times: • Supply chain network design. • Cellular manufacturing.	Flow model economics: • Scheduling. • Level loading. • Setup reduction. • Variability reduction. Replacing forecasts with demand: • Postponement. • Pull systems like 3C and kanban. • Vendor-managed inventory (VMI). • Demand Flow. • Information technology.	
	PM shortcomings addressed	Efforts to reduce process cost across several companies may require subprojects or entirely new projects using the singular project management methodology. Multiple process cost reduction efforts increases the need for singular methodologies that benchmark best practices in the technical areas that come into play in reducing process cost.		

SCM maturity	Stage V of the SCM maturity model for Tasks 4 and 5 requires new behaviors in most companies. Despite this obstacle, attaining this level offers the best opportunity for implementing process improvements in the supply chain.	
Terminology		
3C alternative to MRPII	Decomposition (forecasting)	Demand Flow
Demand-driven supply chain	Disintermediation	Flexibility
Focused factory	Forecast error	Hedge stock
Heijunka	Independent, dependent demand	Inert stock
Kaizen	Lean enterprise	Lean manufacturing
Level plant loading	Lot operation cycle time	Lumpy demand
Mass customization	Matrix bill of material	Min-max
Mixed-model production	P:D ratio	PDCA
Periodic replenishment	Postponement	Product tree
Promotion	Pull system	Push and pull systems
Push system	Rapid replenishment	Replenishment cycle time
Sell-source-ship (3S)	Single minute exchange of dies	Six Sigma
Synchronized supply chain	*Takt time*	Two bin system
Stakeholders	Such process improvements should involve upstream and downstream partners in the supply chain. A multicompany process design team should execute the process.	

Table 15.9 Define Linkages (4.1)

4.1.1 Inputs	4.1 Define Linkages		Executing
	4.1.2 Process Elements		4.1.3 Outputs
Demand-Driven Potential Assessment (5.3) Process Root Cause Identification (5.3)	**Process definition**	Using requirements from the process design, define linkages required for the supply chain and the timing of their implementation. Distinguish between short- and long-term requirements. Identifying the right linkages is an iterative process done in parallel with design development.	Linkage Requirements Project Plan Change Requests
	Approaches and techniques	Requirements analysis. Process re-engineering. Feasibility studies.	
	PM shortcomings addressed	Inadequate technical capability and misunderstood technology are directly addressed.	
	SCM maturity	Use of the appropriate technology can enable achievement of Stage IV or V for Task 4 Managing Supply Chain Information.	

Terminology		
Advance planning system (APS)	Available to promise (ATP)	Business process management (BPM)
Configurator	Constant cycle (fixed cycle) reorder model	Capable to promise (CTP)
Continuous replenishment planning (CRP)	Constant quantity (fixed quantity) reorder model	Customer relationship management (CRM)
Data warehouse	Distribution requirements planning (DRP)	Drum–buffer–rope
Echelon	Efficient consumer response (ECR)	Electronic Data Interchange (EDI)
Forecastable demand	Hosted software vendors (HSV)	Integration
Joint replenishment	Merge-in-transit	Milk run
Point of sale (POS)	Point-to-point integration	Proactive systems
Project manufacturing	Public warehouse	Pull system
Risk pooling	S&OP (sales and operations planning)	Supply chain event management (SCEM)
TCP/IP	Vendor-managed inventory (VMI)	Web services
Stakeholders	Line executives, functional managers, and technical staff should contribute to the development of linkages. The process design team should oversee linkage design. Technical support staff should assist as needed.	

15.5.2.1 *Process Definition for* 5.5 Implement Demand-Driven Supply Chain

Implementing the short-term and long-term visions is essentially a three-step process. The first step seeks to shorten lead times throughout the chain. It relies on outputs from process mapping. The next step uses techniques to implement "flow model economics." This step "synchronizes" operations along the chain. The vision is to eliminate the bullwhip effect and achieve level production levels. The last step is improving the linkages along the chain so information on end-user demand is efficiently transmitted in a timely fashion.

15.5.2.2 *Approaches and Techniques for* 5.5 Implement Demand-Driven Supply Chain

Evolution to a demand-driven supply chain follows a process improvement discipline. There are two basic strategies for becoming more "demand-driven." The first is to shorten the time between the demand signal, usually a purchase, and the point at which a decision to produce is made. The second is to improve communication of demand accurately along the chain, the domain of many software solutions. The following sections describe the techniques available in each stage of this evolution.

15.5.2.2.1 Decision Support Tools

Multicompany efforts to create a demand-driven supply chain require agreed-to business agreements and process design tools. The decision analysis that established the potential to be demand-driven is one example. As the project proceeds to implementation, the results of that analysis will be held up for scrutiny and may have to be adjusted. For example, the effort to convert a decision from forecast-driven to demand-driven might meet obstacles in implementation. We would have to re-evaluate our assessment of demand-driven potential or our approach.

Activity-based costing, described earlier in this chapter, supports business for risk/reward sharing. The application should capture expenses and capital recovery costs and, if appropriate, work them into the prices. The actions that make a supply chain demand-driven also make it flexible. Specifications for the demand-driven supply chain should include the type of flexibility, described in Section 3.5.2, that should be built into operations.

15.5.2.2.2 Long to Short Lead-Time Tools

When we mapped our supply chain in process *5.2 Map Supply Chain Processes*, we discovered long lead-time processes. Herman Miller, discussed in Chapter 4, attacked these lead imes vigorously. Becoming demand-driven requires us to shorten those times as much as possible. Shortening lead time can occur inside the walls of supply chain factories or in the linkages between the factories. Cellular manufacturing works inside the plant. The approach moves from a functional factory layout where like equipment is clustered together to a layout that puts unlike equipment needed for a product together. This cuts in-plant lead times because a cell makes the product in one continuous process and a functional layout requires parts to move from place to place with lead time adding queues along the way. Deciding which products have sufficient volume to justify cells can borrow from the SKU ABC analysis from process mapping.

Supply chain network design might bring suppliers into closer contact with our operation. We also might open distribution facilities or an assembly plant closer to our major customers. At a minimum, we would consider overall lead time in decisions about specifying components and determining their source.

15.5.2.2.3 Flow Model Economics

Supply chains suffer from bullwhip effects and work-in-process inventory because they aren't synchronized. Ideally, each partner in the chain will be able to produce at the same rate as end users consume products. Aircraft companies do this when they set production rates for a particular aircraft model at a monthly rate. Suppliers in the chain synchronize their operations to that rate.

Fixed quantity and fixed sequence scheduling are tools for improving flow economics. A fixed sequence, variable quantity discipline means that replenishment intervals are known. An example is the daily trip of the distributor to the retail store. The distributor restocks what has been consumed, a variable quantity on a fixed replenishment rate. Setup reduction is a common tactic to make smaller batch production on machine tools more economical. A methodical approach minimizes equipment downtime, reducing the economic batch size. A number of measures are addressed at removing variability from the supply chain. Level loading is one attempt at this. Others seek to improve the reliability of all processes, avoiding the need for contingency inventories in case things don't go well. Another way of removing variability is replacing unreliable suppliers.

15.5.2.2.4 Replacing Forecasts with Demand

Shortening lead times and adopting flow model economics can be done without large technology investments. Replacing forecasts with demand can also be "low tech." However, in high-volume environments it is likely to be an application where systems play an important role. For example, short-term measures can utilize postponement. This strategy takes advantage of commonality among products delivered to end users. It does this by "postponing" a commitment to a final product configuration until the latest time possible. For products where a few components make a variety of products, this can be an effective way to displace forecasts with actual demand in replenishment decisions. Demand flow is a way to implement this intent

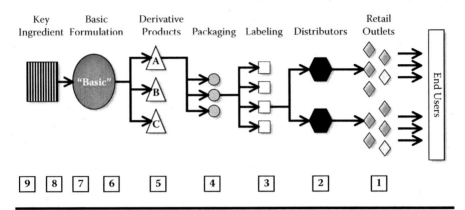

Figure 15.6 3C approach to the demand-driven supply chain.

by modeling final assembly like a sandwich shop in which final products are built to order. This is a valuable tool when the products are customized for each customer.

Pull systems essentially signal—by some means—upstream operations when consumption occurs downstream. The *kanban* is a card that provides this signal in Japanese factories. It authorizes the upstream operation to bring another predefined fixed quantity of material. Vendor-managed inventory (VMI) is like the grocery distributor described earlier. Replenishment to established levels is left to the vendor, often a distributor of "C" inventory items.

A technique called 3C (consumption, capacity, and commonality) provides a framework that should find wider application.[4] It has particular value when multiple products have common components and accurate forecasts for final product demand are illusive. 3C reduces dependence on forecasts for replenishment decisions and has the elements one must address on a journey from forecast-driven to demand-driven.

Another supply chain example shown in Figure 15.6 helps explain 3C. This is a V-type product example since it begins with a simple formulation called "Basic" that is reshaped into distinct configurations based on packaging and labels. Like the postponement approach, 3C capitalizes on the commonality (one of the Cs) inherent in product structures like Basic's. "A" products built on common modules (e.g., automobiles) should also consider 3C.

The other Cs in 3C are consumption and capacity. Consumption refers to the demand-driven property in 3C since end-user consumption drives replenishment decisions. This is achieved by identifying "consumption centers" that are links in the chain. Each consumption center triggers replenishment orders at fixed intervals called the "time between pulls" (TBP) from upstream sources. The simple "rule" in 3C is to replenish only what has been consumed since the last replenishment. So, the order quantity equals the amount consumed.

Table 15.10   3C Alternative Method for Replenishment

	Units			
	Product A	*Product B*	*Product C*	*Target for Basic*
"Basic" required per unit from BOM	4	10	2	4000[a]
Capacity per week (MSR)	1000	50	500	

[a] Equals 4 units A × 1000.

Capacity, the last C, sets 3C target inventories. The method provides 100 percent certainty there is no stockout. This is done by establishing a safety stock level base that accounts for consumption during the time between pulls plus the lead time for the order. This amount is based on the maximum sales rate (MSR) during that period. The MSR is usually expressed as units per day or week. So, if the reorder frequency is five days and the lead time is ten days, the target inventory would be the maximum consumption rate, or capacity, times fifteen days. The fixed interval variable quantity approach assures regular flow; one knows that product will move at every interval as long as there is consumption. If there is no end-user consumption, no replenishment will occur, limiting inventory build up without end-user demand.

The data in Table 15.10 illustrates how to derive a replenishment rule for manufacturing the Basic Formulation (Level 6), labeled "Basic" in Figure 15.6. This is the raw material for the three derivative products in Figure 15.6, Products A, B, and C. With data from the bill of materials, or BOM, Table 15.10 shows how much Basic is required for each derivative product. This is four units for each unit of Product A, ten units for Product B, and two units for Product C. Conventional practice would have us forecasting all the end items for A, B, and C to decide how much Basic to produce. 3C takes a simpler approach. The rule is based on the frequency that Basic will be produced (the TBP), which is weekly. The capacity feature of 3C requires us to determine how much Basic could ever conceivably be consumed in the TBP period (one week). This capacity would assume that the most intensive user of Basic is 100 percent of product demand. In this case, this is Product A. If nothing but Product A were sold, 4000 units of Basic would be required. For Product B, this figure is 500 units; for Product C, it is 1000 units. This assumption is conservative since Products B and C will also be sold in any given week.

So, the business rule is that Basic replenishment be sufficient to reach the target inventory of 4000 units plus initial requirements to cover the lead time for Basic. If downstream demand has "pulled" or consumed 1500 units of Basic in the past week, then 1500 units would be ordered. If none were pulled, zero units would be ordered. No rule could be simpler. The 3C method also builds in reserve safety stock of Basic to populate the chain with initial inventory and to account for Basic's lead time. Essentially, the amount consumed equals the amount reordered and the customer demand is satisfied.

One reaction might be that targeting so conservatively will result in excess Basic inventory. The reality is that Basic will be consumed as it is produced so that actual cycling inventory levels will never reach 4000 units plus the lead-time component. Also, the methodology allows for cutting back on the target inventory since the 100 percent assumption is highly conservative, and the peak consumption for Product B and C is far below that for Product A.

How does one determine the "capacity per week" for each product? If there is a manufacturing constraint, it could be in Basic production or even that of the key ingredient supplier (Level 8). If supply chain capacity is not limited by physical constraints, then the constraint is the maximum sales rate of all the products that use Basic. For most T- and V-type products, internal constraints are unlikely in downstream processes like assembly, packaging, and labeling. For a T-type product, the chief consumption center will be at the very end of the chain closest to the end user. A T-type product supplier seeking to provide VMI services to retailers with a broad customer base could use 3C to assure inventory is on hand. For example, in Figure 15.6, the Key Ingredient supplier could manage its finished goods with 3C replenishment rules.

The supplier of a component to A-type assembly manufacturers like Dell or General Motors could provide reliable, responsive VMI services to customers using 3C. Forecasts from the suppliers would establish initial inventories and be the basis for target inventories, providing a competitive advantage in selling to these customers. Perhaps the greatest value of 3C is to V-type supply chains like our example in Figure 15.6. Forecasting is really difficult to do well and labor intensive because there are so many final product SKUs. 3C offers an attractive alternative to synchronize the supply chain in the face of variable lead-time and replenishment cycles, preventing inventory build up and lost sales due to outages. Reducing lost sales addresses market mediation costs described in Section 4.2 that arise from mismatches in supply and demand.

15.5.2.2.5 Define Linkages (4.1)

Technology is placed here because it enables the demand-driven supply chain by improving efficiency in planning operations and exchanging information. We defend our placement of IT because technology should support the demand-driven supply chain, not be the main event in its implementation. This is consistent with philosophies adopted by the IT frameworks summarized in Section 9.7.

Table 15.9 summarizes our coverage of linkages for the demand-driven supply chain. IT applications should be coordinated with the steps listed earlier. For example, it may be tempting to purchase an application that provides supply chain "visibility." However, it may be futile unless the non-technical solutions described earlier aren't considered first.

15.5.2.3 Project Managemet Shortcomings Addressed by 5.5 Implement Demand-Driven Supply Chain

Like *5.4 Reduce Material Cost*, success in this process demands that the obstacles described in Chapter 9 be absent. This multicompany effort should be run like a startup enterprise, with flexibility and a willingness to change. The likelihood that technology will be a product of the effort requires an understanding of technology by one's own company and its partners. It also requires the technical competence to implement that technology not only in one's own company but also in partner organizations, as depicted in Figure 9.1.

15.5.2.4 SCM Maturity for 5.5 Implement Demand-Driven Supply Chain

Implementing the demand-driven supply chain is indicative of Stage IV and V SCM maturity. Stage IV is primarily cost-reduction focused. Stage V brings additional sophistication, taking into account marketing strategy and utilizing risk/reward sharing among partners.

15.5.2.5 Terminology for 5.5 Implement Demand-Driven Supply Chain

Terminology focuses on Glossary terms related to techniques for implementing the demand-driven supply chain.

15.5.2.6 Stakeholders for 5.5 Implement Demand-Driven Supply Chain

A process design team, supported by employee front-line teams, should complete the process design and test the solutions. All partners in the supply chain whose operations are affected are stakeholders. For longer-term measures like systems and facility changes, providers of outside services will likely support the effort.

15.5.3 Outputs from 5.5 Implement Demand-Driven Supply Chain (5.5.3)

The principal output is a new process that makes use of actual demand for decision making along the supply chain. The supply chain should rank high on both customer-facing and internal-facing performance measures. Customer-facing metrics include delivery, fill rate, perfect order percentage, and lead time. It should also be more flexible and cost-effective. Change requests are another output for the process. These are part of the loop closing needed to update progress on fulfilling the strategy and making needed changes.

Notes

1. Doug Hicks adopted the convention of using "abc" rather than "ABC" to describe focused use of activity-based costing for decision making. This avoids building expensive but seldom used activity-based accounting systems (what he calls ABC).
2. Jack B. ReVelle, John W. Moran, and Charles A. Cox, *The QFD Handbook* (New York: John Wiley & Sons, 1998).
3. R. Bruce McAfee, Myron Glassman, and Earl D. Honeycutt Jr., "The Effects of Culture and Human Resource Management Policies on Supply Chain Management Strategy," *Journal of Business Logistics* (2002): 1–18.
4. Miguel Fernández-Rañada, F. Xavier Gurrola-Gal, and Enrique López-Tello, *3C: A Proven Alternative to MRP II for Optimizing Supply Chain Performance* (Boca Raton: St. Lucie Press, 2000).

Appendix A

Summary of Inputs and Outputs for a Supply Chain Project

This table summarizes inputs and outputs for the supply chain project. Most entries in the "Inputs/Outputs" column are output products of the processes where they are listed. Inputs are identified along with their source.

Section	Process #	Process Name	Inputs/Outputs	Where Used
12.1	1.1	Charter the Supply Chain Effort	Customer and Product Briefing (external input)	1.1, 1.3
			Strategy (external input)	1.1, 1.3
			Environmental Briefing (external input)	1.1, 1.3, 1.4
			Issues (external input)	1.1, 1.3, 1.4
			SCM Charter Elements	1.2

(continued on next page)

Section	Process #	Process Name	Inputs/Outputs	Where Used
			Project Management Charter Elements	1.2
12.2	1.2	Develop Project Plan	SCM Plan	1.3
			Project Management Plan	1.3
12.3	1.3	Define Spheres	Enabling Process Definition	1.4
			Supply Chain Sphere Definition	1.4
12.4	1.4	Define Activity Systems	Activity System Designs	1.5, 1.6, 2.4, 3.2, 3.3, 3.4, 5.1
12.5	1.5	Align Organization	Organization Design	2.1, 2.3, 2.4, 3.1, 3.4
12.6	1.6	Develop Collaboration Strategy	Collaboration Strategy	2.3, 2.4, 3.1, 3.2, 3.3
12.7	1.7	Control Changes	Implementation Progress Various inputs from 1.4, 2.5, 3.5, 3.7, 5.1	
			Environmental Updates (external input)	
			Review Meetings (external input)	
			Partner Inputs (external input)	
			Changes	1.2, 4.1, 5.4, 5.5
12.8	1.8	Close Phase	Deliverables	
13.1	2.1	Plan Organization	Organization Implementation Plan	2.2

Section	Process #	Process Name	Inputs/Outputs	Where Used
13.2	2.2	Acquire Staff	Staff Acquisition (external input)	2.2
			Staff Resources	2.3, 5.1
13.3	2.3	Organize for Activity System Implementation	Implemented Organization Plan	2.4
			Organization Plan Implementation Progress Reports	2.5
13.4	2.4	Implement Metrics	Project Control Metrics	2.5
			Supply Chain Metrics	5.1
13.5	2.5	Control Schedule	Organization Changes	2.1
			SCM Change Requests	1.7
			Project Management Change Requests	1.7
14.1	3.1	Plan Communications	External Communications Plan	3.2, 3.3
14.2	3.2	Implement Supplier Base Plan	Multicompany Organization Design — Supplier Base Implementation	3.4
			Collaboration Plan Change Suggestions (suppliers)	3.1
14.3	3.3	Implement Customer Base Plan	Multicompany Organization Design — Customer Base Implementation	3.4
			Collaboration Plan Change Suggestions (customers)	3.1

(continued on next page)

Section	Process #	Process Name	Inputs/Outputs	Where Used
14.4	3.4	Install Multicompany Organization	SCM Subprojects	3.5, 3.6, 3.7, 5.1
			Multicompany Project Staffing Requirements	3.5, 5.1
			Multicompany Risk Sharing Plan	3.5, 3.6, 5.1
14.5	3.5	Plan Risk Sharing	Partner Business Arrangements	3.7, 5.1
14.6	3.6	Acquire Multicompany Resources	Staffed SCM Projects, Subprojects, or Project Extensions	1.7, 5.1
			Staff Plan Exceptions	1.7
14.7	3.7	Verify Partner Scope	SCM and Project Management Change Requests	1.7
15.1	5.1	Plan Process Improvements	Process Improvement Initiation	5.2
			SCM Change Requests	1.7
15.2	5.2	Map Supply Chain Processes	Process Analysis	5.3
15.3	5.3	Identify Root Causes for Cost	Process Root Cause Identification and To-Be Process Design	5.4, 5.5
			Action Plans	
15.4	5.4	Reduce Material Cost	Reduced Material Costs	
15.5	5.5	Implement Demand-Driven Supply Chain	Implemented Supply Chain Operations	4.1
15.6	4.1	Define Linkages	Linkage Requirements	5.5

Appendix B

SCM Project Responsibilities

The Responsibility Assignment Matrix lists the SCM processes and suggested assignments. Its purpose is to clarify "who does what" in the project.

Legend	
A	Accountable: Has decision-making authority. Assigns responsibilities. Is accountable for project results.
C	Consulted: Provides input to those responsible or accountable. Tests solutions to confirm feasibility.
I	Informed: Provided with progress reports or information on the products of the project.
R	Responsible: Assigned to complete certain project processes.

Section	Process #	Process Name	Project Manager/ Project Office	Company Steering Committee	Multicompany Steering Committee	Supply Chain Design Team	Sphere Design Team	Process Design Team	Company Internal Departments	Partner Internal Departments
12.1	1.1	Charter the Supply Chain Effort	R	A					C	
12.2	1.2	Develop Project Plan	R	A		C			C	
12.3	1.3	Define Spheres	I	A		R			I	
12.4	1.4	Define Activity Systems	I	C		A	R		C	C
12.5	1.5	Align Organization		A		R	C		I	
12.6	1.6	Develop Collaboration Strategy	I	A		R	C		I	C
12.7	1.7	Control Changes	R	A	I	I				
12.8	1.8	Close Phase	R	A		I				
13.1	2.1	Plan Organization	A	I		R			C	
13.2	2.2	Acquire Staff	A	I		I				
13.3	2.3	Organize for Activity System Implementation	R	A					C	

13.4	2.4	Implement Metrics	A	A		R	C		A	C
13.5	2.5	Control Schedule	R	A						
14.1	3.1	Plan Communications	I	A	C	R			C	C
14.2	3.2	Implement Supplier Base Plan	I	A		R	C		C	C
14.3	3.3	Implement Customer Base Plan	I	A		R	C		C	C
14.4	3.4	Install Multicompany Organization	I		A	R			C	C
14.5	3.5	Plan Risk Sharing	I	I	A		R			C
14.6	3.6	Acquire Multicompany Resources	R	I	A				C	C
14.7	3.7	Verify Partner Scope	R	I	A					
15.1	5.1	Plan Process Improvements	R	A	C			C	C	I
15.2	5.2	Map Supply Chain Processes	I	I	A	C		R	C	C
15.3	5.3	Identify Root Causes for Cost	I	I	A	C		R	C	C
15.4	5.4	Reduce Material Cost	I	A	C	C		R	C	C
15.5	5.5	Implement Demand-Driven Supply Chain	I	A	C	C		R	C	C
15.6	4.1	Define Linkages	I	A	C	C		R	C	C

Glossary

In this Glossary, terms defined elsewhere are in *italics*.

3C: Alternative to MRP. A method that uses *capacity, commonality,* and *consumption* as a basis for control of material in the supply chain. The technique decreases the dependence of the supply chain on forecast accuracy by shifting inventory decision to considerations of actual demand and capacity. APICS uses the term "fixed reorder cycle inventory model" to characterize similar replenishment systems.

3S: Sell–source–ship. A supply chain characterization in which the seller doesn't hold inventory. Once an order is placed, the seller channels orders to single or multiple sources. This is the opposite of the buy–hold–sell model in which the seller does hold inventory.

5S: In lean production systems, the requirements of an efficient workplace. Components include the following:

1. Sort: Remove the items not needed and assure that those that are needed are present.
2. Simplify: Arrange items to be ready for use.
3. Scrub: Clean up the work area.
4. Standardize: Sort, simplify, and scrub daily.
5. Sustain: Follow the first four Ss.

(Adapted from John H. Blackstone Jr., *APICS Dictionary,* 12th ed., APICS—The Association for Operations Management, 2008)

ABC inventory classification: Division of inventory into groups based on decreasing order of annual dollar volume (annual units × projected volume). "A" items are 10 percent to 20 percent of items but 50 percent to 70 percent of dollar volume. "B" items are about 20 percent of items and 20 percent of dollar volume. "C" items are 60 percent to 70 percent of items but only 10 percent to 30 percent of value.

The classification points to places where attention can be focused for improvement. The same principle can be applied to suppliers, customers, and markets. In classification efforts, one must decide at what level the classification should be completed. This will depend on the product's *configuration.* (Adapted from John H. Blackstone Jr., *APICS Dictionary,* 12th ed., APICS—The Association for Operations Management, 2008)

ABC/ABM: Activity-based costing/activity-based management. A method to plan, measure and control expenses associated with managing and monitoring the supply chain; specific techniques for assigning cost in business processes to activities. ABC is seen to overcome many of the shortcomings of conventional accounting methodologies.

ABCD analysis: Technique for analyzing technical and administrative functions. "A" activities add value to the customer and require decision-making discretion. "B" activities require decision making but don't add value. "C" activities don't require decision making but do add value. "D" items don't require decision making and don't add value. The classification is useful for process analysis and deciding how to remove or automate activities.

absorption accounting: An accounting approach that allocates a portion of fixed costs to products. Such allocations are often arbitrary making decisions based on these costs problematic. *Activity-based costing* is an alternative.

action plan: A plan that defines a *project* or *projects.* They are part of *portfolios, programs,* or *initiatives.*

activity (project management context): An element of work performed during a project. It has an expected duration, cost, and resource requirement. An activity can be subdivided into tasks. Activity definitions describe what has to be done to produce deliverables. Formerly called a "work item." (Adapted from Project Management Institute, *Combined Standards Glossary,* 3rd ed., PMI, 2007)

activity, cost driver: A cost object in *activity-based costing* to which variable and fixed activity costs are assigned. Examples include a unit of output or capacity like cost per unit of production, cost per order, cost per machine-hour, or cost per labor-hour.

activity system: A term originated by Michael Porter in defining networks of activities that provide a sustainable competitive advantage. These networks can constitute a supply chain. An activity in this context is a feature of the company's strategy that makes it distinctive. Activities, in turn, are supported by supply chain and other company processes.

adaptability: A SCOR metric that is a component of the agility performance attribute. It includes both upside and downside adaptability.

Wikipedia defines the term as the ability of a supply chain to adapt itself efficiently and fast to changed circumstances. Such a chain is able to fit its behavior as its environment or parts of the system itself change.

agile enterprise: Companies that employ rapid customer/supplier partnering to achieve a short product development life cycle. Agility merges competencies in cost, quality, dependability, and flexibility. (Adapted from John H.

Blackstone Jr., *APICS Dictionary,* 12th ed., APICS—The Association for Operations Management, 2008)

APICS: International not-for-profit offering programs and materials for individual and organizational education, standards of excellence, and integrated resource management topics. Formerly called American Production and Inventory Control Society; now, the Educational Society for Resource Management.

application area: With respect to project management, an application area is a discipline where project management theory and practice applies. This book adapts SCM to project management. Other example application areas include construction, defense acquisition, and software development.

APS: Advanced Planning System. System that plans actual logistics and production over short-term, immediate, and long-term periods. Can be separate from or built into MRP/ERP systems. The APS can generate different scenarios for decision support. Components include demand planning, production planning, production scheduling, distribution planning, and transportation planning. (Adapted from John H. Blackstone Jr., *APICS Dictionary,* 12th ed., APICS—The Association for Operations Management, 2008)

as-is: The current state, such as how processes in the supply chain process are currently performed.

ASQC: The American Society for Quality Control.

assemble-to-order: An environment where products or services are assembled after receipt of an order. This is useful where there are a large number of options consisting of common components. A basket of groceries is an example. Made-to-order computers are another. In a *VAT analysis,* this approach might be tried for "T" type product structures. (Adapted from John H. Blackstone Jr., *APICS Dictionary,* 12th ed., APICS—The Association for Operations Management, 2008)

ATP: Available to promise. The uncommitted portion of inventory and planned production maintained in the master schedule. (Adapted from Project Management Institute, *Combined Standards Glossary,* 3rd ed., PMI, 2007)

auctions online: Online negotiations among qualified suppliers. Usually facilitated by software applications.

autonomation: Automated shutdown of a production line or other operation when an abnormality or defect occurs. (Adapted from Project Management Institute, *Combined Standards Glossary,* 3rd ed., PMI, 2007)

Balanced Scorecard: An approach to measurement that cascades measures from the top down through the organization. The method uses four perspectives to achieve balance: financial, customer, internal business, and innovation and learning.

bar coding: An automatic identification technology that uses parallel dark bars and spaces to represent characters. Bar coding is often an important element in automating the tracking of material in the supply chain.

barrier: An element that limits a supply chain from achieving higher levels of performance. Unlike *constraints,* they may be managed or mitigated in a supply chain design project.

baseline: Approved plan for a project, work breakdown structure, work package, or schedule activity. Used with descriptor like "cost baseline" or "schedule baseline." (Adapted from Project Management Institute, *Combined Standards Glossary,* 3rd ed., PMI, 2007)

batch-and-queue system: Refers to a production management system that relies on large batches of material. This leads to large queues while waiting to complete a production step. Such systems are characterized by high work in process inventory and low velocity production.

BCP: Business Continuity Planning. Formal processes that include analysis of processes, organizations, and systems, a risk analysis of those processes and systems, and response plans to assure their continuity. A DRP for information system servers, networks, and application software is a subset of BCP. The acknowledgment of the need for business continuity planning has grown out of DRP efforts.

benchmarking: A search for those best practices that will lead to superior performance. Benchmarking is usually executed with those who perform a targeted activity the best, regardless of the industry they are in. Internal benchmarking makes comparisons within an organization, such as developing best practices from several stores that perform similar functions.

BOM: Bill of materials.

BPM: Business process management. Broadly, BPM focuses on improving business processes rather than functions or costs. Narrowly, BPMI (Business Process Management Initiative) is a non-profit group promoting open standards for information technology used in business processes.

BPMI: Business Process Management Initiative.

BPMN: Business Process Modeling Notation. A set of standards for graphically expressing business processes. The standard facilitates understanding among process stakeholders.

BPO: Business process outsourcing. Contracting out for support services beyond information technology. Examples include Human Resources, Finance and Accounting, and logistics services.

BPR: Business process re-engineering. A fundamental rethinking of redesign of a process based on customer requirements that ignores function (departments, organization, units, company boundaries) and product constraints. (Adapted from John H. Blackstone Jr., *APICS Dictionary,* 12th ed., APICS—The Association for Operations Management, 2008)

branding: Vision, position, "space" in the market. Establishing a brand name is a primary way to compete in many industries. SCM can support the strategy for establishing a brand "image."

bread man: A term applied to "automatic" replacement of inventory by third-party logistics providers, normally distributors. The analogy is the bread man who replenishes stock in the grocery store on a regularly scheduled basis. A related term is *"milk run."* The term can also apply to types of vendor-managed inventory.

buffer: An inventory used to decouple operations in the supply chain. A buffer ahead of a constraint protects the constraining operations against loss of inputs.

bullwhip effect: A term that describes the phenomenon in which small changes in final demand for a product produce wide swings in production upstream in the supply chain. APICS defines this condition as "nervousness."

business model: A model answers questions like the following: "Who is the customer?" "What does the customer value?" "How do we make money in this business?" "What is the underlying economic logic that explains how we deliver value to customers?" A *strategy* defines how the organization competes. Competing effectively requires being different from your competitors. (*Source:* Joan Magretta, "Why Business Models Matter," *Harvard Business Review*, May 2002, 87–92)

capacity: The capability of the supply chain to perform its function that considers product design and mix. Capacity can be determined over near-term, intermediate, and long-term time horizons. (Adapted from John H. Blackstone Jr., *APICS Dictionary,* 12th ed., APICS—The Association for Operations Management, 2008)

capacity strategy: A strategic choice for adjusting strategy to business levels. A "leading" strategy adds capacity in anticipation of demand. A "lag" strategy waits until the demand has materialized. A "tracking" strategy attempts to match capacity and demand. (*Note:* Such a strategy should consider product life cycle position and profitability.) (Adapted from John H. Blackstone Jr., *APICS Dictionary,* 12th ed., APICS—The Association for Operations Management, 2008)

carrying cost: Cost of holding inventory expressed as a percentage of the product cost. Components include the cost of capital, obsolescence, shrinkage, insurance, taxes, spoilage, and storage/handling.

cash-to-cash cycle time: The time between payments to suppliers for product components to the time customers make payments. This parameter has become an important measure of supply chain performance, reflecting both financial and inventory management process performance. Most have negative measures ranging from 30 to 80 days. Some, notably Dell, has a positive cycle time, meaning it collects payments from customers before it has to pay suppliers.

category management: A structure that focuses on management of products or product families. With respect to SCM, this could also include incoming material, production planning, and distribution shifting away from a structure based on commodities or manufacturing plants.

cause and effect diagram (fishbone diagram): A tool that uses a graphical description of contributing elements to identify root causes of process variation.

CCR: Capacity constrained resource. Any supply chain resource that, if not actively managed, will limit the throughput of the chain. In *3C*, capacity is used in setting replenishment rules. (Adapted from John H. Blackstone Jr., *APICS Dictionary*, 12th ed., APICS—The Association for Operations Management, 2008)

cellular manufacturing: A manufacturing process that produces families of parts within a single line or cell of machines with operators who work only within the line or cell. The cellular concept is applicable to administrative and technical processes. In this context, it means clustering unlike operations to increase processing *velocity.*

certified supplier: A supplier that has been approved for providing defined components for manufacturing or distribution. Certification levels may have varying criteria related to quality management, such as needs for quality control. Suppliers are often qualified before financial terms are negotiated.

channel: A group of businesses, or channel *partners,* that take ownership title to products or facilitate exchange during the marketing process from the original buyer to the final buyer. Effective SCM requires an understanding of the needs of each customer and segment and the correct channel to reach them.

channel equity: Affiliations and relationships among enterprises along the supply chain that improve value for participants. (Adapted from John H. Blackstone Jr., *APICS Dictionary*, 12th ed., APICS—The Association for Operations Management, 2008)

channel master: The single, most powerful company in a supply chain. The channel master dictates terms of trade for the channel. The presence of a master depends on the nature of the industry and competition. Channel mastery is often the goal of SCM programs.

charter: A document that authorizes a project. It enables the project manager to apply resources to project activities.

chase replenishment method: A planning method that seeks to maintain a stable inventory level while varying production or replenishment quantities. Companies may combine chase and level production methods. 3C is an example of a chase replenishment method. (Adapted from John H. Blackstone Jr., *APICS Dictionary*, 12th ed., APICS—The Association for Operations Management, 2008)

CLM: Council of Logistics Management.

co-destiny: A supply chain that has evolved from intraorganizational to interorganizational management. Also called a *Stage 3 supply chain organization.* (Adapted from John H. Blackstone Jr., *APICS Dictionary*, 12th ed., APICS—The Association for Operations Management, 2008)

COE: Center of Excellence. A formal or informal committee that focuses on benchmarking and continuous improvement. Has expertise in identifying project management tools.

collaboration: CGR Management Consultants (CGR) defines it as joint planning and execution of supply chain activities. These activities can range from new product development to day-to-day operations. Collaboration includes all aspects of the relationship related to physical movement, information sharing, financial flows, and exchange of intellectual property. Collaboration is also defined as internal between people and functions and external between supply chain companies.

The Supply-Chain Council defines collaboration as "a relationship built on trust that is benchmarked by the commitment to the team objective and where consensus may not always be achievable but where nothing takes place without the commitment of all involved."

collaboration software: Applications in this category, also referred to as "groupware," are classified at three levels:

- communication tools (e-mail, faxing, conferencing, Web publishing),
- electronic conferencing tools (Internet message boards, instant messaging), and
- collaborative management tools (work flow, project management systems, electronic calendars).

(Adapted from *Wikipedia*)

collaborative execution systems: Category of application software that enables the effective coordination and flow of information across the entire value chain. Automates tasks required to manage each transaction and to provide real-time visibility to information. Collaborative executive systems are designed to improve productivity and reliability.

collaboratory: A term coined by participants in a Supply-Chain Council SCOR update technical committee. It refers to the entity that includes the business, cultural, and system environment needed to build and operate a linkage between partners.

component: A part, element, or piece of a complex whole. With respect to project management, these include portfolios, programs, projects, and business strategies. (Adapted from Project Management Institute, *A Guide to the Project Management Body of Knowledge [PMBOK Guide]*, 4th ed., PMI, 2008)

configuration: The arrangement of components specified to produce an assembly. Configuration has a major impact on supply chain design. For example, different configurations affect *postponement* strategies. In application of the *3C* approach, configuration determines commonality among end items.

configurator: A system used by design-to-order, make-to-order, or assemble-to-order companies. They enable direct customer or sales engineer configuration of the product. Configurators can generate solid models, drawings, costs, and bills of material. (Adapted from John H. Blackstone Jr., *APICS Dictionary,* 12th ed., APICS—The Association for Operations Management, 2008)

consignment: A shipment by a common carrier.

Terms of a contract in which a supplier is not paid until the goods are used or sold. (Adapted from John H. Blackstone Jr., *APICS Dictionary,* 12th ed., APICS—The Association for Operations Management, 2008)

constant cycle (fixed cycle) reorder model: An inventory reorder pattern with fixed time intervals and variable quantities, like *3C.* Advantages include the following:

- Better for close operations with minimal transportation requirements.
- Can take advantage of EOQ economies for operations involving high setup costs.
- Fast, doesn't require counting or tracking of inventory.
- Simplicity. Compatible with visible signaling. Examples are the two-bin system and *Kanban* approaches.
- Easier to predict time requirements once orders are placed.

A disadvantage is that the model can cause excess inventory in the system. It is better for low-cost, "C" items. Some companies expense items in this category.

constant quantity (fixed quantity) reorder model: An inventory reorder pattern with fixed quantity delivered at variable time intervals, like *kanban.*

Advantages include the following:

- Establishes a regular rhythm in the supply chain.
- Decreases variability from uncertainty about schedules.
- Can take advantage of setup economies when setup times depend on sequence. An example is paint lines where different color sequences require different setup efforts.

Disadvantages arise when variation in quantities can cause production to run behind. One must also track production through the chain, with a requirement to know usage at various points to signal correct quantity. The approach fits higher-value "A" items.

constraint: Any element that prevents a system from achieving a higher level of performance. Constraints can be of many kinds, including physical steps in production and the limits on customer desire for the product.

An element that limits the supply chain from achieving higher level of performance. Among the types are physical, policy-related, financial, or process constraints. Some supply chain re-engineering will face firm constraints that limit design options. *Barriers* are similar to constraints but can be addressed and mitigated in the process design. The *theory of constraints (TOC)* provides concepts and tools for managing constraints in a supply chain.

control points: In the *theory of constraints (TOC),* these are strategic locations that are tightly planned and scheduled. Other work centers are not, simplifying scheduling and control. (Adapted from *APICS Dictionary,* 10th ed.)

COQ: Cost of quality. COQ may be viewed as a subset of *activity-based costing* and can provide the information necessary to drive service improvements and reduce costs. Components of COQ usually include appraisal, prevention, detection, and correction. Correction can include internal (before the sale) and external (after the sale) components.

Core competence: An organization capability that can be applied to a variety of core and end products. The capability is usually technology-based but can also be competence in facets of supply chain management.

cost driver: In activity based costing, volume variable used to calculate the total cost of an activity. The activity cost may be express in (cost)/(unit of volume). The unit of volume used is the cost driver.

C_p, C_{pk}: Process capability and the index of capability, respectively. This is the ability of a process to produce outputs that conform to specifications. Typically, a process is considered "capable" when capability or the capability index are 1.33 or greater. This means the variation in the process is less than the specification range. C_p = (upper – lower specification limit)/6s, where s = standard deviation of process output. C_{pk} = (mean – nearer specification)/3s.

CPFR: Collaborative Planning, Forecasting & Replenishment. A set of standard business processes used for supply chain collaboration. The term is a trademark of the sponsoring organization, the Voluntary Interindustry Commerce Standards (VICS) Association.

CPIO: Chief process improvement officer. A senior management role to lead the re-engineering of processes. Facilitates process improvement across internal and external boundaries.

critical path: The series of activities that determines the duration of a project. It is the longest path through the project. The Critical Path Method (CPM) is a technique to predict the project's duration by analyzing the path of activities with the least amount of scheduling flexibility. (Adapted from Project Management Institute, *Combined Standards Glossary,* 3rd ed., PMI, 2007)

CRM: Customer relationship management. "CRM aligns business processes with customer strategies to build customer loyalty and increase profits over time." (Quoted from Darrell K. Rigby, Frederick F. Reichheld, and Phil Schefter, "Avoid the Four Perils of CRM," *Harvard Business Review,* February 2002, 101–9)

Computer applications that deal with the "front office" interface between the company and its customers.

CRP: Continuous Replenishment Planning. The practice of partnering between distribution channel members that changes the traditional replenishment process from traditional purchase orders based on economic order quantities, to the replenishment of products based on actual and forecasted product demand.

CSCMP: Council of Supply Chain Management Professionals. A worldwide professional organization of logistics personnel. Formerly the CLM, it has contributed heavily to the discussion of supply chain issues.

CTP: Capable to promise. The ability to commit to orders with available capacity and inventory. (Adapted from John H. Blackstone Jr., *APICS Dictionary,* 12th ed., APICS—The Association for Operations Management, 2008)

CTQ: Critical to quality. A feature in a product or service that's important to customers. Such a feature can be translated to processes for delivering the feature. The term is used in connection with Six Sigma efforts to improve processes.

customer: A person or organization who decides to purchase a product or service or who receives a product or service if no purchase is involved, such as an internal customer for information. An *end user* is the person or organization that uses or consumes the product or service. The end user is not necessarily the customer or buyer.

customer-centric organization: An organization structure built around customer segments. Desirable when segments have different requirements, style-driven products with short product lives requiring fast responses, and higher margin products. (*Source:* James B. Ayers, *Handbook of Supply Chain Management,* 2nd ed., Auerbach Publications, 2006)

customer-centric supply chain: Supply chains or organizations whose construct centers on the requirements of targeted customer segments. Alternatives are functional and product-centric supply chains.

customer-partner: A customer or end user organization with which a company has formed a partnership. (Adapted from John H. Blackstone Jr., *APICS Dictionary,* 12th ed., APICS—The Association for Operations Management, 2008)

customer–supplier partnership: A relationship characterized by cooperation and trust. Suppliers typically guarantee quality and help the customer reduce costs and improve quality. (Adapted from John H. Blackstone Jr., *APICS Dictionary,* 12th ed., APICS—The Association for Operations Management, 2008)

cycle time: CGR views cycle time as a property of processes along the supply chain. The minimum theoretical cycle time for a product's supply chain is the sum of individual process cycle times.

Cycle time reduction is achieved through process re-engineering including new technology along the chain. Examples include automated sharing of information about final demand, introducing postponement through product design, and automation in production processes.

Lead time is a market-oriented property that is driven by competitive forces. A competitor that works to reduce cycle time can enjoy the benefits of having the shortest lead time. *Throughput time* is a synonym.

data warehouse: A repository for data organized in a format that is suitable for ad hoc query processing. Data warehouses are built from operational databases used for day-to-day business processes. The operational data is "cleaned" and transformed in a way that is amenable to fast retrieval and efficient analysis. A single-purpose data warehouse is sometimes referred to as a "data mart."

DCF: Discounted cash flow. A method of financial analysis that recognizes the time value of money as measured by the cost of capital. DCF is used to convert capital costs into "equivalent uniform cash flows." This makes it possible to combine expense and capital items when weighing capital investments.

decomposition (forecasting): A method of forecasting where data is divided into trend, seasonal, and cyclical components. Another component may be random—where no pattern exists. Forecasts are made using each component. (Adapted from John H. Blackstone Jr., *APICS Dictionary*, 12th ed., APICS—The Association for Operations Management, 2008)

decomposition (WBS, IDEF): Breaking a category down into lower levels for sharper definition of requirements. The term can apply to project deliverables, scope, activities, tasks, and projects. IDEF decomposes functions in a supply chain in a similar way. (Adapted from Project Management Institute, *Combined Standards Glossary*, 3rd ed., PMI, 2007)

deficiency, discrepancy: Failure of a quality system to comply with requirements.

DELIVER processes: Processes to provide finished goods and services to customers. These processes are components of SCOR and the CSCMP's *Supply Chain Management Process Standards*.

deliverable: Any measurable, tangible, verifiable outcome, result, or item produced to complete a project or part of a project. Often refers to a work product delivered to and approved by a sponsor or customer. (Adapted from Project Management Institute, *Combined Standards Glossary*, 3rd ed., PMI, 2007)

demand: End-user requirements for a product or service. This is what would be consumed if sufficient product were available at prices that yield a profit. End users aren't necessarily purchasers who pay for a product. A "customer" may buy a product or service on behalf of the end user. Demand can be independent, like an end item not linked to another item, or dependent, when it is a component of another item. Derived demand arises from sales of products where the item is consumed such as steel in automobiles or washing machines in new homes.

demand chain: A term sometimes applied to the "outgoing" side of the business. Supply chain, in this context, only applies to the "incoming" side. To the end user, all activities to produce the product or service are part of the *"supply chain."*

Demand Flow: A technique to speed product final assembly. Demand Flow uses the concept of a "pile of parts" that can be assembled in response to actual customer orders. The term is trademarked by the John Costanza Institute of Technology.

demand-driven supply chain: A term developed by CGR that applies to supply chains that use tools that enable decisions to be made on the basis of actual customer demand rather than forecasts. The extent to which a supply chain is "demand-driven" is measurable. Most supply chains will require some level of forecasting for advanced planning. However, it is desirable to reduce dependence on these forecasts. APICS uses the term "demand-chain management" to describe a similar environment.

design team: A team, usually of operations managers involved in included supply chain processes, that designs new supply chains. Design teams may be called upon to develop spheres, activity systems, requirements for IT systems, and process improvements.

disintermediation: The elimination of echelons or stages in the supply chain. This can reduce cycle time and operating expense.

DMAIC: "Define, measure, analyze, improve, and control" improvement cycle used by Six Sigma practitioners.

downstream: The end of the supply chain nearest to end users. *Upstream* refers to the beginnings of the supply chain, probably suppliers of components or raw materials.

driving force: A strategic planning concept developed by Michel Robert. The concept holds that there is one and only one driving force around which a company competes. Company management may acknowledge this; however, often it does not.

DRP: Distribution requirements planning. Replenishment procedures at distribution control points. Can use MRP logic or other rules.

drumbeat: The pace at which an organization produces product. Used to pace all the operations in a factory or in a supply chain. Similar to *Takt time.*

drum–buffer–rope: In the *theory of constraints (TOC)*, a generalized process to manage resources to maximize throughput. The "drum" sets the pace of production to match the system's constraint. "Buffers" placed at constraints protect the system from disruption and uncertainty. The "rope" communicates between the constraint and the gating operation that controls release of work into the system. The model can be applied at work center, factory, and supply chain levels. *Takt time* is also a term applied to the "drum."

echelon: A term that refers to layers of distribution or to stages in the process. Each echelon can include the storage, transportation, and handling of the product between the source (presumably a factory) and its point of use. A trend is toward reducing echelons to speed the supply chain and reduce its cost. Also, competitors at any echelon may seek to add services, squeezing out other echelon levels.

E-commerce: Electronic commerce has come to mean many different things to many different people. Originally, the term meant selling things online. The term has evolved to mean conducting business online, which can include customer service functions, sales, marketing, public relations, advertising, and more.

ECR: Efficient Consumer Response. Refers to technologies to match supply and demand in the retail sector.

EDI: Electronic data interchange. The computer-to-computer transmission of business information between trading partners. The information should be organized in standard file formats or transaction sets following guidelines administered by the Uniform Code Council (UCC). Standards have been developed for all regular business-to-business communications, including purchase orders, invoices, shipping notices, and funds transfer. By eliminating the clerical, mailing, and other costs associated with paper-based information, EDI reduces costs, time delays, and errors.

EMI/ESI: Early manufacturing involvement/early supplier involvement. Inclusion of the manufacturing department and suppliers in product design. The result is a more producible and durable design.

ENABLE process: A process that prepares, maintains, or manages information, trading partner relationships, or other factors to support planning and execution processes. Enable processes are operations-centric in that they support production for most, if not all, products and markets. These processes are components of SCOR and the CSCMP's *Supply Chain Management Process Standards.*

Enable sphere: A *sphere* made up of *ENABLE processes* that support product-producing spheres.

end user: The person or organization that uses or consumes a product or service. The end user is at the end of the supply chain. The user is not necessarily the *customer* or buyer of the product or service.

engineer-to-order: Products that need unique engineering design, customization, or new materials. Each order results in a unique bill of material, some unique part numbers, and custom routings. (Adapted from John H. Blackstone Jr., *APICS Dictionary,* 12th ed., APICS—The Association for Operations Management, 2008)

EOQ: Economic Order Quantity. A fixed order-quantity model that determines the amount of an item to be purchased or manufactured at one time. The model minimizes the combined costs of acquiring and carrying inventory. When production rates are closer to consumption rates, as in a synchronized supply chain, the production quantity approaches infinity, essentially continuous operation.

EPC: Electronic product code. Any of several methods for identifying a product. The most complete can identify unit items from specific manufacturers.

ERP: Enterprise resource planning. ERP systems are comprised of software programs that tie together all of an enterprise's various functions, such as Finance, Manufacturing, Sales, Distribution, Procurement, and Human Resources. This software also provides for the analysis of the data from these areas to plan production, forecast sales, and analyze quality. The core of most ERP systems is an *MRP system*.

EVA: Economic value added. The dollar amount of value added by an enterprise over a specified period of time. EVA takes into account the capital employed in the business. The term is trademarked by Stern Stewart. Synonym: *residual income.*

event: An occurrence in the supply chain that triggers the need for action. *Supply chain event management* refers to software solutions that monitor operating data to determine whether such an event has occurred.

EXECUTION process: A SCOR process that changes the state of material goods. It includes scheduling/sequencing, transforming products through manufacturing processes, and moving products.

executive information system: Software providing operating information for direct access by executive users.

extended product: Those features of a product that aren't part of the base, or physical, product. Many supply chain attributes are extended product features like availability of product, method of delivery, customer service, ability to return the product, and so forth. (Adapted from James B. Ayers, *Handbook of Supply Chain Management,* 2nd ed., Auerbach Publications, 2006)

facilitating processes (project management context): Processes that may or may not be needed, depending on the needs of the project. These are likely to be performed intermittently or as needed. Examples include *staff acquisition, risk response planning, team development,* and *solicitation of suppliers.*

five focusing steps: A five-step *theory of constraints* (TOC) process to continuously evaluate the production system and market mix to make the most of the system constraints:

1. Identify constraints in the system.
2. Decide how to exploit the constraint.
3. Subordinate non-constraints to the constraints.
4. Elevate the constraints in the system.
5. Return to step 1 if the constraint is broken.

(Adapted from John H. Blackstone Jr., *APICS Dictionary,* 12th ed., APICS—The Association for Operations Management, 2008)

flexibility: The ability to change or react to internal or external changes with little penalty in time, effort, cost, or performance. Categories of flexibility include product mix variation, volume variations, labor flexibility, design-change flexibility, and routing flexibility. (*Source:* David M. Upton, "The Management of Flexibility," *California Management Review,* Winter 1994, 72–89)

float: In supply chains, the time required for payments to suppliers to be completed.

In project schedules, the time an activity can be delayed without affecting the completion of the project. Activities on the critical path have no float.

focused factory: A concept originated by Wickham Skinner arguing that factories or parts of factories perform best if they are designed to fulfill customer requirements as efficiently as possible. The focused factory uses manufacturing capability to support strategies for competing.

forecast error: The difference between actual and forecast demand, stated as an absolute value or a percentage. Forecast errors are used to adjust production and inventory plans in supply chains with high dependence on forecasts for decision making.

forecastable demand: Applies to certain patterns of demand that contain enough history to provide a forecast of future demand. The opposite is *"lumpy"* demand for which forecasting isn't possible.

freight forwarder: This is a manager or handler for the shipment of goods. The responsibilities of a freight forwarder include arranging shipment details and completing documentation. Because of their brokering role, freight forwarders have a good understanding of market trends and insurance and transport alternatives.

front-line team: A group of people working in a process that test new designs and provide recommendations for process design and changes.

functional organization: An organization structure built around functional tasks like marketing, accounting, manufacturing, and customer service. Works best where product lines are narrow or mature businesses. Not a good alternative where speed is required or products and customers have diverse requirements. (*Source:* James B. Ayers, *Handbook of Supply Chain Management,* 2nd ed., Auerbach Publications, 2006)

functional product: A category of product with lower margins and low uncertainty regarding demand. The supply chains for these products should be designed for the lowest possible cost. See *innovative product.*

fuzzy front end: Refers to the beginning of the development cycle, when new product and service concepts are not clear. Many organizations are defining processes and systems to manage the "fuzziness" of the front end of new product development cycle.

glass pipeline: A term describing a supply chain in which the visibility over the status of the product is high. One is able to track physical movement through the pipeline easily.

globalization: Doing business across international boundaries.

GMROI: Gross margin return on investment. A financial performance measure that incorporates sales, profit margin, and assets employed. It is calculated by multiplying the traditional gross margin by the ratio of net sales to average inventory: (gross margin/net sales) × (net sales/average inventory).

greenfield vision: An ideal state based on specifications for future operations. The greenfield should ignore constraints inherent in the current situation. It should serve as a "stretch" target for implementing improvements in the supply chain. The use of the greenfield approach is based on the premise that, without ambitious targets, only incremental change will occur.

hedge inventory: A form of safety stock implemented for a specific period. Reasons can include interruptions due to strikes, price increases, or a currency re-evaluation. (Adapted from John H. Blackstone Jr., *APICS Dictionary*, 12th ed., APICS—The Association for Operations Management, 2008)

Heijunka (production smoothing): A principle for adapting supply chain production to fluctuating customer demand. The principle is a pillar of "lean" systems. The Japanese word *Heijunka* (pronounced *hey-joon-kah*), means literally "make flat and level." Customer demand must be met *with the customer's preferred delivery times* but customer demand is "bumpy," and factories prefer "level," or stable production. So, a manufacturer needs to try and *smooth out* these bumps in production.

The main tool for smoothing is frequent changing of the model mix on a given line. TPS advocates small batches of many models over short periods of time, requiring fast changeovers. (Adapted from Frederick Stimson Harriman at www.fredharriman.com)

horizontal accounting: A term that relates to system- or *activity-based costs*. Costs are expressed "horizontally" along a process that moves between "vertical" budgeted cost centers. The principle is also applied to collecting project costs and measuring earned value when multiple organizations contribute to producing deliverables in a work package.

HSV: Hosted software vendors. A model of offering software packages over the Internet. The term has supplanted "ASP." Applications can be in categories such as accounting and CRM or vertical solutions for specific industries. (Adapted from *Infoworld*, January 20, 2003, 35)

hybrid inventory system, hybrid production system: Replenishment procedures that combine approaches. For the hybrid inventory system, some replenishment would be at fixed intervals and variable quantities. For the hybrid production system, some use level production planning; others use the *chase production method*. (Adapted from John H. Blackstone Jr.,

APICS Dictionary, 12th ed., APICS—The Association for Operations Management, 2008)

IDEF: Integrated Computer-Aided Manufacturing (ICAM) definition methods are used to perform modeling activities in support of enterprise integration. The original IDEF methods were developed for the purpose of enhancing communication among people who needed to decide how their existing systems were to be integrated. The technique of decomposing a process into activities is useful for supply chain process analysis. The product is a "node tree" of supply chain process functions. IDEF0 modeling is supported by Visio software.

implosion: The process of determining where a component is used in the product line. Implosions can be single level, showing only the parents of the next higher level; or multilevel, showing the ultimate top-level parents. Also "where used list." Opposite of "explosion." Supports implementation of *3C* approach to replenishment decision making. (Adapted from John H. Blackstone Jr., *APICS Dictionary,* 12th ed., APICS—The Association for Operations Management, 2008)

incentive arrangement: Contract calling for sharing costs and rewards between a buyer and seller. Elements include target cost, target profit, and sharing arrangements. (Adapted from John H. Blackstone Jr., *APICS Dictionary,* 12th ed., APICS—The Association for Operations Management, 2008)

independent, dependent demand: Independent demand is driven by end user or customer needs. It comes from outside the sphere or enterprise. Dependent demand is derived from independent demand and triggers replenishment within the sphere or enterprise.

inert stock: A term used by CGR to define slow-moving categories of inventory. Components can include defective items, obsolete items, "stranded" odd quantity components with no demand, and *"lumpy"* demand items. The inert category can be a large portion of total inventory. Reducing it may require a concerted effort on several fronts.

initiative: A broad program to improve supply chain operations. Initiatives can last several years and evolve with changing requirements. An initiative can have multiple projects. A synonym is *program.*

innovative product: An innovative product has high margins and uncertain demand. The supply chain for such products should be designed for responsiveness to demand, rather than efficiency. See *functional* product.

integrated supply: An alliance or long-term commitment between two or more organizations for the purpose of achieving specific business objectives by maximizing the effectiveness of each participant's resources. The relationship is based upon trust, dedication to common goals, and an understanding of each other's individual expectations and values.

integration: The extent to which components of the production process are inextricably linked. A software design concept that allows users to move easily between applications.

inventory turns: The number of times each year that the inventory turns over. It can be in units but is more often in dollars. It is computed by dividing the average inventory level into the annual cost of goods sold.

issue, issues log: Issues are questions that define the scope of the supply chain strategy. A running list keeps track of these issues and the response implicit in the strategy. Issues are often tracked in categories like Financial, Organization/Measures, Product Development, Processes, and so forth.

ITIL: Information Technology Infrastructure Library. A comprehensive document set that has become a *de facto* standard for managing IT functions.

Jikoda: Japanese term for the practice of stopping a line when a defect occurs. (Adapted from John H. Blackstone Jr., *APICS Dictionary,* 12th ed., APICS—The Association for Operations Management, 2008)

JIT: Just in Time. A philosophy of manufacturing based on planning elimination of all waste and continuous improvement of productivity. It encompasses the successful execution of all manufacturing activities required to produce a final product, from design engineering to delivery, and including all stages of conversion from raw material onward. The primary elements of JIT are to have only the required inventory when needed; to improve quality to zero defects; to reduce lead times by reducing setup times, queue lengths, and lot sizes; to incrementally revise the operations themselves; and to accomplish these things at minimum cost. In the broad sense, it applies to all forms of manufacturing, job shop, and process as well as repetitive. (Adapted from John H. Blackstone Jr., *APICS Dictionary,* 12th ed., APICS—The Association for Operations Management, 2008)

joint replenishment: Coordination of lot sizing and order release for related items. The purpose is to take advantage for setup, shipping, and quantity discounts. It applies to material ordering, group technology production, and distribution. The commonality component of the *3C* approach is a form of joint replenishment. (Adapted from John H. Blackstone Jr., *APICS Dictionary,* 12th ed., APICS—The Association for Operations Management, 2008)

Kaizen: A Japanese word that means, loosely translated, constant improvement.

Kanban: A method of JIT production that uses standard containers or lots sizes with a single card attached to each. It is a pull system in which work centers signal with a card that they wish to withdraw parts from feeding operations or suppliers. The Japanese word kanban means card, billboard, or sign. The term is often used synonymously for the specific scheduling system deployed in the *Toyota Production System (TPS)*. (Adapted from John H. Blackstone Jr., *APICS Dictionary,* 12th ed., APICS—The Association for Operations Management, 2008)

Kano model: The model describes three different types of quality: (1) basic, items that one assumes is part of a product; (2) performance, the customer will be able to articulate this type of quality and can be captured by surveys; and (3) excitement, a quality that is unexpected and cannot be articulated by the customer. The supply chain has the potential for assuring all three types of quality. (*Source:* Jack B. ReVelle, John W. Moran, and Charles A. Cox, *The QFD Handbook*, John Wiley & Sons, 1998)

key characteristic: A feature whose variation has the greatest impact on the fit, performance, or service life of the finished product from the perspective of the customer. Key characteristics are a tool to help decide where to focus limited resources. They are used for process improvement purposes. Key characteristics may or may not be "critical characteristics" that affect product safety.

key process parameter: A process input that is controllable and that has a high statistical correlation with the variation in a part key characteristic. Key process parameters are most effectively determined by the use of designed experiments.

knowledge management: Refers to efforts to capture the "knowledge" resident in an organization. Such efforts are often centered on information technology. Some have dismissed knowledge management as a fad but the concept has value in supply chain management across multiple enterprises.

lead time: CGR's view is that lead time is associated with a product or service delivered by the supply chain. It is "imposed" on the supply chain by the competitive environment. It is driven by customer expectations, supply chain innovations, and competitive pressure.

All these factors are in constant motion, moving toward "faster, cheaper, better." Competitors that can't deliver products and services within the established lead time will likely perish. Competitors that have the shortest lead time have an advantage.

lean enterprise: A term coined by James Womack and Daniel Jones (originators of the "lean" terminology) to extend the idea of "lean manufacturing" along the value or supply chain, including upstream and downstream partners. The enterprise focuses on removing operations that add no value to the customer and adding those that do. Such operations are not confined to product-producing ones. The lean enterprise is operationally synchronized with end user demand. (Adapted from John H. Blackstone Jr., *APICS Dictionary*, 12th ed., APICS—The Association for Operations Management, 2008)

lean production: Production approach based on using multiskilled workers, highly flexible machines and very adaptable organizations and procedures to manufacture an increasing variety of products while continually decreasing costs. "Lean" means more productive use of labor, material, and inventory along the supply chain.

legacy systems: A network or hierarchical database system usually running on a mainframe. Replacement of legacy systems is often a motivator for installing new supply chain information systems. Implementing supply chain improvements may be limited by the capabilities of legacy systems.

level (of a product): Components of product structure. Each level is coded with the end item as the 0 level. Level 1 has level 0 components; level 2 has level 1 components, and so forth. Also see decomposition. (Adapted from John H. Blackstone Jr., *APICS Dictionary*, 12th ed., APICS—The Association for Operations Management, 2008)

Level 1 processes: SCOR and the CSCMP's process models have five core management processes: PLAN, SOURCE, MAKE, DELIVER, and RETURN. There are separate definitions in this Glossary for each.

Level plant loading: Efforts to reduce variability in production at the business unit and supply chain levels. Level plant loading is considered a best practice for achieving effective supply chains. *Drumbeat* and *Takt time* are related terms.

Limiting operation: The operation with the least capacity. A supply chain bottleneck that may be protected by establishing buffer inventories. (Adapted from John H. Blackstone Jr., *APICS Dictionary*, 12th ed., APICS—The Association for Operations Management, 2008)

LOE: Level of effort. A support type activity that is hard to measure and doesn't produce end products. It is usually characterized as a uniform rate of activity. (Adapted from Project Management Institute, *Combined Standards Glossary*, 3rd ed., PMI, 2007)

logistics management: Logistics management is that part of supply chain management that plans, implements, and controls the efficient, effective forward and reverse flow and storage of goods, services, and related information between the point of origin and the point of consumption in order to meet customers' requirements. (*Source:* www.cscmp.org)

lot operation cycle time: Length of time from the start of setup to the end of cleanup for a production lot at a given operation. Includes setup, production, and cleanup. (Adapted from John H. Blackstone Jr., *APICS Dictionary*, 12th ed., APICS—The Association for Operations Management, 2008)

LTL: Truckload/less than truckload carriers. Carriers that cater to the needs of different classes of shippers. Truckload-only carriers generally serve larger shippers. LTL carriers generally serve smaller shippers.

lumpy demand: An infrequently occurring demand that can't be forecast. The usual result is a need to carry an insurance level of stock. Also called "discontinuous demand."

MAD: Mean absolute deviation. The average of absolute values of the deviations between observed and expected values. MAD can be calculated to evaluate forecasting processes as the difference between actual sales and forecasts.

MAKE processes: Processes that transform material into finished products. These processes are components of SCOR and the CSCMP's *Supply Chain Management Process Standards.*

make-to-order: A production environment where the product is made after receipt of the order. The product is often a combination of standard and custom items. Make-to-order is similar to *assemble-to-order.* (Adapted from John H. Blackstone Jr., *APICS Dictionary,* 12th ed., APICS—The Association for Operations Management, 2008)

make-to-stock: An environment where products are finished before receipt of a customer order. The customer orders are filled from stock. Production orders replenish the stock. (Adapted from John H. Blackstone Jr., *APICS Dictionary,* 12th ed., APICS—The Association for Operations Management, 2008)

manufacturing strategy: The concept that manufacturing can support other strategies for competing, such as product, marketing, and financial strategies. A related term is a "supply chain strategy" where supply chain design contributes to competitiveness.

market mediation cost: A term originated by Marshal Fisher that refers to the cost of mismatches between supply and demand. Mismatches are too much or too little supply for the actual demand. Too much produces market mediation costs in the form of write downs; too little results in lost sales (also a market mediation cost).

marketing mix: Components of a strategy aimed at a particular market: product, price, promotion, and place (or *supply chains*).

mass customization: Creation of individual variations of a high volume product with many options for configuration.

matrix BOM: A method for identifying common components. Components are arranged on one dimension, end products on the other. This is a useful tool for establishing commonality in applying the 3C methodology.

Maturity Model: A framework for measuring progress toward some goal. The model consists of descriptive "levels" to help users assess their progress toward higher levels of maturity. Harold Kerzner's Project Management Maturity Model (PMMM) has five levels: common language, common processes, singular methodology, benchmarking, and continuous improvement.

merge-in-transit: A technique for combining order components from various sources while those components are in transit from sources to customers.

MES: Manufacturing execution system. An MES is a manufacturing software application. MES focuses on execution and management of production processes. MES provides synchronization of the following as they are used to make the product: labor, machinery and equipment, tooling, other resources, for example, power, raw material, and work in process inventory. MES usually operates in time increments from subshift to real-time.

MES applications may serve as interfaces between MRP scheduling applications and machine controllers. They also collect quality and production data.

milestone: A significant event in the project often associated with completion of a deliverable. (Adapted from Project Management Institute, *Combined Standards Glossary,* 3rd ed., PMI, 2007)

milk run: A transportation link in the supply chain characterized by regularly scheduled shipments to or from one or more points. These can encompass upstream suppliers or downstream customers. By combining shipments, more frequent shipments are economically feasible. The milk run lowers the incremental cost of filling an order by establishing continuous flow in the supply chain.

min-max: A type of order point replenishment where the reorder point is the "min" and the "max" sets the order quantity.

mixed-model production: A production scheme where the production line product mix matches what is sold each day.

MRO: Maintenance, repair, and overhaul. A class of activity occurring after the sale of the product. MRO often demands special supply chain design and can be an important factor in the success of long life products.

Maintenance, repair, and operations (or operational). Refers to operations and material required to maintain an asset like a building or a product. Often refers to low-cost items.

MRP, MRP II: Materials requirement planning. A concept developed in the 1970s to make use of high-speed computers to model the requirements of material for a manufacturing operation. Basic components in manufacturing include a bill of materials, inventory data, and a production schedule. MRP and *ERP* systems are viewed as methods for planning all resources of a manufacturing company. MRP addresses operational planning in units, financial planning in dollars, and has simulation capability. Output from MRP is integrated with financial reports, purchase commitments, shipping budgets, and inventory projections. "Closed loop" MRP implies feedback to keep plans valid with regard to constraints like capacity. (Adapted from John H. Blackstone Jr., *APICS Dictionary,* 12th ed., APICS—The Association for Operations Management, 2008)

multilevel-where-used: Depiction by component of all the intermediate and final products where that component is used. Such a display forms the basis of replenishment rules using *3C*. (Adapted from John H. Blackstone Jr., *APICS Dictionary,* 12th ed., APICS—The Association for Operations Management, 2008)

network diagram: A logical display of project activities. It shows sequence and dependencies among activities.

OE: Operational excellence. A term used by Michael Porter in discussions of strategy. His contention is the OE is a necessary but not sufficient condition for sustained competitiveness. It reflects the belief that "you can't save your way to prosperity." Porter advocates the development of activity systems to distinguish the company from its competitors.

operating cycle: The time period, usually in days, required to purchase materials, manufacture product, and sell it. It is calculated by adding the inventory conversion period to the receivables conversion period. (Adapted from John H. Blackstone Jr., *APICS Dictionary,* 12th ed., APICS—The Association for Operations Management, 2008)

operation: A step in a process. Can include a changing of physical configuration, a quality control action, temporary or long-term storage, an administrative task, or transportation.

optimization: The application of operations research tools to a supply chain function. Examples include distribution planning (warehouse location and transportation planning) and planning a scheduling production. Optimization technology applies in complex supply chains and when the potential for improvement justifies its use.

order penetration point: The point in a product's flow where an item is earmarked for a particular customer. Downstream processes are driven by customer orders; upstream processes are driven by forecasts and plans. Moving the penetration point further upstream in the supply chain is the mission of creating a demand-driven supply chain. The concept is related to *postponement.* (Adapted from John H. Blackstone Jr., *APICS Dictionary,* 12th ed., APICS—The Association for Operations Management, 2008)

organizational complement: Needs that arise from the introduction of general-purpose technologies like IT or electric motors: better-skilled workers, increased levels of teamwork, redesigned processes, and new decision rights. (Adapted from Andrew McAfee, "Mastering the Three Worlds of Information Technology," *Harvard Business Review,* November 2006, pp. 141–9)

partner: An entity with which one does business, either upstream or downstream in the supply chain, whose performance is important to your success. The relationship between you and the partner may or may not include *partnering.*

partnering: A management approach used by two or more organizations, often but not always a buyer and a seller, to achieve mutual business objectives by maximizing the effectiveness of each partner's resources. Partnerships can take a number of forms from arms-length sharing of information to acquisition. Examples include collaboration in design, measures to reduce cost, and simplified replenishment procedures. See *Stage 3 supply chain organization.*

partnership classification: A classification of partnerships has three dimensions: purpose, direction, and choice. The purpose defines whether the partnership creates new space or not. Direction refers to the supply chain. Horizontal means partners are at the same echelon. Vertical is a partnership along the supply chain— probably between customer and supplier. Choice refers to the relative strength of each partner. A "many to one" means your company has many competitors and seeking a partnership with a dominant partner. (*Source:* James B. Ayers, *Handbook of Supply Chain Management,* 2nd ed., Auerbach Publications, 2006)

P:D ratio: According to the *APICS Dictionary,* 12th ed., "P" is the manufacturing lead time. "D" is the customer required delivery time. If the ratio exceeds 1.0, the customer order will be delayed or production will start as a result of a forecast (make-to-stock).

The demand-driven supply chain approach argues that different segments of the supply chain can be driven by either forecasts or actual demand. In general, actual demand is more desirable than forecasts. In this book, we use *cycle time* to refer to processes for manufacture and distribution and *lead time* as a market-driven requirement for delivery.

PDCA: Plan–do–check–act. Also called the Deming or the Shewhart Cycle for implementing process improvement. Also plan–do–study–act, another interpretation favored in later years by Deming. (Adapted from *Wikipedia*)

PDM: Product data management. Systems are processes used to track the history of product designs.

performance-based pricing: Basing prices on value to the customer, not necessarily what the product costs. The supply chain can influence value to the customer. Applies specifically to "innovative" products as opposed to "functional" ones where prices are cost-driven in competitive markets.

period order quantity: A replenishment lot size that is equal to requirements for a fixed period of time. Hence, the quantity is constant but the number of orders varies depending on demand. Order and holding costs are equalized. (Adapted from John H. Blackstone Jr., *APICS Dictionary,* 12th ed., APICS—The Association for Operations Management, 2008)

periodic replenishment: Aggregating requirements to place deliveries of varying quantities at evenly spaced time intervals, rather than variably spaced deliveries of equal quantities. The term *"fixed cycle"* also refers to this method. The *"milk run"* is also a tool for implementing this approach. (Adapted from John H. Blackstone Jr., *APICS Dictionary,* 12th ed., APICS—The Association for Operations Management, 2008)

phase: A project phase is a collection of logically related project activities, usually culminating in a deliverable. Phases may be divided into subphases and components. A phase is a component of the project life cycle. (Adapted from Project Management Institute, *Combined Standards Glossary,* 3rd ed., PMI, 2007)

PLAN processes: Processes that balance supply and demand. Plan processes cover long-range planning at the supply chain level. PS, PM, PD, and PR cover shorter-term planning for SOURCE, MAKE, DELIVER, and RETURN. SCOR and the CSCMP's models contain this process.

PMMM: Project Management Maturity Model. A five-level model developed by Dr. Harold Kerzner. The levels are common language, common processes, singular methodology, benchmarking, and continuous improvement.

point-to-point integration: Building a customized computer connection. The software for such integration is usually expensive to build and maintain. When systems change on either side of the connection, expensive changes are needed.

portfolio, PPM: A set of initiatives or projects being pursued to improve supply chains. Portfolio management is deciding the priority of the projects and making resources available for their completion. PPM stands for Project Portfolio Management.

postponement: A product and/or supply chain design strategy that shifts product differentiation (or the *order penetration point*) closer to the end user. The approach encompasses identity changes such as assembly or packaging. (Adapted from *APICS Dictionary*)

PPM: Project portfolio management. Deciding the priority of the projects and making resources available for their completion.

price-taker: A buying organization that typically takes the low price every time. Generally requires a functional supply chain in the face of competitive alternatives. Prices often become the basis for selection in online auctions.

proactive systems: An approach to designing information systems to focus on the needs of decision makers. The approach may rely on computer-based tools to disseminate the needed information. Non-computer-based approaches may also be used.

process: A planned series of actions or operations that are linked together. (Adapted from John H. Blackstone Jr., *APICS Dictionary*, 12th ed., APICS—The Association for Operations Management, 2008)

process, process group (project management context): A series of actions bringing about a result. A process either manages the project itself (a project management process) or creates the output of the project (a product-oriented process). In the former group are Initiating, Planning, Controlling, and Closing process groups. Project management processes call for project management knowledge and practice expertise. In the latter are Executing processes. Executing processes call for application area knowledge and practice expertise. (From *The American Heritage Dictionary of the English Language*, 3rd ed., Houghton Mifflin, 1992; and Project Management Institute, *A Guide to the Project Management Body of Knowledge [PMBOK Guide]*, 3rd ed., PMI, 2004)

process map: A picture of a process flow using symbols.

process owner: The central figure in organizations organized around processes. Owners are charged with end-to-end responsibility and authority for a cross-functional process.

product group, product line, product family: A grouping of products or SKUs for planning and forecasting requirements.

product life cycle: A well-known marketing concept that holds that products pass through phases in their market lives. The phases are inception, growth, maturity, and decline. The presence of the product life cycle has implications for supply chain design.

product pipeline, product funnel: Visual models of the way new products are developed. The concept infers a repetitive pattern for producing products. SCM should be a part of the product development process.

product tree: A graphical representation of the product and its SKUs. The tree can also show manufacturing locations and multiple geographic markets for the same or a similar SKU.

product-centric organization: An organization structure built around different product lines. Preferred in cases of multiple products with different technologies, homogeneous customer bases, capital intensive, and cost-driven businesses. (*Source:* James B. Ayers, *Handbook of Supply Chain Management,* 2nd ed., Auerbach Publications, 2006)

product-centric supply chain: Supply chains or organizations whose construct centers on the production of products. Alternatives are functional and customer-centric supply chains.

product-producing sphere: A sphere that produces products for external customers. The other type is an *enable sphere* that provides a support service. The product-producing sphere is a "business inside the business." It merits its own supply chain design.

program: A group of related projects managed in a coordinated way. A synonym is *initiative.* A program can include project and ongoing operations work. For example, a new product program includes product design (a temporary project) and ongoing manufacturing and sales (an operation). (Adapted from Project Management Institute, *Combined Standards Glossary,* 3rd ed., PMI, 2007)

progressive elaboration: A property of projects that arises from the "temporary" and "unique" nature of projects. At the beginning of a project, the resulting product, service, or result is defined broadly. As the project proceeds, the final result is "progressively elaborated" through updating of project components like schedule, cost, and scope. (Adapted from Project Management Institute, *Combined Standards Glossary,* 3rd ed., PMI, 2007)

project: An organized change effort usually associated with an initiative or program, with a manager, budget, objectives, and schedule. A project is temporary and produces a unique product, service, or result. Several projects may support an *initiative* or *program. Action plans* define the goals for the project. (Adapted from Project Management Institute, *Combined Standards Glossary,* 3rd ed., PMI, 2007)

project life cycle: A collection of generally sequential project phases needed for control of the project. Life cycle phases generally include the initial phase, intermediate phase, and final phase. Different industries define these differently. For example, the construction industry might call the initial phase "feasibility" and the final phase "turnover and startup." A software project might start with "business requirements" and finish with "test and deploy." (Adapted from Project Management Institute, *Combined Standards Glossary,* 3rd ed., PMI, 2007)

project manager: A person responsible for managing a project. The project management function may rest with an individual for smaller projects and with a larger *project office* for larger ones. The project manager function coordinates the logistics involved in the project, including the activities of steering committees, design teams, and employee teams testing new ways of working.

project manufacturing: Manufacturing processes designed for large, often unique products requiring custom design. These processes require flexible processes and design changes. (Adapted from John H. Blackstone Jr., *APICS Dictionary,* 12th ed., APICS—The Association for Operations Management, 2008)

project (program) office: A permanent line function for project managers with expertise in project management processes and tools, a repository of lessons learned, and a champion for project management methodology. A project office can administer a larger supply chain project. (Adapted from Harold Kerzner, *Strategic Planning for Project Management: Using a Project Management Maturity Model,* John Wiley & Sons, 2001)

promotion: A term used by CGR to describe *risk pooling* to lower inventories. In promotion, products, product families, or SKUs are moved higher in tree (promoted) to concentrate demand.

PSM: Provider service model. A tool for defining the staffing requirements to meet defined service objectives. Often used in managing the staff required to support operations focused on delivering services.

public warehouse: A warehouse that is rented or leased. Services are provided under contract or on a fee-for-service basis. (Adapted from John H. Blackstone Jr., *APICS Dictionary,* 12th ed., APICS—The Association for Operations Management, 2008)

pull system: In production, replenishment only when items are taken for use as a result of a pull signal. For material control, an issue of material is made only in response to a pull signal from a using entity. Similarly, in distribution, pull signals come from the downstream warehouses close to the end user. Such practices are essential to implementing the *demand-driven supply chain.* (Adapted from John H. Blackstone Jr., *APICS Dictionary,* 12th ed., APICS—The Association for Operations Management, 2008)

push and pull systems: Production control systems are often described as "push" where decisions are based on forecasts or "pull" where decisions are based on actual demand. A *demand-driven supply chain* is an example of a pull system. Most organizations try to move from "push" to "pull" replenishment.

push system: In production, replenishment from a schedule driven by forecast requirements. In material control, it is the issue of material based on forecast requirements. In distribution, replenishment is based on forecasts. (Adapted from *APICS Dictionary*)

QFD: Quality function deployment. A system engineering process, which transforms the desires of the customer/user into the language required at all project levels to implement a product. QFD also provides the glue necessary, at all project levels, to tie it all together and to manage it. Finally, it is an excellent method for assuring that the customer obtains high value from the product, actually the intended purpose of QFD. Developing a "house of quality" provides a structured approach. The *voice of the customer* encompasses what end users want from the product or service.

QRP: Quick response program. A system to speed information flows through the supply chain. The purpose is to respond rapidly to changes in customer demand. Also *rapid replenishment*. (Adapted from John H. Blackstone Jr., *APICS Dictionary,* 12th ed., APICS—The Association for Operations Management, 2008)

qualitative risk analysis: Use of tools to identify the probability and potential outcomes of high, moderate, and low risk conditions and set priorities for mitigation and response planning. (Adapted from Project Management Institute, *Combined Standards Glossary,* 3rd ed., PMI, 2007)

quality standard: A set of rules for those seeking to qualify under the standard. Standards are either general or industry-specific. Standards bring consistent practice to large numbers of participants in the supply chain.

quality threshold: The expected features of a product and its supply chain. Any participant must at least operate at the threshold to maintain market share. Those falling below the threshold lose market share and may have to exit the business.

quantitative risk analysis: Measurement of probability distributions and potential results to calculate a distribution of possible outcomes.

RAM: Responsibility assignment matrix. A matrix that identifies roles in a project for participants by type of responsibility.

rapid replenishment: Denotes frequent or fast response to signals for inventory restocking. Rapid replenishment enables demand-driven supply chain approaches.

rate-based scheduling: A method for scheduling production that matches demand as expressed by a periodic rate, such as units per day or week. *3C* sets its replenishment rules as the maximum rate of consumption to protect against outages.

real-time locating systems: Systems consisting of various technologies like RFID that track supply chain material as it moves along the chain.

re-engineering: Analysis, redesign, and implementation of process changes. Can involve new technology, new methods of performing process steps, and organization change to support the process. The idea of re-engineering should not be confused with downsizing or staffing cutbacks, although they may occur in conjunction with process change. Also business process re-engineering.

replenishment cycle time: The total time from the moment a need is identified until the product is available for use. The *APICS Dictionary*, 12th ed., uses "lead time" to define this. The *Dictionary* also refers to lead time as the time to perform steps in a process. Here, we refer to cycle time as a physical property that defines the minimum time a process takes if steps are performed consecutively. Lead time is a market-determined property, or expectation by customers for performance. Reducing cycle time is one way, among others, to reduce lead time.

representative product: A typical product flowing through a process that is used as the basis for process design. The concept is applied in designing manufacturing cells.

requirement: A condition or capability (or the written statement of) needed to solve a problem, reach an objective, or to satisfy some contract, standard, or specification. There are different types including functional, user, and business requirements.

requirements, functional: Functional requirements describe the system's behavior and the information the system will manage.

residual income: A method of combining the cost of capital assets and working capital with operating expense in calculating supply chain cost. The method converts asset value to equivalent uniform annual cost using discount rates and asset lifetime.

RETURN processes: Processes addressing return and receipt of products for repair, overhaul or refurbishment, or for resale. Includes post-delivery customer support. These processes are components of SCOR and the CSCMP's *Supply Chain Management Process Standards*.

reverse logistics: The processing of returned merchandise from end users. This process includes matching returned goods authorizations, sorting salvageable, repairable and non-salvageable inventories. Reverse logistics may be a neglected function in supply chain design. The flows involved reverse typical flows of physical goods, information, and funds in the supply chain.

RFID: Radio frequency identification. Emerging technology that uses passive (short range) or active (battery powered long range) tags to identify inventory items. RFID allows for distance reading of product information. Frequently deployed along the supply chain for rapid processing of operating information.

risk: An uncertain event or condition that could have a positive or negative effect on a project's objectives. Risk identification determines what risks might affect the project; a risk management plan will help manage project risks. (Adapted from Project Management Institute, *Combined Standards Glossary*, 3rd ed., PMI, 2007)

risk analysis, risk impact analysis: A formal analysis of risk, or uncertainty, that leads to formal response plans. Components typically include listing threats, vulnerabilities, probabilities, and impacts.

risk pooling: The process of reducing risk among customers by pooling stock, reducing the total inventory required to provide a customer service level. CGR uses the term *promotion* to describe movement up the *product tree*, resulting in pooling the risk of outages at lower levels of inventory. (Adapted from John H. Blackstone Jr., *APICS Dictionary*, 12th ed., APICS—The Association for Operations Management, 2008)

rolling wave planning: A technique that uses *progressive elaboration* to refine activity cost and schedule estimates as a project proceeds. Early activities are planned to a low level in the WBS; later estimates are kept at a higher level and refined when more information becomes available. (Adapted from Project Management Institute, *A Guide to the Project Management Body of Knowledge [PMBOK Guide]*, 4th ed., 2008)

S&OP: Sales, (inventory), and operations planning. Processes for matching supply and demand. Usually an intermediate (one to three months) planning horizon. Also refers to a category of software to perform these tasks.

safety factor, safety stock: Factor used to calculate the amount of inventory required providing for uncertainty in forecasts. This is a numerical value based on a service standard, such as 95 percent certainty that orders will be filled. The factor usually ranges between 1 and 3 and is applied to the mean absolute deviation (MAD) or standard deviation (σ) to compute the safety stock required.

The need for safety stock is reduced from *risk pooling*, more frequent replenishment, or taking advantage of commonality among SKUs using the *3C* methodology.

SCC: Supply-Chain Council. A trade association of companies interested in SCM. The Council was incorporated in June 1997 as a not-for-profit trade association. The Council offers members an opportunity to improve the effectiveness of supply chain relationships from the customer's customer to the supplier's supplier.

SCEM: Supply chain event management. Software feature that monitors supply chain transaction data for predefined "exceptions" or events that require intervention. An example could be a late order. In such a case, the SCEM software would alert designated parties to inform them and suggest interventions.

SCM: Supply chain management. Design, maintenance, and operation of supply chain processes for satisfaction of end user needs. (*Source:* James B. Ayers, *Handbook of Supply Chain Management,* 2nd ed., Auerbach Publications, 2006)

The design, planning, execution, control, and monitoring of supply chain activities with the objective of creating net value, building a competitive infrastructure, leveraging worldwide logistics, synchronizing supply with demand, and measuring performance globally. (*Source:* John H. Blackstone Jr., *APICS Dictionary,* 12th ed., APICS—The Association for Operations Management, 2008)

SCM encompasses the planning and management of all activities involved in sourcing and procurement, conversion, and all logistics management activities. Importantly, it also includes coordination and collaboration with channel partners, which can be suppliers, intermediaries, third-party service providers, and customers. In essence, SCM integrates supply and demand management within and across companies. (*Source:* CSCMP Web site)

SCO: Supply chain orientation. A term coined by the University of Tennessee Supply Chain Research Group. It is a management philosophy that recognizes the implications of proactively managing both the upstream and downstream flows of products, services, finances, and information.

scope: The sum of the products, services, and results to be provided by a project. *Product scope* includes the features and functions in the products and services produced by the project. *Project scope* is what has to be done in the project to produce those features and functions. (Adapted from Project Management Institute, *Combined Standards Glossary,* 3rd ed., PMI, 2007)

SCOR, SCOR-model: Supply-Chain Operations Reference-model. An activity model developed by the Supply-Chain Council to standardize descriptions of supply chain processes.

SCPM: Supply chain performance management. Used to describe software that tracks supply chain operations. Includes supply chain event management (SCEM). (*Source:* ARC Advisory Group)

SDLC: Systems development life cycle. A process for continuous improvement of systems. Different companies may use different cycles. One such cycle includes initiation, requirements definition, design, building/coding, testing, and operations and maintenance. (Adapted from *Wikipedia*)

segmentation: Breaking the market down into definable subcategories. For instance, Coca-Cola may segment its audience based on frequency (one can a month or five cans a day), location (Bangkok or Bangladesh), and many other criteria. Supply chains should be designed with the differing needs of multiple segments in mind.

SFIA: Skills for the Information Age. A framework that defines different levels of skill in over seventy categories related to information technology management areas.

SIPOC: Supplier–inputs–processes–outputs–customers. A tool used by teams to describe their processes. Commonly applied in Six Sigma efforts. Can also display customer requirements.

Six Sigma: Sigma is a letter in the Greek alphabet. The term "sigma" is used to designate the distribution or spread about the mean (average) of any process or procedure.

> For a business or manufacturing process, the sigma value is a metric that indicates how well that process is performing. The higher the sigma value, the better. Sigma measures the capability of the process to perform defect-free work. A defect is anything that results in customer dissatisfaction. The sigma scale of measure is perfectly correlated to such characteristics as defects-per-unit, parts-per-million defective, and the probability of a failure/error.

> A Six Sigma capability means no more than 3.4 parts per million defects. Six sigma programs have become more general in their approach, reflecting overall efforts to make improvement as well as error-free production.

SKU: Stock-keeping unit. An inventory item whose status is maintained in an inventory tracking system. In the distribution system, different SKUs may represent the same item at different locations. Pronounced "*skew*." (Adapted from John H. Blackstone Jr., *APICS Dictionary,* 12th ed., APICS—The Association for Operations Management, 2008)

SMED: Single minute exchange of dies. A theory and the techniques for performing setup operations in fewer than ten minutes, the number of minutes expressed in a single digit. The SMED philosophy is important in moving from "batch-oriented" to "flow-oriented" supply chains.

SOAP: Simple Object Access Protocol. A protocol for exchanging *XML*-based information over the Internet through *Web Services* that allow each system to send and receive needed data.

SOURCE processes: SCOR and the CSCMP's model processes related to incoming material and services.

SOW: Statement of work. A narrative description of products or services to be supplied, often part of contract terms.

SPC: Statistical process control. A set of techniques and tools that help characterize patterns of variation. By understanding these patterns, a business can determine sources of variation and minimize them, resulting in a more consistent product or service. Many customers are demanding consistency as a measure of high quality. The proper use of SPC provides a powerful way to assure that the customer gets the desired consistency time after time.

specification: A description of performance required from the supply chain for a process based on an evaluation of the as-is condition. The specification only states what is required, not how that goal will be reached.

sphere: A description of entities derived by dividing complex supply chain operations for the purposes of improvement. A sphere consists of market-product-operations combinations, or "businesses within the business." There are two types of sphere: *product-producing* (has external customers) and *enable* (provides support to multiple product-producing spheres and has internal customers).

A related but not synonymous term from the Supply-Chain Council is "threads." (*Source:* James B. Ayers, *Handbook of Supply Chain Management,* 2nd ed., Auerbach Publications, 2006)

sponsor: An executive champion for a supply chain improvement effort. The level of the individual will depend on the level of the project: functional (department level), business unit level, or supply chain level.

Stage 3 supply chain organization: Stage 3 refers to the multicompany organization needed to implement supply chain level changes. A common goal, multicompany staffing, a third- party "honest broker," creative win–win contracting, and a senior management steering committee mark Stage 3. Stage 2 refers to company-level processes. Stage 1 to department level processes. APICS uses the term "outpartnering" to describe this structure.

stage gate approach to product development: Formal processes used for the development of new products and services in companies of all sizes, including the following:

1. Clearly defined stages in which specific tasks are undertaken.
2. The development of compelling, comprehensive business cases, rigorous, and demanding.
3. Go/no go decision points at the end of each stage using clearly defined measurable criteria.
4. The objective review of actual versus planned performance for every new product, after its introduction to the marketplace.

(Adapted from Robert G. Cooper, *Winning at New Products,* 2nd ed., Addison-Wesley Publishing Company, 1993)

steering committee: An executive level group responsible for SCM projects. The steering committee makes decisions and sets policies. Membership depends on the levels represented: level 1 is functional, or departmental; level 2 is the business unit level, level 3 is the multicompany or supply chain level. The steering committee is responsible for project results. It will also make important organization-related decisions. A project may have two steering committees. The first is inside the company that initiates the project. Later, a multicompany steering committee may oversee intercompany relationships including processes and terms of agreements.

strategic sourcing: The use of the overall acquisition function as a tool for strategic improvement rather than one focused on transactions only. Involves both cost reduction and quality improvement from better purchasing and effective partnerships across the supply chain.

strategy: The ways in which the company will be different from competitors. Strategy is different from a *business model* that defines the customers, their needs, and the underlying economic logic for the organization. (*Source:* Joan Magretta, "Why Business Models Matter," *Harvard Business Review*, May 2002, 87–92)

subproject: A smaller portion of a larger project. A subproject is likely to be managed just like a stand-alone project. (Adapted from Project Management Institute, *Combined Standards Glossary*, 3rd ed., PMI, 2007)

supplier clustering: Deliberate sourcing from suppliers within a small geographic area to gain economies in shipping. (Adapted from John H. Blackstone Jr., *APICS Dictionary*, 12th ed., APICS—The Association for Operations Management, 2008)

supply chain: Life cycle processes comprising physical, information, financial, and knowledge flows whose purpose is to satisfy end user requirements with products and services from multiple, linked suppliers. (*Source:* James B. Ayers, *Handbook of Supply Chain Management*, 2nd ed., Auerbach Publications, 2006)

The global network used to deliver products and services from raw materials to end customers through an engineered flow of information, physical distribution, and cash. (*Source:* John H. Blackstone Jr., *APICS Dictionary*, 12th ed., APICS—The Association for Operations Management, 2008)

supply chain design: According to the *APICS Dictionary*, 12th ed., facets of design include selection of partners, location and capacity of warehouse and production facilities, the products, the modes of transportation, and supporting information systems.

supply chain strategy: The idea that supply chain design should support overall strategies for competing.

synchronized supply chain: A general vision of having all links in the supply chain producing at the same rate as customer demand. Obstacles include coordination, batch size limitations in production, and inability to share information. However, synchronization is a useful goal as it is likely to provide high levels of customer service at low cost relative to unsynchronized supply chains. The term is somewhat synonymous with a *lean supply chain.*

Takt time: The interval that sets the pace of production to match the rate of customer demand. It is the "heartbeat" of the lean production system. The term is derived from the German expression for a metronome beat.

target costing: A strategic profit planning and cost management system that incorporates a strict focus on customer wants, needs, and values, and translates them into delivered products and services. A variation is using cost as a design criterion in product development.

target inventory system: A periodic review, constant interval method used in a min-max inventory system. Reorder of the variable quantity occurs at the min point in a quantity that doesn't exceed the max inventory. (Adapted from John H. Blackstone Jr., *APICS Dictionary,* 12th ed., APICS—The Association for Operations Management, 2008)

task: May be the lowest level of effort on a project. Not included in a work breakdown structure but could be part of the decomposition of work by individuals responsible for the work. The meaning and placement of the task level can vary by project or by the software tool used. (Adapted from Project Management Institute, *Combined Standards Glossary,* 3rd ed., PMI, 2007)

TBC: Time-based competition. A strategy that emphasizes time as a way to achieve competitiveness. Components include lead time reduction for product or service delivery and faster product introductions. (Adapted from John H. Blackstone Jr., *APICS Dictionary,* 12th ed., APICS—The Association for Operations Management, 2008)

TCO: Total cost of ownership. All the costs associated with buying, supporting, and operating a product or a component. The TCO concept calls attention to the importance of purchase price relative to other factors such as logistics, quality, and service.

TCP/IP: Transmission Control Protocol/Internet Protocol. The communications protocol used by the Internet.

TEU: Twenty-foot equivalent unit. A standard container twenty feet long, eight feet wide, and eight feet high. A TEU is a measure of cargo capacity; trade statistics are often reported in TEU equivalents.

Third-party logistics provider: A company specializing in performing logistics-related services for its customers. Examples include warehouse, transportation, and product assembly. Also called 3PL.

Thread: A multi-entity supply chain that uses different Level 2 SCOR execution processes. For example, a make-to-stock company supplies a make-to-order company.

Throughput: In the *theory of constraints (TOC),* the rate in units of time at which the system generates money through sales. It excludes inventory building. (Adapted from John H. Blackstone Jr., *APICS Dictionary,* 12th ed., APICS—The Association for Operations Management, 2008)

to-be: The future state, or how a supply chain process will be performed in the future. Determined after examining trade-offs between an ideal goal *(green-field)* and constraints standing in the way of implementing that ideal.

TOC: Theory of constraints. A portfolio of management philosophies, management disciplines, and industry-specific "best practices" developed by physicist Dr. Eliyahu M. Goldratt and his associates. Applicable components include managing supply chain bottlenecks, drum–buffer–rope, and costing concepts.

total cost: The sum of variable and fixed costs divided by the number of units produced. (Adapted from John H. Blackstone Jr., *APICS Dictionary,* 12th ed., APICS—The Association for Operations Management, 2008)

TPM: Total productive maintenance. A systematic approach for minimizing machine "downtime" resulting from unexpected breakdowns. TPM emphasizes the role of the machine operator who becomes more involved with routine checks and fine-tuning. TPM enables machinery to operate more efficiently and reliably, decreasing the risk of a "broken link" in the supply chain.

TPS: Toyota Production System. A manufacturing process model developed by Toyota that contributed to its reputation for quality in the auto industry. TPS was built on three key factors that differentiated it from practices being employed by their competitors in the auto industry: (1) reduced lot sizes, leading to production flexibility; (2) controlling parts required in production to enable them to be provided when and where they are needed for specific tasks; and (3) arranging production equipment in the order that people work and value is added instead of grouping by equipment function. All these elements involved suppliers and customers to some extent.

TQM: Total quality management. An approach that involves all employees in continually improving products and work processes to achieve customer satisfaction and world-class performance. TQM is generally associated with "bottom up" incremental improvement.

traceability: An attribute that allows for ongoing location of items in the supply chain.

tracking signal: A signal that forecasting techniques should be re-evaluated. (*Source: Handbook of MRP II and JIT*)

transfer pricing: The pricing of goods and services between entities in the supply chain. These entities can be internal or with outside organizations. Supply chain partnerships require agreements on pricing.

trigger, trigger events: An indication that a risk has occurred or is about to occur. A trigger may activate a risk response or a replanning of supply chain operations.

TRIZ: Russian acronym for theory of incentive problem solving. TRIZ is a methodology for eliminating conflicts that arise in product design. (*Source:* Jack B. ReVelle, John W. Moran, and Charles A. Cox, *The QFD Handbook*, John Wiley & Sons, 1998)

two-bin system: An inventory rule that calls for a new order when one bin (either real or conceptual) runs out. The second bin then becomes the source of new requirements. The reorder quantity is equal to the bin size and depends on lead times and usage quantities. The method is one of the simplest to implement and lends itself to visual approaches.

upstream: A reference to the "front end" component and raw material suppliers in the supply chain. *Downstream* is the end of the supply chain nearest to end users.

value chain: The functions in a company that are the source of strategic advantage. It stems from the many discrete activities a firm performs, including those associated with the supply chain. Value is created through cost efficiencies or differentiation from competitors. A measure of value is the profitability of the enterprise. Trading partners in a supply chain will add varying levels of value to the customers and end users. (Adapted from Michael E. Porter, *Competitive Advantage: Creating and Sustaining Superior Performance*, The Free Press, 1985)

variable costing: An accounting approach to support management decision making. Variable costs normally consist of direct labor and material plus variable overhead. Fixed overhead, which is allocated, is not included, although it is included in the cost of goods sold, the basis for inventory costing.

Variable costing is more valid in making decisions related to make or buy, economic order quantities, and other decisions. Supply chain design may transform variable into fixed costs. For example, a *"milk run"* will be made regardless of a decision to replenish for any single SKU. Therefore, the reorder cost (including transportation) assumption related to the decision should be reduced accordingly.

The approach is consistent with the *theory of constraints (TOC)*, which maintains that operating expense is relatively fixed over a range of production.

VAT analysis: Analysis of product structure from the *theory of constraints (TOC)*. A "V" structure has a few raw materials and many products. An "A" structure has many raw materials and a few end products. A "T" structure has numerous similar finished products assembled from common components. Describing the product structure in these terms is a start toward supply chain design. (Adapted from John H. Blackstone Jr., *APICS Dictionary*, 12th ed., APICS—The Association for Operations Management, 2008)

velocity: A term that describes how much time a unit of production spends in actual process steps as a percentage of total time in the process. Low velocities mean much of the time required for processing is spent in waiting on value-adding steps in the process. A goal of supply chain design is often to increase velocity. The term is increasingly applied to administrative as well as physical processing.

virtual enterprise: A team of individual companies organized to meet a market opportunity as if they were all part of the same company with a common goal.

virtual value chain: The virtual, information-based equivalent of the value chain model where value is created by gathering, selecting, synthesizing, and distributing information. (From Jeffrey F. Rayport and John J.

Sviokla, "Exploiting the Virtual Value Chain," *Harvard Business Review*, November/December, 1995)

voice of the customer: A component of QFD that captures customers' requirements as the basis for design of a strategy, product, service, or process.

VMI/VMR: Vendor-management inventory/vendor-managed replenishment. The practice of partnering between distribution channel members that changes the traditional replenishment process from distributor-generated purchase orders, based on economic order quantities, to the replenishment of products based on actual and forecasted product demand.

Some practitioners view VMR as an enhancement of VMI, requiring more collaboration.

VPN: Virtual private network. A private network that uses Internet technology. It is only accessible by authorized users. It is seen as a cost-effective alternative to dedicated lines.

wall-to-wall inventory: A technique in which material enters a plant and is processed into finished goods without entering a formal stock area. Also four-wall inventory. (*Source:* John H. Blackstone Jr., *APICS Dictionary,* 12th ed., APICS—The Association for Operations Management, 2008)

waste, Muda: Any activity that doesn't add value for customers. In lean manufacturing and broader applications of lean philosophy to service areas, the seven forms taken by waste, including the following:

- overproduction (too much or too early),
- waiting or queuing in the process,
- transportation/unneeded movements,
- processing/poor process design,
- motions or other activities that don't add value,
- inventory, and
- defective scrap or rework.

(Adapted from John H. Blackstone Jr., *APICS Dictionary,* 12th ed., APICS—The Association for Operations Management, 2008)

WBS: Work Breakdown Structure. A *decomposition* of project elements usually stated as deliverables that organizes and defines the total work scope of the project. Descending levels add detailed definition to the project work and include both internal and external deliverables. (Adapted from Project Management Institute, *Combined Standards Glossary,* 3rd ed., PMI, 2007)

Web services: Supply chain applications delivered over the Internet. These reduce the cost and complexity of forming links between supply chain partners and customers for products in the chain. They use shared standards to speed the job of developing links.

WERC: Warehousing Educational & Research Council. An international professional association dedicated to the advancement and education of people involved in the management of warehouses and distribution facilities.

where-used list: A listing of "parent" items that use a particular component and the quantity per unit. The list provides the basis for document commonality in applying *3C* methodology.

WIP: Work in progress. Units of production that have started but not finished the production process. Material entering the factory usually starts as raw material, becomes WIP, and then proceeds to finished goods. High WIP levels are characteristic of long *cycle times* or low *velocity* in production.

WMS: Warehouse management system. A system that tracks and controls the movement of inventory through the warehouse, from receiving to shipping. Many WMSs also plan transportation requirements into and out of the warehouse. The WMS allows visibility to the quantity and location of inventory as well as the age of the inventory to give a current and accurate picture of the ATP.

work flow: A class of software application that includes automation of the flow of information according to process rules. Similar to but not as encompassing as a proactive systems approach in which the requirements of decision makers are part of the redesign of the supply chain.

work package: A deliverable at the lowest level of each branch of the *Work Breakdown Structure (WBS)*. Includes schedule activities and milestones. The work package can be a subproject that is broken down into further activities. (Adapted from Project Management Institute, *Combined Standards Glossary*, 3rd ed., PMI, 2007)

world class: Being best in your industry on enough competitive factors to achieve profit goals and be considered one of the best in satisfying customers.

XML: Extensible Markup Language. This is a flexible cousin of HTML, the format for Web pages. HTML just describes how the document will look. XML describes what's in the document and is not concerned about the display but the organization of the information. XML enables transfer of data among databases and Web sites without losing descriptive information. It also speeds searches because the search engines can look at tags rather than lengthy text. A standard syntax is required in order for companies to share information. (*Source:* Eileen Roche, "Explaining XML," *Harvard Business Review*, July/August 2000, 18)

yield: The amount of acceptable product or material available after the completion of a process.

yield management: Using price and other promotions to maximize the return on investment. Usually infers a fixed capacity, such as airline seats, that is filled with customers from segments paying different prices.

Bibliography

Anderson, David L., Frank F. Britt, and Donavon J. Favre. "The Seven Principles of Supply Chain Management." *Supply Chain Management Review* (April 2007): 41–6.

Armstrong, David, Monte Burke, Emily Lambert, Nathan Vardi, and Rob Wherry. "85 Innovations." *Forbes*, December 2002, 124–210.

Ayers, James B. *Handbook of Supply Chain Management.* 2nd ed. Boca Raton: Auerbach Publications, 2006.

———. *Making Supply Chain Management Work: Design, Implementation, Partnerships, Technology, and Profits.* Boca Raton: Auerbach Publications, 2002.

———. "Supply Chain Strategies." *Information Strategy: The Executive's Journal* (Winter 1999): 2–10.

Ayers, James B., and David R. Malmberg. "Supply Chain Systems: Are You Ready?" *Information Strategy: The Executive's Journal* (Fall 2002): 18–27.

Ayers, James B., and Mary Ann Odegaard. *Retail Supply Chain Management.* Boca Raton: Auerbach Publications, 2008.

Ayers, James B., Craig Gustin, and Scott Stephens. "Reengineering the Supply Chain." *Information Strategy: The Executive's Journal* (Fall 1997): 13–8.

Beavers, Alex N. *Roadmap to the e-Factory.* Boca Raton: Auerbach Publications, 2000.

Bensaou, M., and Michael Earl. "The Right Mind-Set for Managing Information Technology." *Harvard Business Review* (September/October 1998): 119–28.

Bermudez, John. "Supply Chain Management: More Than Just Technology." *Supply Chain Management Review* (March/April 2002): 15–6.

Bhote, Keki R. *Strategic Supply Management: A Blueprint for Revitalizing the Manufacturer–supplier Partnership.* New York: AMACOM, 1989.

Blackstone, John H. Jr. *APICS Dictionary.* 12th ed. APICS (The Association for Operations Management), 2008.

Bolstorff, Peter L. "From Chaos to Control with SCOR Metrics." *CSCMP Supply Chain Quarterly* (Quarter 2/2008): 65–73.

Bovel, David, and Sheffi Yossi. "The Brave New World of Supply Chain Management." *Supply Chain Management Review* (Spring 1998): 14–22.

Bowersox, D.J., and David J. Closs. *Logistical Management: The Integrated Supply Chain Process.* New York: McGraw Hill, 1996.

Burt, David N. "Managing Suppliers Up to Speed." *Harvard Business Review* (July/August 1989): 127–35.

Camp, Robert C. *Benchmarking.* Milwaukee: ASQC Quality Press, 1989.

Cavinato, Joseph L. "What's Your Supply Chain Type?" *Supply Chain Management Review* (May/June 2002): 60–6.

Cliffe, Sarah. "ERP Implementation: How to Avoid $100 Million Write-Offs." *Harvard Business Review* (January/February 1999): 16–7.

Cooper, Robert G. *Winning at New Products*. 2nd ed. Reading, MA: Addison-Wesley, 1993.

Cooper, Robin, and W. Bruce Chew. "Control Tomorrow's Costs through Today's Designs." *Harvard Business Review* (January/February 1996): 88–97.

Council of Supply Chain Management Professionals (CSCMP). *Supply Chain Management Process Standards*. 6 vols. CSCMP, 2004.

Dyer, Jeffrey H. "How Chrysler Created an American *Keiretsu*." *Harvard Business Review* (July/August 1996): 42–56.

Eisenhardt, Kathleen M., and Shona L. Brown. "Patching: Restitching Business Portfolios in Dynamic Markets." *Harvard Business Review* (May/June 1999): 72–82.

Feitzinger, Edward, and Hau Lee. "Mass Customization at Hewlett-Packard: The Power of Postponement." *Harvard Business Review* (January/February 1997): 116–21.

Feld, Charlie S., and Donna B. Stoddard. "Getting IT Right." *Harvard Business Review* (February 2004): 72–79.

Fernández-Rañada, Miguel, F. Xavier Gurrola-Gal, and Enrique López-Tello. *3C: A Proven Alternative to MRPII for Optimizing Supply Chain Performance*. Boca Raton: CRC Press, 2000.

Fisher, Marshall L. "What Is the Right Supply Chain for Your Product?" *Harvard Business Review* (March/April 1997): 105–16.

Fisher, Marshall L., Janice H. Hammond, Walter R. Obermeyer, and Ananth Raman. "Making Supply Meet Demand in an Uncertain World." *Harvard Business Review* (May/June 1994): 83–92.

Fites, Donald V. "Make Your Dealers Your Partners." *Harvard Business Review* (March/April 1996): 84–95.

Geary, Steve, Paul Childerhouse, and Denis Towill. "Uncertainty and the Seamless Supply Chain." *Supply Chain Management Review* (July/August 2002): 52–61.

Gilliland, Michael. "Is Forecasting a Waste of Time?" *Supply Chain Management Review* (July/August 2002): 16–23.

Goldratt, Eliyahu M., and Jeff Cox. *The Goal*. Croton-on-Hudson, NY: North River Press, 1984.

Goldratt, Eliyahu M., and Robert E. Fox. *The Race*. Croton-on-Hudson, NY: North River Press, 1986.

Hagel, John III, and John Seely Brown. "Your Next IT Strategy." *Harvard Business Review* (October 2001): 105–13.

Hamel, Gary and C.K. Prahalad. The Core Competency of the Corporation. *Harvard Business Review* (May/June 1990): 79–90.

———. "Strategic Intent." *Harvard Business Review* (May/June 1989): 63–76.

Harbison, John R., and Peter Pekar. *Smart Alliances: A Practical Guide to Repeatable Success*. San Francisco: Jossey-Bass, 1998.

Hauser, John R., and Don Clausing. "The House of Quality." *Harvard Business Review* (May/June 1988): 63–73.

Haverly, Richard C. and James F. Whelan. *Logistics Software*. 1998 edition, vol. 1. Council of Logistics Management (compact disc).

Hayes, Robert H., and Gary P. Pisano. "Beyond World-Class: The New Manufacturing Strategy." *Harvard Business Review* (January/February, 1994): 77–84.

Hayes, Robert H., and Steven C. Wheelwright. *Restoring Our Competitive Edge: Competing through Manufacturing.* New York: John Wiley & Sons, 1984.

Hayes, Robert H., Steven C. Wheelwright, and Kim B. Clark. *Dynamic Manufacturing: Creating the Learning Organization.* New York: Free Press, 1988.

Hicks, Douglas T. *Activity-Based Costing: Making It Work for Small and Mid-Sized Companies.* 2nd ed. New York: John Wiley & Sons, 1999.

House, Charles H., and Raymond L. Price. "The Return Map: Tracking Product Teams." *Harvard Business Review* (January/February 1991): 92–100.

Iansiti, Marco, and Jonathan West. "Technology Integration: Turning Great Research into Great Products." *Harvard Business Review* (May/June 1997): 69–79.

Imai, Masaaki. *Kaizen.* New York: Random House, 1986.

International Institute of Business Analysis (IIBA). *A Guide to the Business Analysis Body of Knowledge (BABOK).* Release 1.6, 2006.

Johnson, Bradford C. "Retail: The Walmart Effect." *The McKinsey Quarterly*, no. 1 (2002): 4042.

Juran, J.M. *Juran on Quality by Design.* New York: The Free Press, 1992.

Kaplan, Robert S., and David P. Norton. "The Balanced Scorecard—Measures That Drive Performance." *Harvard Business Review* (January/February 1992): 71–79.

Kennedy, James E. Implementing Enterprise Software toward the Multicompany Environment. In *Handbook of Supply Chain Management,* 2nd ed. (Boca Raton: St. Lucie Press, 2006), 441-9.

Kerzner, Harold. *Project Management: A Systems Approach to Planning, Scheduling, and Controlling.* 7th ed. New York: John Wiley & Sons, 2001.

———. *Strategic Planning for Project Management: Using a Project Management Maturity Model.* New York: John Wiley & Sons, 2001.

Kim, W. Chan, and Renée Mauborgne. *Blue Ocean Strategy.* Boston: Harvard Business School Press, 2005.

———. "Creating New Market Space." *Harvard Business Review* (January/February 1999): 83–93.

Kumar, Nirmalya. "The Power of Trust in Manufacturer–Retailer Relationships." *Harvard Business Review* (November/December 1996): 92–107.

Lee, Hau L. "What Constitutes Supply Chain Integration?" *IEEM Network News*, Stanford University School of Engineering, Summer 1998.

Lutz, Robert A. *Guts.* New York: John Wiley & Sons, 1998.

Magretta, Joan. "Why Business Models Matter." *Harvard Business Review* (May 2002): 87–92.

McGrath, Rita Gunther, and Ian C. MacMillan. "Discovery-Driven Planning." *Harvard Business Review* (July/August 1995): 44–54.

McAfee, Andrew. "Mastering the Three Worlds of Information Technology." *Harvard Business Review* (November 2006): 141–9.

Melik, Rudolf. *The Rise of the Project Workforce: Managing People and Projects in a Flat World.* Hoboken, NJ: John Wiley & Sons, 2007.

Moberg, Christopher, Kate Vitasek, Theodore L. Stank, and Abré Pienaar. "Time to Remodel." *CSCMP Supply Chain Quarterly* (Quarter 3/2008): 36–48.

Monden, Yasuhiro. *Toyota Production System.* Norcross, GA: Institute of Industrial Engineers, 1983.

Morris, Steven A., and Denise Johnson McManus. "Information Infrastructure Centrality in the Agile Organization." *Information Systems Management* (Fall 2002): 8–12.

Murray, Alan. "Intellectual Property: Old Rules Don't Apply." *Wall Street Journal*, August 23, 2001, A1.

Narus, James A., and James C. Anderson. "Rethinking Distribution: Adaptive Channels." *Harvard Business Review* (July/August 1996): 112–20.

Nelson, Emily, and Evan Ramstad. "Hershey's Biggest Dud Has Turned Out to Be Its New Technology." *The Wall Street Journal*, October 28, 1999, A1.

Nyman, Lee R. *Making Manufacturing Cells Work.* Detroit: Society of Manufacturing Engineers, 1992.

Office of Government Commerce (OGC). *The Business View on Successful IT Service Delivery.* Great Britain: OGC, 2006.

Petroff, John N. *Handbook of MRPII and JIT: Strategies for Total Manufacturing Control.* Englewood Cliffs, NJ: Prentice-Hall, 1993.

Poirier, Charles C. "Achieving Supply Chain Connectivity." *Supply Chain Management Review* (November/December 2002): 16–22.

———. The Path to Supply Chain Leadership. *Supply Chain Management Review* (Fall 1998): 16–26.

Poirer, Charles C., and Stephen E. Reiter. *Supply Chain Optimization: Building the Strongest Total Business Network.* San Francisco: Berrett-Koehler, 1996.

Porter, Michael E. "Strategy and the Internet." *Harvard Business Review* (March 2001): 62–78.

———. "What Is Strategy?" *Harvard Business Review* (November/December 1996): 61–78.

———. *Competitive Advantage: Creating and Sustaining Superior Performance.* New York: The Free Press, 1985.

———. *Competitive Strategy: Techniques for Analyzing Industries and Competitors.* New York: The Free Press, 1980.

Project Management Institute. *Project Manager Competency Development Framework* (*PMCD*). 2nd ed. PMI, 2007.

———. *Combined Standards Glossary.* 3rd ed. PMI, 2007.

Project Management Institute Global Standard. *A Guide to the Project Management Body of Knowledge (PMBOK Guide).* 4th ed. PMI, 2008. American National Standard ANSI/PMI 99-001-2008.

———. *Organizational Project Management Maturity Model Knowledge Foundation* (*OPM3 Knowledge Foundation*). PMI, 2008. ANSI/PMI 08-004-2008.

———. *Practice Standard for Work Breakdown Structures.* 2nd ed. PMI, 2006.

———. *The Standard for Portfolio Management.* 2nd ed. PMI, 2008. American National Standard ANSI/PMI 08-003-2008.

———. *The Standard for Program Management.* 2nd ed. PMI, 2008. American National Standard ANSI/PMI 08-02-2008.

Ptak, Carol A., and Eli Schragenheim. *ERP: Tools, Techniques, and Applications for Integrating the Supply Chain.* Boca Raton: CRC Press, 2000.

Quinn, Frank J., Morgan L. Swink, and Charles C. Poirer. "The Sixth Annual Global Survey of Supply Chain Progress." *Supply Chain Management Review* (October 2008).

Rayport, Jeffrey F., and John J. Sviokla. "Exploiting the Virtual Value Chain." *Harvard Business Review* (November/December 1995): 75–85.

ReVelle, Jack B., John W. Moran, and Charles A. Cox. *The QFD Handbook.* New York: John Wiley & Sons, 1998.

Rice, James B. Jr., and Richard M. Hoppe. "Supply Chain versus Supply Chain: The Hype and the Reality." *Supply Chain Management Review* (September/October 2001): 46–54.

Rigby, Darrell K., Frederick F. Reichheld, and Phil Schefter. "Avoid the Four Perils of CRM." *Harvard Business Review* (February 2002): 101–9.

Riggs, David A., and Sharon L. Robbins. *The Executive's Guide to Supply Chain Management: Building Supply Chain Thinking into All Business Processes.* New York: AMACOM, 1998.

Ritter, David. "We Must Never Break the Chain," in *The Supply Chain Yearbook* (New York: McGraw-Hill, 2001), 199–200.

Robert, Michel. *Strategy Pure and Simple II.* New York: McGraw-Hill, 1998.

Roche, Eileen. "Explaining XML." *Harvard Business Review* (July/August 2000): 18.

Ross, David F. *Competing through Supply Chain Management: Creating Market-Winning Strategies through Supply Chain Partnerships.* Chapman & Hall Materials Management/ Logistics Series. New York: Springer, 1997.

Ross, Jeanne W., and Peter Weill. "Six IT decisions Your IT People Shouldn't Make." *Harvard Business Review* (November 2002): 85–91.

Roztocki, N., and K.L. Needy. "An Integrated Activity-Based Costing and Economic Value Added System as an Engineering Management Tool for Manufacturers," in *1998 ASEM National Conference Proceedings,* Virginia Beach, VA, October 1–3, 1998, 77–84.

Skinner, Wickham. "The Focused Factory." *Harvard Business Review* (May/June 1974): 113–21.

Supply-Chain Council. SCOR Quick Reference, Version 9.0, 2008.

———. Supply-Chain Operations Reference-model, Overview, Version 9.0, 2008.

———. Supply-Chain Operations Reference-model, SCOR Overview, Version 9.0, 2008.

Tinnirello, Paul C. *Project Management.* Boca Raton: Auerbach Publications, 2000.

Turbide, Dave. "What Is APS?" *Midrange ERP* (January/February 1998).

Upton, David M. "What Really Makes Factories Flexible?" *Harvard Business Review* (July/ August 1995): 74–81.

———. "The Management of Flexibility." *California Management Review* (Winter 1994): 72–89.

Upton, David M., and Andrew McAfee. "The Real Virtual Factory." *Harvard Business Review* (July/August 1996): 123–33.

Walton, Mary. *The Deming Management Method.* The Putnam Publishing Group, 1986.

Wheelwright, Steven C., and Kim B. Clark. *Revolutionizing Product Development.* New York: Free Press, 1992.

Womack, James P., and Daniel T. Jones. "Beyond Toyota: How to Root Out Waste and Pursue Perfection." *Harvard Business Review* (September/October 1996): 140–58.

———. "From Lean Production to the Lean Enterprise." *Harvard Business Review* (March/ April 1994): 93–103.

INDEX

Index